Russian Eyewitness Accounts of the Campaign of 1807

Russian Eyewitness Accounts of the Campaign of 1807

Compiled, Translated and Edited by
Alexander Mikaberidze

Foreword by James Arnold

FRONTLINE BOOKS, LONDON

Russian Eyewitness Accounts of the Campaign of 1807

This edition published in 2015 by Frontline Books,
an imprint of Pen & Sword Books Ltd,
47 Church Street, Barnsley, S. Yorkshire, S70 2AS
www.frontline-books.com

ISBN: 978-1-84832-762-7

For more information on our books, please visit
www.frontline-books.com, email info@frontline-books.com
or write to us at the above address.

Printed and bound by CPI Group (UK) Ltd, Croydon, CR0 4YY

Typeset in10/12.25 point Plantin MT by JCS Publishing Services Ltd,
www.jcs-publishing.co.uk

Contents

Illustrations

Foreword

Napoleon Bonaparte's masterpiece, the battle of Austerlitz on 2 December 1805, was a terrible defeat for the Russian army. Twenty-seven-year-old Tsar Alexander I was present at and contributed to the debacle. Yet there was little official reaction to the calamity in St. Petersburg or Moscow, thus allowing the Tsar and his generals largely to escape blame. Instead, most Russians blamed the Austrians. Defiant in defeat, Alexander refused to ratify a peace treaty with France. The next year, when Prussia forced a new war on France, Russia allied with Prussia and sent its armies westward to confront Napoleon again. The ensuing collisions took place in Poland. Chastened by his experience in 1805, Alexander stayed home during the autumn and winter. His absence allowed military professionals to conduct the campaign.

The Russian army of 1806–07 was an army in transition. Alexander's father, Tsar Paul I, had insisted upon perfection of appearance and robotic ability to perform drill. Alexander tolerated limited reforms. The army had learned from its defeat at Austerlitz. It entered Poland with a new organisational structure featuring permanent divisions, which was a step towards a future featuring a French-like army corps structure. On a tactical level, Russian infantry utilised the same array of formations as every other European army: column, line and square. However, there was increasing emphasis on open order combat, necessary training to contest French skirmish superiority. The 1806–07 campaign would witness the army's light infantry, its jagers, repeatedly displaying exemplary conduct while serving as the army's advance and rear guard. The superbly-mounted cavalry regiments fought bravely, but flaws in doctrine, training and organisation prevented them from accomplishing as much as their imposing numbers promised. Likewise, the artillery suffered from numerous deficiencies, including an absence of standardised doctrine, the use of inefficient regimental guns, and the lack of joint training with infantry and cavalry. In 1806, the armies assembling for the Polish campaign were assigned fifty-three artillery companies totalling 624 guns. The sheer weight of fire coming from so many artillery pieces made it a formidable battlefield force.

When the Russian army met Napoleon in 1806, the French emperor had just won an overwhelming victory over Prussia. He and his army appeared invincible. Then came a seemingly implausible reversal of fortune when an inexperienced Russian army, riven by command dissension, inflicted a pair of severe checks at Pultusk and Golymin. Napoleon's opponents rejoiced to see the 'Corsican Ogre' falter as he retired to winter quarters to lick his wounds. The Russian armies were not done. Flush with his success at Pultusk, General Bennigsen assumed overall command of the Tsar's forces and launched a surprise offensive. It compelled Napoleon to abandon winter quarters and begin a gruelling campaign. Napoleon's brilliantly-conceived strategic envelopment miscarried. A five-day all-out pursuit finally brought the Russians to bay on the snow-covered ground of Eylau. Here over 140,000 French and Russian soldiers fought a terrible battle. They displayed surpassing courage and moments of inspired leadership, but also committed costly blunders as victory trembled in the balance. The battle inflicted nearly 60,000 casualties. Then and thereafter, both sides claimed victory, but what was absolutely clear was that for the first time in his career Napoleon had met a foe capable of effectively resisting him.

The winter of 1806–07 provided little breathing space for the exhausted armies. A series of battles blunted a Russian offensive and attention turned to the fortress city of Danzig. Spring 1807 brought renewed campaigning as once again the Russians launched a surprise offensive during which Bennigsen almost destroyed a major French force. Instead came Napoleon's counter-offensive leading to the battle of Heilsberg. Four days later occurred the decisive encounter at Friedland, followed by the fateful meeting on 26 June 1807 between Alexander and Napoleon on a raft in the middle of the Niemen River outside of Tilsit. The Russian people had made an enormous sacrifice to fight Napoleon. After Tilsit, they asked why. Over the coming years, Tsar Alexander would answer by exhibiting an implacable determination to bring down the French tyrant.

Russian eyewitness accounts provide nuggets of solid, primary source history, reminders of the limitations of these sources, and insights into the human condition when warriors engage. Alexander Benckendorff is utterly convincing as he describes Russo-Prussian friction as the two allies uneasily try to coordinate campaign strategy. It is an important theme that will recur in 1813. Otto Löwenstern's letter describing Eylau is a good reminder how participants in a battle have a limited, and often incorrect understanding of the course of a battle. Levin Bennigsen's informative, detailed report about Eylau provides another demonstration of how generals try to explain away misfortune to their superiors. Sergei Volkonskii's account of Friedland showcases some of the internal frictions in the army. It is amusing to learn that one faction referred to officers who had achieved promotion during Emperor Paul's time as 'the Gatchina Rareripes'. For English-language readers, much of our knowledge about the Russian army comes from the pen of the British busybody, Robert Wilson. Wilson had a high self-regard. Alexander Obolenskii provides a delightful detail, writing that the Russians nicknamed Wilson 'the Beacon' because he always surmounted the highest terrain to view the battle.

Most published history of the Napoleonic Wars portrays Russia's warriors as walking muskets: stupid, inflexible, but brave. Their leaders are usually viewed as inept at best. In this volume, as well as in his similar publications, Alexander Mikaberidze gives voice to the Russian experience. His invaluable work portrays a very different reality.

James R. Arnold
Lexington, Virginia
Autumn 2014

Preface

The War of the Fourth Coalition holds a particular place in the history of the Napoleonic Wars. Fought in the wake of Napoleon's triumphant campaign of 1805, this war had solidified French control over central and parts of eastern Europe through a brilliant campaign against Prussia in October 1806 and a prolonged but ultimately victorious conflict with Russia in late 1806 and the spring of 1807. The war culminated in the Treaty of Tilsit that marked a turning point in the Napoleonic Wars. In the wake of his triumphs at Austerlitz, Jena and Friedland, Napoleon emerged as the master of almost all western and central Europe, with a free hand to do whatever he liked toward recreating Europe according to his own designs for the benefit of France, himself and his family.

Much has been written on this campaign over the last 200 years. The historiography of the War of the Fourth Coalition, however, tends to focus on Napoleon's short but triumphant campaign against Prussia in the autumn of 1806. The Franco-Russian War, sometimes referred to as the Polish Campaign as Napoleon himself styled it, received relatively scant attention from historians. Most of what has been written on this campaign comes from German (Eduard Höpfner, Oscar von Lettow-Vorbeck, etc.) and French (G. Lechartier, Paul Foucart, Adolphe Thiers, Jean Thiry, etc.) historians, with occasional contribution from English/American ones. Lorraine Petre's *Napoleon's Campaign in Poland, 1806-1807*, originally published in 1901, remained the standard account of the campaign for much of the century, supplemented by Christopher Summerville's general survey in 2005,[*] and was only superseded in 2011 with the publication of the second volume of James Arnold and Ralph Reinertsen's excellent study of the campaign.[†]

Yet, with the exception of Arnold and Reinertsen, the existing studies betray a clear partiality towards the French – they tend to rely on French sources and explore the campaign from the French point of view. This is partly the result of the paucity of Russian sources but partly of the linguistic

---

[*] Christopher Summerville, *Napoleon's Polish Gamble: Eylau and Friedland, 1807* (Barnsley, 2005).
[†] James Arnold and Ralph Reinertsen, *Crisis in the Snows: Russian Confronts Napoleon: The Eylau Campaign, 1806-1807* (Lexington VA, 2007); *Napoleon's Triumph: La Grande Armée versus the Tsar's Army. The Friedland Campaign 1807* (Lexington VA, 2011).

difficulties, administrative hurdles and political and ideological rivalries that combined to create a substantial dearth in Western translations of Russian accounts of the Napoleonic Wars. Consequently, the Russian side of the story is largely lost in the existing narratives. As Arnold aptly pointed out, Russian 'soldiers have passed into history as walking muskets: stupid, inflexible, but brave. [Russian] leaders are recalled as inept'.* Until now the vast majority of Russian sources remained inaccessible to and overlooked by Western scholars and only a handful of them have been translated into English or French. The present book features two dozen Russian sources, from which only a handful has been accessible in English or French: the memoirs of Levin Bennigsen came out in French in 1908, Nadezhda Durova's memoir was translated into English in 1988, Denis Davydov's memoir in 1999, Alexsey Yermolov's in 2005 and Eduard von Löwenstern's in 2010.

Even in Russia, historians have long ignored the 1806–07 campaign, which tends to be sandwiched between the brief mentioning of the Russian defeat at Austerlitz and the much more detailed exploration of the Patriotic War of 1812. Alexander Mikhailovskii-Danilevskii's *Opisanie vtoroi voiny imperatora Aleksandra I s Napoleonom v 1806-1807 g.*, originally published in 1846, remained the sole in-depth Russian study on this campaign until the turn of the twenty-first century.† The first decade of the twenty-first century saw the publication of two new studies – V. Shikanov's *Pervaya Polskaya kampaniya 1806-1807* (2002) and I. Vasiliev's *Nesostoyavshiisya revanch: Rossiya i Frantsiya, 1806-1807 gg.* (2010) – which have now become the standard Russian narratives of the war. These authors did their best to explore both sides of the war and have mostly succeeded in their efforts. But their works still suffer from common problems of heavily relying on existing publications and failing to consult original archival sources. There is still no Russian-language anthology of primary sources on the 1806–07 campaign.

Russian Eyewitness Accounts of the Campaign of 1807 is the first title to bring together letters, diaries and memoirs of Russian participants of the campaign. It offers but a glimpse of vibrant memoir literature that exists about this campaign but has been long inaccessible and underutilised. We do hope that this selective coverage will not detract from the overall value of the book.

---

* Arnold and Reinertsen, *Crisis in the Snows*, xv.

† In addition to Mikhailovskii-Danilevskii's work, there are several articles and booklets on the various parts of the campaign: for example, B. Kolyubakin's booklet *Preissich-Eylauskaya operatsiya. Srazhenie u Preussisch-Eylau 26-27 ianvarya 1807* (St. Petersburg, 1911) or articles by N. Morozov on the battles at Guttstadt and Friedland published in *Voennyj sbornik* in 1907. More recently there were several articles published in the Russian journals *Imperator* and *Zeughaus*. The unpublished manuscript written by Karpov (preserved at the Russian State Military Historical Archive) is almost entirely based on the works of Mikhailovskii-Danilevskii and Höpfner.

The book is organised in chronological manner starting with the aftermath of the Russian defeat at Austerlitz. It is divided into seven chapters that contain a selection of excerpts from over two dozen memoirs and diaries. In selecting material, we sought to include memoirs, diaries and letters to present a variety of viewpoints, ranging from a commander-in-chief to a humble non-commissioned officer. These narratives are naturally subjective and occasionally imprecise but they are indispensable if we want to understand how their authors went about their normal existence and experienced the war that became the turning point in their lives. We believe that these documents show the other side of the coin: providing an unique insight on the Russian side of the war, how and why decisions were made and what Russian officers and soldiers experienced as they slowly progressed towards victory. Due to space limitations, we were unable to include those memoirs that dealt with operations on the sidelines (i.e. the siege of Danzig) and many official documents, including some battle reports and Journals of Military Operations. Unlike the first two instalments of this series, this volume features excerpts from three British participants in the campaign – Robert Ker Porter, George Jackson and Robert Wilson. We made the exception of including them because these men were eyewitnesses to events that are not as well described in the Russian accounts. Thus, Ker Porter left a vivid description of the fête given in honour of Peter Bagration on his return from Austerlitz. George Jackson maintained close contacts with Russian officers in Bennigsen's army and his diary reflects information supplied by them. Robert Wilson participated in the campaign and was eyewitness to the fighting, leaving vivid recollections of it. But instead of citing Wilson's famous 'Brief Remarks . . .' which was published three years after the war, we decided to include excerpts from the less-consulted journal that Wilson had kept during the campaign. This book features only a small part of Bennigsen's three-volume memoirs. In translating Bennigsen's memoirs, we have consulted both the French and Russian editions that noticeably differ, with the Russian version omitting many passages and entire chapters.

Every book is a result of joint effort and I am grateful to many individuals for their support and assistance. While working on this book I frequently remembered (and chuckled at) the great stories that Professor Donald D. Horward told his graduate students of his visit to the 1970s Poland, and especially of his epic trip to Pultusk. I am very grateful to Donald Graves who supported my original idea of an anthology of Russian memoirs and proposed it to Frontline Books. Without him, this book probably would not have been published. The publisher, Michael Leventhal, quickly saw the value of the proposal and agreed to publish not just one but three volumes of Russian memoirs, and I am very grateful for his willingness to launch this unique series. My editor Stephen Chumbley patiently waited for the delivery of the manuscript, offering support and encouragement throughout the past two years. Stephen Summerfield kindly allowed me to reproduce excerpts from his translation of Eduard von Löwenstern's memoir while Paul A. Strietelmeir generously shared his time and knowledge to translate Bennigsen's memoirs, which will be eventually published as a separate book. Greg Gorsuch has kindly translated General Uvarov's battle reports that I discovered at the Russian State Military Historical Archives but unfortunately they did not make it into the final version of the manuscript. I am thankful to Boris Megorsky, who frequently pointed me in the right direction and helped me procure several sources that remain inaccessible in the West.

Last but not least, I am indebted to my family: to my sons Luka and Sergi for being perfect little boys and allowing me to carry on writing, and to my wife Anna for her constant encouragement, ceaseless aid and support for all my undertakings.

This book is dedicated to my friends and colleagues from the Institute on Napoleon and the French Revolution – Kenneth Johnson, Karen Reid and Jason Musteen, and in memory of Jack Sigler, whose friendship I will always cherish.

Editor's Note

Dates in original Russian documents are given in the Julian calendar, which was effective in the Russian Empire at the time. For this book, I converted dates into the Gregorian calendar and provided them in brackets. At the same time, whenever the author himself included date conversions in his memoirs, I kept them intact and they are oftentimes shown in parenthesis or separated by a dash. Russian sources often cite old measurements (sazhen, pud, versta, and so on), which I have converted to modern measurements.

The reader should not be surprised to see various numbers attached to Russian names. There were often several officers with the same last name serving in the Russian army and, consequently, numbers were attached to their last names to distinguish them. To distinguish between the uhlan (especially Polish) regiments in the Allied and Russian armies, I have used 'lancer' for units in the French army and 'uhlan' for those in the Russian service.

The source for each memoir is indicated by a short title at the end of the cited text while full bibliographic details of the sources are listed at the back of the book. I tried to stay as true to the original text as possible, which entailed retaining authors' use of contemporary measurements and older names for locations.

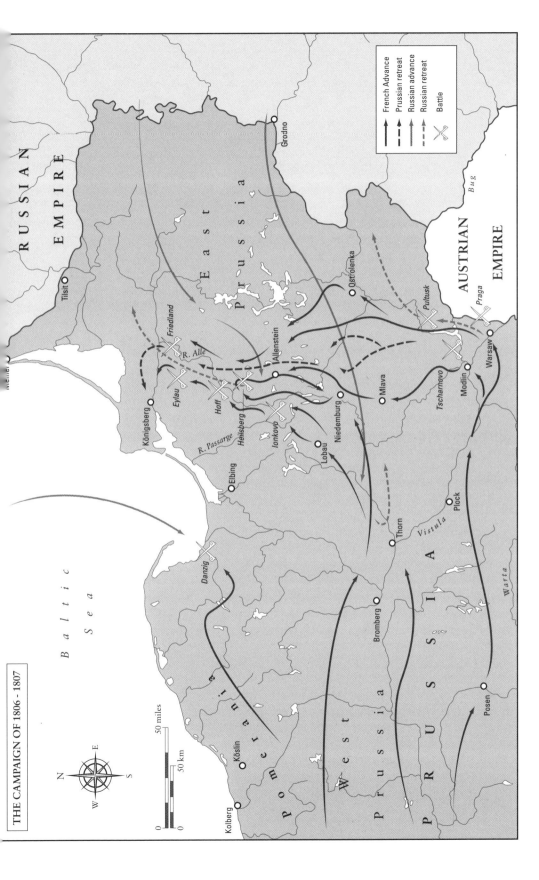

THE CAMPAIGN OF 1806 - 1807

N
W — E
S

50 miles
50 km

Baltic Sea

RUSSIAN EMPIRE

Memel

Tilsit

Königsberg

Elbing

Danzig

Kolberg

Köslin

Pomerania

West Prussia

PRUSSIA

Posen

Bromberg

Warta

Vistula

Plock

Thorn

Modlin

Warsaw

Praga

Tscharnovo

Niedemburg

Lobau

Ionkovo

Heilsberg

R. Passarge

Hoff

Eylau

Friedland

R. Alle

Allenstein

Mlava

Pultusk

Ostrolenka

East Prussia

Grodno

Bug

AUSTRIAN EMPIRE

French Advance
Prussian retreat
Russian advance
Russian retreat
Battle

1

The Eclipse of Austerlitz

In 1805, after three peaceful but anxious years, Europe found itself once more in the abyss of war. The War of the Third Coalition had once against pitted France against a coalition of European states, the Holy Roman Empire, the Russian Empire, the United Kingdom, Naples and Sweden. But unlike the earlier Coalition wars, which lasted for several years, the War of the Third Coalition proved to be brief and decisive. It began in earnest in late August and ended just three months later in the battle of Austerlitz on 2 December. Austerlitz was the masterpiece of Napoleon's military strategy. Despite the numerical superiority, the Russo-Austrian army was decisively defeated and the Third Coalition suffered a deadly blow. Two days after the battle, the Holy Roman Emperor Francis sued for peace. Although Emperor Alexander of Russia remained defiant, his army was shattered and had to withdraw to Russia. The French lost some 9,000 men, of whom 1,300 were killed, but the Allied army suffered around 27,000 casualties. The Russians sustained most of the losses, with over 21,000 killed, wounded and captured and 133 guns lost. Looking at the flower of the Russian military lying scattered across the blood-soaked fields, Napoleon is said to have remarked, 'Many fine ladies will weep tomorrow in St. Petersburg!'

The moral and political impact of the battle of Austerlitz on Russia was profound. On the morning of the battle, Napoleon famously welcomed 'the sun of Austerlitz' as it rose above the December mists. But, for Russia, it was truly 'the eclipse of Austerlitz'. For the past hundred years, the Russians were accustomed to the victories of their army over the Turks, Swedes and Poles, as well as the French in 1799, and believed it was invincible. Austerlitz shattered such illusions. Alexander was the first tsar to command the field army since Peter the Great, which only further heightened the Russian sense of defeat on the fields of Moravia. Indeed, the disastrous conclusion of the battle shocked Russian society. Writing from St. Petersburg, Joseph de Maistre commented that the 'battle of Austerlitz had a magical effect on public opinion . . . and it seems that the defeat in a single battle had paralysed the entire empire.'* The Russian nobility initially refused to believe the extent of the defeat. But as the

---

* Joseph de Maistre, *Peterburgskie pisma* (St. Petersburg, 1995), p. 61. Similar information in Correspondence of Olry, in *Istoricheskii Vestnik*, 147 (1917), p. 433.

news arrived and the nature of the defeat became known, Austerlitz led to a strong upsurge of nationalism and calls to continue the war in order to restore the honour of Russia.

Alexander Eyler

The grandson of the well-known scientist Leonard Eyler, Alexander Eyler had enlisted in an artillery regiment at an early age and served with distinction during the Russo-Swedish War in 1790. Transferred as a lieutenant to the Life Guard Artillery Battalion in 1796, he participated in the 1805 campaign and distinguished himself at Austerlitz, earning the Order of St. Anne (3rd class).

On 2 December there was a battle at Austerlitz, the first one for the [Russian Imperial] Guard. We were all just thinking of how we must not let Napoleon escape from us. The Guard, consisting of six battalions, two cuirassier regiments and two artillery companies, was initially supposed to form the reserve of Prince Bagration's corps but soon found itself on the front line and was among the first to open fire at the French, whom we initially mistook for our own men due to the distance; yet, the very first cannonball that tore through our ranks quickly dispelled our illusions and the battle commenced in earnest. [General Mikhail] Miloradovich's column, which was on the left flank of the Guard, fled without firing a shot* and left us, just barely 5,000 men strong, to hold ground against some 30,000 Frenchmen under the direct orders of Napoleon himself. No wonder then that our forces were routed, driven across the gully and scattered [across the fields]. But the Guard itself did not flee; it rallied around the Life Guard Grenadier Regiment that had just arrived on the battlefield. At last dusk fell and we were all delighted that Napoleon did not pursue us. Overall, the Guard fought with a great spirit, with infantry charging with bayonets three times and the cuirassiers launching two charges. But the enemy prevailed through his sheer might . . .

The fast-approaching night allowed us to retreat without further losses. We marched to Halych, on the border with Hungary. On one of the bivouacs I fell asleep amidst a heap of stones and had my horse stolen after the thief cut the reins that I was holding in my hand. We had no bread or forage, and soldiers had to pay a chervonetz [gold coin] for just two pounds of bread; the French captured many of our supply transports while my wagon had to be abandoned with all my possessions still in it because its horses had been harnessed to the Emperor's [Alexander's] carriage to save it from the enemy. I had nothing but

---

* Eyler is unfairly harsh in his criticism of Miloradovich's troops who did their best to hold the centre of the Russian positions.

what I was wearing, not even a clean pair of undergarments to change. We spent six days in Halych, having virtually no bread, food or forage. Some of us survived by digging up potatoes but most simply starved; horses were fed rotten hay from the roofs of local houses.

Meanwhile, Austria concluded a humiliating peace with Napoleon and we resumed our march in the most dreadful conditions. [Fortunately], in Hungary, we were received very well, cared for and fed well. But marching across mountains and crossing rivers and rivulets without bridges in December proved to be particularly arduous. Our marching route ran across Krakow and Brest-Litovsk to the old road to St. Petersburg, but we did it by forced marches, which, together with the starvation that we experienced in Halych, resulted in the loss of many excellent men and horses . . . This campaign is noteworthy because in just seven months we covered over 4,500 verstas [4,800 km]* in forced marches and endured a battle where we suffered complete defeat and were forced to suffer from insufferable hunger and other hardships for two weeks . . . [From the Russian text in A. Eyler, *Zapiski*]

Pavel Grabbe

Not even sixteen years old in the autumn of 1805, Pavel Grabbe was born into a minor noble family from the province of Lifland. One of eleven children, he lost his father early in his life while his mother fell into a debilitating hypochondria, leaving the children to fend for themselves. Fortunately, Dowager Empress Maria Feodorovna took notice of the Grabbe family and helped Pavel and his two brothers to enrol in the Cadet Corps. Pavel proved to be a good student, later recalling that 'my main teachers were the ancients, especially Plutarch, whom I encountered early on and whose unassuming stories introduced me to a new world, important ideals and the greatness of human beings. I read voraciously everything I could lay my hands on, whether it was good, bad or downright corrupting.' In September 1805 Grabbe graduated from the Cadet Corps with the rank of sub-lieutenant and was assigned to the 2nd Artillery Regiment that was with the Russian army marching to engage the French.

I caught up with my regiment one march away from Warsaw and found many pleasant individuals in it. We passed Warsaw in a full parade and, although I was at my designated spot, I barely saw anything. There were vast numbers of people in the streets; balconies and windows of homes were sparkling with beauties dressed in their best dresses. All around me I kept hearing comments, 'Look, just look at that officer, he is just a child', followed by further laments

---

* Nowadays, the direct route (by car, on major highways) from St. Petersburg (Russia) to Brno (Czech Republic) is 1,720km long.

and observations on how unacceptable it was to send children to war. I was so embarrassed by this that my face turned red and looking down onto the road, I crossed the entire city [without looking up]. At that age (I was not even sixteen years old) I was so diminutive that my name was invariably followed by the nickname 'little'. [Fortunately] over the next three years, filled with hardships and challenges, I grew in stature, reaching the height of ten vershoks* but remained scrawny for the rest of my life.

I was assigned to the company of Captain Chuikevich. My memories of him contain nothing pleasant. We marched to Moravia through Silesia and this blessed region left a delectable impression on me with its general orderliness, abundance and the touching generosity of the local population. Mountains, which I saw for the first time in my life, astonished and captivated me with their unusual and striking sights.

General Ivan Nikolaevich Essen's column, where [my company served] was hurrying to join the main [Russian] army that was concentrated at Olmütz. At Weisskirchen [Hranice], we left the paved road and moved towards Prerau [Přerov] amidst dreadful mud that disordered our artillery after just one march. We still had to make two more marches to Austerlitz. But we soon received the news that the [decisive] battle [at Austerlitz] was lost and the fugitives from various regiments, of frightful appearance, revealed the depth of the disaster we had suffered.

And so it was that I experienced the first adversities of life that made me leave behind my adolescence and acquire a sense of my own capabilities and the necessity of applying them without outside advice or direction.

Essen's column hurried to follow the [main Russian] army during its retreat across Hungary. Because of the exhaustion of the horses, my company commander was unable to remove all of his caissons and had to leave two of them at Prerau, ordering me to lead thirteen artillerists in acquiring, if necessary by force, sufficient number of horses and rejoining the army. Just as our army departed and I was about to assume my first command, the alarm was sounded all across the town: the French outposts were approaching. In desperation I decided to abandon my palubas, as we called large ammunition transports back then, and flee together with my men. The main road seemed too dangerous, so we rushed into the mountains. We soon caught up with some regiments from Essen's column that were also hurrying to move deeper into the mountainous range. Several French

---

* Vershok is an old Russian measurement of length, equal to 4.45cm (1.75in). In eighteenth/nineteenth century Russia, height was given in arshins (one arshin equals 71cm/28in) and vershoks. Since the height of an adult human being was rarely under two arshins (142cm/55in), Russian writers usually simply indicated how many vershoks tall they were. Grabbe's reference to ten vershoks (44cm/17in) should be added to his height in arshins: 44cm + 142cm = 186cm.

dragoons, who pursued our officer, approached us but there were too many of us for them to attack, and we were already preparing to defend ourselves. Travelling across minor and very difficult roads, all the while staying up in the mountains, we managed to get to Weisskirchen that was located in a valley below. It was not known whether the French had captured this town or not, yet our salvation depended on the answer to this question. We were soon joined by ammunition and treasury chests from various regiments. A feldwebel* and several men from the Moskovskii Grenadier Regiment volunteered to descend into the town. It was agreed that a musket shot would serve as a signal that the enemy were present in the town. Moved by their self-sacrifice, I decided to join them. [Upon entering the town, we found that] the French had not arrived yet, but were expected any minute. While our detachment was descending from the mountains, we went to the city hall to request provisions. Despite the extraordinary circumstances, we found the city officials at their posts, calmly writing at their desks as if it was peacetime. Not without clamour and threats, not to mention complying with tedious forms that could have delayed us and delivered to the enemy, were we able to secure all that we requested. It was here that for the first time in my life I was astonished by this remarkable character trait of the Germans, who phlegmatically follow the established order of things even if it could be advantageous to the enemy. But this trait also had a more honourable side to it, because it also testifies to the conscientious performance of one's duty . . .

Just as the threat of captivity dissipated, I was seized by the fear of responsibility and [the sense of] indignity of failing my very first assignment and continued to experience them every minute of our movement until we rejoined the army at Biala, as I recall, in Galicia. Feeling embarrassed, I showed up in front of our artillery commander [General] Rezvyi, who received me cheerfully and understandingly, consoling me that all the artillery palubas had to be abandoned in the mountains. I was soon transferred to another company, commanded by Fedor Maksimovich Schulman. Here I found myself in a great band, just like a family, which is not infrequent when it comes to the artillery.

Our army crossed the [imperial] borders and our company was assigned winter quarters between Ustyluh and Vladimir in the Volhynia.

Thus ended my first campaign that involved simply marching, all on foot and in late autumn and early winter, which proved to be very difficult considering my age. [General Mikhail] Miloradovich's exploit at Krems and of [Prince Peter] Bagration at Amstetten were the subjects of our conversations during respite and became the best educational experiences of that time. [From the Russian text in P. Grabbe, *Zapiski* . . .]

---

* Senior non-commissioned officer in a company.

Alexsey Yermolov

By the age of twenty-nine, Alexsey Yermolov was already the veteran of three campaigns, having fought against the Poles in 1794, the Persians in 1796 and the French in 1805. Like many other Russian noblemen, he began his career in the Russian Imperial Guard but later studied in the Artillery and Engineer Cadet Corps. He was arrested in 1799 for association with freethinkers and alleged participation in a conspiracy against Emperor Paul I. He spent two years in exile in Kostroma before the new Emperor Alexander I pardoned him and allowed him to return to military service. Yermolov transferred to the artillery, serving in a horse artillery company during the War of the Third Coalition in 1805. He distinguished himself at Amstetten and Austerlitz for which he was promoted to colonel in July 1806.

In the armistice [the French] concluded with the Austrians, it was mentioned that the Russians could retreat without molestation but the time and direction were indicated by what the French called à journées d'etapes.* We had no need for such patronising permission since the enemy did not risk following us into a country like Hungary in late autumn. They could not have been certain that Austria, having Archduke Charles' and Archduke Ferdinand's troops ready at Znaim, might not consider breaking the armistice, placing Napoleon in a difficult position.

Thus, our army moved along bad roads in terrible weather in one of the poorest regions of Hungary, passing through Kaschau and Eperies, and, having crossed the Carpathian Mountains near Bartfeld, descending into Galicia near Dukla. Our army was met in the most friendly fashion throughout Hungary, nothing being refused to relieve our exhausted troops. The local nobles greeted the commander-in-chief with complete respect. Two celebrations were organised, and, to our surprise, there were many who wished to entertain themselves after so shameful a defeat almost as though the enemy had lost and been destroyed.

Looking at our troops, the Hungarians were surprised that the French could defeat them; their annoyance was visible but they did not embarrass us with compassion. They thought the only reason for our defeat must have been the betrayal of the Austrian generals, and this alone showed how they trusted us! Not knowing that I understood Latin, they spoke openly about the Austrians and I heard praise for only a few of them.

During the battle of Austerlitz, Lieutenant-General Essen's corps had been a short march from the battlefield and it retreated along a different route, rejoining us in Galicia. Heavy artillery, dispatched to the fortress of Olmütz,

---

* Yermolov's note: I saw the commander-in-chief, who, as he dispatched a courier off to St. Petersburg, said the following to him: 'I graciously ask the commanders of the advance forces of the main French army to give permission for our free passage'.

also rejoined us successfully. Alexander was not with the army and left for Russia at Gödding.

[The battle of Austerlitz] was accompanied by so many strange incidents. I heard the opinions of many notable officers on this battle but none of them had a clear understanding of it and they agreed only on events they had not witnessed. Histories of this battle will certainly be written but it will be difficult to completely trust them and it will be easier to describe some local actions rather than how they related and connected to each other. It can be said about Austerlitz that each part of the army was instructed to operate separately, on condition that it would neither await nor support other elements, indeed it might have been better if we forgot that there were other Russian troops on the battlefield at that same moment.

Thus, Fate placed us, divided and without any mutual support, in front of an enemy, wary of Russians, but who dared to be a vanquisher. A Russian should never forgive the defeat at Austerlitz and the heart of each Russian should burn with a desire for vengeance!

In mid-January [1806], our army returned to our frontiers and established itself in Volhynia. The headquarters was at Dubno. After passing through Prussia's Polish territories, General of Cavalry Michelson's army encountered no enemy forces and returned to our frontiers. General of Cavalry Bennigsen assumed command.

We remained in Volhynia until the spring; following the arduous campaign, the much-needed rest revealed hidden troubles in our reduced army. I was attached with my company to the 3rd Division of Lieutenant-General Baron von der Osten-Sacken, deployed near Shavel in Volhynia.

Awards were soon distributed for the last campaign. Many received generous awards for Austerlitz alone; I was decorated with the Order of St. Anna (2nd class) for the campaign, since it was impossible to award me with a lesser decoration. Finally, based on the commander-in-chief's and Uvarov's excellent recommendations, I was promoted to colonel, bypassing a more senior officer in rank. I had to consider this as a great honour, although I had already served in the same rank for over nine years. [From the Russian text in A. Yermolov, *Zapiski*]

Robert Ker Porter

The humiliating defeat at Austerlitz rocked Russian society and made it search for a hero to rest its hopes and aspirations on. In this environment, Prince Peter Bagration, who commanded the Russian advance and rearguards and held the Allied right flank at Austerlitz, became one of the most celebrated commanders in the army. His determined struggle at Schöngrabern and Austerlitz brought him immense popularity and he was among the few who emerged from the defeat with their careers unscathed. His name and exploits stood in stark contrast to many others, including Emperor Alexander's actions during the battle. Bagration arrived at St. Petersburg in late January 1806 and settled at Countess Gagarina's house on the bank of the Neva River. He was received as a national hero and showered with awards and receptions. As his fame spread throughout the empire, Bagration made public appearances with the Emperor and served as guest of honour at numerous events. In late February, he travelled to Moscow, where the English Club, one of the most prestigious social clubs in Russia, offered a special dinner 'in honour of his late gallant conduct with the armies.' It was arranged on 15 March 1806 and its lavishness and lustre exceeded every expectation. The English traveller Robert Ker Porter, who happened to be in Russia at this time, was able to attend these festivities and left a fascinating account of them. Years later Leo Tolstoy used this event in his famous novel War and Peace.

After six days and nights of weary travel, we arrived at Moscow on the twenty-ninth of February: but the weather being foggy, so entirely enveloped the city as to conceal a view from us which, I am told, for magnificence is not exceeded in Europe.

On delivering our letters of introduction, we were welcomed with all the courtesies of friendship; and at the first salutation, [we] were made to forget, by the true politeness of this generous people, that we were strangers. I have heard it said that hospitality is a mark of barbarism. On what this opinion is grounded I cannot guess: but certainly it had not its foundation at Moscow, for I never saw, in any part of the world, such general polish of manners as in this city. Their hospitality appears to me to arise from a confidence in the friend who gives the introduction that he will not recommend any person unworthy of their notice; not doubting this, their benevolence hesitates not to receive the introduced with kindness: and from their love of society, if he prove agreeable he soon finds himself on the most easy and pleasant terms with a large and elegant acquaintance. Hence, I am led to consider this disqualifying remark on hospitality, as one of those commonplaces which the ignorant adopt on the faith of others; and those others, if they be equally unreflecting, can only promulgate the like dogmas, as an excuse for some failing in themselves.

Fortunately for us, our arrival and Prince Bagration's was nearly at the same time. We received cards from the English club* (an association only so in name, not three of our nation belonging to it), inviting us to a dinner which they gave to the prince in honour of his late gallant conduct with the armies. The house appropriated to this entertainment was a palace which formerly had been the residence of Prince Gagarin. Its suite of splendid

---

* The Club opened on 24 July 1802 and had over 400 members. 'Iz istorii Moskovskogo Angliiskogo Kluba', *Russkii arkhiv*, 27/2 (1889), p. 87.

saloons, and the great marble hall in which dinner was served, were fitted up with the most unsparing magnificence. At half past two o'clock the governor, General Baklashov and Prince Bagration entered. The latter was immediately surrounded by all in the room, eager to express their joy at his presence, and congratulations to their country in being yet blessed with the preservation of such a man. He is below the middle stature; of a dark complexion, deeply tinged with the climates in which he has served. His eye is small, quick and penetrating. His nose, a very high aquiline; and his face perfectly Georgian (he being of that country), expresses the most charming affability and sweetness. His demeanour is in unison with his countenance, being demonstrative of a modesty as winning as it is admirable in so idolised a character. He was dressed in a uniform wholly of green, covered with the insignia of many orders, stars, and a red ribbon.

The dinner was conducted with the nicest decorum; and the healths of the emperor and Prince Bagration were drunk with the greatest enthusiasm. In fact, I never saw a society of Russians so animated; and more than once it reminded me of similar meetings in honour of our glorious friend and hero Sir Sidney Smith.* Indeed the sentiment was so much the same, and the idea of one great man so naturally suggested those of others, that several of the Russian nobility present asked me if it were not like the fetes we dedicate to our heroes. I acknowledged the resemblance; but inwardly gave them the palm of general politeness; a grace in which this assembly far exceeded ours: I never in my life experienced so much attention as was there paid to us as strangers and Englishmen. Three quarters of an hour finished the repast; previous to which a band of singers from a regiment quartered in the city, sang an air in honour of the prince. The words, I here present to you in a prose translation:

Friendship unites us here. Joy captivates each heart!
Truth herself declares, that he is the hero
Who sacrifices himself to the Emperor and the empire,

---

* Sir William Sidney Smith (1764–1840) was one of the most colourful characters of the period. Arrogant and flamboyant by nature, Smith was also daring and ingenious. His adventures led him to various parts of the world fighting Republican and Imperial France. The French captured him in 1798, but Smith staged a remarkable escape from the Temple prison in Paris. In 1799, he commanded the British fleet in the Eastern Mediterranean and was instrumental in defeating Napoleon's troops in Syria. Smith captured vital French siege guns, making it impossible for the French to capture Acre. In addition, he transported a Turkish army to fight the French at Aboukir. In 1805, he became rear admiral and two years later took part in naval actions against the Turks. In November 1807 he oversaw the embarking of the Portuguese prince regent and royal family for Rio de Janeiro and was appointed commander-in-chief on the coast of South America in February 1808. He was recalled the next year, made vice admiral in 1810 and served in the Mediterranean for the next four years.

Despising envy and malice, and
Who dedicates himself to justice.

Chorus – Let us entwine him a crown of laurels, for he merits wearing it.

Unassisted by fortunate circumstances,
He wrested honour from the arms of peril.
He added not a single ray to the glory of Russia,
But surrounded it with thousands of beams.
Hope dawned wherever he appeared.
Enemy failed to make him shrink,
And with a few he overcame many.

Chorus – Let us entwine him with a crown of laurels, for he merits wearing it.

Hero's soul is satisfied with gratitude alone,
All other recompense is foreign to his feelings.
He despises luxury and pride, and all the vanities of the world.
To serve mankind is his aim, and its happiness his reward.
They, who reap the renown of virtue, lose it not in the grave.

Chorus – Let us entwine him a crown of laurels, for he merits wearing it.

[English text in Robert Ker Porter, *Travelling Sketches in Russia and Sweden*]

Philip Vigel

The author of acerbic but highly insightful memoirs, Philip Vigel was celebrating his twentieth birthday when he was assigned to the Russian diplomatic mission to China. Thus, he was absent while the Russian army campaigned in Moravia and learned about the Russian defeat at Austerlitz only upon his return to Moscow in March 1806.

Despite the Great Lent, Moscow turned out to be joyous and boisterous. [It was greeting the returning Russian warriors] and Prince Bagration, virtually the only commander who had defended the honour of Russian arms [at Austerlitz], had arrived to bask on his laurels, accompanied by numerous young men from prominent families who had befriended him during the last campaign. Of these men I only saw, at Prince Sergey Fedorovich Golitsyn's house, Prince Sergey, Golitsyn's third son, who had been injured in the head and wore a rather beautiful and coquettish black bandage. Numerous festivities, featuring adulatory poems, were held in honour of Bagration and his companions . . .

I left Moscow on 24 March and arrived at St. Petersburg on the 28th, after a ten-month absence. I found public attitudes in St. Petersburg to be rather different from Moscow's. The [Muscovites] allowed themselves to castigate the Tsar, even ridicule him, and shower profanities on his vanquisher, derisively calling him Napoleoshka. But in St. Petersburg, public attitudes were much more reserved: everyone felt that the humiliation experienced by the head of the state must inexorably be shared by the entire state. The resentment of our powerful foe was also much more deeply felt and more decorously expressed. [People] tried not to show much despondency, instead they took on brave airs and sought to explain [Napoleon's] victory as a turn of luck rather than skill. There was a general desire for a new war. Noble youth, which had been raised by the émigrés and took part in this campaign, despised [Napoleon] not as much because he was the enemy of our fatherland but rather because it saw him as a diminutive lieutenant who dared to seize the throne of the Grand Louis. These young men spoke haughtily and menacingly of their future battle exploits, which became subjects of surreptitious ridicule by some who as if unintentionally called these men 'zéro' instead of 'héros' and referred to the numerous St. Anne swords* that had been issued [in the wake of Austerlitz] as 'jackass swords': 'âne' instead of 'Anne'. Our Sovereign [Alexander] must have been content with the sentiments expressed by high society, the court and the guard, even though it was French royalism, and especially obsequiousness, that was taking on the hues of [Russian] patriotism. On the other hand, the supporters of England pointed to this nation as the anchor of our salvation and English influence in our affairs only further increased. It was from this time that I began to abhor [England]: I found it offensive that we were among the nations that these arrogant islanders, who reside beyond the continental dangers, recruit to fight for their own advantages.

[. . .]

The [Russian] government spent the entire summer of 1806 preparing for a new war against Napoleon. The great hardship that Russia [traditionally] endured – its numerous, one may even say countless, army – only further increased that year . . . But no one complained: everyone saw that political prestige, independence and every security of the state required it . . .

After the meeting in Berlin [in 1805], not just a political alliance but rather a genuine friendship tied Emperor Alexander and King [Frederick William III] of Prussia. As it befitted him, Napoleon gave [Frederick William] Hannover, a foreign land that did not belong to him, but he also formed a German confederacy called the Confederation of the Rhine and declared himself as its head, thus isolating Prussia from Germany. Subsequently, Prussia had numerous reasons for dissatisfaction with France while Russia continually

---

* The fourth class of the Order of St. Anne, granted for valour in military service, featured a cross borne on the pommel of an edged weapon.

instigated her to war. And so, having two hundred and fifty thousand of the best troops and with Russia making robust military preparations, Prussia did not wait long to declare war. This news was received ecstatically in St. Petersburg.

Prussia's material resources were vast, finances were in order, troops fresh and superbly drilled; but this composite kingdom lacked moral strength, except for memories of the victories of Frederick the Great and enthusiasm for their courageous, kind and beautiful queen. Its founder [Frederick the Great] left an important legacy to Europe but he also contributed to the debasement [of Prussia]: even when fighting the French, defeating and despoiling them, he still continued to embrace everything that eventually brought destruction to the ancient monarchy [in France]. During the peaceful half of his reign he sought to acculturate his half-barbarian [poluvarvarov] subjects by turning them into Frenchmen and endeavoured to undermine religion, and consequently morality, among them. His dissolute and weak-willed successor [Frederick William II], having dispatched his aged commander the Duke of Brunswick with a braggardly manifesto, pompously rose in arms against the revolution only to flee ignominiously from Verdun. He then recognised the [French] republic and lived in peaceful agreement with the [French] terrorists and even accepted the defrocked Abbe [Emmanuel] Sieyes as a [French] envoy to his court. Under both the old and the new Frederick Williams,* Prussia, hiding in its northern corner [of Europe], snickered over futile but honourable efforts of its rival, and one time overlord, Austria [against France] and refused to offer a helping hand to her. Meanwhile, doubt and unhappiness spread freely in the realm founded and uplifted by its godless king [Frederick the Great]. The worm of immorality kept eating away at this young and fast growing tree, so why is it so surprising that it fell down from a single strike of lightning? We had all forgotten the shameful campaign of Frederick William II and were instead expecting for Rossbach.† In early October, instead of Rossbach, we got Jena. ‡

Napoleon had never experienced such a successful and magnificent campaign: at his first touch, entire fortresses fell without any resistance; entire fleeing [Prussian] corps fell into his hands. The Prussian disgrace reddened our faces and each Prussian defeat was felt like a dagger piercing our very own hearts . . . [From the Russian text in Ph. Vigel, *Zapiski*]

---

* Frederick William II ascended the throne of Prussia in 1786, upon the death of Frederick the Great. Frederick William III inherited the Prussian crown in 1797.

† At the battle of Rossbach, on 5 November 1757, Frederick II crushed the Franco-Imperial armies. The battle is considered one of Frederick's greatest victories.

‡ Fought on 14 October 1806, the twin battles of Jena-Auerstädt resulted in the complete destruction of the Prussian forces and French victory in the war. By 25 October, the French troops were already in Berlin, where Napoleon arrived on the 27th.

Alexander Benckendorff

Alexander Benckendorff, the future chief gendarme of Russia, was born into a prominent German family and his father served as the military governor of Riga under Emperor Paul. After receiving education in a Jesuit boarding school, he was enrolled in the elite Life Guard Semeyonosvkii Regiment in 1798 at the age of seventeen. After serving in the Caucasus in 1803–4 and on the island of Corfu in 1804, Benckendorff was promoted to the Guard staff captain and made a flügel adjutant to Emperor Alexander I. In late 1806, Benckendorff was officially appointed as a duty officer to General Peter Tolstoy and sent to represent Russian interests at the Prussian court. He reached Prussian territory amidst the ongoing disastrous campaign against Emperor Napoleon, who had crushed the Prussian armies at the battles of Jena and Auerstädt and was busy occupying the kingdom.

Upon my arrival in Königsberg, I received the news of the [Prussian] defeat at Jena. In just one day, in effect, in just a few hours, the fate of the Prussian monarchy was resolved. This [Prussian] army, which was so confident of its perfection, so well drilled, so rich in its [military] theory, found itself assailed on all sides and surrendered its arms almost without resistance. Berlin soon fell and everyone fled or surrendered; I found the Prussian king [Frederick William III] and Queen [Louise] at Graudenz [Grudziądz], where, protected by the Vistula River, they considered themselves somewhat safe from the enemy pursuit.

What amazed me the most was the air of imperturbability on everyone's faces [at the Prussian court]. There was certain idleness and apathy everywhere, with the Prussian generals discussing the complete destruction of their army with the same indifference and composure with which they drafted plans for drill manoeuvres at Potsdam for the past forty years. The old general [Friedrich Adolf Graf von] Kalckreuth,* the [die-hard] enemy of [Karl Wilhelm Ferdinand] Duke of Brunswick and several other Prussian generals who commanded troops at Jena, assumed a certain air of sarcasm and indifference and was seemingly pleased with the degradation that covered the uniform that he had grown old wearing. I exploited his sentiments to secure his trust and learn everything that his jealousy sought to conceal. I learned from him details of battles and shameful capitulations of various corps as well as about the remaining resources at the disposal of Prussia. I hurried to provide these details to the Emperor [Alexander].

Only the [Prussian] queen had the appearance of a person who fully appreciated the scale of this disaster and the depth of the fall in the wake of

---

* Born in 1737, Kalckreuth was a Prussian generalfeldmarschall who had served with distinction in the War of the Bavarian Succession (1778–9) and the Prussian invasion of the Netherlands in 1787.

her brilliant stay at Stettin. She bitterly cried every time she saw me, as my presence seemed to have reminded her of her previous grandeur and maybe even reproached for her great propensity to follow Russia's policies and for the influence that she ill-used to make the decision for war. She was the only one who was genuinely distressed yet she also preserved her courage and when false-hearted, or weak-willed, advisers urged the king to entrust himself to the magnanimity of the conqueror [Napoleon], hers was the voice of honesty that urged him to choose hardship over dishonour.

Meanwhile, disastrous news kept arriving from all across the kingdom: the remnants of the [Prussian] army that survived at Jena kept surrendering to the mercy of the victors; Prince [Eugen Friedrich Heinrich von] Württemberg surrendered with his 17,000 men at Halle; at Frankfurt-am-Oder, the old [Generalfeldmarschall] Wichard Joachim Heinrich von Möllendorf chose the shameful glory of discrediting his seventy years of service to the vagaries of battle and was not ashamed to surrender his sword together with some 12,000 men entrusted to his command.* Only [Gebhard Leberecht von] Blücher continued to valiantly defend the honour of the Prussian army and fight unfalteringly, yielding only to the superior [French] forces and greater talent of Marshal [Karl] Bernadotte who blockaded him in Lübeck; Blücher lost his corps only after a series of bloody combats. [Meanwhile,] the fortress of Magdeburg surrendered without resistance, Stettin delivered its keys to the enemy while Kustrin, the almost impregnable fortress, fell upon the arrival of the first French outposts.

So many catastrophes, so much cowardice [malodushie], unfolding so swiftly was unprecedented in times of war and seemed so bizarre that if effectively paralysed any [Prussian] desire to defend [themselves]. Just one month after the start of the campaign, the [Prussian] army, capital and the most important fortresses were all lost. The king [Frederick William] decided to appeal for peace. I learned about it from Generalfeldmarschall† Kalckreuth and upon seeing tears on the queen's face. So I deemed necessary to request an audience with the king and, even though I had no instructions on this occasion, I informed the king how surprised the Emperor [Alexander] would be to hear about the start of [Franco-Prussian] negotiations. He tried to deny that negotiations had started and sought to assure me that his aide-de-camp went to the French headquarters only to discuss the [possible] exchange of prisoners of war. I pretended that I believed him and observed that it would be beneficial for Prussia to trust wholeheartedly in the formidable alliance with the Emperor [Alexander] rather than to surrender to the conqueror who

---

* Benckendorff seems to be mistaken since Möllendorf surrendered at Erfurt, not Frankfurt-am-Oder.

† Kalckreuth was still a general in the autumn of 1806 and received the rank of Generalfeldmarschall after defending Danzig in 1807.

was notorious for his perfidy and whose demands were infinite; besides, our troops had already departed from the borders of Russia and it was too late to countermand this decision. He asked whether I could confirm all of this and I responded that I vouched for every single word that I had uttered. He then opened the door and departed, having instructed me to visit the queen. I found her sitting on a chair next to the door. She had heard our conversation and was pleased with my speech as her opinion matched mine. [She told me that] she would give me a letter for the Emperor [Alexander] in which she would inform him of everything. She assured me that she concealed nothing and all of her efforts were directed to end negotiations that [the Prussian court] had opened with Napoleon. That same evening she delivered this letter to me via her lady-in-waiting and I immediately conveyed it to St. Petersburg, together with the latest news about successes of the French army.

So, the [Prussian] king, having made the decision [to end negotiations] against his ministers' suggestions, ordered the last remaining [Prussian] resources to be committed [to wage the war]. General [Anton Wilhelm von] Lestocq was instructed to rally under his command the surviving [Prussian] troops that were scattered across Old Prussia. These numbered just 17,000 men, the survivors of over 200,000 warriors that comprised the king's army at the start of the campaign. [From the Russian text in A. Benckendorff, *Vospominaniya* . . .]

Levin Bennigsen*

By 1806, the 61-year-old Leontii Leontievich (Levin August Theophile) Bennigsen had more than forty years of military service. Born in Hanover, he began his service in the Hanoverian Guard and took part in the concluding campaigns of the Seven Years War. He later entered Russian service and distinguished himself fighting the Turks, Poles and Persians. Emperor Paul I promoted him to lieutenant-general in 1798 but this did not prevent Bennigsen from participating in the conspiracy that assassinated the emperor. Despite this, Bennigsen's career did not suffer under Paul's son, Alexander, who appointed him the military governor of Vilna and promoted to general of cavalry in 1802. During the War of the Third Coalition in 1805, Bennigsen commanded a reserve corps in north-western Russia and was not involved in the Russian debacle at Austerlitz. The following year he was tasked with leading his corps to support Prussia against France, although this was made impossible by the brilliant French victories at Jena-Auerstädt in October 1806. After commanding Russian forces during the bloody campaign in Poland in 1806–7, Bennigsen spent four years in retirement at his estate near Vilna and

---

* Translated by Paul Strietelmeier.

maintained close correspondence with Alexander Borisovich Fock, who urged him to start writing memoirs of the past campaign. Bennigsen agreed, noting that he wanted to write them 'not because I feel the need to clear my name, which does not require it at all, but rather to further extoll Russian arms'.

I hasten, General [Fock], to acknowledge the reception of your letter. You reproach me for having neglected my correspondence with you since the Peace of Tilsit. I was at fault, I admit; but the circumstances under which I found myself excuse this delay. I sent you, over the course of the war, my ongoing opinion concerning all major events which took place. After the peace, I promised to favour you with certain bits of information, their result and sequence, as well as all of the details of my operations. I will keep my word and am currently organising those papers which relate to the war. This occupation has contributed to the interruption of our correspondence, which I resume today with pleasure and interest.

I will not respond separately to the majority of the questions which you have posed to me, General, and which seem to me to be personal, as the following correspondence before you will serve as a response. I limit myself to repeating to you that, far from bidding for the command of the army, I requested on several occasions to be spared from it. If, on the one hand, my sense of pride was flattered to be a commander-in-chief in a fight upon which the eyes of Europe must be fixed, as this fight could decide her fate, on the other hand, I had not lost sight of the responsibility to which I had exposed myself toward my sovereign and the entirety of a great nation. If one reflected on the circumstances in which we found ourselves and on the unforeseen catastrophes, which with a single blow had confounded all calculations, changed the plan and the theatre of war, as well as the operations, one could not delude oneself concerning the great difficulties which I had to overcome during the glorious career which I experienced. The combination of experience and comparison proved that the least mistake would result in the immediate invasion of our frontiers. It was the moment when fortune and audacity seemed to decide and triumph over all wise and prudent measures with which one opposed them, and each instant rendered these measures more necessary, which alone could make up for the too great disparity between of means between the two sides, a disproportion which need not be attributed at all to the superiority of enemy resources, but to the new combinations which events had created and to the respective plans and intentions of the two adversaries.

Napoleon, having succeeded in overwhelming Prussia, kept his forces concentrated and announced his intention to invade Russia, and the latter was only equipped to render assistance to an ally in a distant theatre. I need not tell you – for you will see it in our correspondence – that our court could not expect to fight with our forces alone anything more than a defensive war [ne pouvait s'attendre à rien moins qu'à soutenir avec ses forces seules une guerre pour sa défence].

Nothing was prepared for this scenario; consequently, a single battle lost, a single event like the last campaign of 1805 in Austria had provided at Ulm and Austerlitz, and as Prussia had just offered at Auerstädt, Jena, etc., that is the least reverse would have incalculable consequences for Russia, the more so as the war against the Turks was soon to ignite and had become inevitable, a war whose outcome had to be decided on the Vistula.

Add to all of these considerations that I had to act against Napoleon, the greatest captain of our time, against all the marshals of France, of which the majority had already commanded armies with distinction and the greatest success, against an army that was always victorious and accustomed to deciding a war with a single battle, moreover an army infinitely superior in numbers, especially at the opening of the second campaign, as I have already told you and as you will be convinced, in the following correspondence, by actual documents.

In the wars against France in which Russia had taken an active part, she had until this point only been an auxiliary power; the theatre of war had always been so distant that losses, as considerable as they may be, could not have any dangerous consequences for Russia. [In earlier wars], her task was limited to fighting with force and efficacy the common enemy, so as to realise the goals of the coalition, to assure the safety and independence of the states of Europe. Nowadays, she is forced to make war directly on her own frontiers against all the combined forces of France, the majority of the princes of Germany, Holland, Italy, etc., while the imperative of her own safety imposed altogether different duties.

How could one foresee, even believe that Russia, who in all the preceding wars had so loyally helped her allies with formidable armies, would be abandoned by these same forces she had aided? That Austria would remain neutral and allow the best moment to put the French army under the greatest pressure and reclaim the influence that she seemed to have lost without hope of return to pass? That Russia would have nothing to hope for in terms of diversion that could be undertaken by England, and that Sweden, too weak and too disconnected from immediate events to be able to act effectively alone, would remain more fidgety than active, more harmful to herself than helpful to the common cause? Finally that all of these Prussian forces, this great and beautiful army which for so long seemed to serve as a boulevard against the French, would disappear (so to speak) in eight days? – That all of the fortresses, even Magdebourg, Stettin, Küstren, etc., which should have stopped the advance of the enemy, or, if it advanced, would have greatly weakened the [French] army due to the detachments it would have had to deploy in order to besiege them, surrendered at the first sight of enemy forces, without the least resistance? – That these fortresses, once fallen, the French Emperor, placing there only weak garrisons, taken from auxiliary troops, and having nothing more to fear at the rear of his armies, would immediately be able to march with not only the national forces [French army?], but also with a considerable number of allied troops against Russia, before she had had time to exploit her great resources and assemble proportional forces on the frontier?

This state of things – the total abandonment in which Russia found herself – naturally had to displace, or rather place out of her reach, the primary goal of her path and conduct. It was not a question of her reducing France herself, to the point of being able to place limits on the preponderance that France had acquired over the rest of Europe. It was no longer anything but to maintain the integrity of the Russian Empire and to conserve her influence in Europe, in order to maintain the means of being useful to her friends and allies. There were two roads to achieving this end; peace negotiations or war.

Emperor Alexander, judging Europe according to the purity of his intentions, again hesitated to believe the pusillanimity and passive resignation of the other parties of interest and preferred to risk war. His troops delivered battles such that would have been able to re-animate the failing courage of his allies. But finally recognising frustration in his last hopes, and having no hope for foreign assistance, he believed it necessary that his brave nation sacrifice its previous disinterested views that favoured its allies and decided to seize on the first opportunity to negotiate.

Such was the real situation, especially at the beginning of the second campaign. I will have the occasion to convince you, in the following, that nothing is less founded than the opinion, instantly accepted [accrédité un instant], that after the battle of Friedland Russia found herself in such a critical position that she had been obliged to make peace. The exaggerations of the French bulletins, about which I will speak to you one day at greater length, and the falsities scattered about in this respect had not been able to alter the reality of the situation for a moment. When the course of my correspondence with you leads us to the period of this action, you will make your own judgment about the importance of this battle and you will be convinced that the loss of Friedland, which only cost our army 4,830 men, was too insignificant to attenuate the Russian forces, to influence later operations and to be, as many believed at the time, the cause of the peace that followed closely (I have sufficiently explained the reasons that motivated it), all the more so since the considerable reinforcements, which were gathering in the interior of the Empire, were already on the march, not far from our frontiers and soon to enter the theatre of war. I will speak of these reinforcements in greater depth in my following correspondence; you will see that the great resources and the Russian forces found themselves again spared for the defence of the country, and you will learn at the same time the reasons that impeded the arrival of these reinforcements, before the beginning of the second campaign. [From the French text in Levin Bennigsen, *Mémoires* . . .]

Imperial Manifesto, 30 November 1806

By late 1806, Russia was the only continental power still capable of fielding a major army against Napoleon. The Austrians had been vanquished the year before and the Prussian army had been virtually annihilated in the autumn of 1806. Russians learned memorable lessons at Austerlitz and in the following months they began rapidly reorganising their military forces. In late November, on the eve of a new campaign against France, Emperor Alexander called for the creation of new forces to support the war effort. The Imperial manifesto proclaimed the establishment of new forces of 'territorial armies' or 'militias' that were designed 'to exist only during the time of public danger'. The manifesto specified that 612,000 men had to be called up to serve in these militia forces, one of the largest mobilisations of militia forces Russia undertook in the first half of the nineteenth century. Russia's first effort at militia forces was only partially successful, as local authorities struggled to mobilise, outfit, train and maintain the prescribed number of recruits; ultimately fewer than 230,000 militiamen were mobilised. But the Russian authorities did acquire valuable experience that they put to use during Napoleon's invasion of Russia in 1812.

The events that have spread over Europe the horrors of bloodshed and desolation from an insatiable thirst of conquest and aggrandisement in the present usurped government of France, are manifest to the whole world. Our endeavours to set bounds to this evil, and to preserve the tranquillity and integrity of powers in alliance with us by pacific measures, all proved ineffectual. The perfidy with which the common enemy violates the sanctity of treaties and the rights of nations, threatening Europe with universal devastation, compelled us, at last, to take up arms in support of neighbouring kingdoms. The series of disasters that befell the Austrian armies obliged that monarchy to conclude a disadvantageous peace, on terms dictated by the ambition of the conqueror, and the dire necessity of circumstances. After this, Prussia, vainly attempting to check the mischief by the establishment of general and solid peace through the means of negotiation, notwithstanding all her sacrifices for the sake of preserving an alliance with France, notwithstanding all her compliances with the demands of this common enemy, could not long remain exempt from the calamities of war. Lulled into a state of delusive security by the prospect of a peace, which she vainly hoped to enjoy, and the mistaken confidence she reposed in a treacherous ally, she was suddenly plunged into the very abyss of ruin. The armies of Napoleon, falling on the Prussian troops before they had been able to unite, defeated them, made an easy conquest of the defenceless capital, and seized the greatest part of the provinces of that kingdom.

In such a state of affairs, seeing this neighbouring power, which divided the western borders of our empire from France, destitute of all means of defence, it became indispensably necessary for us to advance our armies, under the command of Field Marshal Count Kamenski, for the defence of our territories, menaced on that side with an hostile invasion; and, having implored the protection of the Almighty, who ever espouses the cause of the just, we ordered every effort to be made for the defeat of this dangerous assailant, who, in the proclamations he has published, carries his audacity so far as openly to threaten that he will extend his triumph even inside our dominions.

At the commencement of this inevitable war, the whole burden of which, after the total overthrow of our allies, devolves upon our country, we consider it our first duty to redouble our unceasing efforts for the preservation of the tranquillity and integrity of our empire, by augmenting and collecting the armed force of a faithful, brave, and magnanimous people, entrusted to our administration by Almighty Providence.

The misfortunes, which have so rapidly overtaken the neighbouring powers, evince the present necessity of recourse to unusual means, to great and vigorous measures, which can only be carried into effect by a zealous attachment to our country, by a manly firmness of spirit, and a true sense of national honour. A people really inspired and actuated by sentiments of that description, arming in a body, may raise an insurmountable rampart against every hostile attack, however formidable. Neglect in providing for their internal security by such general armaments during the present contest with France, in opposition to her system of plunder and conquest, has been attended with the most pernicious consequences to Austria, and hastened the downfall of Prussia. Their fate was determined by the loss of a few battles; after which the enemy meeting no obstacle, and dreading no opposition from an unarmed populace, suddenly forced his way through the interior provinces, spread devastation and terror by his rapid and violent depredation, destroyed the scattered remains of a routed army, and effected a total overthrow of their empires. The bravery of the Russian troops, and the victories which their unexampled firmness, for the course of a century past, has gained over every foreign foe, to the remotest corners of the earth, the trophies still existing in various parts of these realms which have been extended by their achievements, and the recollection of the glory they have thus acquired, affords us the strongest ground to hope that on the present occasion, under the dispensations of Providence, whose blessings attend the arms of the just, all the machinations of our enemies may be confounded, and that the only traces they leave behind them upon our soil will be their own graves.

The immense tract of country upon which these armies must act occasioning many difficulties in the way of their speedy and mutual co-operation for the defence of an extensive frontier, the evident danger which would arise in case (which God forbid should ever be the case) the enemy might penetrate into the interior of our empire, compel us to adopt the most efficacious measures to avert it, by the establishment of a general temporary armed militia, which may be ready in all quarters at a moment's notice, to support the regular troops, and able to oppose to the enemy at every step the invincible force of the true sons of their country, united for the preservation of their most valuable enjoyments.

In such arduous circumstances we refer with the fullest confidence to the distinguished order of the hereditary nobility of our empire, by whose faithful services in the field of battle, and extensive sacrifices both of life and property, Russia has been elevated to her present greatness, to that order which, by examples of heroism has on all occasions animated and assisted the subordinate members of the empire to participate in the salvation, defence, and glory of our country. The memorable proofs of patriotism and of loyalty displayed in ancient and modern times by the nobility of Russia, and their well-known readiness on every occasion, where the common good requires their exertion, to obey the summons of their sovereign, and to meet with spirit every toil, and every danger for the service of the empire, convince us how cordially, zealously, and efficaciously, it will co-operate with us for the speedy and successful completion of such a provisional armament or militia, as is indispensably required, and now ordained for public security, according to the regulations annexed hereto.

We are likewise well assured that our faithful corporations, notables, merchants, townsmen, as well as the crown peasants and free farmers will unite their efforts to bear the common burden of this important public duty for the defence of Fatherland, our Holy Faith, and for individual well-being.

May the servants of the church of God offer up in concert with ourselves, and all our faithful subjects, the most fervent prayers towards the Supreme Disposer of Events, that he may shed his divine favour on our effort to avert the common danger, to vanquish, and exterminate the foe, and to restore the blessings of peace and tranquillity in the heart of our Fatherland.

The formation of the internal troops or militia, to exist only during the time of public danger, is to be carried into effect on the following plan:–

I. On the Establishment of the Provisional Troops or Militia.

Each province [gubernia], both on the frontiers and in the interior, shall arm such a number of its inhabitants, for its proportion of the provincial territorial army [gubernskoe zemskoe voisko], or militia, as is specified in the annexed table.

The several provinces joined in the table, compose a district [oblast'], and the united provincial troops of those respective provinces compose the district territorial armies [oblastnoe zemskoe voisko] or militia.

The numbers of such district territorial armies is fixed at seven.

The commanders in chief of the district territorial armies are to be appointed by the sovereign, from persons whose known fidelity, services, and merits, entitle them to public confidence.

The commanders of the provincial territorial armies are to be chosen by the nobility of each province, out of persons who have distinguished themselves in military service, and, if possible, residents of the same province. In case the nobility should not elect, the commander-in-chief is to nominate them.

The subordinate officers of the provincial territorial armies, that is of the various units consisting of a thousand, five hundred, and so on [uezdnye tysiachnye, piatisotennye i drugie], are likewise to be chosen by the nobility of the province out of their own body; if practicable, out of persons who have served with honour in the field, or in default of them, out of such as have not served, and out of other classes. In case of non-appointment by the nobility, the commander of the provincial territorial army appoints.

After the publication of this manifesto, the Civil Governors shall, without delay, make up lists and reports of the inhabitants of every estate, in their respective provinces, and furnish the most accurate copies of the same, according to forms prescribed, with all expedition to the commanders in chief of districts, and to the commanders of the provincial territorial armies who shall be appointed.

II. On the Levy and Equipment of the Militia.

The Civil Governors, with the marshals of the nobility, determine according to these lists and the registers of the peasants belonging to the crown, and to landholders, with those of inhabitants of towns, what proportion of peasants of each description, and of citizens, is to be levied to fill up the number specified in the paper.

The Assemblies of the Nobility being furnished by their respective heads with notice of the number of men required for this provisional public service, determine according to their enrolments how many each is to furnish. When this specification is made up, every landholder or owner of serfs must provide, in the space of two weeks, his quota of men, completely equipped, as far as practicable, armed with firearms, and consisting, where such can be found, of people accustomed to the use of them; that is, jagers [egerya], volunteers [okhotniki], etc.; clothing them suitably to the season, and furnishing each man with three rubles in money; they are also to prepare provisions sufficient to maintain them all for three months.

At the same time, the crown villages and all other towns must provide, without delay, their respective quotas of men for the provincial territorial army [gubernskoe zemskoe voisko] out of such as are fit to bear arms, equip them in the same proportion with clothes and money, and furnish also three months' provisions.

The corporations in cities, at their meetings, immediately after the publication of this manifesto and the enrolment of the provincial troops in their respective provinces, must require, in proportion to their means, circumstances, and zeal, for the public good of every citizen, contributions of money, food, or other articles necessary for the clothing and equipment of soldiers. Reports of these public contributions will be given to the Civil Governors, to the commanders of provincial troops, and to the commanders in chief of the district territorial armies, and by them immediately presented to the Sovereign.

For the safe custody of such offers and contributions, whether from the order of nobility, or from the corporation of cities, the most convenient and effectual means are left to their own disposal to arrange. Proper places for the purpose will be allotted by the commanders of provinces, and the commander-in-chief of the district.

Free persons of every estate, whom a regard to their country may induce to engage as volunteers in its service, and to join, without delay, these corps of provincial troops, will be received into them by the commanders of provincial territorial armies.

Every inhabitant of provinces, who have in their houses muskets, cutlasses, sabres, pikes, or arms of any other description, over and above what each may require for the equipment of the militia, or for his own individual use, is required to deliver them up for the public service; in country places, to the marshals of the nobility and commanders of the troops belonging to the divisions [uezd] where they reside; and, in cities, to the councils [duma] and to the magistrates. Such donations will be accepted with suitable acknowledgments; and, on the receipt of them, those who take them will give a proper certificate, and report the same to the commanders of the provincial troops.

Powder, cannon, cannonballs, and all other military stores, which cannot be provided by individuals, shall be furnished out of the imperial arsenals or government magazines. The commander-in-chief, and the provincial commanders, will use their utmost endeavours to procure everything necessary within their respective provinces, and the civil officers are bound to render them every assistance.

To form and strengthen this body of militia, an adequate number of regular troops will be allotted, under the direction of the provincial commander.

III. On the Regulation of the Militia.

The commander-in-chief of a regional territorial army [oblastnoe zemskoe voisko] shall carry into effect, according to the instructions given him, all the measures tending to the public security: the orders he gives are to be fulfilled by subordinate officers in the places under his control with the same exactitude, fidelity, and expedition as the commands of the Sovereign.

Persons who distinguish themselves by particular proofs of zeal are to be immediately reported to us, that they may receive promotion proportionate to their merits.

Under his control are placed the commanders of the provincial troops and the civil governors as far as relates to the superintendence of the provincial territorial armies.

To the commander of the provincial troops are subjected in all respects the marshals of the nobility in provinces and districts, and they are to fulfil his orders. To him likewise are subjected the civil officers and magistrates of all descriptions, as far as relates to the completion of measures tending to the public security; all subaltern officers of the militia are likewise under his control.

That all these measures may be carried into effect with the utmost promptitude, the strictest submission and good order are required, and the slightest instances of disobedience to superiors, injurious to the public welfare, must meet with speedy and severe punishment. To provide, therefore, against an evil pregnant with such imminent danger to the empire, the commander-in-chief is hereby invested with power to arrest and deliver up to a court-martial any person guilty of disobedience and of breach of fidelity (or of the special oath which will be administered to these militia troops), and the sentences of the court-martial will be put into instant execution, though they extend to the deprivation of life. When, by the blessing of the Almighty, our efforts, in conjunction with those of our faithful subjects, for the defence of our country, and the defeat of its haughty enemies, shall have been crowned with wished-for success and the danger with which we are now threatened shall pass away, then with hearts full of gratitude toward the Providence that protects us, these our troops shall lay down their arms and return to their homes and families, saved by their courage, there to enjoy the fruits of peace so gloriously acquired. We likewise solemnly pledge our Imperial word, and impose upon ourselves the sacred obligation, as the representative of a grateful country, to bestow graces and favours, and to reward with honour, and those marks of distinction due to eminent merit and services, all the true-born sons of Russia, who, on the present occasion, may display their zeal by acts of personal courage, by the sacrifices of their property, or by other deeds essentially conducive to the public good. The names of all such champions, in their country's service, will be celebrated with just admiration by posterity, and enrolled in the annals of immortal fame.

Specification of the Numbers of People, divided by districts, to be Supplied to form Temporary Internal Militia in Each Province

1st District

	Number of Militiamen in Each Province
St. Petersburg	11,000
Novgorod	19,000
Tver	30,000
Olonetsk	6,000
Yaroslav	24,000
Total	**90,000**

2nd District

	Number of Militiamen in Each Province
Estland	8,000
Lifland	20,000
Courland	12,000
Pskov	20,000
Total	**60,000**

3rd District

	Number of Militiamen in Each Province
Vitebsk	23,000
Mogilev	25,000
Smolensk	30,000
Chernigov	33,000
Total	**111,000**

4th District

	Number of Militiamen in Each Province
Moscow	29,000
Tula	29,000
Kaluga	24,000
Vladimir	29,000
Ryazan	29,000
Total	**140,000**

5th District

	Number of Militiamen in Each Province
Orlov	19,000
Kursk	23,000
Voronezh	18,000
Kharkov	15,000
Total	**75,000**

6th District

	Number of Militiamen in Each Province
Kiev	21,000
Poltava	26,000
Kherson	4,000
Ekaterinoslav	8,000
Total	**59,000**

7th District

	Number of Militiamen in Each Province
Kostroma	15,500
Vologda	11,000
Nizhnii Novgorod	16,500
Kazan	16,000
Vyatka	18,000
Total	**77,000**

In total, in seven districts – 612,000

The provinces not listed in this table are to supply contributions of provisions, arms and ammunition. [From the Russian text in *Polnoe sobranie zakonov*, XIX, No. 22.374]

2

The Winter Campaign, December 1806

The War of the Fourth Coalition, as the campaign of 1806–7 eventually became known, began rather disastrously for the Allies (Britain, Prussia, Sweden, Saxony and Russia). Prussia, which could have had a decisive effect on the outcome of the war in 1805, had dithered until the autumn of 1806 when King Frederick William III was at last forced by his hawkish advisors, led by his beautiful wife Louise, to intervene in the fighting. Yet, the war was over just a few weeks later. In early October Napoleon invaded Saxony and scored a brilliant victory at Jena and Auerstädt (14 October) where the Prussian army effectively collapsed. Less than two weeks later, Napoleon made a triumphant entry into the Prussian capital, Berlin. With his army in tatters, Frederick William was forced to leave his capital for East Prussia where he eagerly awaited news of the arrival of Russian troops. Napoleon soon turned his attention to these Russian forces, which, under the command of General Baron Levin Bennigsen, were marching to support their Prussian allies. In worsening weather, which turned the roads into mud, the Grande Armée marched into Poland, forcing the Russians to withdraw over the Vistula. The French cavalry occupied the former Polish capital city of Warsaw on 28 November. A second Russian army, under General Fedor Fedorovich Buxhöwden, advanced to confront the French. On 26 December, at Golymin, the French caught up with the Russian rearguard, under General Prince Dmitry Vladimirovich Golitsyn, whose troops were too exhausted to march further. Golitsyn also had to hold the town and await General Fabian von der Osten-Sacken's troops, who were in danger of being cut off. With a total of about 16,000–18,000 men facing the corps of 38,000 men under Marshals Augereau and Murat, the Russians held out until nightfall and then withdrew. On the same day, 12 miles away, General Bennigsen decided to attack Marshal Jean Lannes's corps of 20,000 men with his 40,000–45,000 men at Pultusk. Both sides claimed a victory, but Bennigsen, who would later claim that he had been faced by Napoleon with 60,000 men, left the field to Lannes.

At the end of December both sides settled down into winter quarters. Napoleon needed the time to put his army, which had now been campaigning for over a year, into order. The Russians settled into winter quarters around Königsberg, and took this respite to reorganise and replenish their forces. Due to the ongoing bickering between Bennigsen and Buxhöwden, Emperor Alexander decided to grant the overall command of the Russian armies to Field Marshal Mikhail Kamenski, an experienced but frail commander who had been enjoying retirement at his rural estate for the past few decades. Kamenski's appointment, however, did not last long. Just days after arriving in the theatre of war, he abandoned his post, claiming ill health. Soon thereafter Buxhöwden was also recalled, leaving Bennigsen in command.

Faddei Bulgarin

A man of contradictions, Faddei Bulgarin (Jan Tadeusz Bulgarun) was born into a Polish noble family in the Polish-Lithuanian Commonwealth in 1789. Just three years later, the Second Polish Partition changed his life's trajectory. His father, a die-hard Polish nationalist and republican, actively participated in the resistance to the Russian invasion and was exiled to Siberia. The young Bulgarin was educated in St. Petersburg, where he studied at the famed Land Noble Cadet Corps. Upon graduation in 1806, Bulgarin enlisted in the Grand Duke's Uhlan Regiment and participated in the spring campaign of 1807 in Poland, distinguishing himself at Friedland. After distinguished service during the Russo-Swedish War of 1808–9, Bulgarin retired with the rank of sub lieutenant. By then, Napoleon had already established the Duchy of Warsaw and the news of reforms and transformations taking place in his homeland certainly excited the young Bulgarin. In 1811, he left Russia for Warsaw, where he enlisted in the French service and was assigned to the 2nd Lancer Regiment of the Vistula Legion. In 1812 he served in Spain before being sent to Russia, where he distinguished himself fighting Russians; he later claimed* that it was he who had helped the French discover fords across the Berezina River that allowed Napoleon's army to escape from Russia. In 1813, Bulgarin distinguished himself in Germany, including at the battle of Bautzen, where, as he later claimed, Napoleon himself took note of him, entrusted him with a mission and later rewarded him with promotion to captain and the Legion of Honour. In 1814 he was captured and returned to Russia, where he underwent a remarkable transformation, becoming an ardent supporter of the reactionary policies of the imperial court and an active agent of the secret police. He emerged as one of the most prominent literary figures in Russia, contributing to many

---

* In his memoirs Józef Załuski, of the Imperial Guard's Polish Chevau-Légers, recalled that 'the first ford on the Berezina was discovered by an officer of the 8th Regiment of Lubinski with the help of a few lancers. This officer was Bulharyn, who later became the famed Russian writer.' Józef Załuski, *Wspomnienia o pułku lekkokonnym polskim gwardyi Napoleona I* (Krakow, 1865), p. 273.

leading newspapers and literary journals and publishing some of the earliest Russian historical novels, which enjoyed considerable popularity both at home and abroad. Yet Bulgarin's unscrupulous manners also made him the most odious figure in the Russian literary world and he was the target of much criticism and ridicule.

The entire city of St. Petersburg and all of Russia eagerly awaited news from our army that was fighting the French. The first news filled our hearts with joy. Before our departure [from St. Petersburg], we celebrated two complete victories over Napoleon himself at Pultusk and Preussisch-Eylau, and several brilliant victories over his marshals at Golymin, Mohrungen, Lopachin, Nasielsk, etc. It is rather amusing that Paris and all of France were celebrating these very victories as well! French bulletins heralded crushing defeats of the Russians while the Russian reports announced the complete defeat of the French! We saw no French bulletins in Russia and consequently had every right to celebrate our victories. But Europe was at a loss.

[...]

The Russian army, which entered [east] Prussia [in late 1806], was divided into two strong corps, or, as they were referred to then, into two armies. The first army was led by General of Cavalry Baron Leontii Leontievich Bennigsen while the second was commanded by General of Infantry Count Fedor Fedorovich Buxhöwden. Our armies were already in Prussia and Baron Bennigsen's forces had already fought several advance-guard combats with the enemy when, on 16 November 1806, a new commander-in-chief was appointed – Field Marshal General Count Mikhail Fedorovich Kamenski, who hastened to arrive to the armies and found Bennigsen on the Narew, in the vicinity of Pultusk, while Count Buxhöwden's army was approaching the Vistula, in the direction of Ostrolenka. Having taken command of the armies, Count Kamenski reported to His Majesty the Emperor that his forces consisted, based on rosters, of 159,000 men.

Thus the attention of all Russia and, indeed, of all Europe was drawn to just three individuals: Kamenski, Bennigsen and Buxhöwden. Count Kamenski was then seventy-eight years old, having been born in 1738. He studied at the Land Nobility Cadet Corps and graduating as a corps sergeant at the age of nineteen, he enrolled in the army with the rank of lieutenant in 1757. Back then the cadet corps was what a military academy is today, so the cadet received a higher military education, which Kamenski, upon his graduation, continually perfected, delving into various fields of science and reading military theorists. That same year [1757], he transferred with the same rank to the artillery, and a year later, rose to the rank of captain. Passionate about the art of war, bored by idleness and eager to earn some experience, Kamenski sought [Imperial] permission to serve as a volunteer in the French army, where he served for two years under the command of the famed Marshal [Victor François, Duke de] Broglie, fighting against the allies of [the Prussian King] Frederick the Great during the Seven Years War. When Russia entered the war, Kamenski hastened to the army of [Peter] Saltykov and took part in all actions in 1760–1, earning the rank of colonel and the post of general-quartermaster-lieutenant (which corresponds to the present-day corps quartermaster). By his twenty-ninth birthday Kamenski already enjoyed a brilliant reputation in the army and society: [he] owned a family estate with three thousand serfs, and was graciously received at the court and by all the powerful grandees.

At the conclusion of peace with Prussia and then on the accession to the throne of Empress Catherine II, Kamenski visited Berlin and met Frederick the Great several times, who, you might say, tested his military knowledge and, surprised by Kamenski's combination of mind and scholarship with unusual fervour and a certain savageness of imagination, he even referred to him as 'est un jeune Canadien, qui est pourtant assez civilise', meaning 'this a young Canadian savage, but he is civilised enough'.*

Choosing persons to keep company with the heir to the throne, Empress [Catherine] allowed Kamenski to attend His Highness Grand Duke Paul Petrovich, which is certainly the best proof of how highly regarded he was at this time. Until 1769, Kamenski was still known only as a gallant and knowledgeable officer but the war against Turkey [the Ottoman Empire] that began that year gave him an opportunity to demonstrate his far superior abilities. He arrived at the army of Prince Golitsyn already in the rank of major-general, and commanding the vanguard, he contributed to the defeat of the grand vizier of the Crimean Khan and the capture of the [fortress of] Khotin. Transferring to the command of Count Panin, and then to Count Rumyantsev, Kamenski continued to distinguish himself in command of a separate corps, earned his promotion to the rank of lieutenant-general, and greatly contributed to the conclusion of the famed Peace of Küçük Kaynarca [in 1774].

Thus, Kamenski became renowned throughout Russia. He returned to St. Petersburg with [the Order of] St. George 2nd class, with the ribbons of the [Orders of] St. Anna and of St. Alexander, and with the reputation of a skilful commander and fearless warrior. During the Second Turkish War [1788] Kamenski joined the army with the rank of general-en-chef and, commanding a corps, he crushed the hordes [orda] of the Crimean Khan, earning the Order of St. Vladimir 1st class [in 1789]. Yet, despite Kamenski's victories and acquired fame, Empress Catherine II, knowing his violent temper and cruelty towards the vanquished, refused to entrust him with the command of the main army after the death of Prince Potemkin [in

---

* Frederick was referring to the fierce Iroquois or the Six Nations, who during the French and Indian War (the North American part of the Seven Years War) supported Britain (Prussia's ally) against the French.

1791], and instead confirmed the choice made by [Potemkin] shortly before his death. Thus General Kakhovskii became the commander-in-chief, even though he was junior in rank to Kamenski, who was reprimanded for disobeying the posthumous orders of Prince Potemkin by intending to claim command of the army based on his seniority. Yet, if we follow the letter of the law, Kamenski was correct since it is illegal to bequeath armies as if they were one's own property, without special [Imperial] permission, and, until the new appointment, the command always belonged to the most senior in rank. Kamenski was offended by such treatment and left the military service, returning to his estates. Emperor Paul, upon his accession to the throne, recalled Kamenski to the court, gave him the Order of St. Andrew the First-Called (in March 1797), promoted him to the rank of field marshal (in April 1797) on the coronation day and granted him the title of count. Yet in December 1797, Kamenski was suddenly discharged from the military. He returned to his estates and remained idle until 1806.

Both biographers of Count M. F. Kamenski and everyone who knew him agree on his character traits. He undoubtedly was a learned man and a skilled tactician. The great Suvorov, with whom Kamenski had an eternal and implacable enmity, used to say: 'Kamenski knows tactics, but I know the practice.' Kamenski's personal courage bordered on insanity and even his enemies confirmed the truth of his words when he stated that he would be glad to know how it feels to fear death! His mind was deep and insightful, but all his laudable qualities were overshadowed by his extraordinary temper and intemperance in anger that drove him to cruelty, extraordinary pride, recklessness, perversity and impatience in dealing with people, whom he frequently insulted for no reason. Neither comrades not subordinates liked Kamenski, and all feared meeting him. During my last year at the [Cadet Corps] I met [Kamenski] on several occasions. He came to observe us during training and recreation, and spoke, joked and even played with the cadets. He was of rather small stature, lean and covered with wrinkles; he wore a Prussian-style uniform, with which he was dismissed by Emperor Paul I. Unusually thick and heavy eyebrows, with eyes shining like burning coals underneath them, added certain ferocity to his face. He was abrupt in his conversation and had rather quaint manners, whether because he was imitating his arch-enemy, Suvorov, or by nature; despite his advanced age, he seemed vigorous and agile in all his movements.

What made the Emperor appoint him commander-in-chief? Everyone was lost guessing, but the more experienced people were saying that it was done to excite the national spirit, to revive the memories of the glorious time of Catherine the Great, which was sacred to the people. It was in this spirit that the great Derzhavin praised the appointment of Kamenski, whom he described in his verses as 'the sword bequeathed [to us] by Catherine'. So Kamenski was employed in the same way as the Turks use the banner of [the Prophet] Muhammad – for its appearance. Kutuzov, whom Catherine II called her general, and about whom Suvorov wrote in his report about the capture of Izmail: 'General Kutuzov advanced on my left wing but was my right hand,' was removed [from command] and appointed (in October 1806) as the military governor of Kiev . . . Although Kutuzov was not responsible for the defeat at Austerlitz, he was held responsible for it and it was feared that his appointment to command the armies might have a bad effect on the troops. Besides, Kutuzov, who was considered a man of extraordinary cunning, had numerous enemies, who feared his influence.

So we faced a great challenge: could Kamenski, a 78-year-old man who had never commanded armies and who earned his reputation commanding small detachments during wars against the unlearned Orientals, resist the genius of Napoleon? At that time I heard from many that, due to his intensity of character and impatience, Kamenski was unsuitable to the post of commander-in-chief, for which one of the most important qualities must be unshakable composure. It seems for the very purpose of constraining Kamenski's ardour that particular arrangement, which we will discuss below, had been devised.

The next man facing Napoleon was [Baron] Leontii Leontievich* Bennigsen, on whom all our hopes were based. Bennigsen was originally from Hanover, born into a wealthy baronial family. In 1806 he was sixty-two years old, having been born in February 1745. He enlisted in the Hanoverian service as a page at the age of ten; by fourteen, he was already an ensign in the Hanoverian Foot Guards. In 1762, at the age of seventeen and already a captain, he participated in the last campaign of the Seven Years War. After the war, Bennigsen retired with the rank of lieutenant-colonel, married and inherited his family's vast estates upon his father's death. But he was a soldier in his heart and soul and peaceful life was onerous for him. The glory of the Russian arms fascinated him and, in 1773, he entered Russian service in the rank of premier-major, first assigned to the Vyatskii Musketeer Regiment and later transferred to the Narvskii Regiment. I mentioned these regiments purposely since they were proud of the names of the great men who had served in their ranks. Napoleon had invented a perfect tool for maintaining martial spirit in the regiments when he ordered that the famous men must be posthumously kept on the regimental rolls of units where they had served. In 1777, Bennigsen was promoted to lieutenant-colonel of the Kievskii Light Horse Regiment and, in 1788, he became a colonel and appointed commander of the Izyumskii Hussar Regiment. Under Empress Catherine II, the position of regimental commander was very important, because a colonel was not just a complete master of his unit but, one might say, its absolute lord, selecting its officers and managing it without almost any oversight. During the war

---

* Bennigsen's original name was Levin August Theophile.

against the Turks, Bennigsen was dispatched, with his regiment, to the famed Army of Ekaterinoslav commanded by Prince Potemkin. He distinguished himself in numerous actions, especially during the assault on Ochakov, and was promoted to brigadier. In 1792, Bennigsen was given command of a flying detachment in Lithuania to protect Byelorussia. Excelling throughout the Polish campaign, Bennigsen was awarded the order of St. Vladimir (3rd class), a golden sword [for gallantry] with diamonds, the Order of St. George (3rd class), was granted a hereditary estate with 1,080 serfs in the Minsk province, and was promoted to major-general.

Seeking further fame and military exploits, Bennigsen, after the conquest of Poland, transferred to the army of Count [Pavel] Zubov who was dispatched in 1796 to fight Persia. He contributed to the capture of [the fortress of] Derbent and was rewarded with the Order of St. Anne (1st class). For the next ten years Bennigsen did not bare his sword but was still promoted to lieutenant-general in 1798 and to general of cavalry in 1802. In November 1805, Bennigsen was given command of the Army of the North, with which he departed to Germany to eventually join up with Kutuzov but did not arrive in time for Austerlitz and returned to Russia upon the conclusion of peace.

Thus, Bennigsen had never served either as a commander-in-chief nor as a corps commander in wartime and his abilities as a military commander could not be properly judged by his previous service. He was brave and enterprising, but if one considers that his main accomplishments came as a detachment commander against the Polish confederates, that is, the rebellious nobility and a small number of regular troops who were inexperienced, poorly armed and led by men with limited understanding of the art of war, then Bennigsen's former successes could not have served as sufficient guarantees of future victories, especially in a war against such a commander as Napoleon. Yet everyone recognised that Bennigsen had a broad knowledge and that although he had not had a classical education due to enlisting in the army at an early age, he had still acquired a thorough understanding of strategy through reading, thinking and practising. Nature created him as a warrior, endowing him with a passionate love for the art of war, quickness of mind, military eye, extraordinary courage, rare audacity and remarkable composure. Bennigsen was of tall stature but rather lean, and had expressive facial features and a quick glance. His imposing and dignified appearance, lordly manners and constant composure inspired respect and aroused instinctive confidence in his superiors, peers and subordinates. Back then it was rumoured that Bennigsen had submitted a report in which he critically reviewed the 1805 campaign and the battle of Austerlitz, and presented a plan for a future war against France. I do not know what has become of these important documents but I have heard about their existence from a person close to Bennigsen, General of Artillery

Alexander Borisovich Fock. Those who knew Bennigsen well claimed that he was a man of an extremely subtle mind and insinuating when he needed it, and that he nurtured inordinate ambition within himself, and therefore a great many feared him, just as they did Kutuzov.

General of Infantry Count Fedor Buxhöwden, originally from Lifland, was fifty-six years old [in 1806] and just as Bennigsen, he had followed his passion for the art of war and embarked on a military career in 1764. Little is known about his early years of service. In 1769, during a war against the Turks, he, undoubtedly still in the junior ranks, had somehow earned particular goodwill from the famous Feldzug-meister General Count Gregory Grigorievich Orlov, who appointed him to his suite and took him on his travels through Germany and Italy. By 1783 Buxhöwden was already a colonel and, after 1787, Her Imperial Majesty's flügel adjutant. This was a particularly noteworthy distinction because back then, the number of flügel adjutants was quite small and this position was granted only to those who were closest to Her Imperial Majesty and enjoyed her special grace and confidence. By then Buxhöwden already had the Cross of St. George (4th class) and commanded the Kexholmskii Musketeer Regiment. In 1789, in the rank of brigadier, Buxhöwden took part in the Swedish War, serving on the galley fleet and distinguishing himself on several occasions; he earned the [Order of] St. George (3rd class) and promotion to major-general, keeping his position of Her Majesty's flügel adjutant. In 1790 Buxhöwden distinguished himself in land operations against the Swedes and, upon the conclusion of the peace, he was granted the ribbon of [the Order of] St. Anna. During the Polish War of 1793–4, he commanded a division, earned confidence and favour of the great Suvorov, who, for his distinction during the assault on the suburb of Praga, appointed Buxhöwden commandant of Warsaw and the governor of all conquered Poland. For this war, Buxhöwden received the Order of St. Vladimir (2nd class), ten thousand rubles and a prosperous estate in Lifland, which was given him in hereditary possession.

Upon his accession to the throne, Emperor Paul appointed Buxhöwden as the military governor-general of St. Petersburg (by then he was already a lieutenant-general) but in late 1798 Buxhöwden was discharged from military service and retired to Germany. Emperor Alexander, upon inheriting the throne, recalled him and appointed him as the governor-general of [the Baltic] provinces, with authority over the troops deployed there. In 1805 Buxhöwden was ordered to lead a corps by forced marches to Olmütz to join Kutuzov, which he promptly accomplished. He then fought honourably in the battle of Austerlitz, commanding our left flank. Buxhöwden enjoyed a reputation as a brave warrior and enterprising general, but he never received a classical education, never commanded an army and never operated independently against the enemy. Buxhöwden was fat and clumsy, rather brusque in dealing with subordinates, and had a stubborn and unyielding temper. His greatest merit lay in the favour shown to him by Suvorov, who never erred in choosing his companions. At that time just saying that a general was 'Suvorov's favourite' sufficed to excite unlimited trust in him among the troops.

These then were the three key individuals who stood at the forefront of the war in 1806. It was rumoured that Count Bennigsen and Buxhöwden were given secret instructions to counter and constrain Count Kamenski's rashness, and that Count Kamenski, although serving as commander-in-chief, was instructed or encouraged to consult on important occasions with both his assistants, Bennigsen and Buxhöwden, who commanded separate corps under his direct command.

Neither the bad time of the year, nor impassable roads or complete lack of supplies prevented Russians from launching, in November 1806, military movements on the banks of the Vistula River, not far away from Warsaw, where the headquarters of the French army was located, and where Napoleon, who was then in Poznan, was expected to arrive any day. The Russian forces, as already mentioned, were divided into two armies; Buxhöwden had not yet arrived at the Vistula when Bennigsen had already moved forward, intending to make a swift flanking movement to capture Thorn, where General Lestocq and the Prussians were located, or at least establish direct communications with him. But Marshal Ney anticipated Bennigsen and drove Lestocq out of Thorn, which caused Bennigsen to fall back to Pultusk to join Buxhöwden. Prior to 13 [26] December, only minor skirmishing between the Russian and the French advanced guards occurred, although the steadfastness that Count Osterman demonstrated at Naselsk had shown the French that fighting the Russians would not be easy. [From the Russian text in F. Bulgarin, *Vospominaniya*]

Denis Davydov

The future renowned soldier, poet and symbol of Russian hussar bravado Denis Davydov was just twenty-one years old when the news of the defeat at Austerlitz shocked Russian society. A scion of a distinguished Russian noble family, he was already serving in a cavalry unit and dreamt of military exploits and glory, especially after his brother distinguished himself at Austerlitz, was wounded seven times and fell into French captivity where he in fact met Napoleon. Davydov was eager to fight and ready to go to extremes to get his transfer to the field army.

On 4 [16] July 1806, I was transferred from the Byelarusian Hussars, where I served as a rotmistr [captain], to the Life Guard Hussar Regiment, where I received the rank of lieutenant. In late September, I arrived in St. Petersburg and immediately moved to Pavlovsk, where my squadron was quartered.

The squadron commander [B. Chetvertinskii] was a longtime friend of mine and one of the culprits in my transfer to the Guard while my comrades-in-arms were all excellent lads. We lived well and our regimental life was filled more with camaraderie than ceremony, more with stories than business, more with gold on top of sabretaches [as we gambled] than inside them, more with champagnes (and consequently, plenty of debts) than sadness . . . We were always cheerful and in high spirits! Perhaps, these days I would have been deeply grateful for such a fate and wished nothing more but I was just twenty-two years old and burning with ambition, tired of inaction and languishing out of abundance of life. Moreover, my position with respect to my comrades was truly unbearable. I left the [Chevalier Guard] regiment [in September 1804] without having fired a single shot and spent the next two years in the [Belorusskii] regiment, which saw no active service, only to transfer back to the Guard that had just returned from Austerlitz. I reeked of mother's milk while they smelled of burnt gunpowder. I spoke of my zeal and was, in return, shown battle scars, which I always found enviable, or awards that flattered me.

At last, we received the news of the Prussian army's defeat at Jena. There was plenty of talk about sending troops to the aid of our defeated ally, and Field Marshal Count [Mikhail] Kamenski was recalled from his village estate to take command of the army. This news livened me up. Like a madman I rushed to the capital to see if there was any way I could wriggle myself into his adjutants or, at least, be assigned to some regular regiment that was being sent abroad.

All my efforts proved to be in vain. I could not find anyone who could vouch for me, in fact I could not even find a single person who could share the passionate feelings churning inside my heart. Everywhere I went, the poetry that burned in my soul and eyes was greeted with a prosaic mot, 'It does you credit!' – 'Oh, spare me! I do not seek praise but am asking for help: do not let me languish in garrison service and court balls; let me breath fresh air!' – 'But you do know that the Emperor does not favour volunteers' [was a constant refrain]. I considered this sacrilegious word ['to volunteer'] as a libel against the Emperor, considering it to be impossible for a Russian Tsar not to like those eager to rush to fight. And thus, all of my efforts proved futile.

Meanwhile, columns of grandparents and grandmothers, uncles and aunts, as if part of Napoleon's army, were assaulting Suite No. 9 at the Hotel Severnaya, where Field Marshal [Kamenski] was staying. Everyone kept asking him about their relatives, all such requests were satisfied and, to my great chagrin, I had to witness many of my acquaintances and friends making preparations for their departure to the army.

Finally, desperation drove me to take an extreme step: On 28 November, at four o'clock after midnight, I put on my uniform, got inside a carriage and drove directly to the field marshal's apartment. I chose this later hour to anticipate another column of relatives that was preparing for a new assault at dawn. Besides, every eccentric loves unconventional things and a <u>nocturnal raid</u> [original emphasis] of a young lieutenant, lacking connections and patronage, on the elderly but very lively, ardent and obstinate Field Marshal was clearly outside the rules of conventional behaviour, even against good sense. Everyone was deep asleep at the courtyard and inside the hotel. Suite No. 9, accessible via a steep, narrow and barely-lit staircase, was on the third floor. At the entrance to the aforesaid suite was a small corridor, dimly lit by a glowing lantern. The weather was cold. Approaching the suite I wrapped myself in a coat and leaned against the wall in anticipation of someone coming out of upper chambers so I could follow them into the antechamber that was filled with the loud snoring of the Field Marshal's burly orderly.

The first fervours of my determination soon began to diminish as I examined myself, looked around the barely-lit corridor and considered the lateness of the hour I had chosen to present myself to this esteemed individual. I also mulled over the almost childish wilfulness that characterises all old men when they wake up, which would have been augmented by the unbridled impulses of anger that Field Marshal Count Kamenski was well known for. After giving it some thought, I threw off my cloak that made me look like Abellino* or Fra Diavolo, and decided to seek the resolution of my predicament in uniform.

I soon heard the door opening and a little old man, fresh and cheerful, appeared before me in a robe, with a white rag tied around his head and unlit candle in his hand. It was the Field Marshal himself. Seeing me, he stopped. 'Who are you?' he asked. I introduced myself. 'Who are you visiting?' – 'Your Excellency.' He quickly glanced at me, walked along the corridor to the lantern, lit his candle, and on the way back, told me, 'Come with me.' I followed him; he remained silent and walked with a candle in front of me. Before entering the bedroom, out of respect for the old man, I decided to halt until he specifically called upon me. Noticing my intention, he said angrily, 'Come along.' I stepped inside the bedroom. The Field Marshal fixed the candle in a candlestick, which stood on the table beside the bed, and asked me, 'So what do you want?' I told him about my desire to take part in the war. He flushed, started walking with rapid strides to and fro and speaking almost in a frenzy: 'What is this torment! Every greenhorn feels compelled to show up here and ask to be appointed to the army, when I have not been yet appointed myself! I am exhausted from all these requests! Who do you think you are?' I repeated my name. 'Which Davydov?' [he inquired]. I mentioned my father's name. He then relented, recalling his amity towards my father and even my grandfather. He began to name my relatives, almost

---

* A brigand, the main character in the Swiss writer Heinrich Zschokke's romance *Abällino der grosse Bandit* which was first published in 1795.

getting as far as my ancestor Minchak Kasaevncha, the scion of the Golden Horde and patriarch of the Davydov family. He approached me and told me good-naturedly, 'I recall that you had to leave the Guard against your will. Why? Tell me the truth, just as you would to your deceased father.' I told him about my youthful adventures with all the frankness of my character and years.* He listened attentively, sometimes smiling, occasionally frowning . . . When I finished, he shook my hand and said: 'Well, my dear Davydov! I will ask about you this very day. I will tell the Emperor about everything: how you broke into my chamber – who has heard of such a thing!? – in the middle of the night and burst into my chamber, and how I initially mistook you – forgive me – for a ruffian . . . True, I initially thought you intended to shoot me! To tell the truth, I was never afraid of death, especially now, in my old age; but you did look very suspiciously. Just admit it!' I apologised for my audacity in bothering him in such an unusual hour. 'No, no, on the contrary,' he countered with ardour, 'I loved your exploit, for it reveals boundless assiduity; here is a passionate soul, here is a [fervent] heart . . . I know it, I feel it!'

So I bade goodbye to the Field Marshal and returned home full of hopes for success. My heart was full of joy and dreams wandered into my head; I already envisioned myself commanding a regiment and winning important battles; by the time I laid down in my bed, I was already the vanquisher of Napoleon and could not catch any sleep because of this emotional turmoil. At this youthful age hopes can oftentimes been mistaken for actuality!

In the morning, the Guard and the entire city were already talking about my foray on the Field Marshal; and yet I still heard nothing from him. The following day, at nine o'clock in the morning, I went to his hotel to find out about my fate. The street was jammed with carriages and coaches. I entered the rooms, full of officials, and stopped near the lintel. Soon it was [military] review hour. The Field Marshal came out to get to his carriage and upon seeing me, he approached and embraced me, then took me aside and said, 'I have talked about you [to Emperor Alexander], dear Davydov! I asked him several times to have you as an aide-de-camp but he was refused on the pretext that you have yet to serve in the regiment. I must confess that judging by the sovereign's words and expressions, it would be impossible to get you what you so desire. You must find some other way and believe me, no matter how you find a way to reach your goal, I will always gladly accept you and will give you an opportunity to prove yourself.' With these words he disappeared while I remained standing dumbfounded! But when a procession of the <u>chosen ones</u> [original emphasis] began to follow him and pass by me, I glanced at them, shrugged my shoulders and gave a devilish grin!

[. . .]

---

* Davydov was transferred from the Guard for writing satirical poems.

I had long enjoyed the friendliest relations with my squadron commander and was therefore warmly received by his sister, who was back then a rather prominent personality. Spending time at her gorgeous and luxurious home, which was [regularly] visited by princes, foreign ambassadors and notable personalities, I developed a wide network of acquaintances. My search for Suite No. 9 at the Hotel Severnaya soon became the subject of detailed conversations in that part of the capital that, out of idleness, sustains itself on gossip of whatever kind it may be. The house of Maria Antonovna Naryshkina, as one of the most fashionable estates, belonged to this circle. As soon as I entered her living room, everyone turned to me with questions about the incident and no one wondered any longer about my daring raid on the crazed old man.

This exploit, which was described as 'extraordinary', elevated me in the eyes of this powerful woman. After all the exclamations, with which I was showered, she finally told me, 'Why did you have to take such risks? You should have chosen me as your champion and your wish would have been fulfilled a long time ago.' You can imagine how thrilled I was to hear this! I told her that there was still time and that her attention and involvement would only serve as a guarantee of success. She promised to intercede on my behalf; she might have assumed that there were prospects of something 'extraordinary inside me and hope that the future glory of the protégé would eventually shine on the patroness as well; I kissed with great delight her lovely hand and returned home feeling the same excitement as on my return from the Hotel Severnaya. Yet, two days later I learned that all my hopes were dashed by the order not to deprive me of the joy of drilling and yawping in front of my squad.

It seemed that my fate had been sealed and that Providence had refused to liven me up with her smile. So what had happened? First, Valuev, the messenger, arrived with the news of the Field Marshal [Kamenski's] illness and his departure from the army. Two days later arrived another messenger, Count Vasiliev, with the news of Bennigsen's victory at Pultusk. The Emperor then appointed Prince Peter Ivanovich Bagration to command the advance guard of our field army that was entrusted to General Bennigsen. So what impact could the Field Marshal [Kamenski] or [our victory at] Pultusk, Bennigsen or Bagration have on the poor hussar lieutenant who kept walking with a whip inside the manège* or drinking with his comrades? The former, who was never refused in anything, was denied his request concerning me; Bennigsen did not even know that I existed; I knew about Pultusk only from a map; and I had only a passing acquaintance of Bagration: hello, goodbye, and that's it!

On the day of Count Vasiliev's arrival, I went to St. Petersburg to see my brother and had little hope for the success of Prince Bagration's petition on

---

*   Riding school.

my behalf; I was convinced that even if he decided to intercede, he would be refused. Having learned about his appointment to the army, I did not even think of asking him to take me as his adjutant. But here is how my wish was fulfilled.

The Prince, having been informed of his appointment by the Emperor himself and receiving permission to take several Guards officers, decided to visit Naryshkina that very morning in order to ask her if she wanted him to take her brother (my squadron commander), as he had already served with distinction under the Prince's command during the Austerlitz campaign, was sincerely devoted to him and always stated that he would refuse to follow anyone else to the army. Naryshkina immediately agreed to the Prince's offer, adding that he would do her a great favour if he agreed to take with him Denis Davydov as well. Back then, a single word of this woman was akin to a command and the very next day Prince [Bagration] went to the Emperor and I still cannot conceive how he was able to achieve what the Field Marshal [Kamenski] himself had failed to accomplish despite all of his efforts. On the day of this fateful decision, I, unaware of anything that was transpiring, went, as usual to have lunch with Naryshkina and her brother. Upon seeing me, she hastened to tell him that her brother was going with Prince Bagration [to the army]; I quivered upon hearing this news; Boris Chetvertinsky, who loved me like a brother and knew very well how great was my desire to join to go to the army, asked her: 'And what about him?' – pointing at me. – 'Oh, him? [Sadly] another rejection,' she replied. I turned pale upon hearing this. Noticing my reaction, she became alarmed, rushed to me and said, 'I beg your pardon, I just wanted to tease you. You are going to the army!' I do not remember what happened next but I was later assured that I almost threw myself into her embrace. I could not eat anything during lunch. It felt as if fire, not blood, ran in my veins and my head was spinning upside down.

After lunch I rushed to Prince Bagration, who was supposed to return his post in the evening. He lived in the home of Prince Gagarin on the Dvortsovaya [Palace] Embankment. By the time of my arrival, his carriage was already at the porch.* I am still ashamed of my weakness – even though I was sure that the Prince did not deceive Naryshkina about the Emperor's permission for my departure to the army, and that Naryshkina did not lie to me, I still could not bear any possible disappointment and preferred to remain in ignorance rather than learn the truth that could have been devastating for

---

* Davydov's note: I found three officers with the Prince. It is rather strange that of them all, I am the only one who survived the war. Prince Bagration himself died at Borodino; Prince Mikhail Sergeevich Golitsyn was killed at Landsberg in 1807; Count Grabowskii was killed at Krasnyi in 1812; and Count St. Priest was killed at Rheims in 1814.

me! And so?! Instead of asking the Prince whether I was indeed appointed to him and when should I depart, I escorted him to the carriage and bid farewell to him without uttering a single word about myself! Only after he was already gone did I feel ashamed of myself and went to Count Lieven, who served as the director of His Imperial Majesty's field chancellery, who informed that I was indeed appointed as adjutant to Prince Bagration and that a relevant order would be issued the following day.

Leaving St. Petersburg on 3 [15] January, I caught up with Prince Fedor Gagarin, who served as cornet in the Chevalier Guard Regiment, near Pskov and then travelled with him to Vilna. Upon arriving there we found many wounded officers of the Guards but I can only remember [Philadelphis] Ryndin, who rose to major-general before getting killed in 1829, [Ange Hyacinthe Maxence] Baron de Damas, who had a very good mastery of the Russian language and later served as the minister of war and of foreign affairs of France, and still later tutored the Duke of Bordeaux,★ [Pavel] Pushchin (who is now in retirement with the rank of major-general), Friedrichs (who is now Master of the Horse at the [imperial] court), Mandryka (who is now a major-general) and others. All these officers were dispatched to train the newly formed infantry regiments. We wanted to rest for a few days in Vilna and enjoy balls and other local amusements before proceeding to our final destination. But upon learning that the army was expected to fight a decisive battle at any moment, my blood boiled once more and I left Vilna immediately.

Passing through Skidzyel, I stopped by at Ozerki to visit Shepelev, who then was a colonel and was tasked with forming the Grodnenskii (now Klyastitskii) Hussar Regiment; there I found my former squadron commanders and my friends Stepan Bibikov, Alexander Davydov, the everlasting major but later glorious General [Jacob] Kulnev, [Ivan] Gorgoli, met Fedor Rudeger, my fatherly commander during the [Polish] campaign of 1831 that so justly brought him great renown; he was then, it seems, a staff rotmistr and maybe a rotmistr in the Grodnenskii Regiment.† While in Grodno, I also visited the wife of Colonel Borozdin (who died as the general of cavalry). He, just like Shepelev, had finished organising the Finlyandskii Dragoon Regiment and were already at Lyck, across the border. [From the Russian text in Denis Davydov, *Voennye zapiski*]

★ The Duke of Bordeaux was Henri Charles Ferdinand Marie Dieudonné d'Artois, the posthumous son of Charles Ferdinand, Duke of Berry and grandson of Charles X of France. After his grandfather's overthrow in 1830, he became known as the Comte de Chambord and was the Legistimist pretender to the throne of France for almost four decades.

† Rudeger was promoted to staff rotmistr in March 1805 and was promoted to major in November 1807.

Mikhail Kamenski

When he received the Imperial request to lead the Russian armies in Poland, the elderly Kamenski was already in poor health but his ambition seems to have been burning strongly enough since he accepted the command. Yet, after arriving at Pultusk and looking into the army affairs, his health only deteriorated further, prompting him to note the following in a letter to Emperor Alexander.

I am too old for the army. I almost completely lost my vision. I barely can ride a horse but not out of laziness as it is with others. I am unable to find any locations on the map and am unfamiliar with this region . . . I am signing documents without even knowing what they are about. [From the Russian text of Kamenski to Alexander, 22 December 1807, in Mikhailovskii-Danilevskii, *Opisanie vtoroi voiny . . .*]

Alexander Benckendorff

Still in Graudentz with the Prussian royal family, Benckendorff did his best to bolster Prussian spirits in the wake of the crushing defeat at Jena-Auerstädt. He urged King Frederick William III to remain steadfast and trust in his alliance with Russia, whose armies were already moving through Poland to support Prussia.

General Bennigsen, at the head of 60,000 men, entered the provinces of Prussia and approached Warsaw but the king [Frederick William III of Prussia], on the advice of his generals, decided to change their direction and move our army towards Osterode, hoping to protect old Prussia and use this position to compel the French to take up winter quarters. [The Prussians] tried to conceal from me that Napoleon's army was at Kalisch and the King, without informing me, sent individual orders to our division commanders instructing them to turn to Osterode. I considered it my duty to hasten to meet General Bennigsen and warn him about everything, as I was convinced that the Prussians would try to conceal from him the actual situation on the ground and, consequently, Bennigsen, being unable to receive in timely fashion instructions from St. Petersburg, might find himself in a serious predicament. I asked the [Prussian] king permission to leave and sought out his aide-de-camp to learn where I could find General Bennigsen. When he perceived my intentions, he sought to gain time by not giving me directions and instead assuring me that the leading elements of our forces were already in Warsaw. Because of this untruthful statement he forced me to undertake a rather lengthy journey, hoping that by the time of my belated arrival our columns would have already changed their direction in accordance to the [Prussian] king's orders. But he had failed in his enterprise because none of our division commanders followed these orders since they only obeyed orders coming from the commander-in-chief.

Upon arriving in Warsaw, I found the Prussian commandant in a rather strange state of mind. He was fearful of everything and was afraid to leave his furniture, his cellar and did not have the courage to order the evacuation of neither the gunpowder that the Poles coveted nor the weapons that [the Poles] desired to capture and use against us.

I immediately left for the meeting with General Bennigsen, whom I found only at Lomza. He was thrilled [v vostorge] to learn from me about the actual state of affairs and was convinced that he must continue his advance to Warsaw without counting on the weak Prussian reinforcements. However, his situation was rather precarious by then: he had departed from our borders in order to reinforce the strong [mnogochislennuyu] Prussian army and intending to engage the enemy in central Germany. Instead, he could no longer have support of the Prussian army while the enemy was threatening our very own borders. Some units in [Bennigsen's] army were not fully reorganised and everything that he hoped to accomplish calmly with the help of the [Prussians] now had to be undertaken hastily and by our own efforts.

General Bennigsen acted quite worthily and did not quail in these difficult circumstances. Instead, he decided to lead his weak army against Napoleon, who had just routed a 200,000-strong army and overthrown the Prussian monarchy in astonishing fashion. At that moment, Napoleon truly seemed to be an indomitable giant.

General Bennigsen's army comprised the divisions of General Count [Alexander] Osterman[-Tolstoy],* Prince [Dmitrii] Golitsyn,† General [Fabian von Osten-]Sacken‡ and General [Alexander] Siedmioraczki.§ In total, it included twenty-four infantry and twelve cavalry regiments.¶ Bennigsen took up winter quarters in the vicinity of Pultusk and dispatched General Siedmioraczki to Praga, the suburb of Warsaw on the eastern bank of the Vistula River. General [Mikhail] Barclay [de Tolly] marched with a strong detachment to Plock while Count [Karl] Lambert, with the Aleksandriiskii Hussar Regiment and the Cossacks, departed from Warsaw to conduct reconnaissance and intercept French couriers. Thus, just one jager regiment

---

* Commanded the 2nd Division.
† Commanded the 4th Division.
‡ Commanded the 3rd Division.
§ Major-General Siedmioraczki was the chef of the Byelozerskii Musketeer Regiment and commanded the 6th Division.
¶ Bennigsen's army corps consisted of the 2nd, 3rd, 4th and 6th Divisions that, on paper, had 71,680 men (2,443 officers and 69,237 rank-and-file) of whom some 60,000 were present.

stayed behind to guard the bridge across the Vistula and maintain order in the streets of Warsaw.

Such was the situation in which General Bennigsen awaited orders from St. Petersburg and observed the enemy movement. The King of Prussia [soon] arrived at Pultusk and was shown [the Russian] regiments deployed in the vicinity of the town. He was very pleased with this review and departed for Königsberg, where the [Prussian] Queen was expected to arrive.

Meanwhile, St. Petersburg received the news of the Prussian defeat and the threats our army was now exposed to. His Imperial Majesty the Emperor [Alexander] ordered the formation of a corps from the divisions of General Peter Essen and General Dmitrii Dokhturov, and place it under command of General Friedrich Wilhelm Buxhöwden, who was given an order to depart immediately [with his troops] and join the army of General Bennigsen. Another corps, under the command of General [Roman] Anrep, also began to be formed at Grodno.

Count [Peter] Tolstoy* arrived with the army in capacity of a general for special assignments [general fo osobym porucheniyam] and the Emperor's delegate [doverennoe litso] while General [Bogdan] Knorring was Quartermaster-General. But the army needed a commander-in-chief because General Bennigsen had instructions to not be subordinate to General Buxhöwden, even though the latter enjoyed seniority in rank. General Knorring was senior to both of these generals but only had the authority to advise them, while General Count Tolstoy was instructed to submit precise reports on proceedings to the Emperor.

Finding a commander-in-chief was a difficult task. After the disastrous day of Austerlitz, General Kutuzov had fallen in the eyes of high society and especially in the opinion of the Emperor.† Popular opinion soon called for the recall of the old Field Marshal Count [Mikhail] Kamenski who had been in retirement for some fifteen years. The Emperor acquiesced to the public demand and Count Kamenski departed from St. Petersburg taking with him the best of the younger generation. The army was thrilled [v vostorge] by this choice, even though it did not fully understand what was behind it. The field marshal was known only by the cruelties that he had done in Moldavia, Poland and Finland, but he was always known as a firm and harsh man, and such a reputation, deemed to be a sign of rigour and strength of character,

---

* Peter Tolstoy had the rank of lieutenant-general and commanded the Life Guard Preobrazhenskii Regiment in 1803–7. In 1805, he was given command of a corps dispatched to Pomerania but was forced to return in the wake of the Allied defeat at Austerlitz. In 1806 he was sent to the Prussian corps where he served as Russian liaison to King Frederick William III before being sent as the personal representative of Emperor Alexander to the Russian army.

† The disgraced Kutuzov was appointed the military governor of Kiev in late 1806.

compelled [many] to consider him as the only individual who was capable of standing up to Napoleon and ensuring the much-needed unity of the army that included generals envious of each other, young officers and barely-experienced [neobstrelyannykh] soldiers. The entire army eagerly awaited his arrival. Meanwhile the enemy, stationed at Kalisch to prepare an uprising in Poland, advanced to Warsaw, where General Lambert had already fought a cavalry skirmish with the enemy troops.

Being assigned to Count [Peter] Tolstoy, I was sent to Grodno to deliver all the recent news to the Field Marshal, who had arrived there, and to urge him to travel to Pultusk. Upon arriving there I was astonished by the terror [uzhas] which he had instilled in the members of his suite. I accomplished my mission and assured [Kamenski] that the soldiers were excited to see him as their commander-in-chief. He hastily completed his preparations and departed that same evening: wishing to accompany him, I sent a messenger to Pultusk to warn Count Tolstoy who came out to meet us at Byelostock.

Everyone liked [Kamenski's] liveliness, even his ill-temper, and everything he said [seemingly] instilled hope in people. He graciously greeted Count Tolstoy and [briefly] stopped at Ostrolenka in order to deal with some matters; upon his arrival at Pultusk, [Kamenski] received the news that Napoleon was at Warsaw where he had been welcomed enthusiastically [by the Poles] and that the French were already repairing the bridge [over the Vistula].

The Field Marshal was too skilled in the art of war to expect that he would be able to defend the crossing on the Vistula when the enemy threatened in multiple places. So he chose to concentrate his forces which, in accordance with General Bennigsen's first disposition, had become too dispersed. Napoleon, in order to anticipate this movement, quickly moved forward and attacked our corps piecemeal.

The Field Marshal moved to Nowe Miasto, where General Bennigsen gathered the larger part of his army [corps] while its forward elements were already in direct contact with the enemy. A report from an outpost deployed in Czarnowo informed Bennigsen that Count Osterman bravely defended himself and was forced to fall back in the face of superior enemy forces only after a battle that lasted late into the night.*

The following day the Field Marshal [Kamenski] arrived at Czarnowo, where he was greeted by the rapturous shouts of 'hurrah' by a part of Count Osterman's division that, having displayed unrivalled gallantry in action, demonstrated a superb poise in the ranks. Returning to Nowe Miasto in the afternoon, the Field Marshal soon had to leave it and, after a hard fight, the enemy troops occupied this town in the evening. An order was issued instructing General Bennigsen's corps to withdraw and concentrate at Pultusk and take up a position there while General Buxhöwden's corps was to gather

---

* The battle at Czarnowo took place on 23 December.

at Makow. General Anrep's corps, which was marching to join the army, was on the left bank of the Narew and had built bridges to maintain constant contact with the left flank of the [Russian] position at Pultusk.

The Field Marshal spent the night at the outposts, despite the dangers of being captured by the enemy's forward detachments. The following day he travelled to Golymin: terrible mud slowed down the movement of our columns, and especially the artillery. Kamenski could see that horses could no longer haul cannon and even the efforts of 300 men were not sufficient to drag everything that got stuck in the mud; during this march we lost more than seventy cannon that had to be abandoned in the mud.

Count [Peter von] Pahlen, with a rearguard consisting of his Sumskii Hussar Regiment and two regiments of infantry, fought before Golymin but was forced to turn in the direction of Makow. The approach of the enemy forces compelled the Field Marshal to proceed to Pultusk. In the evening he passed amidst the bonfires of our bivouacs and the joy which his presence induced among the rank-and-file, seemed to have inspired him to fight and engendered the most alluring aspirations in us.

Our position was located in front of Pultusk, on the right bank of the Narew. The left flank was closely adjacent to a steep riverbank while the right was anchored on all but impassable woods. Thus our retreat could be carried out either through Pultusk, where bridges were built across the river, or on the road to Ostrolenka, along the right bank of the Narew. The mud, which so complicated troop movements, could negate any orders and paralyse any other general but Napoleon. Horses perished on roads and that little part of artillery that still accompanied the French army was hauled by the oxen; mud surrounded our positions like a genuine fortification.

General Buxhöwden, who was still at Makow, received the order to move to Pultusk in such a manner as to arrive to the right flank of our position by noon and join the action. As a result of our attacks and superiority of artillery the enemy would be thus weakened. [Buxhöwden] was supposed to leave a strong detachment at Makow to observe the movements of a French corps that Count Pahlen was following. When the battle commenced, General Anrep was expected to cross the Narew River and attack the right flank of the enemy columns. With all these arrangements made and orders issued, we left the field marshal so he could rest, and went to sleep, expecting a battle on the morrow and feeling certain in our success. At 4 o'clock in the morning Colonel [Semen] Stavrakov* suddenly woke us all up and informed us that the Field Marshal had seemingly lost his mind and was about to leave the

---

* Benckendorff is mistaken – in 1806, Stavrakov was a lieutenant-colonel of His Imperial Majesty's Suite on the Quartermaster Service, the precursor of the Russian General Staff. In late 1806 Stavrakov served as a brigade-major in the Russian headquarters and was later attached to Count Peter Tolstoy, distinguishing himself at

army. Count Tolstoy rushed to see Kamenski, and all of us followed him. [We found] the Field Marshal restlessly pacing around the room. Tolstoy asked him whether he had received any news of the enemy. Kamenski answered in the negative but declared that he had no confidence in inexperienced generals and untrained army; that he was, therefore, departing and washing his hands of the whole matter; that he had already issued necessary orders on the retreat of our corps to the Russian border; and, finally, that he had allowed the abandonment of cannon and wagons in order to save the troops.

These words struck us like a bolt of lightning; tears streamed down our faces and we could not understand such a sudden change of mind. Count Osterman and General Bennigsen, who had also been forewarned, tried expressing their objections to the unworkable enterprise [Kamenski] had proposed but the Field Marshal became so furious that he abruptly bid farewell to all of us, rushed to his carriage and left us all dumbfounded by what we had just seen and heard. No one was able to explain what precisely caused such a shameless clouding of the mind and compelled a man, so jealously protective of his own name, to betray his duty and abandon his command after orders had already been issued to fight a battle, in which success was completely assured.

This unparalleled event can be considered as one of the greatest turns of good fortune for Napoleon: it seemed that Heaven itself safeguarded his plans and undermined all the virtues of the force that opposed him. The gallantry of our troops, the trust they felt towards their commander-in-chief, his prudent dispositions and especially the outcome of that day served as unequivocal evidence of the defeat that Napoleon would have suffered. The limited amount of artillery that he could commit to this battle, the wretched state of his cavalry and the fine condition of ours – all of this would have assured our complete victory. Pultusk should have marked the limit of Napoleon's military victories and become the triumph of Field Marshal Kamenski.

Just as Kamenski departed, the enemy appeared at the edge of the woods in front of our left flank. General Bennigsen decided to accept battle with his army corps and offered Count Tolstoy to travel at once to General Buxhöwden, assure him with regards to the field marshal's orders that had caused such anxiety and suggest joint operations in the battle as it was agreed in the initial dispositions. I accompanied the Count on this trip. We found General Buxhöwden's corps still at Makow. He was marching to Pultusk to arrive by the time specified by the Field Marshal but upon receiving his second order, he turned back. It was noon and General Buxhöwden, citing the fatigue of his troops, refused to move any further even though

---

Eylau (awarded a golden sword for gallantry), Heilsberg (attached to Duty General A. Fock) and Friedland, where he garnered the Order of St. George 4th class.

the distance from Makow to Pultusk was no more than two miles.* At the same time, General Anrep, having received the startling order from the Field Marshal, destroyed the bridges [on the Narew River] and could no longer participate in the battle.

In the evening we received the news that the French had been repelled in all directions and that General Bennigsen held the field of battle; our losses were considerable only on the left wing. [During the battle] the enemy deployed several times in attack columns but was [each time] repelled by our artillery while in many places our cavalry pursued him to the extent that the mud permitted it. One wonders what would have been left of the French army if the Field Marshal commanded that day and carried out the converging movements of corps of General Buxhöwden and General Anrep.

Contrary to expectations, the victory at Pultusk did not produce satisfactory results: the following night General Buxhöwden retreated to Novogrudok while General Bennigsen moved to Ostrolenka. General Anrep continued his earlier movement. Pleased that he was not pursued, Napoleon also fell back to Warsaw where he announced his victory [at Pultusk]. Thus, two armies had moved away from each other and scouts on both sides could not locate them. Napoleon took up winter quarters which he protected with the corps of Marshal Ney and the corps of Bernadotte, the right part of which extended to Mohrungen.

The news of the glorious day at Pultusk soon reached Field Marshal Kamenski. He turned back and reached the army at Ostrolenka. He intended to resume his command but Count Osterman was the first to declare that he was no longer worthy of this honour and that he must beseech the mercy of the Emperor and conceal his shame in the provincial wilderness. Despairing, the Field Marshal departed once more, taking with him the scorn of the entire army. The Emperor [Alexander], having learned about prudent and decisive leadership of General Bennigsen who corrected, as much as he could, the foolishness of Count Kamenski, recalled General Buxhöwden and entrusted the overall command of the army to General Bennigsen. [From the Russian text in A. Benckendorff, *Vospominaniya* . . .]

George Jackson

Serving as the British chargé d'affaires to the Court of Prussia, Jackson followed King Frederick William and Queen Louise to Königsberg, where he maintained close relations with many senior Prussian and Russian civil and military officials, who kept him appraised of most recent developments.

---

* Buxhöwden refers to German *meile*. Nowadays, the shortest route from Makow to Pultusk is 20km (12 miles) long.

Jackson's diary, therefore, offers unique insights into the internal dynamics of the Prussian court and Russian headquarters.

Königsberg, Thursday, January 1

The history of Bennigsen's victory, as we now know for a certainty, is this. Kamenski was attacked and supposed to be wounded. He then left the army 'in a huff', after conferring the command on Buxhöwden, with orders to retreat as far as their own frontiers. Bennigsen had similar directions, which he executed as far as Pultusk, but there made a halt, declaring that he would retreat no further, but would await there the enemy's attack; which soon after commenced, under Murat, Lannes, and Davoust [*sic*]. Nothing, however, can be more unsatisfactory than Bennigsen's letters; for at the same moment that we are congratulated on a great victory, we are informed that the victor is in full retreat, and that Lestocq has been beaten back from village to village!

January 2

Colonel Sontag arrived here from Ortelsburg yesterday evening. He reached the Russian headquarters on the 21st [December], but Kamenski, who had joined the army only the preceding night, refused him permission to remain there without an order from St. Petersburg. Sontag, therefore, proceeded on towards Lestocq's corps, but had hardly reached Mlawa when he learnt that the French had forced the post of Soldau. He then returned to Pressnitz, whence he struck off to Ortelsburg, which he left on the 30th, hearing, he said, that Lord Hutchinson had arrived; but he had got tired of headquarters, I fancy, for the Prussians hardly pass a day without fighting. To all appearances, they are left entirely to their fate by the Russians, of whose movements Sontag knew nothing since he left Pultusk.

A letter from Buxhöwden, brought here today by a Russian officer, says that Kamenski had gone off *sans dire gare*, that he had ordered Lestocq to retreat to Johannisburg, and that he himself intended gaining the Bug. This has caused as much consternation as displeasure; for all this part of the country is thus left at the mercy of the enemy, and everybody is hastening to get off. The poor queen [Louise of Prussia], owing to her illness, will wait till the last moment. The Radzivills stay here *en tous cas*. For my part I shall wait till the last. When the officer left Buxhöwden, he was at Novogorod, but he knew nothing of a second supposed victory gained by that general.

It is now ascertained that the loss of the French in the battle of the 20th, at Pultusk, was very considerable. Bennigsen and Buxhöwden were separated by the overflowing of the Narew, which obliged the former to go eighteen German miles about, by Tycoczyn, to re-effect a junction. Upon the news reaching St. Petersburg, orders were sent to Kamenski to remain at Grodno. Buxhöwden was recalled, and the entire command given to Bennigsen, who, by the last accounts, was at Novogorod, Lestocq being at Drengfurth.

January 3
My intention is now to follow the king [Frederick William of Prussia]. I had an idea when the first account of the victory was brought of being the bearer of it, but I no longer flatter myself with the hope of anything of that sort from hence. Hitherto I have been more sanguine than most persons, but if Lestocq's army be annihilated, and at present it seems almost impossible that it should be otherwise, a peace, if peace it may be called, will doubtless be the instantaneous result – that is, if Bonaparte should be inclined to grant any terms at all.

Yet in Russia they seem to be making some stir, and one man in every hundred is obliged to serve. The formation of a militia is ordered in Courland and Livonia; but the experience of the past month is so striking, that the most hopeful person cannot look for much advantage from these measures.

The jealousies, the personal piques that exist among the Russian commanders are most discouraging. But for these squabbles, Bennigsen's affair might really have acquired some right to the name of a victory.

January 4
General Zastrow told me to-day that Kamenski had not entirely quitted the army, but that he went about from division to division, without any settled plan, and that his behaviour, generally, was so extraordinary that, unless he was insane, it could not be accounted for, especially after the flattering assurances he had given the king on his first arrival.

[Zastrow] was very unreserved in his conversation and went so far, even, as to say that it would have been much better for Prussia had Russia said plainly, 'Arrangez vous comme vous pouvez,' than to promise her assistance and then leave her in the manner the Russian generals were now doing. 'Had she not,' he said, 'given us the assurances she did, we should, at least, have known "à quoi nous en tenir, et tant bien que mal," should have settled things at once.' [English text in George Jackson, *Diaries and Letters* . . .]

Levin Bennigsen

Leading one of the Russian army corps (and later the entire Russian army) in Poland, Bennigsen found himself facing ever-challenging circumstances. Logistical difficulties were soon compounded by poor weather and escalating bickering with other senior officers. The arrival of the new commander-in-chief, Field Marshal Mikhail Kamenski, only further constrained him. After the war in Poland was over, Bennigsen spent four years in retirement at his estate near Vilna and maintained a close correspondence with Alexander Borisovich Fock, who served in Bennigsen's headquarters and urged him to start writing memoirs of the past campaign. Bennigsen agreed, oftentimes sending long letters and excerpts from his memoirs to the general.

On 27 September/9 October 1806, finding myself at Medjiboje, in Podolie, 100 verstas from the Dniester, and destined to serve against the Turks in case of a war, I received via feldjäger a writ from the Emperor, of the 23rd/4th of the same month, in the most gracious and flattering terms, by which His Majesty honoured me with the command of an army corps, composed of four divisions: the Second, under the orders of Lt.-Gen. Count Osterman, the Third under Lt.-Gen. Sacken, the Fourth under Lt.-Gen. Prince Golitsyn and the Sixth under Major-General Siedmioraczki. At the same time His Majesty asked that I make haste to arrive at Grodno as quickly as possible. These four divisions added up to 60,000 men, combatants and non-combatants, with which I was destined to bring aid to the King of Prussia against Napoleon.

I left the next day, the 28th/10th, and arrived at Grodno on 3/15 October where I already found Prussian commissaries, Major-General Chlebowski and Stein's private councillor, whom had been sent by the King to regulate the march of my corps. I added to them my chief of staff General [Fabian] Steinheil, and we worked ceaselessly for a convention for this march across Prussian territory. According to this convention, the soldiers had to be fed at their stopping point, that is to say by their hosts, and forage had to be supplied by the inhabitants as well, wherever our troops passed, all of it being at a fixed price. This convention was sent to the respective courts, for the confirmation of the two sovereigns. We could not even see the need of magazines on the right bank of the Vistula, because I had, without stopping, to march via Silesia and cross the Elbe to reach the theatre of war.

I worked while waiting for the necessary measures for my army corps to cross the frontier and received the order to accelerate my march as much as possible, but without fatiguing the troops too much, and to follow all orders that His Majesty the King of Prussia saw fit to give. But the circumstances soon changed: instead of a long march to reach the theatre of war, the disasters that befell the Prussian army required not only a complete change in the operational plans, but precautions and the greatest action on our part to arm for the defence of our own frontiers; circumstances we certainly had not foreseen and for which we were not as well prepared. We shall see that on this occasion the resources of Russia, when it was a question of a war that threatened its frontiers, as well as the depth of support which a beloved sovereign could expect, by all of the sacrifices that the Russian nation made at that time with the greatest enthusiasm.

Several days before leaving Grodno, I received the news of the unfortunate incidents at Auerstädt, Jena and Halle, upon the 2nd/14th and 5th/17th October. This unfortunate news was no less speedy in arriving at St. Petersburg, from which came the orders to hold my army in place as concentrated as possible, and not to pass the Vistula so as not to expose unnecessarily my brave troops.

At the same time General Buxhöwden received the orders to assemble four other divisions in Lithuania: the 5th under Lt.-Gen. Tuchkov, the 7th under Lt.-Gen. Dokhturov, the 8th under Lt.-Gen. Essen III and the 14th under Lt.-Gen. Anrep. These four divisions amounted to almost 40,000 men. General Michelson, who had already commenced hostilities against the Turks, received orders to release General Essen I immediately with two divisions, which only amounted to 17,000 men, having been obliged to leave many men behind. This general was ordered to march on Brest to cover our frontiers.

Such were the initial arrangements made by Russia. Before going further, it seems necessary that I make some mention of the enemy forces, which were advancing to invade our frontiers. According to authentic intelligence [renseignements], the forces of the different corps of the French army, crossing the Rhine, were as follows.

	Men
The Guards under Marshal Bessières	12,000
Augereau's 7th Corps	11,400
Bernadotte's 1st Corps	16,800
Lefebvre's 9th Corps	12,000
Davout's 3rd Corps	34,000
Soult's 4th Corps	30,600
Lannes' 5th Corps	23,400
Ney's 6th Corps	22,200
Total:	162,400
Cavalry Reserve under the Grand Duke of Berg	20,400
Guard Reserve under General Oudinot	8,000
Total French Troops:	190,800 men

It was with these numbers that the French began their war against Prussia in the first days of October in 1806. [. . .] After having crossed the Oder, the French began a winter campaign against the Russians and Prussians with an effective force of 143,040 men. When the French arrived on the Vistula, the Russians only had 60,000, and the Prussians 10,000 men to oppose the French.

On 22 October/3 November, my army corps proceeded to cross our frontiers in four columns at Jalowka, Grodno, Olitta and Jurburg. I myself left on 27 October/8 November. I arrived on 29 October/10 November with my headquarters at Ostrolenka, finding there the Emperor's aide-de-camp, Benckendorff, who had been sent from St. Petersburg to join the King of Prussia and found that [the Prussian king] had sent me dispatches from

Graudenz, dated 25 October/6 November, in which His Majesty was so gracious as to provide me with news on the various unfortunate affairs his army had suffered, of the loss of Stettin and Küstrin; finally, that the French were marching quickly on the Vistula, in two columns, of which one was marching via southern Prussia and the second via Pomerania and western Prussia. His Majesty made known to me his desire to mass the Russian and Prussian troops between Osterode and Soldau, behind the Drewenz, as from such an advantageous position we could oppose the progress of the French in Prussia [ancienne Prusse] or just as easily push the French back should they cross the Vistula. At the same time His Majesty invited me to join in correspondence with his cavalry commander, Count Kalkreuth, who commanded Prussian troops at that time, so as to act in concert during our operations. Given the distance between our defenceless borders and the four divisions under General Buxhöwden and those of General Essen, I felt it my responsibility to inform His Majesty that if I moved with my corps into position between Osterode and Soldau, the French column marching on Warsaw could cross our borders without the least resistance. As it was essential for me to protect our frontiers against invasion, and that the orders of the Emperor, obliged me to never lose sight of that fact in my operations, I requested that His Majesty the King agree to the measures that I found indispensable in my position, and according to which I had already given the necessary order for the march of my columns. The orders that I gave in this respect were as follows:

One division under General Siedmioraczki to Prague. He will push a detachment through Warsaw under the orders of Colonel Yurkovskii, composed of five squadrons of the Alexandriiskii Hussar Regiment, a regiment of Cossacks, a battalion of jagers and two cannon in order to take up a position at Blonie, on the Posen road, and at Kazun on either the Petrokow or Breslau roads. (In Petrokow as in Posen and in numerous other villages in grande Pologne, insurrections fomented by the enemy had already broken out.) Colonel Yurkovskii will hold his line of light troops on the Bzura River. This detachment will serve to observe the enemy column, which is directing its march on Warsaw and must inhibit it and at the same time the insurgents cannot move toward Warsaw before the arrival of the French army.

General Siedmioraczki will place a detachment on the right bank of the Bug, from the Austrian border to the Narew; he will establish a chain of light troops on his right along the length of the Vistula, halfway up the Plock road.

Major-General Barclay de Tolly, commanding the advance guard, will go to Plock; he will have under his orders his regiment of jagers, a regiment of infantry, five squadrons from the Polish Light-Horse Regiment, two regiments of Cossacks and the horse artillery company under Prince Yashvil. The majority of his detachment will occupy the environs of Plock and Plonsk; his line of Cossacks on his left will connect with General Siedmioraczki's line. On his right, on the side of Thorn, it will connect with the Prussians. In order to control the cordon on this side, he will remain in constant contact with General Lestocq.

General Barclay will deploy groups of light troops across the Vistula to make patrols and bring news of the enemy. Lt.-Gen. Sacken will occupy the distance from Mlawa to Soldau and Gilgenburg with the 3rd Division. Lt.-Gen. Count Osterman will occupy the environs of Ciechanow with the 2nd Division. Lt.-Gen. Golitsyn will occupy the environs of Pultusk, where my headquarters will be established.

In this position I could concentrate my four divisions in two days and move in force wheresoever the circumstances required. I made my report to the Emperor on these arrangements that the King had deigned to approve. The Prussian corps, under the orders of General Count Kalkreuth, found itself in the local reserve cantons [cantonments] between Saalfeld and the Soldowka River, and the chain of his advance-posts deployed on the Vistula from Danzig up to the environs of Plock. General Lestocq, who currently commanded the advance posts, sent out detachments on the left bank of the Vistula, to gain some concrete news on the enemy approach; one of these attachments, led by Major Mutius, spotted two officers from the enemy headquarters in the small village of Bromberg, on reconnaissance with an escort; the officers were taken prisoner and the escort dispersed. Two days later, the approach of the advance guard of Lannes' corps forced all of the detachments to re-cross the Vistula and General Lestocq ordered the bridge below Thorn burned on 4/16 November.

Along with my report to the Emperor that I sent from Ostrolenka, I wrote a letter to the Minister, M. Budberg, on 30 October/11 November concerning a matter, which in the subsequent period and throughout almost the entire war caused me the greatest burden and which often presented obstacles to my operations. It concerned the measures needed to provision my army. I can serve as an example that often the arms of the enemy are not as redoubtable to a general as the annoyance of suffering from want of the means that an army on offensive operations requires; they irrevocably lose precious time, and the public, ignorant of these circumstances, always ascribe the regrettable results to the fault or inaction of the general. We will have more occasions to persuade ourselves of that truth, when I have arrived at the siege of Danzig, where the lack of supplies kept me nailed to the same position. At the time I wrote my letter to the minister, it was still only a question of barely keeping the army supplied, but one will see in following that it was not the only issue concerning supplies and magazines for which Russia was not even remotely prepared in this unanticipated war. One will see that she lacked, from this side of the empire, all the means that must be prepared in advance and that an active war urgently demands so that a general can act vigorously.

At the end of my letter I attempted to fix the minister's attention on the critical state of the forces we had available to oppose the incoming torrent that menaced us. I insisted on the necessity of taking timely measures [à temps] to render us capable of a vigorous resistance. The situation was all the more important as all of our reports assured us that the French army, moving against us quickly, surpassed greatly not only the forces at my disposition, but even those that we could gather with time. Determined by circumstances, the government addressed itself to the nation, which prepared itself with the greatest eagerness and enthusiasm to the formation of 612,000 militiamen,⋆ other than the gifts that individuals offered in money, horses, wheat, arms, etc., for the defence of the fatherland. In the manifesto published in Petersburg, you will find exposed the manner in which the levy [draft] was conducted and the distribution thereof across different governments in the empire. Moreover, one finds that this number would be even more considerable and, in dismissing a section of the draft already taken, we reduced it to 215,000 men that the nation effectively furnished, but that the great distances of the empire hindered the timely arrival of these troops.

On 31 October/12 November, I arrived at Pultusk with my headquarters; my first concern was to find subsistence for my army. Not finding a magazine anywhere, having no resources to procure one, no wagons attached to the army to transport supplies, the roads additionally being so bad as to be impassable, the peasants' horses already either worn out or too weak to carry the necessary load, I received daily complaints about the lack of supplies under which the troops were suffering and that the regiments were required to send troops into villages to take the necessary supplies by force. Due to this extreme encumbrance, I addressed myself to the governor of Warsaw, Baron de Köhler, asking him to deliver the necessary supplies from the Warsaw magazine or the surrounding countryside, if only for the division occupying Praga and the surrounding region; but he responded that he was unable to meet my demands and that all he could do was furnish at most one or two days' supplies for General Siedmioraczki's single division. I sent the original letter to the minister, M. de Budberg, in Petersburg, depicting the quandary in which the army found itself and praying he could work toward the means by which we could escape this critical state.

[Thus] even the aid of provisions in an allied country, for which we would fight, was lacking. As of my arrival in Warsaw, I offered to send out large detachments to take as much as possible from the considerable magazines in many places not far from Warsaw, on the left bank of the Vistula, before the arrival of the enemy; but they evaded that proposition on the pretext that they could not consent without the express permission of the King, and yet there was not enough time to wait for a response from His Majesty, a response that

---

⋆ See Imperial manifesto of 30 November 1806 in Chapter 1.

certainly would not have been in the negative. In this way, all of the magazines fell into the hands of the French, and augmented our suffering. The bad intentions of the commanders of these magazines manifested itself again at Plock, where they hid from General Barclay de Tolly the amount of provisions that was actually there, at a moment when it was very difficult to supply his army, and it was only when we were about to quit the Vistula that they opened the magazine and we found such a great amount of provisions that we could not transport them all for lack of time and wagons. In the end, our predicament regarding provisions grew daily in an allied country, a country that had an abundance of supplies.

In an interview I had at Tilsit with the Prince of Neuchâtel [Alexander Berthier], during the peace negotiations, he said to me: 'we enjoyed fifty per cent greater advantages in this war [nous avons eu 50 pour 100 sur vous dans cette guerre], because for us it was a war of invasion and permitted us to make requisitions in all of the conquered states.' I felt the weight of this truth throughout the war.

On 4/16 November, I went to Warsaw to speak with the military governor of the city, Baron de Köhler. He greatly feared an uprising by the inhabitants of Warsaw, which contained 60,000 souls and which one could already regard as the heart of insurrection, as soon as the French made themselves the masters. We agreed to remove all military munitions from the city to the Vistula, then to the Bug and then the Narew for use by the Russian army. We still found in the shops of the merchants from Danzig lead, and sugared almonds in large-enough quantities; I commandeered and carried away those as well. The Prussian artillery, which was in Warsaw, was split up amongst different units in the city and deployed in the open squares while the rest was near the bridge over the Vistula; the entire garrison had to be assembled every night in different houses so as to be able to leave the city on the first signal.

General Siedmioraczki was ordered to quickly build batteries on the right bank of the Vistula below Praga, the better to defend that passage from the French. A very gracious letter, which His Majesty the King of Prussia wrote to Prince Joseph Poniatowski and by which he charged him to organise a bourgeois guard to maintain order in the city, contributed greatly to the tranquillity that reined during the evacuation by the Prussians and the French occupation. Prince Poniatowski, nephew of the last King of Poland, knew how to profit from the consideration which he was shown and handled it with great prudence and wisdom.

On 5/17 November, the advance guard of Lannes' corps arrived at Podgorze, across from Thorn, where General Lestocq had his headquarters; the commanding general send a representative with a letter to the magistrate, by which he summoned the city and demanded that they quickly deliver all the defences on the right bank of the Vistula, and, moreover, several thousand servings of bread and meat, etc., and if not provided, he would bombard the city and reduce it to ashes. General Lestocq sent the emissary away with the response that he could not permit the city to fulfil the least demand of the French general. The emissary had just left the city when cannon fire began.

The next day, all of Marshal Lannes' corps, 18,000 men strong, arrived at Thorn, which was bombarded again, but without effect, and they made more attempts to encourage General Lestocq to surrender the city; Lestocq rejected all these propositions with dignity and firmness. There were even discussions between General Lestocq and General Victor, and after that with Marshal Lannes on a small island on the Vistula. The French generals employed all of their eloquence to engage General Lestocq to retire from the city and from the Vistula, but he remained firm in his resolution to defend his position. The generals therefore parted and Marshal Lannes subsequently bombarded the city again; the effect was of no consequence. Whilst waiting, the enemy cut down trees and transported timber from the Brahe on the Vistula for the construction of a bridge. General Lestocq devised a plan to deprive the enemy of as many of these resources as possible. Bülow's battalion of fusiliers acquitted itself well in this task, taking and destroying twenty-six boats. The enemy, then, fatigued by the resistance offered by General Lestocq, reneged on his plan to cross the Vistula at Thorn and continued his march on Warsaw on the left bank of the river. Shortly after the departure of Marshal Lannes' corps, Marshal Augereau's corps passed by the same road across near Thorn. At this time the city was once again bombarded, albeit weakly.

On 6/18 November, I returned to Pultusk, where shortly thereafter I received a letter from His Majesty the King of Prussia from Osterode, from 10/22 November, in which His Majesty deigned to inform me that General Duroc had arrived by order of Emperor Napoleon, with propositions for an armistice, but the conditions were of such a nature that His Majesty was not certain if he should consent, and as for the rest, it was withheld from me . . . General Duroc had to return to his master the next day. The King further informed me that he thought it his duty to inform me of these circumstances, ultimately so that, supposing that in the wake of the refusal the enemy could quicken his march, I could take the time to take the necessary measures. General Duroc effectively left Osterode on 11/23 November, and the King arrived at my headquarters in Pultusk on 12/24 November.

The conditions of the armistice that Duroc had proposed were that the King yield all fortresses still occupied by Prussian troops on the Oder and the Vistula until the peace, the foundations of which were not mentioned, that he abandon his alliance with Russia, that he close his ports to the English, and that he arranged that Russia also, whether she liked it or not, close her ports to the navigation and commerce of Great Britain.

In your last letter you judged, as a true soldier [en vrai militaire] and as I should expect from your wisdom, the principle that I had adopted to not defend the passage of the Vistula. Let us forgo all the criticisms that have already appeared; it would be useless to refute them . . . It is sufficient to know, the war having hardly having ended, there appeared a mass of essays, descriptions, even histories, to convince one that messieurs the authors held on the object of being the first to speak, but not to speak the truth or research the circumstances that drove events. A soldier, who with attention and map in hand examines the position of the two armies, will only find one issue that major considerations rendered indispensable.

The army corps under my orders was then only 60,000 men strong, as I have already said, including non-combatants, and those of the Prussians, under the orders of Lieutenant-General Lestocq, only 10,000 men. The course of the Vistula, from the Austrian frontier to Graudenz, covers a distance of nearly 45 German lieues. Would I not have committed a terrible fault if I had scattered my troops to defend the passage of this river against an army twice my size, and again on such an extended line, even if one wished to suppose that the fortresses of Graudenz and Danzig defended the lower Vistula? Observe that neither General Buxhöwden nor General Essen had arrived at their destinations with their corps.

The large French army, favoured by the inhabitants of the country and whose troops had already arrived in Warsaw in force [forces considerables], could only have the goal of forcing the Vistula and, in scoring a victory between this river and the Narew, to favour an insurrection of the previously Polish provinces and even, in its final result, to oblige the army of General Michelson to retreat from the Turkish front.

Add to that that in defending the Vistula I would have had to occupy the principal bridges in force, where the enemy would have tried to effect their passage and especially those where the enemy was probing [faisait des demonstrations]; the latter were principally at Warsaw and Thorn; but at the same time the French were preparing the necessary timber for a bridge on the Netze; they could use it to access the Vistula and either ascend or descend that river, according to the place they deemed it necessary. In defending these two widely separated points 30 miles apart, I risked not having the forces to oppose the French at any point between Thorn and Warsaw. In order to effect it, the French only needed three days; two for the construction of the bridge and one for the passage. It was no great trouble to hide for 48 hours their march either on Warsaw or Thorn or some other place they occupied. Continuing to threaten both Warsaw and Thorn, they could have gained another day or two and not only built a bridge, but have made one or two marches, without me being able to take the necessary measures to defend against a passage. I was therefore exposed to the danger of my army being cut in half and suffering a decisive defeat. Moreover this passage could be easily forced at Warsaw, across from Praga, under the protection of several large-calibre batteries; I therefore had to retain a large force concentrated on this bank.

Everything I have just said is without doubt more than enough for me to have renounced the defence of the Vistula, without the following consideration, which always had to enter into my consideration, supporting that conclusion.

The events at Ulm were too fresh to escape my memory; the left wing of the Austrians rested on Ansbach and Beyreuth, one would believe it to be perfectly secure, while the French, far from respecting this neutral country, traversed it and in turning the left flank of the Austrians, managed to destroy their flank, which gave place to the unforeseen results. Here, my left wing rested on Galicia. Should I not have feared that the French, if I stretched out too far on my right, would traverse Galicia to turn my left wing? Should I not have taken measures against this eventuality that could have ruined all? Look at the map and look at the open path the French would have had and say what must have happened. No help could arrive for me; all had been obliged to rush to the defence of our own country. If therefore I needed to preserve the principal part of my forces at the extremity of my left wing, how could I stretch myself on my right and defend so enormous a distance as was discussed above?

It was during the King's stay at Pultusk that His Majesty confided the command of his troops in myself, placing at their head, in the place of the cavalry general Count Kalkreuth, Lieutenant-General Lestocq, a soldier of the greatest merit, who, in the preceding wars, had already served with brilliant distinction. In this war, having always commandeered a separate corps, composed of Russian and Prussian troops, he achieved the greatest reputation. I must further add that General Lestocq, by noble and just behaviour, knew first off to gain the confidence of his Russian troops, such that all those who found themselves under his orders felt honoured and still speak of this brave General with the greatest attachment and gratitude.

The King informed me that he had sent Major de Goltz into Silesia with order to form a corps composed of the troops still in fortresses, of men who, after various engagements, had ended up in that province, and of new recruits being raised there. This corps could have always withdrawn into the fortresses and could have constituted a considerable force. It could have made powerful diversions, which could have forced the French to commit considerable bodies of troops [again the word is *corps*, but unless used for the French I am variously translating it as corps or as some variant of 'bodies of troops'], but I know not who impeded this plan so wisely conceived. We had assembled so few forces that the Bavarian corps, which moved into Silesia, defeated it and forced the rest to take refuge in Bohemia. The majority of fortresses gave themselves up one after the other; on 1 December, the enemy began to weakly bombard Glogau and, on 2 December, the fortress had already surrendered. Breslau surrendered on 6 January, after a defence of almost four weeks. On 10 January, the enemy arrived before Schweidnitz; this fortress only held out until 16 January, when she gave up as well. I will speak to you at the appropriate time about events occurring in Silesia. His Majesty, after having conferred with me on future operations, left Pultusk on 14/26 November for Osterode.

The Prussian troops were already in the position I indicated above; the entirety, excepting the garrisons in different fortresses and those still in Warsaw, consisted of six battalions of fusiliers, eight regiments of infantry of the line, fifty squadrons and nine battalions of artillery. The combined army remained for some time in this position. General Barclay had several parties of Cossacks swim across the Vistula; they ran into some scraps [petites affaires] that all ended up well enough and each time they brought back prisoners, as many officers as soldiers, from whom we learned that Prince Murat, with a portion of the cavalry reserve, and Marshals Davout and Lannes with their corps were marching on Warsaw. We then learned that Davout's headquarters [quartier general] had arrived on 9 November (new style) in Posen and that he had continued, on 16 November, his march on Warsaw.

Colonel Yurkovskii also sent us several prisoners taken in scraps at the advance posts. On 12/24 November, the French arrived at Sochaczew and the detachment under their orders was obliged to retreat to Blonie, where on 13/25 November there was another advance-post skirmish, costing ten men [de part et d'autre], over which Colonel Yurkovskii retreated to Warsaw. The city was evacuated by the Prussian troops on 14/26 November in the greatest order and the bridge over the Vistula was burned. On 15/27 November, a detachment of French cavalry entered Warsaw. On this occasion the inhabitants were peaceful, which one must attribute, as I said before, to the wise preparations of Prince Joseph Poniatowski. General Siedmioraczki had already received orders to hold fast at Praga and defend the passage of the Vistula. The Prussian garrison that left Warsaw was still 4,000 men strong; but as the regiments that composed it were made up of Poles, the majority deserted in Galicia, when they arrived on the Bug, which forms the frontier between Prussia and Austria at this point.

At first I did nothing to change my position and I could have held there if General Siedmioraczki, to whom I confided the left wing of my position as well as the defence of the passage of the Vistula at Praga, had not hurriedly left his position on 19 November/1 December against my explicit orders; he retreated on the false news that the French were already marching via Galicia to turn his flank. The French in Warsaw were soon informed by the inhabitants of Praga, and they did not hesitate to exploit the misunderstanding of our general, as they crossed the Vistula to occupy this post. When I received General Siedmioraczki's report at Pultusk, the French had already occupied Praga in force, which I could no longer retake without a useless effusion of blood.

Murat found himself at Warsaw at that time as well as Marshal Davout's and Lannes' corps, whose forces greatly surpassed my own; we also knew that all the other army corps were approaching the Vistula.

As a consequence of the previously-noted circumstances, the passage of the Vistula at the extremity of my left wing was a real possibility, and I had to fear that the French would take advantage of the situation and attack my isolated forces before I had time to concentrate my corps. Therefore I could no longer hold my position on the Vistula and I had identify, without loss of time, the means by which we could cover our frontiers from the banks at Brest [du côte de Brest], where our General Essen had not yet arrived.

In the hope that the French had not yet been informed of the approach of General Buxhöwden with his corps and that they were following me with the intensity they usually threw into their operations, I opted to retreat toward the reinforcements that he was leading. To this effect, I directed the march of different detachments from their cantonments, on 20 November/2 December, to Rozan and from there to Ostrolenka, where I hoped General Buxhöwden could join me with at least a portion of his corps; I planned on luring the enemy to the plains in the area and where the Prussian corps under the orders of General Lestocq should also be [devait se render de même]. But this strategy did not succeed.

On 24 November/6 December I received the news that the enemy was pushing no further and they had contented themselves to fortify the bridge at Praga by works on which they made a certain number of inhabitants work. I therefore resolved to return to Pultusk. On the following map [not reproduced here], you will see the position my corps took in two lines in tight cantonments [cantonments serrés], so that the troops could be concentrated promptly [en deux fois] in 24 hours beneath Pultusk, on the right bank of the Narew. A reserve of twelve battalions was placed along the river near Pultusk.

Lt.-Gen. Count Osterman, to whom I had given command of the left wing of my corps in place of General Siedmioraczki, occupied the environs of Sierock and Czarnowo to defend the passage of the Wkra River, where it flows into the Narew, and to stop the enemy for as long as necessary to concentrate the army at Pultusk.

General Barclay de Tolly was sent to Nowe Miasto with the advance guard to occupy the Wkra River; his advance posts on his left linked up with those of General Count Osterman, and on his right with those of General Lestocq, whom I had ordered to retreat from Thorn to Strassburg on the Drewenz River. The General arrived with his headquarters on 24 November/6 December at Gollub and the next day at Strassburg. Renouncing the defence of the Vistula, I could no longer hold Thorn; I had to save the troops, and those that I left there for its defence would have been irrevocably lost, as the place was not sufficiently fortified for a garrison to hold for very long.

On 25 November/7 December, Colonel Rusanov of the Aleksandriiskii Hussar Regiment was sent with his squadron and a company of the 4th Jager Regiment under the orders of Captain Kulich to reconnoitre the enemy positions from Pomichowo by Modlin up to Zakroczyn. On his return, he found the enemy had cut him off with infantry. He decided to charge the infantry, sabre in hand, which he succeeded in doing without considerable losses; but the company of jagers was quickly surrounded by the enemy, which believed they could no longer escape. Captain Kulich, in his critical position, didn't lose his cool; he knocked over those that approached his front, took two small batteries and forced the enemy to retreat toward the Vistula; there they jumped into boats where they lost more men from the fire of our jagers.

Meanwhile the enemy had occupied the Pomichowo Road, which our jagers had to recross. But Captain Kulich was informed, and this enterprising officer, having already fought from the morning until 3 o'clock that afternoon and seeing that he was low on ammunition, decided to retreat via the forests, passing by the village of Wronna and happily reached Kolozomb, where he crossed the Wkra River and joined up with a detachment from General Dorokhov. In this affair, which brought great honour to Captain Kulich, we only lost twenty-six men killed, wounded or missing. Due to the report I made on the conduct of this officer, the Emperor, sent him the Order of Vladimir (4th class), and the Prussian King the Ordre de Mérite [Pour le Mérite]. But this brave officer was never able to enjoy these honourable decorations, as he had the misfortune to be killed at the battle of Czarnowo, where he once again distinguished himself.

On 29 November/11 December, Colonel Grekov XVIII went on reconnaissance with his regiment of Cossacks via Zakroczyn, where he found an enemy detachment in wait to ambush General Dorokhov's detachment. Grekov surprised the enemy detachment, killed several men, took one officer and fifteen *jagers à cheval* prisoner and dispersed the rest.

Almost eight days after my return to Pultusk, General Buxhöwden installed himself and his corps around Wyssoko-Mazovetsk, where he placed his headquarters. I sent Lt.-Gen. Count Tolstoy to instruct him to use one of his divisions to relieve my troops along the left bank of the Narew, to occupy the distance on the Bug from the Austrian frontier to the mouth of the Narew, so that I might concentrate my four divisions entirely on the right bank of the Narew. Moreover, it was agreed that he would bring up his three other divisions close enough to the left bank to be able to link up with me at Pultusk if needed within two marches. In this manner we were strong enough to receive battle, that the enemy, in accordance with the information we had received, did not hesitate to present all of their forces. General Lestocq made several attempts to retake Thorn; but already having received word that the enemy had already occupied this city with considerable forces, he wisely renounced these moves and contented himself to establish a chain of advance posts from Bischofswerder to Strassburg, the left wing of which connected with the Russian right, and at the same time he occupied the region between Danzig and Bischofswerder with a flying corps [corps volant]. Soon after we received the news that Emperor Napoleon had arrived at Posen on 15/27 November, and we had to wait from one day to the next to hear of his arrival in Warsaw, which one could consider as the signal of great military events to come.

Meanwhile, I received an edict from the Emperor [Alexander] in which he noted that the consideration of the necessity to form from the two corps, one of them confided to me, the other to General Buxhöwden, a single mass, more formidable in its unity and more able to present a barrier to the enemy's progress, had compelled him to place Field Marshal Count Kamenski at the head of all his troops, ready to act against the French; and that he [Kamenski] would direct military operations and it was he whom we would follow forthwith. This choice had been motivated by the desire and by the virtually unanimous voice of the public and the nation.

The long and highly distinguished service that Count Kamenski had rendered to his sovereigns and his nation gained him this confidence, the most beautiful recompense that a general can enjoy at the end of his career. [Kamenski] had already served as a colonel in the Seven Years War; he had served as a volunteer in the French army during the campaign of 1759. In the wars against the Turks, during the reign of [Empress] Catherine II, he commanded a detached corps with distinction. He combined with this great experience all of the knowledge and instruction necessary for a good and grand general. In his youth he had often been enjoined to serve the functions of a quartermaster-general and he had studied deeply [à fond] the sciences relative to that role. The state would certainly have taken the same good and distinguished service from this man in this great and important war if his advanced age, his infirmities and bad physique from which he suffered, had allowed him the indispensable activity to a commanding general so that he could judge with his own eyes the enemy movements and direct those of his own troops.

On the news, which I had received, that our field marshal had arrived in Lithuania, I sent him a highly detailed report on the state of my corps, accompanied by a map on which I had marked precisely the position of my troops, with a rigorous analysis of the information on the position of different French corps and finally all news that had reached me concerning the enemy's intentions. The field marshal arrived on 7/19 December at Pultusk; Napoleon had arrived in Warsaw during the night of 18/19 December (new style). Lt.-Gen. Count Osterman reported at the same time that the enemy had reinforced himself considerably on our left wing across from him; that he was preparing the necessary materials for the construction of a bridge on the Bug; that by means of a small island at the mouth of the Wkra where this river flows into the Bug, at a small distance from the village of Czarnowo, the passage could be easily forced by an enemy superior in numbers. In consequence we had to wait and see from one moment to the next our left wing forced and Count Osterman obliged to retreat on Pultusk, into the position I had prepared to receive battle.

However, the Field Marshal did not approve of my position or the measures I had taken. The day after his arrival, he sent the twelve battalions I had placed in reserve on the Narew to Nowe Miasto, on the Wkra River, to join the advance guard and he ordered me to go there and take command. His intention was to cross the Wkra with a considerable body of troops at Nowe Miasto, to force the enemy to re-cross the Vistula at Plock and from there to lift the blockade of Graudenz, which the French had already initiated. On 10/22 December, prepared to leave for Nowe Miasto, I went to the Field Marshal to receive his final orders, when we learned from a report by Lt.-Gen. Count Osterman that the small island, of which I have already made mention, had been attacked and taken by Marshal Davout's corps on 7/19 December and that it was occupied by considerable forces; that the enemy was working on batteries, under the protection of which the passage of the small river, which still separated us from the enemy, would by all appearances be forced the next night and that then it would be impossible to hold against the considerable forces facing him. He reported at the same time that according to the unanimous testimony of the prisoners, Napoleon himself was across from him and that they had heard repeated cries of 'Vive l'Empereur!' Marshal Soult and his corps had already crossed the Vistula near Wyszogrod and with him a portion of the cavalry reserve under the Grand Duke of Berg. Marshal Lannes' corps had passed the Vistula at Warsaw and was following Marshal Davout's corps on the Pultusk Road, also with a portion of the cavalry reserve. The corps of Marshal Ney and Bernadotte had already passed the Vistula at Thorn; the first was at Rypin, and the second at the extreme left wing of the French army.

Major-General Count Pahlen, who with his regiment of hussars maintained, at a certain distance, our advance posts in front of our right wing on the Wkra, reported that the enemy was advancing in considerable forces against him. At the same time we received a notice from Warsaw that came to us via Galicia, that the enemy would attack us on 12/24 December at all points to force the passage of the Wkra.

Our field marshal [Kamenski], either not believing all of these reports, or supposing that the enemy was halting his movements on our right, did not retain me at Pultusk. Not only did he change nothing about his dispositions, but moreover he reinforced the advance guard with some troops of the first line and all of the infantry from the second line of the right wing. The next day, 11/23 December, he sent the order to Lt.-Gen. Prince Golitsyn to arrive at Nowe Miasto with the two cavalry regiments that remained with him.

On 11/23 December I arrived at Nowe Miasto at the same time as the enemy was making a reconnaissance, which lent itself to a lively enough skirmish. The evening of the same day the field marshal himself arrived at Nowe Miasto. All of these troops, which I have mentioned, found themselves moving against our centre and right wing, when Napoleon attacked Count

Osterman via the island, which I mentioned earlier, on the night of 11/12 (23/24) December and forced the passage of the Bug. Count Osterman, at the moment the engagement commenced, sent us Colonel Uvarov, aide-de-camp to the Emperor [Alexander], with a report in which he exposed the utter impossibility of holding out against the considerable forces opposing him. Colonel Uvarov was sent back with orders from the field marshal, but was captured by the enemy on the road back. Count Osterman was already retreating, after an engagement that lasted six hours and a beautiful defence that earned him the mark of satisfaction from his sovereign and the admiration of the entire army. As soon as it was daylight, our field marshal himself left for Czarnowo in a small carriage, but almost an hour and a half later he returned back, but on horseback. He could not make it through, finding the enemy already in possession of this location.

At the same time we received reports that our entire line of advance posts had been attacked, and shortly after that, that our principal post, 4 verstas from us on the Wkra River and meant to cover Nowe Miasto, had been attacked and taken; that the four cannon that formed a battery there had been taken and that the enemy was advancing quickly and in force. Our field marshal took it upon himself to move with the troops on the march on our right, and he vested in me his trust to command the rest.

We had good reason to believe that the enemy was waiting for us at Pultusk, where only one unit remained, and which were cut off from the two divisions on the left bank of the Narew. I therefore ordered the entire advance guard to retire down the Strzegocin Road, where our Marshal had ordered us to regroup in lieu of Pultusk. I myself moved within 4 verstas of that place with General Titov, who was with his brigade in a village 4 verstas behind Nowe Miasto, with whom I travelled along the Strzegocin Road. Before leaving I wrote orders to all the generals, who had received the order to advance on our right, to abandon their trajectory post haste, to take the Pultusk road, and to maintain the highest diligence in their march. At 10 in the evening I arrived at Strzegocin, where I found Count Osterman in retreat with his corps; Major-General Count Lambert arrived at the same time with a detachment of cavalry; around one hour after midnight, General Barclay arrived with the advance guard from Nowe Miasto and then General Sacken with the left wing of the first line. Lt.-Gen. Prince Golitsyn with his cavalry regiments and various other detachments – in all twelve battalions and thirty-five squadrons – almost all of the Cossacks and a number of cannon couldn't make it to Strzegocin or Pultusk, as the enemy had cut off that road.

My first concern was to arrange all of the troops that had arrived at Strzegocin in battle formation as much as the deep darkness of the night permitted. After allowing the troops to rest for a bit, I moved them off toward Pultusk in the following arrangement: General Count Lambert, making up the advance guard with his light troops, left at two hours after midnight; at three o'clock, Count Osterman with his troops; at 4 o'clock, General Sacken should have left with several regiments from his division and at 5 o'clock, General Barclay as the rearguard.

General Sacken did not execute his orders exactly; without reason and contrary to the order I had given, he remained at Strzegocin until 6 o'clock, which held up General Barclay and his rearguard. Because of this loss of time we were obliged to abandon more cannon that we need not have lost in roads that had become impassable, due to this fault of General Sacken. The various detachments in the Russian army lost fifty-two cannon altogether in the retreat, that got so sunken in the mud that no matter how many efforts we committed to it, we could not rescue them. The enemy did not follow closely and, according to these dispositions, the march went along in an orderly manner.

After having given all the necessary orders for this march, I left to rejoin the advance-guard, with which I arrived at 9 o'clock at Pultusk, where luckily General Baggovut, who had occupied the distance from Sierock to Dembe, had already arrived. In learning of the retreat of all of our troops from the Wkra River, he had wisely directed his detachment toward Pultusk and had occupied the heights, from which he covered the roads from Sierock and Nasielsk.

Around 11 o'clock, he notified me that the enemy was advancing against him via the Nasielsk Road and that his advance posts were already engaged. We then confirmed that it was General Suchet who had arrived with a division either for a reconnaissance or to occupy Pultusk if we had not already arrived. But General Baggovut made such good use of the terrain that the enemy, despite his superior numbers, was forced to retreat as he could not bring his artillery up the impassable roads while General Baggovut had six 6-pounder pieces. Our regiment of Tatar Light Horse, under the orders of Lt.-Gen. Knorring, distinguished themselves well on this occasion. They overran an enemy cavalry regiment and took seventeen prisoners. The enemy took casualties, especially from our artillery. Our loss was two killed, three wounded. I could not reinforce General Baggovut as I had only arrived with a few troops that barely sufficed to cover the heavy artillery at Pultusk. Moreover I had no knowledge of the enemy's strength. As our troops arrived, I placed them in the previously-chosen positions. Luckily for us, the day passed without any serious engagements.

That evening, at 10 o'clock, our field marshal returned to Pultusk; I went to give my report on all that had passed since his departure from Nowe Miasto, adding that we should consider the appearance of the enemy that day as a reconnaissance rather than an attack, but that we should expect a serious attack the next day by Napoleon himself. Count Kamenski consented to accept battle and inquired if all was ready. I responded that I had occupied my positions as the troops arrived, but that we were still missing a great many, though I still hoped they would arrive during the night, at which our field marshal wrote to General Buxhöwden, who stood with one division at Makow, two miles from Pultusk, and another division under the orders of General Dokhturov at Golymin, to move to the right bank of the Narew, and to Generals Essen III and Anrep, who were on the left bank of the Narew, to move without delay to our aid at Pultusk. The orders were sent and all these troops should have been able to arrive in due time during the next day's action. I retired tranquilly to my quarters near where my soldiers were bivouacked.

Unfortunately, during the night our field marshal became so ill that he could not be placed on a horse to command in person, for which he was changing the dispositions. To this end, he sought me out about three hours before daybreak and gave me a written order, in which he ordered me to retreat quickly with all of the troops under my command toward our frontiers. Given the dispersal of our army, it was easy to foresee the unfortunate consequences of a precipitated retreat; they would have been the same as a lost battle. Fighting, I would at least have gained time for the other troops that were already cut off from me to regain the upper Narew.

I therefore resolved to hold my position and accept a battle rather than risk the safety and interests of our state by a retreat, the consequences of which could not have been anything other than dire. I should add that it was unknown to me that he had sent orders to Generals Buxhöwden, Essen III and Anrep revoking the call to come to my aid, and ordering them instead to march toward our frontiers. These generals received these orders when they were already on the march and not far from the battlefield; thus three divisions could have arrived to aid me during the fight, as you see on the map, and the day would have undoubtedly decided the outcome of this first campaign to our advantage. Finally, despite all of the unfortunate circumstances, by their bravery our troops stood that day against all the attacks executed by the enemy against multiple points.

I will wait to communicate to you the reports that arrived from detachments that were separated from me and attacked that day while on the march. In this letter I will limit myself to relating the Battle of Pultusk and then to reflect on the great results of this memorable day. You will agree that, although the battle was not as deadly as Preussisch-Eylau, the consequences were no less important for Russia, especially after what had happened on the Wkra and of which I have already spoken. It is certain that, without the changes that had taken place relative to the measures I had taken, the Battle of Pultusk would have been more decisive than it was, as the enemy would have run up against seven divisions.

I have already said, General, that I had chosen the position of Pultusk upon my arrival with the army in that country. It had to cover the main road to Ostrolenka, as well as the bridges I had built on the Narew below Pultusk and Zambsk; at the same time it had to ensure free communication with General Buxhöwden's corps. From this position I could move rapidly to secure our borders wherever they were threatened, and I could easily execute the plan conceived before the arrival of our field marshal, that is, moving, after a decisive victory at Pultusk, my principal forces to the lower Vistula to disengage Graudenz and to secure communications with Danzig. To this end I had already hastily established at Soldau, Mlawa, Prasnitz, etc., small magazines that later fell into the hands of the enemy.

I occupied a plain . . . which offered no marked advantage to either party. Bravery, which on every occasion had marked the troops of the armies fighting in this war, and manoeuvre would decide the engagement.

My left wing rested on the small village of Pultusk and my right on a thicket near the village of Moszyn. To cover the Narew and the Grande Route from Sierock to Pultusk, I had pushed a corps under General Baggovut four verstas in front of my left wing, composed of infantry regiments from Stary-Oskol and Vilna, each one three battalions, of a battalion from the Revelskii Regiment, of the 4th Regiment of jagers, of the Polish Tatar Light-Horse Regiment, of two squadrons of the Kievskii Dragoon Regiment, and of a regiment of Cossacks.

The advance guard commanded by General Barclay de Tolly – composed of the 1st, 3rd and 20th Jager Regiments, altogether nine battalions, of the Tenginskii Infantry Regiment (three battalions), and five squadrons from the Polish Light-Horse Regiment – was placed in front of the right wing in the thicket, with six cannon to keep the enemy from turning that wing.

On 14/26 December, around 9 o'clock in the morning, after inspecting the troops that had arrived in bivouac during the night, I received a report from General Baggovut on the enemy approach. We knew that Napoleon was there himself with the corps of Lannes and Davout and a portion of the cavalry reserve under the Grand Duke of Berg [Murat]. Upon hearing this report I ordered my cavalry to advance a thousand paces into the plain in front of the infantry to mask my position until the enemy arrived in force. Marshal Davout moved first against our left; he impetuously attacked General Baggovut's advance corps. Too weak to resist, the latter retreated slightly; but in order to secure the town, and the enemy could have no other end in attacking our left than to take it, I reinforced this corps with three infantry battalions. As this was insufficient, I detached Lt.-Gen. Count Osterman with the Tulskii Infantry Regiment and a battalion of the Pavlovskii Grenadier Regiment; I had already detached, in cavalry, the Izumskii Hussar Regiment and the Kargopolskii Dragoon Regiment. From that moment on the engagement became more serious; we fought a long time with the greatest ferocity on both sides. The battalion of Grenadiers from the Staroskolskii Regiment and a battalion of the 4th Jager Regiment made a bayonet attack against the enemy's central column. At the same time, General [Sergey]

Kozhin,* with the Emperor's Cuirassier's Regiment and two squadrons from the Kargopolskii Dragoons Regiment successfully attacked the left flank of the columns; he overtook an infantry column of about 2,000 men, of whom the greater part were killed and three hundred taken prisoner; among the dead was one Colonel Rosen at the head of the enemy column. On the left of Baggovut's corps a strong enemy column attempted to force his left, passing between a height and the Narew, on the banks of the river; but it was attacked by two battalions of our infantry. A battalion under the command of Major Brewern arrived from General Anrep's division on the left bank of the Narew, with two cannon, flanked the enemy column, which was soon repulsed with losses. General Dokhturov with his Izumskii Hussars Regiment adeptly drew an enemy column onto one of our batteries with a false retreat; the enemy was stopped with losses from this battery's fire. These attacks were so co-ordinated that the enemy was forced to break off and for the moment renounce an attempt to break our left.

Throughout the battle [the French] attached great importance to taking Pultusk. Having already received reinforcements, they renewed their attack against Baggovut's entire line, which was forced to withdraw a second time due to the superior strength of the enemy and retreat to a ravine behind them. But Count Osterman arrived with his detachment; he hastily arranged a few cannon into a battery on a hill behind the ravine. The fire from this battery had a great effect; all the troops threw themselves on the enemy once again, forcing them to retire. General Baggovut pursued them with his entire cavalry supported by the jagers and the Tulskii Infantry Regiment commanded by Major-General [Andrey] Somov for more than 4 verstas. We took nearly 500 prisoners in these attacks and the pursuit of the enemy on our left wing. The success we had was due largely to the good conduct of General Baggovut and to the wise dispositions of Lt.-Gen. Count Osterman.

While these stubborn fights were underway on our left, a large enemy column advanced against our centre, upon which I gradually withdrew my cavalry. I ordered it through our two lines of infantry and it placed itself in a third line behind my right wing, near enough to redeploy if the enemy wanted to attack our centre. But after several volleys by our heavy artillery, the enemy column turned to the left and went to link up with the troops that Marshal Lannes was moving in several columns against our right wing. They traversed the thicket and impetuously attacked our advance guard under the command of General Barclay who was covering our right wing; but too weak in comparison to the enemy's superior forces, Barclay was forced to fall back. I had hidden a battery charged with canister [mitraille] in the brush, whose

---

* Sergey Kozhin commanded the Life Guard Horse Regiment in 1800 and served as chef of His Majesty's Life Guard Cuirassier Regiment until being killed in action in early 1807.

discharge momentarily halted the enemy's ardour. But soon after this battery was taken and General Barclay forced to retreat again.

The General sent one of his aides-de-camp to General Sacken, who commanded our right wing, asking for help. Unable to obtain it even after a second request, he sent the same aide-de-camp, M. Bartholomé, to me, begging that I come myself to the right wing. Although my presence was still necessary on the left wing, where I was, I felt it necessary to concede to General Barclay's request. Barely had I arrived at our centre than I perceived that the enemy had managed to win the brush and come parallel [gagne dans les brousailles la parallele] to our right wing. Afraid of quickly being outflanked, I abruptly changed the order of my line by withdrawing my right wing onto my centre . . . At the same time I reinforced General Barclay with three battalions from the Chernigovskii Regiment, under the command of Prince Dolgorouky V, all three from the second line. This move was a great success, as all of the batteries that were in front of our right wing fired into the flanks of the enemy columns, which were now in the thickets.

At the moment when I saw the enemy had been stopped, I also sent General Barclay the Litovskii Infantry Regiment. Then this General, having closed his ranks, charged the enemy columns at the bayonet. At the same time I pushed forward a battery, supported by several squadrons, which directed a wonderful fire into the thickets; at the same time I sent forward the rest of the cavalry in front of the centre of my first line to contain the enemy cavalry. I had already sent the order to General Count Osterman to move forward all of the infantry on the left wing. These attacks succeeded everywhere; the enemy was forced to concede and retire from the battlefield.

We had fought with the greatest bravery on two fronts, from 11 o'clock in the morning until 7 o'clock in the evening. The musket fire, especially on our right wing, was for six hours more and more sustained and lively [des plus soutenus et de plus vifs]; the lines of infantry were so close so many times that they seemed to blend together, and one saw that our infantry was determined to justify that day, the high opinion concerning their bravery that they have always enjoyed in Europe, but which a few unfortunate affairs in the preceding campaigns had momentarily altered for those that did not understand the heart of the Russian soldier. The French, for their part, habituated to their great captain forcing all before him to retreat, only barely gave ground for the first time at Pultusk, after having redoubled their greatest efforts with uncommon valour. Darkness, the bad weather and hail accompanied by a biting wind kept us from pursuing the enemy for very long and from profiting from our victory as we could have had the fighting ceased before the onset of night.

It is my duty to offer here to General Barclay de Tolly the justice that is due to him. By his distinguished conduct in this action he again affirmed the reputation he already enjoyed in the army. I must also render justice to my chief-of-staff, General Steinheil, who by his talents and vigour on that day, as throughout the course of the war, aided me in the execution of my orders. Colonels Berg and Aderkas, of the staff, also distinguished themselves in this action. I would very much like to name all of those who contributed to the victory of that day, but the number is too great.

I will limit myself therefore to expressing my contentment and admiration that I felt in general regarding the conduct and bravery of the troops that were in that action under my orders. I need not tell you of the part our artillery played in the victory of that day, nor of the conduct of the officers that commanded it, as my relation serves as their praise.

In my first official account it was impossible to determine our losses; but they were effectively around 7,000, as many killed as wounded. The French losses can be evaluated without exaggeration at around 10,000 men, including the 700 men we took prisoner on the battlefield.

I repeat, I was not aware of [Kamenski's] orders that General Buxhöwden's divisions had already received, that they not come to my aide. I therefore found myself during the entirety of the action in the greatest sense of security on that issue, all the more so as a battalion from General Anrep's division arrived in the afternoon on the left bank of the Narew, near the bridge below Pultusk, and as a Prussian chasseur, arriving at the same time, assured me that he had seen with his own eyes General Buxhöwden with General Tuchkov's division marching on the road from Makow to Pultusk and that the cavalry would be on the field shortly. I was all the more obligated to await the arrival of the troops that Lt.-Gen. Count Tolstoy, the duty general of the army, had sent to link up with Buxhöwden, when General Baggovut's was already in action and the battle was becoming general. It was only during the night, when it was all over and I had returned the majority of my troops to their original position, that I officially learned that all these troops I had awaited were already withdrawing to our frontier.

Under these circumstances, what else was I to do? Certainly I could do no other than to also follow the orders given by the field marshal, because what was I exposing myself to by remaining at Pultusk? All of the enemy corps that had been detached to attack our different detachments had not hesitated to spin on their heels, regroup and renew an engagement in which the disproportion of forces would have been too great for me to resist. With regret I decided to withdraw from Pultusk so as to more easily extricate Lt.-Gen. Golitsyn and his troops, who had been cut off from me and from whom I had received no news. To this end, on 15/27 December I ordered my heavy artillery to cross the Narew early in the morning, with an appropriate escort, with orders to march on the left bank of this river to Ostrolenka and to await me there. The road on the left bank is sandy and not so impracticable as on the right bank; moreover I was convinced that the enemy was not following me straight away and that I could part for a while from my heavy artillery. After having gotten our wounded on the move, still capable of being transported, I had the troops move out via the Rozan Road, on the right bank of the Narew. The last troops of the rearguard left Pultusk at 11 o'clock in the morning, without having seen the enemy.

The position in which I found myself that day was certainly awkward and difficult. I had received a clear order to move swiftly to our frontiers, and by consequence not to deliver battle; to what personal responsibility was I exposing myself if I had had the misfortune to suffer a notable loss? The unfortunate results would have been blamed on me; the good intentions I had, relative to my determination to dig in my heels, await and stop the enemy, if only for a day, to buy time for our troops, strewn across the right bank of the Narew, to reach the river, would not have justified the accusation of disobedience that could have been made against me, all the more so as one could prove that I had time to move my own troops across the Narew, on the bridges I had built across that waterway. But as the day turned to our advantage, I was vindicated as much as I would have alternately been condemned. My gracious sovereign, in order to show his satisfaction, decorated me with the second class of the military order [Order of St. George] and gave me a gift of 5,000 chervonets.

Now, General, I pray you take map in hand and determine what the result would have been if I had acted differently, that is to say if I had decided to retreat. First what road would I have had to take? I would have over-exposed my heavy artillery if I had moved it to the left bank of the river as I did after the battle, accompanied by a simple escort, as the enemy that was already near Pultusk would have soon reached it: if I had taken it with me on the right bank, I would inevitably have lost it, as the roads were impracticable at the time; the enemy would have followed me closely, and that which occurred during our retreat from the Wkra would have played out again. Let us examine the result of my retreat with my corps across the Narew, which would have been easier to execute for myself and safer for the troops; but the consequences of such an action would have been appalling. Observe that General Buxhöwden was retreating with two divisions from Makow and General Prince Golitsyn with more than one division, cut off from me, on the road from Golymin to Ostrolenka. Napoleon was there in person with considerable forces on the right of the Narew, very near Pultusk. He would have been, no doubt, informed of the scattered march of the troops that I would have had to move from Pultusk. He who had never failed to exploit his enemies' mistakes, would only have had to move along the Narew by the same road that I had taken for Rozan and Ostrolenka, and move there quickly; our troops, whose march would have been slowed by the artillery on bad roads, would have been hard pressed to cross the Narew and escape an adroit enemy. The results of a marked defeat and a considerable loss of troops on the right bank of the Narew, in the circumstances in which we found ourselves, would have been incalculable. They would not have been limited to the loss of a day; they would become far worse by the entrance of an enemy across our frontiers in Lithuania. I would no longer have been in a state to resist the French army, all the more so as no reserve was near me, upon which I could retreat to be reinforced. The formation of the militia in the Empire had barely commenced. I would not therefore have risked a second engagement so as to not risk the lot of the state by a second and final loss, and I would have been forced to abandon these adjacent provinces to the enemy until I was strong enough to face them.

Although the inhabitants of Russian Poland were well and wisely guided during this last war against the French, they would nevertheless have been forced or convinced to follow in common cause with Prussian Poland against us. This spirit of insurrection would not have failed to spread as though a gunpowder trail through all of the formerly Polish provinces. The entry of a French army in force would inevitably have been the signal, and one could not deny that it would have been very difficult to re-conquer these beautiful provinces quickly, at least without a great effusion of blood.

Therefore you see, General, that the victory that Providence accorded our arms at Pultusk precluded all of these misfortunes and gave us time to gather our forces so as to resist again with vigour the formidable enemy forces. [From the French text in Levin Bennigsen, *Mémoires . . .*]

Robert Wilson

'A very slippery fellow,' as the Duke of Wellington once described him, Sir Robert Wilson was, in fact, one of the most colourful individuals of the Napoleonic Era. Few men saw as much as he did of the wars, fighting in Flanders, Holland, South Africa, Egypt, Poland, Portugal, Spain, Russia and Germany. In 1806, Wilson was sent as the British commissioner to the Russian army and was able to use his contacts at the Prussian court and Russian headquarters to gain keen insights into military and political circumstances. Four years after the Polish campaign Wilson wrote a widely-read book on the Russian army in Poland – Brief Remarks on the Character and Composition of the Russian Army and a Sketch of the Campaigns in Poland in the Years 1806 and 1807 – but he also maintained a private journal where he confided his thoughts and insight that could not be made public.

[Königsberg, 31 December] I fear that the state of affairs is very bad, but hope the Russian general will avoid for the present a general action. He has not above one hundred and ten thousand men (exclusive of fifteen thousand Prussians attached to his orders): but in the spring he will be greatly reinforced, and many powerful contingencies may occur to reduce the strength of the French, who are calculated to have a force of one hundred and seventy thousand effectives in Germany and Poland. General Kamenski who commands the Russians, is a very distinguished officer; and active, notwithstanding that he is seventy-two years of age. He affects to imitate [Alexander] Suvorov, and plays the antics of a semi-savage; but he has the confidence and regard of officers and men.

[On 29 December] at ten o'clock news arrived that the Russians had gained the victory. The king sent round the joyful tidings, and the whole town was in movement to assemble at the palace. A courier had arrived with a note from the aide-de-camp of the king; stating that he had great intelligence to communicate, but that he was coming on slowly from the last post because he had lost his hat in the battle and could not appear before His Majesty in that state. Was there ever anything more ridiculous? What an extraordinary trait for the nineteenth century!

Twenty-four postilions and a hat were sent out to meet the aide-de-camp, and about twelve o'clock he dismounted at the palace amidst the acclamations of the populace. The account was soon circulated that the Russian General Bennigsen had been attacked by the French on the 26th, and had repulsed them with a loss on their side of seven thousand men. Lord Hutchinson went to dine with the king in a major-general's uniform, without a star; his best coat having been sent off. We drove off in Mr. Drussini's barouche. I was the charioteer, and it required some skill in these narrow streets, and on slippery pavement as there had been a sharp frost for forty-eight hours. However, I conducted my charge in safety.

On our return there was a little damp thrown upon our rejoicings. It appeared that General Kamenski, the commander-in-chief of the Russians, had gone to S. Petersburg in disgust and, some pretend, wounded in the previous affair when General Osterman's column was compelled to retreat; and that there was the greatest misunderstanding between General Bennigsen and Buxhöwden, the two remaining chief commanders. Buxhöwden had indeed withdrawn his army to the Russian frontier; and Bennigsen had gained by his own corps of fifty thousand men the battle against Murat, Lannes, and Davoust [*sic*].

It was moreover stated that the Russians were in such want of provisions that Bennigsen himself would be obliged to withdraw to Ostrolenka, twenty-five miles distant from the field of action. The victory of the Russians, however, appeared to be decisive: but we anxiously await the details.

In the evening we went to Madame de Toss' for a few minutes, and then to the play, where the two young princesses went and were very loyally received.

This morning it thaws again. Kit and I are preparing to join the Russians, and we are in anxious expectation of news as to the events subsequent to the battle of the 27th, and the state of General Lestocq's corps; the situation of which previously to that day was critical.

December 31. This morning an officer is arrived from General Buxhöwden, stating that on the 26th he also was attacked, and that he repulsed the French with considerable slaughter. Buonaparte himself was present.

Notwithstanding the gallant conduct of the Russian troops, such is the unfortunate discord prevailing among the generals and so great the want of provisions, that the success to all appearance will have no advantageous consequences. The Russians are retiring upon Ostrolenka, and probably behind the Niemen river, which forms the boundary of the Russian empire. Against this measure the king is remonstrating; because in this case all Russian Poland is given up to the French, and what is of more consequence than the soil, immense magazines will fall into their power. In addition to this, the recruiting for the Prussian army will be stopped: this was going on prosperously, as seventeen whole battalions had been recently formed. Never was there a more extraordinary situation of affairs: in the midst of victory we are experiencing all the evils of defeat. Kamenski has certainly resigned the command. He is truly mad. In the streets of Pultusk he gave too painful evidences of his malady.

If we should be obliged to leave this place the retreat will be direful; the weather being very bad, the roads almost impassable. I pity the poor queen, who must be moved in a litter at this season of the year to be expatriated.

General Lestocq, the Prussian general, and his corps are safe. He has acquired great credit, and defends the country against a very superior force inch by inch. The black hussars have particularly distinguished themselves. In both the Russian battles the French had little quarter given them. I cannot but deprecate this practice: but I approve of the measures adopted by the Russians, who burn all the country which they leave behind them so as to make a desert for the French to pass over, if they can pass. In such conjunctures, when the fate of the world is at stake, trespasses must be committed on the civilising laws of war.

General Rüchel, the Prussian war minister, has been with us to say that the Russians have not resolved to retire behind the Niemen; and that their victory has been so disastrous to the French that Buonaparte is retreating.

God grant that this intelligence may prove true! yet General Zastrow is of a different opinion. All admit that the Russians fought nobly, and remained masters of the field.

[...]

[January 8] It is reported that a council of general officers has declared Kamenski mad, and that the generals Buxhöwden and Bennigsen have had a conciliatory interview. Moreover Lestocq has been considerably reinforced: so that affairs do not wear so unpromising an aspect as they did a few days since.

[. . .]

[9 January] The news from the Russian army is confirmed, that Kamenski has been declared mad by a council of officers. His acts of insanity indeed were so unhappily patent, that no sane man, hearing the evidence, could come to any other conclusion. Also that Generals Buxhöwden and Bennigsen have since had an interview and are reconciled. Fifty squadrons have been added to the corps of the latter, and General Essen, at the head of thirty-five thousand men, has reinforced Buxhöwden. The Finland army, including the S. Petersburg division, is also on the march and will be up in three weeks.

At present the Russian force assembled, exclusive of the Prussians under Lestocq, amounts to one hundred and forty thousand men; and such is the zeal of the people and vigour of the government, that in all the districts two-thirds of the recruits required by the *ukase* are already in training. A late *ukase* of the 30th of December, moreover, regulates for a militia of six hundred thousand men.* [English text in Herbert Randolph, *Life of General Sir Robert Wilson*]

Journal of Military Operations of the Imperial Russian Army

Every Russian corps maintained an official journal of military operations that recorded key movements, operations and battle reports. While most journals remain confined to the archives, this particular journal was, in fact, published shortly after the war in 1807 as part of the government efforts to shape public opinion.

As soon as the corps of His Imperial Majesty, under the command of General Baron Bennigsen, consisting of about 45,000 men,† excepting a part of the 3rd and 4th Divisions, had arrived in the environs of Pultusk, on 13 [25] December after a very fatiguing march (the roads being exceeding bad) and continually harassed by the enemy, the said corps was immediately so posted that its right wing was supported by the village of Mosezina, and the left by the small town of Pultusk, with a view to cover the road of Ostrolenka and the bridges near Pultusk and Zamsk that were built to keep open the communication with General of Infantry Count Buxhöwden.

The advance guard, commanded by Major-General Barclay de Tolly, consisting of three jager regiments (1st, 3rd, and 20th) and supported by the Tenginskii Musketeer and Polish Horse Regiments, took a position on our right wing in the bushes; whilst the detachment of Major-General Baggovut, consisting of the Staroskolskii and Vilenskii Musketeer Regiments, and one

---

* See Chapter 1.
† Bennigsen's corps actually numbered about 60,000.

battalion of Revelskii Musketeers, supported by the 4th Jager Regiment, the Tatar Horse Regiment and two squadrons of the Kievskii Dragoon Regiment, was posted before the left flank to cover the Narew River and the road leading from Sierock to Pultusk. These regiments had no sooner made a movement to occupy their above-mentioned positions than they were attacked about noon by a French detachment under the command of General Suchet. The fighting between the latter and our advanced posts of cavalry commenced and was kept up for nearly three hours, whereupon the enemy was repulsed with considerable loss. It afterwards appeared that this attack on the part of the enemy was only made with a view to reconnoitre.

On the following day, being 14 [26] December, when our troops were in the process of being deployed in order of battle, at 11 a.m., they were attacked by a French army of 60,000 men, commanded by Napoleon in person, and consisting of the corps of Marshals Davout and Lannes, and the detachment of General Suchet.

The first attack was made by the enemy in six columns, under Marshal Davout, with great impetuosity, and directed against our left flank, which consisted of the detachment of Major-General Baggovut, with a view to take Pultusk, to get into our rear, and to cut off our communication with the division of Lieutenant-General Anrep, which was deployed beyond the Narew River, two miles from Pultusk. Soon after this, the advance guard of Major-General Barclay de Tolly, on the right flank, was likewise attacked by six of the enemy's columns.

During these attacks of the enemy, made upon both our flanks, he had posted a chain of mounted jagers, behind whom stood several columns, which were preparing to fall upon our centre, but the enemy's intentions were completely frustrated by the powerful and well-directed effect of our artillery batteries, which were erected before our front.

The impetuous attack made by Marshal Davout with 15,000 men, in six columns, upon both flanks of the detachment of Major-General Baggovut obliged the latter to fall back as he had only between 4 and 5,000 men with him; but in his retreat he checked the enemy's progress with the 4th Jager Regiment, which spread itself before the infantry. In the mean while, Lieutenant-General Count Osterman arrived with the Tulskii Musketeer Regiment and one battalion of the Pavlovskii Grenadier Regiment to support him, and the enemy's further progress was checked. Major-General Baggovut, with the grenadier battalion of the Staroskolskii Musketeer Regiment, and a battalion of the 4th Jager Regiment, then threw himself, with fixed bayonets, upon the centre column of the enemy, by which he had been pressed, whilst Major-General Kozhin, with the His Imperial Majesty's Cuirassier Regiment and two squadrons of the Kargopolskii Dragoon Regiment, penetrated the front and flank of that column, and the result was that the whole column was immediately cut to pieces.

Meanwhile, the other battalions of the 4th Jager Regiment, the Tatar Horse Regiment and two squadrons of the Kievskii Dragoons attacked the enemy's columns that had advanced from the left and compelled them to retreat; however, the enemy, receiving an immediate reinforcement, advanced a second time with impetuosity, but was completely overthrown as we had formed a firm front of the jagers, who had thrown themselves upon the enemy with fixed bayonets, while our cavalry charged the columns and completely routed them.

At the same time, Major-General Dorokhov, with the Izumskii Hussar Regiment, made a premeditated retreat before the other enemy columns, which were on our right, and then suddenly turned about on the left with his regiment, by which well-timed manoeuvre he brought those columns right upon our batteries, which caused great havoc among the enemy.

The rest of our cavalry, which was posted in our front and made occasional attacks upon the enemy, received orders to pass back through our line of infantry, to leave an open field for action and to post itself in the rear. Once this was done, all our batteries opened their fire on the enemy's columns, which were advancing against our centre, but which, in consequence of the successful operation of these batteries, were not only checked in their progress, but also driven back.

The enemy, notwithstanding their being thrice defeated, attempted, on receiving a fresh reinforcement, to repeat their attack on all the points of our left flank, with renewed ardour, and pressed forward upon it with several co-ordinating columns. The detachment under Major-General Baggovut was compelled by the superior force of the enemy to fall back once more, as far as the trench in its rear. But being in the meantime joined by the Muromskii Musketeer Regiment and two battalions of the Revelskii Musketeer Regiment, and Lieutenant-General Osterman having occupied the height in the rear of the trench and opened a brisk fire from the battery deployed thereon, Major-General Baggovut attacked the enemy's columns with fresh ardour and succeeded in throwing them into disorder. At that moment, Major-General Somov rushed upon the enemy with the Tulskii Musketeer Regiment with fixed bayonets, and thus completed their total defeat; the enemy was routed, driven from the field of battle, and pursued until the approach of night. Thus, the enemy's attack on our left flank, in consequence of the intrepidity and judicious dispositions of Lieutenant-General Osterman, terminated, in this quarter, in his own destruction, and the whole corps under Marshal Davout was totally defeated.

During this furious attack upon our left flank, a numerous body of the enemy's infantry, divided into six columns under the command of Marshal Lannes, attempted, by penetrating through the brushwood, to flank our advance guard under the command of Major-General Barclay de Tolly, which had taken up position to cover our right flank. The object of the enemy on this side was to break, or at least to push back our right flank, and by this means to cut off our communication with a part of the corps of Count Buxhöwden that was deployed at the villages of Makow and Ostrolenka. The attack of the French on this side was extremely violent and impetuous. Our advance guard, notwithstanding a display of the utmost valour and intrepidity on the part of its commander, was compelled to fall back, by which movement our battery, which kept in check the enemy's columns on the road from Nowe Miasto, soon fell into the hands of the enemy; but the Tenginskii Musketeer Regiment, together with the jagers, charged the enemy with the bayonet, routed him, and reclaimed the cannon. In the meantime, by order of the commander-in-chief General Baron Bennigsen, a masked battery had been deployed in the brushwood, and the cannon were loaded with canister. A few discharges from this battery killed great multitudes of the enemy and checked their impetuosity. But immediately after, the enemy made dispositions to take the battery from the side, and Major-General Barclay de Tolly was, thus, forced for a second time to give way to their superior numbers. The commander-in-chief [Bennigsen], the moment he observed this movement, immediately ordered to change front and to throw back the whole of the right wing, to prevent an attack in flank, at the same time detaching the Chernigovskii Regiment, and soon thereafter, the Litovskii Musketeer Regiment, to reinforce Major-General Barclay de Tolly.

Major-General Barclay de Tolly, as soon as he had formed a part of the infantry which he had with him on one side and sent orders to Major-General Prince Dolgoruky to march with the Chernigovskii Musketeer Regiment on the other side, boldly rushed forward at the point of the bayonet on the enemy's columns, drove them back, and by this means stopped the advance of the other columns of the enemy which were rapidly coming up. But the French, who still kept a fire of musketry, did not abandon their intention of attacking our right flank until the commander-in-chief took the resolution of attacking the enemy in his turn.

With this in view, he ordered Lieutenant-General Count Osterman to move forward with the remaining infantry of the left wing, while on the right flank twenty squadrons of cavalry were ordered to advance in front of the battery under the command of His Imperial Majesty's Flügel Adjutant Stavitskii, which thus taking the enemy's line of infantry in flank, by a vigorous and well directed cannonade totally routed and dispersed it. In the meantime the remainder of our cavalry was posted in the centre to keep that of the enemy in check. The French fought desperately, but were at length compelled to yield at all points to the uncommon bravery of the victorious Russian warriors, the ability and resolution of their commanders, and the heavy and destructive fire of the artillery.

The battle continued from eleven in the morning until seven in the evening, and did not finish until it was completely dark. The enemy was beaten and defeated at every point. The darkness of the night, the inclemency of the weather, and the fatigue of the troops prevented the pursuit of the enemy.

In this battle we made about 700 prisoners; and, according to the statement of some who were taken the day after, the enemy, besides three generals who fell in the action, lost in killed and wounded about ten thousand men. The total of the loss on our side amounts in killed and wounded to between two and three thousand.

The commander-in-chief [Bennigsen] testifies that the troops of His Imperial Majesty who fought on this day gave inexpressible proofs of valour, and from the generals to the ranks acquired never fading glory by their firmness, intrepidity, and zeal. He mentions in particular terms of commendation the regiments of jagers and all artillery officers, who, as the enemy themselves acknowledge, displayed an uncommon degree of activity and address. [Here follows a lengthy list of officers who particularly distinguished themselves in the above battle.] [From the Russian text in the *Journal of Military Operations of Imperial Russian Army*, pp. 36–59]

Mikhail Petrov

One of four brothers to choose a military career, Mikhail Petrov began his military service in the Smolenskii Musketeer Regiment in 1797. Transferred to the Pskovskii Garrison Regiment, Petrov soon found himself in the Yeletskii Musketeer Regiment with which he had participated in the War of the Third Coalition but avoided the catastrophe at Austerlitz. After wintering in Silesia, he returned to Russia in the spring of 1806 only to be sent back to Poland later that year.

In late August 1806 the Yeletskii Musketeer Regiment, led by its chef Major-General [Alexander] Sukin II, marched from its permanent quarters in Pernau to Riga, where it joined Count [Alexander] Osterman-Tolstoy's division. I was then a staff captain commanding the 1st Musketeer Company while my brother, Ivan, was a captain in charge of the 3rd Grenadier Company.

Having reviewed his regiment in Riga, our division commander, Lieutenant-General Count Osterman, informed all staff and junior officers of his division about His Majesty the Emperor's desire . . . 'to have [officers] reduce their baggage in order to facilitate the movements of the main army during the impending war against the French; therefore [all belongings] need to be placed on pack horses instead of wagons that constrain and delay army movements by reducing additional supplies for frontline horses and jamming narrow roads and crossings'. The letter caused considerable discussions, with many speaking of the utility of the Emperor's request, others wondering what would happen in case of sickness or severe injury, and still others marvelling how they would be able to feed themselves as if they were going to fight in the wilderness. As for myself, I quietly went back to my quarters and pondered His Majesty's gentle approach (he could have [simply] ordered us) that coincided with my own belief in the necessity of destroying the vast multitude of officer carriages that constrained army movements, damaged roads and allowed soldiers to fall behind claiming to be fatigued and willing to assist batmen with officer carriages; I then sorted all of my possessions and kept only two shirts, one (spare) uniform with trousers, two towels and one pair of warm stockings. Everything else – horses, wagon, cellarette, suitcase and the rest of my possessions – I sold, unknown to my brother, at a local flea market, taking whatever price was offered for them so that five hours after I heard of the Imperial request, my batman Yefim Perestrukov, having packed all of mine and his belongings into a simple soldier's knapsack and affixing a copper teapot to his belt, was already standing in front of me, wearing a parade uniform and holding a *batik* [staff] in his hand. 'Excellent, Yefim,' I told him and laid down on straw to take a nap knowing that I had carried out His Imperial Majesty's request as a loyal subject and warrior who was capable of understanding the necessities of the war as it befits an officer, not a mercenary, devoted to his Fatherland.

The following day, after a review, we moved by forced marches towards the Vistula. Along the way Major Turgenev started to mock me for my 'bobyl'-like* decency' and even my own brother sternly reprimanded me for my 'hasty and thoughtless obedience' but I replied that I only benefitted from it since I could be carefree. My batman Yefim was a strong and hardworking man. He marched ahead of my company and, having all the necessary money, he always anticipated my arrival and took care of arrangements so both of us could eat well. Meanwhile other officers' batmen, travelling with their masters' carts, always arrived exhausted after a long journey on poor roads and, subjected to their masters' cursing, had to quickly fuss around to prepare something to subdue their hunger and anger. 'This is just our division marching; let's see what would happen when the entire army converges and starts taking order of battle,' I kept telling myself as I peacefully went to bed, content with my obedience to the rigours of war.

After crossing the Niemen at Kovno, the regiments from our and other divisions began rapid movement on thousands of hired German wagons that the Prussians had gathered from across the Königsberg province to speed up the juncture of the army of Count Kamenski with the [remnants of the] Prussian army that had been crushed by the French on the other side of the Elba River, at Jena and Auerstädt. The war, however, took a turn for the worse: marching to fight the French near the Elba, our field marshal intended to rely on supplies prepared by the Prussian government but we

---

* Bobyl was a cotter or landless peasant; colloquially the term was also used to describe an impoverished and homeless man.

faced unexpected circumstances because [after the Prussian collapse at Jena-Auerstädt] the French army, led by Napoleon, passed through Berlin and Poznan, occupied Warsaw and established its operational line along the right bank of the Vistula River while our army barely managed to establish its outposts along the left bank of the Wkra and the right bank of the Narew rivers, near Sierock and Sochoczyn; thus the areas, where no arrangements had been made to gather supplies, suddenly became the theatre of war for the vast campaign of 1806–7.

In such extreme circumstances and while awaiting deliveries of provisions and other necessities from the Jewish suppliers, our regiments were told to feed their men by tasking company commanders with buying whatever they could find from the local population and using company artel funds to be refunded from state monies issued to the regimental chefs.* Maintenance of each soldier here . . . cost us 35 silver kopecks per day. Throughout the month of November I supplied my company, spending just 12 silver kopecks per day per person. My artelschiks, who on 2 [14] December accompanied me to the regimental headquarters to cover the arrears, brought back loads [propast'] of gold and silver coins because they were given, based on overall regimental expenses, 22 silver kopecks per soldier. After setting aside what was owed to the company artel', I had the rest of the monies distributed to my company soldiers who had gathered in a yard. After discussion among themselves, the company soldiers sent their non-commissioned officers who led platoons,† asking whether I would like to take a share of the surplus money. I replied that I was very grateful to the company for its concern for my wellbeing and, showing them my purse that was quite full because I had recently received my pay, I ordered them to tell soldiers that 'I had sufficient monies and that I were killed in action, these monies, which I earned in the service of His Majesty, should be equally divided among them so they could remember that I never desired anything that I was not entitled to.'

On 11 [23] December the French crossed the Wkra River near Sierock. Our division, commanded by Count Osterman, hastened there to support the advance guard of Barclay de Tolly, which included Osterman's 1st and 20th Jager Regiments. It was there that the commander of the 1st Jager Regiment Colonel [Jacob] Davydovskii distinguished himself after receiving two wounds,

---

* Once a regiment received its funds, the regimental commander or chef distributed them through the company. Each company was divided into four platoons (otdelenie) and artels (artl'); each platoon was further divided into desyatki. The artel served as the centre of the soldier's daily life and its main purpose was to control the soldiers' common resources. Soldiers chose a person in charge of the artel funds and this artel'schik was responsible for buying supplies and managing monies received from the company commander. The platoon (otdelenie) leader (an NCO) actually distributed the provisions and funds to the men.

† See note above.

refusing to leave the battlefield and not weakening his steadfast defence of the crossing over the Wkra. [Sadly], three days later at Pultusk, he sustained this third, and mortal, wound to his shoulder that forced him to leave the field of battle, which we won on 14 [26] December, and eventually died at Grodno. May he rest in peace!

On 12 [24] December our advance guards retreated from the Sierock crossings towards Nasielsk, where the first major battle involving several of our divisions took place. Here my soul endured its first test and it was here that I was able to evaluate myself from within and thank Providence for granting me the privilege of being called a true-hearted nobleman serving in the military host of his glorious Fatherland. For five hours cannonballs, shells and grapeshot ravaged and ripped the ranks on both sides; we were showered in the hail of lead. We retreated to Pultusk where, on 14 [26] December Bennigsen accepted a general battle with Napoleon and repelled the French army, which was pursued by our cavalry throughout the night on the bad roads leading to Sochoczyn.

As memorable it was for us to celebrate the first victory over Napoleon, I will never forget my own triumph over the critics of my strict obedience of [the Imperial request] to destroy [personal] transports in Riga. The memory of this exultation always brings me joy and I will gladly explain what happened. During the battle my batman Yefim was in a ravine in the rear of the army, about one versta from the reserve battle line and upon seeing, as he told me, that 'our lads stood their ground and our cannons began to rumble,' he 'realised that we were prevailing and after spending the entire day since dawn on the battle field, would be quite hungry.' So in the evening he got out of the ravine and showed up in front me with a sack of provisions. I still vividly remember how lovely he seemed to me at that moment, despite a layer of dirt covering him as it did all of us. And so I, having welcomed by my dear Yefimushka with a brotherly greeting for the great favour he had done to me, crossed myself and indulged myself to a cup of vodka [gorelka] and pieces of roasted goose wing. Major Turgenev passed by me at a distance and upon observing my bliss, he stopped scratching his sideburn on his starved and yearning left cheekbone; he passed by me once more, this time closer, emitting coughing sounds from his famished chest. Then, as Yefim began to put the provisions back into his blessed sack, Turgenev approached me and addressed my 'bobyl'-like decency': 'What are you doing, Mikhail Matveyevich?' I replied that I was resting after having my fill of eating and washing away the gunpowder smoke of the battle that we had won. He added, standing in front of me, or to be precise in front of Yefim's sack that had suddenly become so precious to him as well, 'I now understand that you are an intelligent and prudent officer while I, in punishment for my thoughtless mockery of you, survive on thin air alone for the third day already, and it serves me right.'

'So where is your cart,' I asked him, getting up from the ground. 'Near Nasielsk. It was sent, together with hundreds of other officer carriages, on the orders of the army hewaldiger* back to the supply train at Golymin but lost its way and fell, together with the regimental chef's personal carriages and other transports of our division, into the devilish hands of the French. One of my batmen escaped, almost naked, from their captivity and arrived with me just two hours ago.'

'Well, well!' I replied. 'What are you waiting for! Hey, Yefim, get us vodka and all that you have left. [Turgenev,] you are welcome to drink and eat your fill.'

Just as Turgenev ate, I saw my brother Ivan returning with his half-battalion from a detachment and shouting from afar, 'Brother, can you feed me, I have not eaten anything for two days.' So Yefim's sack was opened once more and shared its precious contents with another half-starved critic of my obedience to the gentle and farsighted Emperor. When my brother finished eating, I told him, 'It seems that you too, senior captain in our regiment, must be feeling sorry for not destroying your cart back in Riga like I did.' He replied, 'I am ready to commend your for your prudent action but do not grudge the loss of my carriage since we are now amidst such a war that anyone who succeeds in preserving even a small share of vitality must be congratulated for a great accomplishment.' Meanwhile Yefim prepared a teapot and, in the dark, the three of us drank tea and concluded a preliminary agreement under which Turgenev and my brother joined me to form an artel'. We acquired two pack horses that allowed us to have almost any kind of provisions with a hand's reach so that with bread and salt, and the good old teapot, we could have a little piece of heaven even amidst snowdrifts. [From the Russian text in M. Petrov, *Rasskazy* . . .]

Alexsey Yermolov

Still recovering from the Austerlitz campaign, the newly-promoted Colonel Yermolov found himself in command of the 7th Brigade and spent the late summer and early autumn of 1806 preparing his unit for the new campaign.

Following the recent reorganisation of artillery into brigades and their attachment to infantry divisions, I was appointed commander of the 7th Brigade in Lieutenant-General Dokhturov's division, deployed near Dubno in Volhynia, and also took command of a newly-organised horse artillery company. Vigorous measures, to restore the army following our losses, confirmed

---

* Hewaldiger meant a military police officer. A general hewaldiger was responsible for discipline and order in the army, and, in certain circumstances, had the authority to enforce sentences, including the death penalty. During battles, these officers supervised the assembly and transportation of the wounded.

rumours that a new war was looming. General Baron Bennigsen's army was assigned to assist Prussia.

The army received fresh forces that had not participated in the last campaign and it now comprised:

2nd Division (Major-General Count [Alexander] Osterman-Tolstoy)
3rd Division (Lieutenant-General Baron von der Osten-Sacken)
4th Division (Lieutenant-General Prince [Dmitry] Golitsyn)
5th Division (Major-General Siedmioraczki)

Cavalry was attached to divisions, but, according to circumstances, could serve in detachments. A few Don Cossack regiments were assigned to the army too. In early October, the army crossed the Niemen at Urburg and Olita. Another army of four divisions under Buxhöwden had taken part in the battle at Austerlitz but had been boosted by a large number of recruits. This army entered Prussia via Brest-Litovsk in late November.*

By then, General Bennigsen was already on the Narew and had occupied Praga, a suburb of Warsaw, with his division. A cavalry detachment was deployed along the Vistula, a 12-hour march away.

Meanwhile, Napoleon had completely destroyed the Prussians at Auerstädt. This battle was even more catastrophic than the one the Austrians had lost at Ulm. The Prussians lost almost their entire artillery and a remarkably large number of troops were captured. The remnants of the army were scattered or forced to surrender. The best fortresses in the country were captured, some of them surrendering without resistance. The enemy took Berlin and the Prussian king, with a few hastily-assembled troops, withdrew to Königsberg. The Duke of Brunswick, one of Frederick the Great's famous commanders, had led that shattered army. The previous year, Prussia had hesitated in helping us as though it was concerned that we might eclipse their glory of defeating Napoleon.

Following his success, Napoleon dispatched a special corps to subjugate Silesia, while he led his army towards Warsaw, having been informed about the approach of our troops. We also learned about this movement and both our armies were ordered to halt.

Our armies concentrated at Byelostock and their commanders, having no friendship before, turned into enemies. Their actions were not coordinated and confusion reigned even over trivial orders. And in such a state of affairs, we expected the arrival of an enemy flushed by victory. Our cavalry detachment, previously deployed ahead of us, moved back over the Vistula.

---

* Bennigsen commanded some 70,000 men with 276 guns. Buxhöwden had 55,000 men with 216 guns. In addition, General Essen's corps of 37,000 men with 132 guns was marching from the Dniestr.

Napoleon occupied Warsaw and captured large magazines as these had not been destroyed because we had hoped to use them afterwards too. However, Major-General Siedmioraczki, the commander in Praga, should have either evacuated them or, if there was no time, set them alight to deny the enemy their use. However, he did not consider himself authorised to act and had awaited specific instructions. In addition, he did not destroy the boats that would allow the enemy to cross the river; Siedmioraczki was also concerned that he might be forced to cross the Vistula into Austrian territory close to Warsaw and, therefore, he abandoned Praga and withdrew a considerable distance, leaving cavalry patrols to observe the Vistula.* Our other division, deployed on the right, also had its cavalry on the Vistula, but they did not coordinate their actions; so the enemy, having boats at its disposal, used a place where the Vistula was separated by an island, and constructed a bridge to the right bank. We only noticed this when it was too late and could only deploy our troops when the enemy was already present in force.

At that moment General Field Marshal Count Kamenski arrived to assume command of both armies.† This experienced commander immediately realised our dangerous position, our troops being dispersed over a vast area while the enemy had concentrated and controlled the right bank of the Vistula. Kamenski ordered our troops to rally at once. However, because of the enemy's proximity, we had to pull back some distance in order to do this.

Our troops were suffering from the lack of supplies; the only provisions they had were potatoes, which had to be unearthed far away and required large parties to be detached for this purpose. The troops were sometimes dispatched not to the areas where circumstances required them, but rather where better supplies were hoped to be procured. Villages were devastated everywhere, late autumn and constant rain destroyed roads and there was no assistance from the locals in delivering supplies.

As it slowly retreated, our army concentrated and, although danger forced us to accelerate, some of our troops could not avoid the unequal struggle against the enemy. Major-General Count Osterman-Tolstoy made a stoic stand at Czarnow and Serotsk but, despite his fearlessness and the gallantry of his troops, he suffered considerable casualties, losing several guns. Major-General Count Pahlen was also attacked by superior enemy forces

---

* Yermolov's note: General Siedmioraczki belonged to a group known as the Gatchina officers and he had learned his art of war under Kannabich, who taught the kind of tactics someone shrewdly described as the science of rolling up your coat.

† Alexander was exasperated by bickering between Bennigsen and Buxhöwden. He finally chose Kamenski to lead the united Russian armies. Yet, the new commander-in-chief brought no changes to the army – he kept Bennigsen and Buxhöwden in command and gave them complete freedom of action.

at Lopachin. He was marching to his division's assembly point and was only one and a half miles from it when attacked. How vulnerable our lines of communications were! Count Pahlen could have retreated to Golymin directly by taking advantage of a forest that prevented the enemy from deploying; in addition, he would find reinforcements at Golymin. However, we must credit his prudence because he preferred to overcome greater difficulties by heading towards Chaplitz's detachment near Tsekhanov, which could have been isolated and destroyed. I was attached to this unit with three artillery companies and could easily see that our position at Tsekhanov was ineffectual and was a result of Count Buxhöwden's instructions. Field Marshal Kamenski, having learned about this, reprimanded him for thoughtlessly dividing his forces and ordered our detachment to retreat immediately. However, we could not return because we were exhausted after marching on extremely muddy roads. Fortunately, General Count Pahlen's able resistance prolonged the fighting and he joined us late in the evening and the enemy was not able to prevent us from rejoining at Golymin.

When on the following day we marched there, the enemy advanced along the direct route I mentioned above, but we beat them to it by an hour. Having reached Golymin on 14 [26] December, we encountered Lieutenant-General Dokhturov's 7th Division, Lieutenant-General Tuchkov (I)'s 5th Division and part of Lieutenant-General Prince Golitsyn's 4th Division from General Bennigsen's army.

The enemy opened the exchange of fire. The French had inferior forces, largely of cavalry under Prince Murat. Although the wet ground complicated the deployment of our troops, we took up positions at a road junction and the enemy had even less favourable positions covered by woods and scrub. Against their eight guns, we had up to eighty; the entire 5th Division was moved into reserve, while the enemy had no other skirmishers but some dismounted jagers. We could have easily destroyed Prince Murat but were satisfied by a useless exchange of fire, so Murat took the initiative. They were soon reinforced by artillery which could not be utilised because of the swampy terrain and impassable roads. The enemy infantry faced the same problem and it arrived in inferior numbers. Based on seniority, one might think Dokhturov should have commanded on our side, but in all fairness no one was in charge: when I dispatched a brigade adjutant for instructions, he spent over half an hour meeting at least five generals, yet still could not obtain any orders.

Meanwhile, the enemy made some probes and unexpectedly managed to turn our left flank, only because of a mistake on our part; however, some additional forces soon restored order. Major-General Prince Sherbatov's gallantry should be recognised: when his Kostromskoi Musketeer Regiment was disorganised by heavy casualties and had to retreat, he picked up its standard and rushed forward, leading an attack that drove the enemy back. In the evening, our forces were significantly reduced and gaps in our ranks were visible. It was easy to see that it was an improper way to retreat and that the troops were withdrawing on their own initiative. For some time I did not dare retreat without orders but, seeing it was not necessary to remain, I persuaded Lieutenant-Colonel Prince Zhevakhov to retreat with his two squadrons of Pavlograd Hussars; so we went in the direction in which most of our troops seemed to be heading. After passing Golymin, I turned towards Makov. At the same time, our right flank, Major-General Chaplitz's detachment, noticed that our left flank had already withdrawn and did not expect that Golymin, in our centre, would be abandoned before our last troops retreated; so it carelessly approached the town only to be hit by canister fire. This incident spread confusion, further increased by the darkness, between the troops of the Ekaterinoslavskii Grenadier and the Vladimirskii Musketeer Regiments and they lost two artillery pieces.

Thus ended a battle that brought one benefit to us, since we split the enemy forces and pinned some of them down. But how justifiable was this when we had committed forces that were three times larger than the enemy's? One can imagine what Napoleon would have done in such an encounter.

Some five verstas from Golymin, in the village of Kluchnitzy, I found several of our generals in a local noble's house; naturally, some of them were already asleep and the leftovers of their dinner testified that their nap was not induced by hunger. In such cases, the person who arrives last usually enjoys certain privileges and rights and so those officers, who were still awake, honoured me with a bottle of port. I saw that my companion, Prince Zhevakhov, was not thrilled by this mean greeting.

Although we were neither pursued nor observed during our retreat from Golymin, we abandoned around forty guns, most of them heavy pieces, because of the extreme fatigue of the horses and the impassibly muddy roads. It seemed my company had to share the same fate; however, I found a few horses that had been abandoned by other companies and thus avoided the shame of abandoning a gun without a shot.

A major battle took place at Pultusk on the same day. Napoleon, having concentrated his forces except for Murat's cavalry, approached Bennigsen who could not retreat without endangering his troops and so awaited the enemy. Napoleon tried every means to defeat us; his troops were encouraged by his presence and acted with vigour and courage. Our forces were hesitant since the enemy enjoyed superior numbers. We were driven back at some points and exhausted their forces by resistance, but fortunately the French could not match our artillery since theirs had been left behind because of bad roads; this not only prolonged the battle but also helped us to improve our position. Bennigsen was firm in his resolution and, facing a desperate situation, he called on his last resources, ordering his reserve of two infantry regiments to launch a bayonet attack. Regimental commanders were told that the safety of our troops depended solely on this last endeavour, and the regiments attacked furiously. The French retreated, unable to withstand our bayonets. Their troops lost touch with each other and, being unable to check our success, they fell into a hasty retreat; thus, a part of the enemy's position was suddenly in our hands. It was evening and Napoleon could not correct this failure since he needed time to rally his forces before attempting further attacks. Hence, Bennigsen's firmness turned our desperate situation into a victory. To repulse superior enemy forces led by Napoleon himself was indeed a great feat, but to overwhelm and route them was a glorious exploit that no one had claimed before.

Had we taken advantage of Pultusk we could have liberated Warsaw and the Polish territories belonging to Prussia and driven the enemy across the Oder.

Following Pultusk and Golymin, our armies had to either advance against the enemy or, at least, block their further progress. Buxhöwden should have been the first to do this because his troops had faced inferior enemy forces and even if he had been unable to destroy them, then at least it was unnecessary to flee before them. If he considered retreat essential, then he should have coordinated his actions with General Bennigsen. We had precise intelligence on the enemy's main forces and it would have been better to use the troops that were wasted at Golymin to reinforce Bennigsen and complete his victory. However, Buxhöwden, either because of his row with Bennigsen and a desire to harm him or because of a misunderstanding, kept following the Field Marshal's instruction to retreat which had been issued to concentrate our forces, but which should have been adjusted in the light of events which now clearly showed the benefit of attacking. If one is unable to comprehend this, then one should not command an army. If the common well-being is sacrificed for personal squabbles, then punishment should be administered; in any case, the army would have been relieved of this cruel commander, whose mediocre skills it could not trust, and who was famous only for his courage which can never replace the essential skills of a commander.

On the day of the battle, Field Marshal Kamenski arrived at Golymin at 9:00 a.m. and personally positioned the Malakhov Cossack outposts, having seen the importance of the place where he had ordered the other troops to concentrate. In order not to waste time in correspondence, he dispatched a courier to the chief of staff at Tsekhanov with instructions to return to Golymin to avoid being cut off. The Field Marshal was at Pultusk during the battle; however, after it was over, when new orders based on new circumstances were needed, he declared that he was abandoning the army on the grounds of illness and left for Grodno.

He made an unforgivable mistake: his presence with the army was even more essential because he had not expected Pultusk to end successfully, so following his departure, the disagreement between the commanders could only have had disastrous consequences. The army regretted his decision because it trusted in his experience and reputation. The senior officers agreed that the bickering between commanders would do us no good.

General Bennigsen was unable to exploit his success and had to retreat because Buxhöwden had already withdrawn and exposed our rear to the enemy; therefore Bennigsen moved towards Rozan and crossed to the left bank of the Narew at Ostrolenka.

General Buxhöwden retreated through Makov.* He left a rearguard under Major-General Markov to cover the army while it crossed the river. This movement continued slowly until late into the night. Transports crowded on a long bridge, and the enemy appeared from the nearby forest and took up positions in superior numbers close by. It was impossible to destroy the bridge, yet there was a danger that the enemy would capture it under cover of darkness. With permission from my superior, I dispatched a company with instructions to set fire to two of the suburbs to illuminate the French should they dare attack. The French approached the river twice, probing for fords in a few places, but some forty guns under my command beat them back. French casualties must have been considerable and we were able to destroy part of the bridge.

I was threatened with dire punishment for the harsh measure of setting the town on fire and this matter was discussed at headquarters. Of course, after a nice lunch and rest, some 20 verstas from any danger, it was very easy for them to show magnanimity. They finally accepted my explanation. The rearguard withdrew to Novales, where Dokhturov's division was deployed. The Ingermanlandskii Dragoon Regiment, that he had sent towards Rozan, encountered an enemy cavalry detachment there, failed to halt it and instead brought it back with them to the general's headquarters in a Catholic priest's house near the camp. The general himself was sitting quietly in the window when he suddenly saw French cavalry galloping past the fence. Fortunately, the gates to the house were closed and some movement in the camp frightened the enemy. The house owner was suspected of providing information to the French.

When Count Buxhöwden arrived at the Narew it was frozen, the bridges had been destroyed and there was no communication with the other bank. We remained here for a few days and when the enemy advanced our situation became more precarious with every hour. The enemy might have known our armies were separated by the river and could not support each other. However, it seemed that confusion prevented the French from attacking since they limited their operations to reconnaissance only and Major-General Pahlen's outposts kept them at some distance from us.

General Bennigsen took every measure to re-establish communications between the armies. Ropes were stretched across the river, covered with

---

* Makov is located on the River Orzyc.

wet hay which froze and allowed our infantry to cross to the opposite bank. Bridges were soon constructed and the armies were happily united.

The Tsar was unhappy with the Field Marshal's departure from the army but was elated by the success at Pultusk. The Field Marshal was ordered to remain in Grodno until further instructions. Both armies were placed under command of Bennigsen while Buxhöwden was recalled to Russia.* The army welcomed this news since Buxhöwden had failed to gain the trust of the troops. Whilst few knew of his knowledge and limited skills, everyone felt his unbearable haughtiness and arrogance. [From the Russian text in A. Yermolov, *Zapiski* . . .]

Aleksey Sherbatov

A scion of a wealthy and ancient princely family, Sherbatov was born and raised in Moscow. He was just six years old when he was enlisted in a guards regiment but he did not start actual military service until the age of twenty in 1796 and quickly advanced through the ranks. In 1800, the 25-year-old Sherbatov was already a major-general. Despite his youthful enthusiasm for war, he was not assigned to the Russian forces sent to fight Napoleon in 1805 and thus did not experience the dreadful defeat at Austerlitz. Yet his beloved brother was mortally wounded at this battle, a tragedy that deeply affected him. In 1806, Sherbatov commanded the Kostromskoi Infantry Regiment and was assigned to Bennigsen's corps.

My regiment was assigned to Major-General Barclay de Tolly's brigade. Nothing of interest occurred during our march to the town of Pultusk, where our army had stopped. General of Cavalry Count Bennigsen, commander-in-chief of our army, had established his headquarters here. Since the purpose of these memoirs is to write down and collate all the memories of my life, I do not intend to describe the entire campaign but will instead discuss only the most important events, especially those that I was involved in.

In Pultusk we remained idle for a long time and it was here that we learned about the defeats of the Prussian army in the battles at Jena and other places, and about the rapid advance of the French troops and their approach to Warsaw, which was soon thereafter occupied. The Prussian king [Frederick William III] arrived at Pultusk to discuss the plan of campaign with General Bennigsen.

Public opinion in St. Petersburg accused General [Levin] Bennigsen of indecisiveness and sluggish operations, which is why he was soon replaced by the old Field Marshal Count Kamenski, in whom the public hoped to find

---

* Buxhöwden left the army for Riga and complained to Alexander about Bennigsen's actions. When his appeals were ignored, Buxhöwden challenged Bennigsen to a duel.

another Suvorov. Prior to Kamenski's arrival to the headquarters [glavnaia kvartira], the troops had already began to move in accordance with Count Bennigsen's orders, but as soon as he arrived at Pultusk, Count Kamenski, as it befits anyone taking over authority and due to his quick temper [zapalchivii] and impulsive [oprometchivii] character, found all of his predecessor's orders erroneous and, without carefully considering circumstances, he began to issue new instructions to the regiments, thereby creating a bigger mess.

In the meantime, Napoleon, inspired by his miraculous [chudesnii] victory over the Prussians, advanced rapidly in two columns against us: the lead column under his personal command encountered our army on the fields of Pultusk, where General Bennigsen was already expecting the enemy in battle formation, while the second column, also dispatched to Polustusk, marched via Golymin where it accidentally encountered two detachments [otryad] of our troops, which, under Count Kamenski's orders, wandered [brodili naudachu] in the countryside following unsuccessful clashes with the enemy advance troops and also accidentally joined at Golymin. These two detachments – one under command of General Dokhturov, and another led by Lieutenant-General Prince D. V. Golitsyn, which also included my regiment – observed the enemy movement and sought to stop it in order to prevent the enemy from participating in the battle at Pultusk, which saved our army from a complete defeat.

I must note here that Count Kamenski personally went to the advance guard, commanded by Major-General Barclay de Tolly but before reaching it he became disheartened [poteryal golovu] upon encountering our advance troops that were disordered due to strong enemy pressure [natisk] and immediately returned to Pultusk. He was furious, on the verge of madness, telling Count Bennigsen that there is nothing he could do now to correct the wrongs of his predecessor and therefore he instructed him to operate according to circumstances, while he himself packed up and left for Grodno to supervise new preparations for war.

Upon taking over the supreme command, Count Bennigsen immediately began making preparations for the battle that was expected to take place at dawn. This first decisive battle, which has been described by military historians, had shown to the world that the Russians could hold their own against the French led by the until-then invincible Napoleon. But since our army withdrew from the field of battle at night, we cannot, in all fairness, claim it as our victory, even though our bulletins declared it as such – a victory in battle is usually attested by the ensuing offensive movements, rather than by retreating.

Now let us turn to the battle of Golymin that took place on the same day as the battle of Pultusk and in which I participated. Two days prior to the battle, I followed the Field Marshal's order and marched with my Kostromskoi Infantry Regiment to reinforce the advance guard; along the way, two artillery companies were supposed to join me and move under my protection. This union, however, greatly complicated the movement of my regiment since throughout the night, I had to commit my men to the exhausting task of hauling guns and carriages that got stuck in the mud at every step. After tremendous efforts, I finally reached the destination point N [place not indicated], where my divisional commander Prince Golitsyn also arrived. I was just preparing to rest after such an exhausting march when I learned about the arrival of Count Kamenski and his staff, who, I mentioned above, were returning from the defeated advance guard. After Count Kamenski's departure, Prince Golitsyn remained at this location for the entire day, linking up with several regiments from other divisions that had retreated from various forward points. During the night this unintentionally-created detachment retreated to the town of Golymin, already pursued by the enemy cavalry and abandoning two or three cannon that got stuck in mud and proved to be impossible to remove despite our best efforts. At dawn this detachment arrived at Golymin and was soon joined by the enemy. At the same time, Lieutenant-General Dokhturov, with his division being pursued by the French, happened to be passing through this location. He joined our detachment to repel the enemy attacks. I received the order to occupy the woods on the left flank of our position and my regiment was supported by the Dneprovskii Infantry Regiment and one battalion of the Tavricheskii Grenadier Regiment, and later by two squadrons of the Pskovskii Dragoon Regiment . . .

This was my first battle and, despite having no prior military experience, I was given command of the position where the enemy directed his main attack, seeking to turn our position and cut off our line of retreat to the main army. During the battle my dispositions somewhat reflected my inexperience – at first I occupied the woods as only a novice would do but upon seeing that the enemy anticipated me with his skirmishers and thereby greatly threatened me, I made the fortunate decision to abandon the woods and take up position in the open plain. I must note that my entire regiment consisted of young and previously untested soldiers and that like me, not a single staff or junior officer had experienced war before. Coming out of the woods with its left flank, one of the battalions . . . moving at the head of the column came under fire from the enemy skirmishers, who had managed to get through the woods, became disordered and began to retreat in disorder, veering to the side. This disorder soon spread through my entire detachment because fear, like electricity [elektrism], spread in an instant from the head of the column to its end, and my own regiment became disordered as well. Observing the shameless retreat of this disordered crowd, I galloped to the fleeing standard-bearers of my regiment, jumped off the horse, grabbed a flag and rushed with it to the spot where the detachment had to be rallied. All the other standard-bearers followed me and, in turn, the disordered battalions followed them. Upon reaching the rallying line, I ordered my adjutants to place flags at battalion distances so the soldiers could rally accordingly. This was accomplished at once and other regiments followed this example and disorder was thus extinguished. This incident showed that it was inexperience, rather than cowardice, that was at the root of this momentary disarray and I considered myself fortunate that in my very first battle I was able to save myself and the troops entrusted to me from shameful behaviour. As the result of my dispositions, the enemy was contained until the nightfall. [The French] did not dare to attempt an attack while we remained in defensive position. At last, the French attempted a flanking atack against our left but our entire force began to retreat through Golymin to Makow, where we arrived at dawn and found the corps of Major-General Buxhöwden, which had arrived a few days earlier from Russia to reinforce our army. Here we learned about the battle of Pultusk: General Buxhöwden, despite hearing a powerful cannonade, did not consider it necessary or possible – precise reasons remain unknown to me – to advance with his corps to support Count Bennigsen which could have resulted in a different outcome of the battle. It is possible that this was occasioned by the thorny issue of seniority since General Buxhöwden was senior in rank to Count Bennigsen and therefore was unwilling to be subordinated to him, but he could not take charge of the army either. Soon thereafter he was recalled from the army while General Bennigsen was confirmed as the commander-in-chief.

The following day my regiment joined [Bennigsen's] army near the town of Ostrolenka and was assigned to the advance guard commanded by Major-General Barclay de Tolly, where it remained until the end of the war. For the battle of Golymin I was awarded the Order of St. George (4th class). [From the Russian text in A. Sherbatov, *Zhurnal knyazya Sherbatova* . . .]

'Shameful Behaviour'

Bennigsen, 2 [14] January 1807
His Imperial Majesty received the news that during the battle at Pultusk on 14 [26] December Major-General [Pavel] Potulov, the chef of the Ekaterinoslavskii Cuirassier Regiment, was not present with his regiment and that afterwards, having appeared at his regiment, though it remains unclear where he has been absent, he asked Your Excellency's permission to travel to the supply train [wagenburg]. His Imperial Majesty was very displeased by such news and orders you to immediately conduct a thorough investigation to determine what circumstances could have diverted Major-General Potulov's attention away from his regiment on the day when he should have been entirely focused on remaining with his men. If, upon careful examination of circumstances, this investigation uncovers evidence revealing shameful behaviour of this general, that he had abandoned his

regiment without any reason justifying it and without the permission of his superiors, His Imperial Majesty orders to have [Potulov] sent before the court martial that should be conducted in the most timely manner and a court's decision should be sent to His Majesty's confirmation. The Ekaterinoslavskii Cuirassier Regiment should be entrusted to the command of Major-General Kretov of His Imperial Majesty's Suite. [The court martial uncovered behaviour unbecoming for an officer, although precise details are lacking. Potulov was dismissed from his regimental command on 6 February 1807 and appointed head of the cavalry supplies depot in Moscow. In 1812, he joined the opolchenye (militia) forces and fought at Borodino, Tarutino, Maloyaroslavets and Vyazma, being wounded and earning awards. But he was unable to clear his name and retired in September 1814. The Ekaterinoslavskii Cuirassier Regiment was indeed transferred to the command of Nikolai Kretov who led it until the end of the Napoleonic Wars.] [From the Russian text in RGVIA, f. 846, op. 16, d. 3185, ll. 1-3]

Fabian von der Osten-Sacken

Buxhöwden was not the only one who disliked Bennigsen. General Fabian von der Osten-Sacken loathed him as well (clearly visible in his diary excerpts) and relations between the two generals quickly turned tense during the 1806–7 campaign; eventually Bennigsen had him court-martialled for alleged insubordination. Fabian Vilgelmovich (Fabian Gotlib) von der Osten-Sacken (1752–1837) was born into a family of German barons from Courland; although his family name was Osten-Sacken, he is often referred to as Sacken. After enlisting in the Russian army in 1766, he served in Poland and participated in two Russo-Turkish wars. Promoted to Major-General in 1797, Sacken served in the Russian corps sent to Switzerland and took part in the disastrous battle at Zurich, where he helped to cover the Russian retreat before being wounded in the head and captured by the French. Released in 1800, he became chef of the St. Petersburgskii Grenadier Regiment. In 1805, he commanded a corps in the Grodno and Vladimir provinces and thus avoided the Austerlitz disaster. In 1806, he led one of the columns in Bennigsen's army.

Sacken maintained a diary throughout his service in the Napoleonic Wars, including his captivity in France in 1800. The original, which is presumably lost since Sacken left no direct offspring, was written in German, although Russian and French translations of it had been circulating in private circles in the mid-nineteenth century. A French translation of the diary was at one point owned by the Vorontsov family that allowed excerpts, in a heavily edited form, to be published in a Russian journal in 1900.

The Jews are plundering our army; they ruin the local population and leave our troops in complete misery and hardship. General [Levin] Bennigsen protects them as if they were his own children. His actions only raise suspicions that he shares in their profits.

1 [13] December. A new plan of operations against the enemy has been drafted. The division is split into two parts, one is placed under command of Titov, while Sacken, in charge of the other part, proceeded to Nowe Miasto. This enterprise failed and the troops were bivouacked together for the first time at Nowe Miasto. The 3rd Division returned to Makow, where it took up a strong position. On 5th [17 December,] Sacken received first instructions from [Field Marshal] Kamenski. On the 9th [21 December], Lestocq's courier arrived. Barclay reports that the enemy seized Plotsk. The night of the 11th was spent in commotion. An intense cannonade can be heard. On the 12th [24 December], our posts along the Wkra River were driven back. Field Marshal [Mikhail] Kamenski quickly arrived at Sochocin. He did not allow Sacken to remain with his division but requested him to march at once with one regiment to support Bennigsen at Strzegocin. On the 13th [25 December], at 1:00 a.m., we marched from Sochocin via Strasbourg and reached Strzegocin at dawn. However, Bennigsen already moved to Pultusk. Sacken with the Litovskii and Chernigovskii regiments remained at Strzegocin. [Mikhail] Barclay de Tolly was in the advance guard. In the evening, everyone marched to Pultusk.

The road was so poor that one part of the artillery was stuck in mud. On the 14th [26 December] the troops reached Pultusk at dawn. They were deployed in battle order at once. At 10 o'clock in the morning, the enemy appeared and began his attack but he was repelled at all places with heavy casualties. That night, [strong] wind and snow ended the battle. The enemy retreated.

On the 15th [27 December], contrary to common sense, we retreated during the night, abandoning wounded and sick on the battlefield and [some] cannon [still] stuck in the mud. Complete chaos spread among the troops; everyone, literally, fled headlong as if after a complete defeat. The soldiers had not received bread for two days in a row. Falling from exhaustion, covered in mud, we [finally] reached Rozan.

16 [28] December. Even here [at Rozan] Bennigsen did not feel himself safe. At dawn, he ordered everyone to retreat in utter disorder, and so we marched – without halting anywhere or receiving any food, pillaging villages and noblemen's estates – to Ostrolenka.

We were finally given a break on 17 [29] December. The troops were deployed in a rather astonishing manner – as if [prepared] for slaughter. Everything done or said is completely devoid of common sense. There is a genuine chaos of Babylon.*

---

* Sacken refers to the Biblical story of the Tower of Babel and the chaos that prevented its construction.

18 [30 December]. From the start of the campaign until today no one bothered to inquire about Sacken's opinion on military operations, despite the fact that he is the most senior officer after Bennigsen. The troops crossed the Narew River at dawn and took up position on the left bank of the river.

On the 19th [31 December], the corps moved in one column towards Meshkov, where the tail [the rear units] finally arrived at night. [Local] houses are devastated, soldiers spread around and pillage neighbouring villages. Anticipating the enemy, we always place our soldiers in houses. But now, with the [French] at long distance from us, the soldiers were billeted in their tents in the fields; they are not given any food.

At last, on the 20th [December; 1 January 1807], we occupied our quarters. The 3rd Division is deployed at Czartory. Order is established and pillaging is quickly brought to an end. Our headquarters is set up at Nowograd. [From the Russian text in F. Sacken, *Iz zapisok feldmarshala Sackena . . .*]

Sergei Volkonskii

Sergei Grigorievich Volkonskii (1788–1865) made a brilliant military career during the Napoleonic Wars that came to an end during the Decembrist Uprising of 1825. Born into an ancient aristocratic family, he was the son of General Gregory Volkonskii, who served as the governor-general of the Orenburg region under Catherine II. At the tender age of eight, he was enlisted in military service but began actual service in 1805 when he became a lieutenant in the Chevalier Guard Regiment. He distinguished himself during the 1806–7 campaign in Poland as well as in the Russo-Turkish War of 1810–11. In 1812, he was appointed to the Imperial Suite and served in General Peter Wittgenstein's corps. In 1813–14, he fought at Kalisch, Gross-Beeren, Dennewitz, Leipzig and Laon, winning half-a-dozen awards. By the end of the Napoleonic Wars, he was a major-general in charge of a brigade in the 2nd Uhlan Division. Inspired by the ideas fostered by the Enlightenment and the French Revolution, he joined secret societies that sought to transform the Russian monarchy. He was one of the most active members of the failed Decembrist Uprising in 1825 and was initially sentenced to death but later pardoned and sentenced to twenty years' hard labour with the loss of nobility and titles. He remained in exile in Siberia, unable to return to European Russia, until 1856 when he was included in an amnesty.

In late 1806, a new war erupted against France and anyone from the St. Petersburg youth who could serve rushed to enlist in the field army. I was among these fortunates and was appointed as an adjutant to Count Mikhail

Fedorovich Kamenski, a man of considerable intelligence and military virtues but also a decrepit, arrogant and oftentimes irrationally hot-tempered person.

In November Kamenski departed from St. Petersburg after receiving assurances that the army had been adequately supplied with everything needed for military operations. Upon reaching Riga, then Vilna and Grodno, the sites of main supply depots set up for his army, he realised that everything he had been told was nothing but outright lies. Nevertheless, he continued his trip to the headquarters of Bennigsen's corps located at Ostrolenka. [Upon arriving there] he reviewed the army and found hospitals full of sick soldiers who received no treatment and lacked provisions. [He found] supplies exhausted, transportation – in disarray, soldiers barefoot, and depots insufficiently supplied and without any means to replenish them. In short, the army was in the most dreadful conditions.

These findings, in conjunction with his temperament, plunged Kamenski into an irrational desperation. Already advanced in age, he could not endure the two-day inspection of the forward outposts and was both morally and physically affected. He ordered all the army corps to retreat without a fight beyond Grodno, caring not for the loss of cannon and trains but simply endeavouring to ensure the arrival of troops to Grodno, where he intended to reorganise his entire army. To the sound of the first shorts of the French army taking up positions on the heights near Pultusk, Kamenski got into his carriage with his adjutant (and my friend), Peter Valuev and left the army that was already engaging the enemy.

[...]

Kamenski's flight from the army coincided with the first French attacks on our positions at Pultusk. This battle took place on 14 [26] December 1806. Two days prior to it, the French attacked our dispersed and foolhardily stretched-out advance guard under the command of Count Osterman-Tolstoy at Czarnow, under the command of Prince Dmitri Vladimirovich Golitsyn at Golymin and under General Dokhturov at Makow. These detachments, without any communications between them or reserves to support them, endured fierce fighting and managed to erase the indignity of the defeat of Austerlitz by delaying the enemy for an entire day. During the night they prudently withdrew, each in direction of the forces from which they were detached. But only Count Osterman could retreat to Pultusk while the other two detachments marched to Ostrolenka. I do not have complete details about the battles at Golymin and Makow but do know that at Czarnow, Osterman resolutely resisted the French attacks, marking the beginning of his glorious military career. The battle at Czarnow was bitterly contested indeed and both sides lost considerable men; among the numerous wounded staff and junior officers there were Major-General Prince Shakhovskii, chef of the 20th Jager Regiment, and Colonel Davydovskii, chef of the 1st Jagers, both of them seriously wounded.

Kamenski initially suggested concentrating the entire army near Naselsk but unexpected French attacks from various directions and the dispersion of our detachments forced him to retreat to Pultusk, where part of Bennigsen's corps had taken up position. Our retreat from Naselsk to Pultusk was incredibly difficult on account of mud: cannon, caissons and supply wagons stuck up to their axles in mud and, as I recall, over 100 guns were abandoned without a fight.

[...]

The position at Pultusk was chosen quite skilfully: the heights, which we occupied, had no other approach than across an open rolling plain. Our flanks could not be turned because the left was anchored onto the town and the river while the right flank was protected by the woods that were strongly protected by Barclay de Tolly. Continued French assaults on various points of our positions had been all repelled by our artillery that excelled on that day. The charges of the Leib-Cuirassier Regiment, commanded by Major-General Kozhin, of the Kievskii Dragoon Regiment led by Colonel Emmanuel, and of two squadrons of the Kargopolskii Dragoon Regiment led by Major Stahl, remain the most splendid episodes of that battle. The key to our position was on the left flank so the French assaults were primarily directed there. The Navarinskii and Tulskii Infantry Regiment, defending this flank against the superior enemy forces, began to waver [at one point] but the watchful and prudent Osterman quickly noticed this problem: he set up a strong battery at the edge of the town and deployed the Pavlovskii Grenadier Regiment to defend it, telling these soldiers, 'Here is the spot where you must prove that you are worthy of bearing the name of our late Emperor. Fight to the very last man but defend this battery! I have brought you to a dangerous place but you will earn [eternal] glory here. And since this place is perilous, I will stay with you.' The French soon launched a fierce assault at this location. Despite the hail storm of grape-shot and bullets, we held on to this position. During this fighting Osterman noticed that the grenadiers, who were standing like an impregnable wall, had suffered heavy losses so he ordered them to lay down on the ground while he continued to sit on his horse like a medieval knight. The mitres [shapki] of the Pavlovskii [Grenadier] Regiment still bear bullet holes that they sustained at this battle, where the regiment received its baptism of fire.

Engrossed in my memories of the battle of Pultusk, I have forgotten to explain why I served as an adjutant to Count Osterman on that occasion. After Kamenski's flight from the army, my comrades and I, who had arrived with the Field Marshal from St. Petersburg, initially found ourselves forsaken. My comrades chose to join Bennigsen's staff, but I had not made any decision and did not want to serve in the main headquarters. Deep in my thoughts, I slowly rode towards the sound of gunfire when I encountered a stranger, who proved to be Count Ostermann.

'Who are you?' he asked me.

'Volkonskii' I replied.

'Who is your father?'

'Prince Gregory Semeyonovich.'

'Who are you serving with?'

'I was attached to the field marshal.'

'You are without a post, then?'

'I am looking for one.'

'So serve with me. I started my career serving under your father, and you can start yours under me.'

To start a military career under Ostermann – now that was not an easy temptation to decline. Even now, so many years after the event, I still greatly value this meeting. Thus, the battle of Pultusk marked the start of my military career and serving as Ostermann's adjutant I received a fulsome baptism of fire. From the very first day I got accustomed to the smell of enemy gunpowder, to the whizzing of cannonballs, grape-shot and bullets, to the glistening of the enemy bayonets and the blades of swords. I experienced all the challenges of the military life so that afterwards no danger or exertion could unnerve me.

Bennigsen had undoubtedly won the battle at Pultusk. That same evening he dispatched a messenger to Buxhöwden asking him to join him and undertake a joint offensive against the defeated enemy. But Buxhöwden, whether out of his jealousy towards Bennigsen or following Kamenski's order to retreat, refused to join Bennigsen, forcing him to withdraw after a victorious battle. Bennigsen first moved to Ostrolenka and then to Nowogrod, where, no longer pursued by the French, he had halted. Yet, the army found neither rest nor supplies at this place. Even the main headquarters lacked bread for ten days; meat and potatoes, procured through foraging, satisfied our needs. I recall as on one occasion my batman Vasilii Zverev returned from foraging some distance away with two bags of communion bread that was prepared for church services but was not blessed yet; I shared it with my comrades-in-arms.

During our stay at Ostrolenka, Kamenski returned to headquarters and attempted to reclaim the command of the army but because of his sudden and completely unjustified departure, the generals agreed not to let him resume command and to await the Emperor's new orders from St. Petersburg.

Our army remained idle for some two weeks, continuing to suffer from poor supply services, although the [relative] prosperity of that region and our foraging provided us with sufficient provisions. I must note, however, that foraging is a rather ruinous practice: it completely devastates the area and facilitates numerous abuses, especially the weakening of discipline, among the troops.

During this stay we received Imperial orders appointing Bennigsen as commander-in-chief and removing Buxhöwden, for his failure to support

Bennigsen after the victory at Pultusk, from the command of his corps and other responsibilities . . . Field Marshal Kamenski was deprived of the title of commander-in-chief, denied the right to enter both capitals and ordered to reside, under the watchful eye of the police, at his villages in the Orel province. Since I will no longer talk about him, I think it will be proper to mention the tragic end of his life. He had always been a very harsh landlord and mistreated his serfs and servants, but now, ordered to live at his estate without leaving, he had become completely unbearable. So, as he was inspecting his fields, one of his serfs jumped into the carriage and smashed his head in with an axe, killing him instantly. Such was the consequence of the unlimited rights of a Russian landlord that some people still exalt as representation of fatherly patronage. This was a brutal murder indeed but can it be called an unjustified crime? [From the Russian text of Sergei Volkonskii, *Zapiski* . . .]

Eduard von Löwenstern

The younger brother of Waldemar von Löwenstern, the distinguished Russian major-general and author of insightful memoirs, Eduard left behind one of the most vivid memoirs of the Napoleonic Wars. A gifted writer and keen observer, he enlisted in the army at the tender age of sixteen in 1806 and was sent to the Sumskii Hussar Regiment. Just months after his enlistment, Löwenstern found himself marching to Poland, full of excitement and aspirations.

During the march to Jurburg [where the hussars crossed the Niemen River], I was outfitted and received an exhaustive [supply of] ammunition and a local grey Hussar horse named Koptschik. The joy I felt, in my sky-blue pelisse and yellow dolman, at being able for the first time to let my frisky horse cavort cannot be described in words: the jangling sabre, the spurs, kiwer with flying tassels, the sabre scabbard, the long shabraque hanging down – all of it very dear to me. As I rode across the bridge, the bare sabre in my fist, the pelisse over my shoulder, I was swimming in a sea of joy and bliss.

I rode in the Third Peloton [Platoon] commanded by Staff Captain of Cavalry Shishkin. Sergeant Govorov and Private Galushkin looked after me like brothers. Major Potapov, the Captain of Cavalry, and especially the other officers of the squadron, did nothing to improve my condition which unfortunately worsened with each passing day. I was only fourteen years old when I, as a poor Estonian nobleman with no other prospects, decided to try my luck in the military. I had to devote myself totally to the service no matter how easy or how difficult and cheerfully take on all difficulties without complaining and not make an almost unbearable life more difficult by useless complaining. After we crossed the Niemen, I rarely saw my brother Theodor who was serving in the same regiment as portepee-junker.* As quartermaster, he was usually ahead of me and was much too busy with himself and his own ammunition to have been able to have helped me. Govorov assigned a Hussar, Salei, to help me. We became inseparable. We slept in the same bed. We ate from the same bowl. Our horses always stood together and stayed together like their riders. Oh, what a splendid sensitive heart beats under the coarse coat of a common Hussar! I had to consider myself lucky to have found this coarse but good comrade who always joyfully and happily did anything to please me. Without him I could not have stood difficulties I was not used to. Heaven forbid if one of the officers had noticed that someone was helping me with any little thing! I had to do everything myself. I had to wash and brush my Koptschik myself, feed, water, and saddle him in the bitterest cold, keep my ammunition clean, lubricate and blacken my saddle equipment, sweep the stall, and everything, everything, indeed to do the coarsest work of a common Hussar everywhere. All of the common Hussars loved me and helped me wherever and however they could; my youthfulness touched those coarse, uneducated men.

Insterburg† in East Prussia was the first major town in which the regiment stopped. Our Constable Korolevskii, who knew no German, took me into his quarters as an interpreter. Our host, a lawyer, and his wife took care of us as well as those poor people could. They treated me like their own child, and the old man toasted me so bravely at the evening meal that I became drunk and ill and had to be carried to bed. When taking leave, the lawyer's wife stuffed my pockets full of fruit. Unfortunately, all of those delicious things I had been planning to eat on the boring march I had to throw away upon my arrival at the assembled Squadron, since no one was permitted to carry superfluous things in his sabre scabbard, oat sacks, and coat pockets.

During the whole march, I was in charge of the horse teams and pack horses since I could not be taken to the front because of my inexperience. How often did I envy the Hussars, riding their quiet horses, able to smoke their small pipes while I was intolerably shaken apart by my angry, hot-headed Koptschik; and when totally crazy, that horse was barely controllable. He made mounting especially difficult because he would never stand quietly, and you had to be quick when you wanted to mount in your heavy soaking-wet coat with sabre and saddle bags and loaded with ammunition. What an effort it cost me every time to climb into that high Hungarian saddle and swing my leg over the even higher coat sack. The Hussars laughed at my ineptness. The Captain of Cavalry berated me every time for being the last one in the saddle. I, poor devil, had neither the necessary strength nor the desire.

---

* The designation for an officer candidate.
† Today Chernyakhovsk in the Kaliningrad region of Russia.

In Nordenberg we filed en parade past General [Fabian von der Osten-] Sacken. We rode through Ortelsburg* and met several French fourgons [supply wagons] which had been captured near Jena. Here also came the first news that the Prussians had been totally defeated, and to our surprise that the French had already reached the Vistula. In Janova, a little Polish town, I was sent for the first time to get orders. We non-commissioned officers had to wait for several hours in a dirty damp Jewish house until the Regiment's Adjutant had finished his Boston card game and could check us into the Squadron.

The damnable quagmire, the bad wet weather, the poor Polish peasants, the indescribable filth of the Jews and the cramped quarters caused the march to be exceedingly exhausting for us. My horse blanket, my coat, and my uniform were my bed and pillow. The half-cooked meat distributed by the unwashed hands of the private was eagerly consumed and tasted good.

When – totally exhausted – my steadfastness left me, I would sit in the cold, wet stall next to my Koptschik, and only through tears could I catch my breath in my exhausted lungs. I felt myself completely abandoned and cast out into the big desolate world, no loving, empathetic person, no one who would take pity on my helpless situation! Everything passed over me – then I cried bitter painful tears. Nevertheless, exactly that hopeless situation, that feeling either to have to take care of myself or to become totally abject gave me double the strength. Then I accepted it; I had to be responsible for myself. There was no loving mother here, no affectionate father. Here it was everyone for himself and God for us all! Cheered up by the example of the Hussars, I joined in the happy talk and often forgot my worries in the midst of those wild but good men; then I felt relieved after a good cry and rather content.

[. . .]

After several marches we approached the Vistula; and since we formed the extreme tip of the Vanguard, we were always on the lookout the closer we came to our formidable enemy. Our supply train was supposed to stay behind, but could not since there had been no order telling us where we should go. After several weeks, the detachment to which Theodor had belonged joined us again near Nowe Miasto. They had caught sight of the enemy several times and had gone as far as Thorn. Captain of Cavalry Prince Volkonski had been hit in the head with lead shot by a deceitful Pole. Count [Peter von der] Pahlen† wanted to have that nobleman's house set on fire, but as far as I know this is not supposed to have happened.

In Nowe Miasto the alarm was sounded one night. Everyone hurriedly threw themselves on their horses. My grey, that on such occasions became

---

* Today Szczytno, Poland.
† Pahlen served as the chef of the Sumskii Hussar Regiment throughout the Napoleonic Wars.

so heated that he totally lost his wits, took me against my will into the middle of the Dragoon squadron that was also *pêle mêle* hurrying out of the town. Their looks as they drove me out of their midst with broadsword blows until finally after a long time of being yanked, I could rescue myself. Everyone was screaming; everyone was ranting and making noise in that pitch black night. The hubbub was caused by an enemy post that had moved forward but immediately withdrawn.

We took up our first outposts in Glinavis[?]. Hussars from Captain of Cavalry Samarin's squadron brought a chasseur à cheval prisoner into camp. It was a joke to see the poor devil being led around like a rare monster, cursed, given gifts, having them stolen again and finally turned over to the main headquarters. I heard the first pistol shots in the distance as I was busy having the farrier shoe my horse. Those few shots gave me a hammering heart, that was something so unusual for me, something so strange – honestly, I did not feel well.

A person easily becomes accustomed to everything, especially the noise, the travails and dangers of war. Was it the lack of experience of our leaders or was it fear of the formidable enemy that in a few days had beaten and annihilated the Prussian army – in a word, the mere mention of the word 'French' drove officers and soldiers from sleep and chased them to their horses. A few of them had been in earlier wars and no one knew how to put up outposts, to do reconnaissance of the enemy with Russians or what especially a light cavalry officer otherwise would have observed at various opportunities. Because of this uncertainty, men and horses were unnecessarily alarmed that could have certainly remained in bivouac, now however unnecessarily had to be battle-ready day and night where there really was no need for fear. Thus, I remember having to ride patrol with Cornet Borodovski and when we discovered a dead Frenchman lying on the road, we turned around at a sharp trot. Thus, another time with Cornet Maschmeyer we chased and followed a Lieutenant Joqué for two miles, since the one thought that the other was the enemy, and both detachments stormed breathlessly into camp covered with sweat and dirt. Theodor had already been sent from Glinavis to a lost post and had not yet returned.

On 13 [25] December, the Sumskii Hussars and the 21st Jager Regiment under Colonel Laptyev and Colonel Pirogov with his horse [artillery] company marched to Łopacin. As the sun was going down, we passed the village of Gołotczyzna.* Not far from it we observed our baggage and pack horses running wildly and soon afterwards we recognised enemy riders harassing our servants any way they wished. Count Pahlen immediately deployed several Hussars and Cossacks to save the fleeing supply train. Our people were completely successful, denying the French dragoons their booty. We immediately turned around and passed Gołotczyzna in a sharp trot and

---

* Today 10km from Lopacin.

in order to lighten out load, we threw away the large bundles of hay that [the village of] Ciechanow had provided us with. Before we reached the fields on the other side of the village, we were surrounded on all sides. The manor of the nobleman who had given us false information was immediately set on fire over his head. Soon also most of the village was burning brightly.

The French positioned sixteen cannon near a windmill and began firing specifically at the Hussars. For the first time, I heard the thunder of the cannon and the whistle of their balls. That imposing and horrible play of battle awakened in me a feeling unknown up to then. It was not of horror. It was not of joy. It was not of fear. Maidan, a young Hussar in the Second Platoon, was shot next to me. He was the first man I saw dashed to pieces. His brains and blood splattered me in the face. After our squadron had retreated from the continued cannon fire, we stopped on a small elevation that was quite bushy. From there we clearly recognised the enemy squadrons chasing down the road.

A few moments later, we also went on the attack. Several chasseurs à cheval surrounded Major Potapov. Before we could get to him, he had taken seven sabre blows to the head, luckily none fatal. As I saw my major in danger for his life, without thinking, I leapt into the thick pack and my good [stroke of] genius protected me. I do not know what happened after that. I rode around with the others without knowing what I was doing or what was happening around me. It was pitch black night when that dogged, bloody battle ended. Three dismounted light cannon and several carts with pelisses fell into enemy hands. The Sumskii Hussars' bravery and Count Pahlen's expertise saved the rest. In the middle of the night, we returned over almost impassable roads to our bivouac in Ciechanow where several dragoon regiments sent as reinforcements were waiting for us. To my indescribable joy, I found my brother here, whom I had thought was lost. Through cunning and bravery he had escaped the enemy neat Łopacin.

During the battle near Łopacin, while we were in the midst of heavy cannon fire, a Hussar said in a rather loud voice that [given an opportunity during] the first attack, he would strike down Lieutenant Obosenko [Oboznikov] who had been quite strict with the fellow. Cornet Borodovski, who overheard him, had the courage to have the speaker immediately dismount and sent to the front. The balls hit to the right and to the left and roared over our heads. 'Well, dog, shoot or stab the lieutenant to death,' he called to him, 'if you have the courage; if he stays however, then shoot a ball through your head yourself; otherwise I will have you beaten to death.' The Hussar followed the lieutenant during the entire battle and trembled undoubtedly just as much for his life as for his own. The following day in the battle of Pultusk that Hussar was pummelled to pieces next to me. Colonel [Cyprian] Kreutz and Major Durov, both of whose troops had been detailed, suffered considerable losses.

On the same night, we left our bivouac in Ciechanow without being given any time to rest and continued to march the whole day in closed formation.

Late on the evening of 14 [26] December, we met up with the main army near Golymin. We could hear the thunder of cannon fire coming at us from the right and getting stronger by the minute. Soon cannon-balls also reached our front line. The night was dark and filled with the worst rain and snowdrifts. We were standing in soft mud up to our stirrups. It was almost impossible to distinguish friend from enemy. The [French] 4th and 7th Dragoon Regiments attacked our Hussars in the midst of a terrible din. We were thrown into the first line and driven back quite in disorder. We collided with the Ingermanlandskii Dragoon Regiment that formed the second line. The dragoons did not let us pass and, when we did not want to halt, they even looked as if they wanted to battle us.

But soon the fleeing hussars came together: 'Hurrah Sumskii! Hurrah Sumskii!' they yelled from all sides and sabres and broadswords clattered. Now and then the fires in Golymin, when the flames were driven high by the storm wind, illuminated the bloody battlefield. The trooper from the Second Platoon next to me was stabbed through and through. The head of an enemy rider's horse when turning hit me in the face with his snaffle bit full of foam. I imagined I had been hit by a cannon-ball, at least to have lost my entire head. I began to fall from the saddle and only held myself on with one leg. You can imagine how desperate my situation was. Danger makes one brave – barely in my saddle again, I swung desperately around me and luckily my little saddle sustained several heavy blows. As soon as I caught my breath, I retreated from that tight pack. Only then did I notice how I was bleeding. Looking more closely, I realised that I had a head wound that was, however, superficial and did not even need to be bandaged.

At two in the morning that terrible battle gradually ended. All of the cannon stuck in the mud and we left all of the unlucky wounded for our enemy and retreated to Makow while continuing to fight. During the retreat Captain of Cavalry Samarin and Lieutenant Shakhmantov were taken prisoner. They both escaped from Warsaw, however, and returned to us after the battle of Eylau. Several French prisoners were mercilessly massacred during the march. Most cruelly, a dragoon officer killed one [Frenchman] who had already been captured and had shot at him. Even I – may the Lord forgive me for my sin – let myself go so far that I took after a French officer who only collapsed with the sixth or seventh blow to his face and head. You can hardly imagine how bloodthirsty a man can become when he has seen streams of blood for several hours in a row. You become an irritated animal and could at that moment of insanity rip your opponent to pieces with your teeth.

It was a dark and stormy December night when we bivouaced in and around Makow. Yet again, hideously tired, we found no peace. The morning was barely turning grey when enemy flankers [cavalry skirmishers] began to rush us. The sergeant immediately sent me ahead with our flankers. I, loaded pistol in hand, sabre hanging from my sword knot, mingled with our skirmishers, who found the enemy in a small wooded area not too far from our line. It seemed my opponent, an old ice-grey dragoon, did not want to lose his timeworn life in a skirmish because he was very careful and stayed, as best he could, away from me. I kept my grey in motion as best I could, shot several times and missed. He did the same thing, and we were both happy that the recall signal was sounded, and everyone rode back at full gallop. Only toward evening did we retreat through the city and burnt the bridges behind us.

After an unbearable two-day march, we finally reached Ostrolenka. I was indescribably tired, could barely stay on my horse – since the battle of Łopacin, I had almost never dismounted. The little bit of sleep I got while riding could not refresh me or strengthen me after those trials and tribulations. It was my bad luck that my coat had been stolen, the only one that protected me against wind and weather. I was truly very unhappy. The cold December night, wind and snow drifts increased my nasty situation. Only clothed in my uniform, shivering with cold, I followed the regiment; but Salei, my guardian angel, spurred his horse and in less than half an hour, he returned with a stolen hussar coat which he put around my shoulders in the friendliest manner. I do not know from whom he had stolen the coat, but I wrapped myself in it, thanked my brave comrade and quietly and introspectively followed my squadron. A large part of the army came together under the walls of Ostrolenka; hundreds of battalions and squadrons united and lay there helter-skelter. Munition wagons, field equipment, cannon, soldiers with all kinds of weapons camped on the plain together. Field Marshal [Mikhail] Kamenski left the army and turned over the command to General of Cavalry Baron Bennigsen.

I saw [my brother] Georges for the first time in a long time. He had been promoted to Lieutenant in the Izumskii Hussar Regiment and had lost a horse to a cannon-ball near Pultusk. Georges was one of the handsomest officers in our army. We had just set up bivouac when the horrible words 'to horse and mount' put everyone into motion again. We left Ostrolenka that same night and turned toward Kosläna [?] where we found forage and supplies. We removed our saddles after a long period, cooked ourselves something warm and rested under the open skies in that December night as best we could.

Lieutenant Obosenko with his hussars had captured a convoy of Danzig brandy. All of the field canteens were filled and, as you can imagine, there was no lack of drunkards. On New Year's Eve, I was sent with fifty men on reconnaissance. When we were crossing a frozen river, the ice broke under me and I fell off my horse into the water. The Hussars pulled me out again with a great deal of difficulty, built a big fire and, as best they could, dried out their young comrade whom they all loved.

We left our post on the Narew in order to push on into East Prussia and possibly to chase Marshals Bernadotte and Ney to the devil. In the night, with Polish uhlans, we passed through Byala, where my dear Theodor treated me to delicious pancakes during the march. We went through Arys and Rhein and stayed in Bartenstein* for a few days. We recuperated as well as we could. I had burned my boots in the hot ashes of a bivouac and needed this stop to acquire a pair of big peasant boots, which, though not pretty, when filled with straw were exceedingly warm and gave me a great deal of pleasure. When I was ordering something for an officer in the apothecary in Bartenstein and had to wait a long time, I used the jostling crowd to steal as many raisins and as much brown sugar as I could hide. You can imagine how much pleasure I had enjoying this easily acquired booty in bivouac. We set up bivouac in the courtyard of the Bailiff of Seeburg,† who helped us as best he could. Here I realised for the first time that the vermin – those inseparable fellow travellers of bivouacs and filth – had pursued me in a way that made me feel nauseous. [From the German text in Eduard von Löwenstern, *Mit Graf Pahlens Reiterei gegen Napoleon* . . .]

---

* Today Bartoszyce, Poland.
† Today Jeziorany, Poland.

3

The Road to Eylau

Bennigsen, who had been encouraged by the successes at Pultusk and Golymin, was eager to renew the campaign. In mid-January 1807 he decided to strike at Marshal Michel Ney, who, against Napoleon's orders but forced by the necessity of sustaining his corps in a barren countryside, had scattered his corps over a large area in search of better quarters closer to Königsberg. The Russian offensive began successfully and Ney's corps was forced to give ground. However, this offensive also resulted in the Russian army moving too far away from its bases, and Napoleon saw a chance to encircle his opponent. In January Napoleon conceived a brilliant manoeuvre to turn the enemy flank and destroy Bennigsen's army but a dispatch sent to Marshal Bernadotte detailing the Emperor's plans was captured by a Cossack patrol. Bennigsen, realising he was marching into a trap, immediately ordered his army to withdraw. On 3 February the French caught up with the Russians at Jankovo, but the engagement that followed was inconclusive, and Bennigsen withdrew during the night. Napoleon instructed Marshal Ney to pursue Lestocq's Prussian corps and prevent him from joining Bennigsen. The French army, led by Napoleon himself, pursued the Russians through driving snow, and on 6 February clashed with the Russian rearguard commanded by Barclay de Tolly at Hoff. Once more, after heavy fighting, the Russians retreated. The French again caught up with the Russian rearguard, led by Prince Bagration, on the evening of 7 February near the town of Eylau.

Journal of Military Operations of the Imperial Russian Army

On 7 [19] January Colonel Rostovskii dispatched a detachment, consisting of two companies of the 24th Jager Regiment and two sotnyas from the Kiselev's Cossack Regiment, under the command of Lieutenant-Colonel Vlastov, to the village of Surkvishen where, having arrived after a nightfall, it surrounded an enemy detachment and killed up to 100 men and captured eighteen; our side lost two jagers and one Cossack wounded.

On 8 [20] January, General Lieutenant Prince [Dmitri] Golitsyn, upon learning that the enemy was nearby at the village of Langheim, dispatched there a Cossack detachment from Grekov XVIII's Cossack Regiment, which, upon its arrival, surrounded an entire squadron of French hussars from the 3rd Hussar Regiment, killed some of them and captured fifty-nine hussars, two officers and Captain St. Auben Le Brun.

On the 9th [21 January] the army entered quarters that the enemy had abandoned earlier that morning, around 4 a.m., retreating through Bischoffstein, where a [French] detachment under the command of General Colbert was located, and partly through Schippenbeil. That same day Major-General Markov's advance guard captured one officer and seven soldiers.

On the 11th [23 January] the main headquarters moved to Liebstadt.

On the 12th, General Barclay de Tolly sent a squadron of the regiment of Izumskii Hussars, with about sixty Cossacks, to Passenheim. There this detachment found two squadrons of French cavalry, and attacked and destroyed them entirely, making twenty-nine dragoons and Captains Dervaux and Cachelot prisoner. The same day General Markov, with the advance guard, surprised a detachment composed of three regiments of cavalry, and several hundred soldiers at Lipstadt. We took 270 prisoners, including eighteen officers, among whom was Lieutenant-Colonel Fabre. Three hundred French were killed on the spot.

The next day there was a more serious engagement. Marshal Bernadotte, having gained intelligence of the approach of the Russian army, arrived with all his forces at Mohrungen, and established his headquarters at that place, extending himself half a league before the town upon the road to Lipstadt. General Markov attacked this body with forces too inferior to be able to count upon success. He was repulsed; but having been afterwards reinforced by the division of cavalry under General Anrep, the enemy thought proper to retire. In this very bloody action, the French lost more than 1,000 men, and two standards. We had 700 killed and wounded, but the most serious loss which we suffered was that of the brave General Anrep, who was killed by a sharpshooter in the most unfortunate manner: his loss is regretted by all the army.

While this affair was taking place before Mohrungen, Prince Mikhail Dolgoruky, with his dragoon regiment, marched against the rear of the enemy, and arrived unobserved at the headquarters. There he carried off the equipage of the Marshal (Bernadotte), his servants, his plate, some ladies, and a considerable quantity of money, comprising the contributions levied upon Elbingen; besides which, he made upwards of 400 prisoners. The number of these last increases every moment, and not a day passes without the arrival of more than fifty of them. Three French generals are already in our power: Generals Foultrier and Lasseur were taken by our troops, and the third, General of Division Victor, by the Prussian garrison of Colberg.

After these different actions, which have all terminated in favour of our army, I [Bennigsen] have caused it to advance as far as this place; and have taken a concentrated position in its environs. The right wing is supported by the Vistula River. After seventeen unremitted marches, I thought it necessary to stop for a moment but tomorrow I shall advance again and attack the corps of Marshal Ney. In the meanwhile I have succeeded in driving the enemy from this province, in covering Königsberg, and in throwing a part of the French army into consternation and disorder, the effects of which are already most perceptible. Such are the brilliant results to which our march towards Regal Prussia, and the perseverance and courage with which the troops of his imperial majesty have executed that fatiguing operation, have conducted us. The enemy, surprised in his cantonments, vanquished in every affair, has retreated with a precipitation and a disorder which only too much denote the deplorable condition in which he finds himself.

It still remains for me to make mention of the Prussian army which is under my orders, and to render it the justice which is due to it. Our successes seem to have electrified it. It begins to recover itself a little and to lose that dejection into which its misfortunes had plunged it. Among the rest, the garrison of Danzig has gained an advantage over the Polish insurgents, whom it attacked near Dirschau, and beat them, taking some cannons and their military chest. [From the Russian text in *Zhurnal voennykh deistvii imperatorskoi Rossiiskoi armii*]

Peter Bagration

The task of protecting the Russian army from Napoleon's attack was entrusted to Prince Peter Bagration, who had successfully handled this challenging mission. A veteran of many campaigns, Bagration was born into the royal family of Georgia but spent his entire life in the Russian empire. Bagration was beloved by his troops who admired his cool composure on the battlefield and unassuming demeanour. Bagration's countenance was 'perfectly Georgian', as one British witness described, including the archetypal large aquiline nose that became the subject of many anecdotes. One such amusing story, involving Bagration's adjutant Denis Davydov, has been recorded by the great Russian poet Alexander Pushkin in his diary in 1815. By then, Davydov was already one of the Russian heroes of the Napoleonic Wars, having distinguished himself leading a guerrilla detachment in 1812.

[Bagration had] a large Georgian nose while the partisan [Davydov] barely had a nose to speak of. Once Davydov appeared in front of General Bennigsen: 'Prince Bagration has sent me to inform Your Excellency that the enemy is on our nose [i.e. very close]'. 'Whose nose, Denis Vasilievich?' replied the general. 'If Bagration's, we have enough time to have a lunch. If yours, we have to hurry!' [From the Russian text in A. Pushkin, *Dnevniki. Avtobiograficheskaya proza*]

Fabian von der Osten-Sacken

23rd [December, 4 January 1807]. Bennigsen informs us about rumours that the enemy had crossed the Narew and is at Chervintsy. We remain idle. News is expected from Barclay. We are constantly short of bread. Our actions have become not only hardly comprehensible but straight-out nonsensical. The weather is befitting the autumn and winter has not set in yet.

25 [December, 6 January 1807]. Attempts are being made to construct pontoons near Nowograd but the ice creates serious hurdles to this; a pontoon bridge fails as well. The winter begins at last.

[...]

1 [13] January 1807. Another year has passed in discontent, sorrow, hardship, misery and dangers of every kind. It brought me no pleasure or joy. We entered old Prussia.

14 [26] January. We reached Liepstadt. Learning about the appearance of some enemy patrols, the entire army of over 70,000 men took up battle positions on the heights dominating this town and spent most of the night at bivouacs. The day before, Anrep was killed near the village of Georgenthal while Bernadotte slipped away from us.

15th [27 January]. The army moved to Mohrungen. Sacken's division arrived at Spiegelberg on the 20th and, on the night of 22nd, it reached Jankovo, where the army was deployed in battle order. The enemy made attempts to build bridges over the Alle River. Our army retreats pointlessly, and, as usual, Bennigsen is first to flee.

On the 23rd [4 February], we moved to Wolfensdorf. The enemy, taking advantage of our withdrawal, attacked our rearguard and inflicted heavy casualties on it.

On the 24th [5 February], the army continued its retreat and, on the 25th, it made a night-time withdrawal to Landsberg. The enemy caught up with us around noon. Several combats ended unsuccessfully for us due to poor leadership on our part. [From the Russian text in F. Sacken, *Iz zapisok feldmarshala Sackena* ...]

Eduard von Löwenstern

Having received his baptism of fire in a combat near Łopacin, the young Löwenstern was no longer driven by the enthusiasm that animated him at the start of the war. Instead, he felt completely exhausted by the continued marching, lack of supplies and poor weather.

The deep snow and the cold aggravated our forced marches to Osterode that we had to undertake in order to join Prince Bagration's advance guard that was awaiting us there. Not far from Preusissch-Eylau, I was an orderly for Count Pahlen, who did not have me do anything important the entire day.

The innkeeper's daughter, a cute girl, tried all kinds of tricks to seduce me, but chaste and inexperienced I stayed brave, and was berated as a dumb kid by the girl and not worth the trouble of staying with. Theodor brought me a roasted goose he had stolen from somewhere, since he knew only too well that being an orderly and hunger meant the same thing.

After marching back and forth several times, after innumerable encounters and engagements, we approached the little town of Mohrungen. Through deserters and spies, we had learned that Marshal Bernadotte with his headquarters, suspecting no danger, were spending time in that town unguarded and busy levying contributions. In the dark of the night the Sumskii Hussar Regiment and the Kurlandskii (Courland) Dragoons slipped in as quietly as possible. Exploiting the incomprehensible carelessness of the French, we galloped into the middle of the town, shouting wildly, without finding a single guard post. You can imagine the shock and the horror of the enemy quietly resting there. Because our Colonel Shishkin was slow, our squadron arrived a little too late to hew in. We only got the gleanings of the rich booty. Nevertheless, we had our hands full to capture or cut down the half-clothed French pouring out of the houses. I myself captured fourteen men that night. Yelling 'Pardon', clinging to my stirrups, several of them escaped from me in the throng. Three squadrons led by Colonel of Cavalry Kreutz did not spend much time plundering and taking prisoners but galloped through the other town gate to spread death and destruction in the bivouac out there. Our brave hussars emphatically exploited the initial surprise. In the dark they cut down everyone who resisted them; but soon they were attacked by several hurriedly-pulled together squadrons and driven back. They lost their brave leader Colonel of Cavalry Kreutz, whose horse fell on the ice. He was immediately surrounded and, covered with many wounds, taken prisoner.* During that bloody night, we took over one thousand prisoners, captured Marshal Bernadotte's entire equipage, consisting of four well-packed coaches as well as pack horses and captured all of the contribution money, packed into barrels and loaded on wagons.

Not far from Mohrungen, we bivouacked near an isolated mill. We all had more than enough money but nothing to eat. For two days, I had not had even a piece of bread to eat. The hussars were paying a ducat for a piece of bread. Especially because of the booty from Mohrungen, the value of money had fallen. Exhausted from hunger, wrapped in my coat, I lay down and certainly would have died if Lieutenant Obosenko had not found me and revived me with strengthening soup. The only thing we had plenty of was pork fat, that the hussars hungrily devoured without any bread or salt.

Toward evening, we encountered the enemy near Jonkendorf and the Olviopolskii Hussar Regiment undertook a marvellous attack. On that day, we did not lose a single man; and very seldom did a ball land in our front

---

* Kreutz was released after Tilsit.

line. Early the next morning, the retreat began again. Near Landsberg, a large convoy of brandy was coming our way that had either been sent too early or too late to the army. Since not everything could be quickly drunk, most of the barrels were smashed. Several of our soldiers stayed there, lying dead drunk next to the barrels and ended up prisoners of the enemy. The cannon fire of the enemy pursuing us now was horrific. I saw a cannon-ball mow down eight grenadiers from the Tobolskii [Musketeer] Regiment. [From the German text in Eduard von Löwenstern, *Mit Graf Pahlens Reiterei gegen Napoleon . . .*]

Sergei Volkonskii

After the battle of Pultusk, Volkonskii followed Bennigsen's forces to Osterode, where he spent two weeks in deprivation. At last, in January, the Russian army advanced and fought several combats with the French, including at Mohrungen. In his memoir, written decades after the event, Volkonskii provides only pithy accounts of these engagements, acknowledging that 'time has erased much from my memory'. But he did recall one particular incident of the battle of Mohrungen.

The battle ended in our favour and the French even retreated but [our commander] Anrep was killed at the very end of the battle . . . The battle was marked by a splendid charge of the Sumskii Hussar Regiment and a bayonet melee between the infantry forces. Although, I am wrong to call this a bayonet melee. Eyewitnesses told me that Ekaterinoslavskii Grenadier Regiment was surprised that a column of the French voltigeurs dared to accept a bayonet melee [and make its own advance] 'These underlings are not worthy of our bayonets,' [the grenadiers] said and, reversing their muskets, they drove off the French column with their musket-butts. [From the Russian text in Sergei Volkonskii, *Zapiski . . .*]

Yakov Otroshenko

Staff Captain Otroshenko commanded a company in the 7th Jager Regiment.

We retreated to Liebstadt, where we spent a day in the snow-covered field. Prince Bagration arrived to take over command of the advance guard and the soldiers and all of us [officers] rejoiced: this general had already distinguished himself during the retreat to Austerlitz [in 1805]. On the third day we moved to Mohrungen but the French retreated. We found the field covered with frozen corpses. It was here that General Anrep was killed. After spending the night there, we were preparing to start baking bread the next day when we unexpectedly received orders to embark on another march at once. We walked all night long without halting anywhere. By dawn we reached the town of Jonkowo, where a battle was already raging to the right of us. Since our regiment had no bread, we were allowed to deploy at the nearby village and bake bread. At midnight our regiment was ordered to leave the village and proceed to the left flank of our army. We arrived at our position before sunrise and deployed there. In front of us was a stream with a dam and watermill.

A battalion of the Uglitskii Musketeer Regiment, with two cannon, was deployed on the heights above the dam. Behind this regiment was a pine forest while in front of it, near the dam itself, were the following companies: the 5th, 6th and 8th Companies from the 2nd Battalion of the 7th Jager Regiment while I, with the 7th Company, was ordered to occupy the woods to the right, adjacent to the swamps about one versta [1 km] away [from the dam]. The 1st Battalion of our regiment stood in an open field behind these woods. Behind this battalion was the forest that stretched all the way to the battalion of the Uglitskii Regiment. A road, leading from the watermill, passed by the 1st Battalion towards our main forces while across the road there was a swamp with brushwood. This swamp was also adjacent to the woods which was separated by another boggy area from the enemy positions. Inside this wood was our 3rd Battalion commanded by Captain Kavetskii. This battalion deployed a skirmish line along the edge of the forest and the swamp to the 1st Battalion that was deployed to the right of the 3rd Battalion. During the day the 1st Battalion lit fires and calmly rested on the soft snow that had fallen during the night.

At dawn enemy cavalry patrols appeared on the heights in front of me but my jagers opened fire and drove them back. At noon several enemy cannon appeared and opened fire, across the woods where I was deployed, at the 1st Battalion (my woods were located in a hollow). The enemy cannon soon departed. But for the rest of the day a rumbling cannonade could be heard from the direction of our main forces.

As night fell, a sharp frost set in. Our regimental commander,* already tipsy [navesele], happened to be on the road behind my woods and asked the jagers of my company whether they were cold. Upon hearing their affirmative answer, he ordered fires to be lit in the skirmish line. When I informed him that fires were not allowed in the skirmish line, he angrily shouted at me, 'I order you to immediately light up fires. How dare you argue with me. I will have you arrested!' So I obeyed the order. When the fires lit up the edges of the woods, I went to the skirmish line and, approaching the swamp, asked whether anyone could see what was happening across the marshland. The jager told me, 'An enemy column is advancing directly at us.' I immediately shouted to douse the fires and rallying the nearby pairs [of skirmishers], I ordered them to open fire at this column. The enemy veered to the right and disappeared behind the heights. Leaving my men, I ran along the skirmish line to the right and asked the jagers if they could see anything. I was again

---

* Colonel Pavel Tolbukhin commanded the 7th Jagers in 1804–7.

told that the French were advancing in groups scattered across the swamps. I ordered them to open fire. The enemy, however, moved forward without returning fire. I had to move [my men] back into the woods, where I observed a thick line [of men] passing behind me. Hiding behind a tree, I asked twice who was going there but got no response. Just then a volley was fired at our 1st Battalion. Realising that the enemy had cut me off from the 1st Battalion, I shouted to my men, 'Fall back, jagers!' while the French began to yell, 'Tirer! [Fire!]' I rushed to the edge of the woods, stood behind a tree and waited until all my men came out of the woods, and then ran behind them. I did not lose a single man in my company because the French were shooting in the dark and directed their fire at the 1st Battalion.

Reaching the dam, I saw that our battalion commander had already ordered the bridge to be destroyed. When I informed him that the enemy was already on our side of the stream, he refused to believe me. But turning around he saw heavy musket fire from where the 1st Battalion was deployed and ran to the battalion of the Uglitskii Regiment, ordering it to open fire. The regimental commander was also shouting orders, but there was no enemy in front of us. Instead, he was in the woods behind us. I saw no other recourse but to start retreating as soon as possible before the enemy had captured the road on which we had arrived the previous day. It was too late to reinforce the battalion on the right and the enemy could easily surround us. I ordered my company to turn left and moved to the road. But the French, having routed our 1st Battalion, moved through the woods to this road, where they greeted us with a volley. The French were lodged in the woods at the road's edge but there was an open field, covered with snow, to the left of us. We charged into the woods and fought through the first line of [French resistance] only to encounter another one that inflicted considerable losses on us. Still, we succeeded in driving it back but soon stumbled into the third line of defence that opened a heavy fire on us. We were forced to clear our way with the bayonet. In the process the men became scattered through the woods and lost their way. I found myself with just fifteen soldiers and one non-commissioned officer. Not knowing where the road was leading, I finally decided to move towards the vast glow that I noticed above our main forces during the night. Moving out of the woods into an open field, I came across some Prussian artillery and asked where the Russian army was. Following their directions, I came to the village where our main forces were located. There I found our regimental and battalion commanders and asked them where our regiment was. 'It will gather around here,' they replied. So I kept my men standing next to them. By dawn the entire regiment, which counted no more than 500 men, had rallied.

The army began to retreat. The 7th Jager Regiment was assigned to the rearguard and covered the retreat [of the army] throughout that day. My company was behind our regiment. At the bridge over the Alle River, I organised an ambush behind the buildings and greeted the French with close-range volleys, forcing them to fall back leaving killed and wounded. But I also suffered losses, including a feldwebel,* two non-commissioned officers and five soldiers. Our cavalry was already deployed in three lines behind the village – it was retreating with each line replacing the other. I made my way through the cavalry and rejoined the regiment, which at nightfall camped near the village, on the piles of frozen mud.

The French stayed about three verstas [3km] from us. A vast fiery pillar appeared in the sky above their army – this was the reflection of the fires that the [French] had lit in the valley. But this sight affected our soldiers, who murmured that this was a bad omen for us. At midnight, we were ordered to continue the retreat. We passed the village and stopped at places where other regiments were camped. There was a lot of straw so we all lay down and slept soundly before getting up and marching towards Landsberg. At sunset we bivouacked in an open field and deployed a skirmish line. Yet at night, we were again ordered to leave this position. After marching for several verstas, we halted once more on an open field and remained there until dawn.

At dawn on 26 January [7 February], the enemy approached and a heavy fighting broke out. The French attacked us severely and we were forced to fall back. The road ran through the woods, where numerous barrels with vodka had been damaged and, in places, there were puddles of vodka on the road. I offered my comrade, Captain Pilipenko, to organise an ambush with our two companies and offer the French a snack of lead. [He agreed] and we almost finished deploying when a Cossack galloped by shouting, 'Jagers, fall back, the enemy has already moved around the woods'. So we hastened to retreat and upon emerging from the woods, stumbled into the French infantrymen. We had to resort to our bayonets to fight through. As we were trying to get away from the enemy, our artillery generously showered us with grape-shot which claimed quite a few men; those moving through the village to the left suffered even more than us. We lost many men, including Major Dreyer and four company commanders, Atreshkov, Ulitin, Mikheev and Bobruika, all of whom were captured. By sunset we approached the town of Preussisch-Eylau, where infantry regiments replaced us and the 7th Jager Regiment, after passing through the town [Eylau], took a position two verstas away from it, on the road to Königsberg. [From the Russian text in Y. Otroshenko, *Zapiski* . . .]

Alexsey Yermolov

The commander-in-chief received the order to advance into Prussia and, in late December, the army marched for Kolno, Byala, Johanesburg and beyond. Three vanguards were established and the largest of them was given to

---

* A senior non-commissioned officer.

Major-General Markov, while Major-General Barclay de Tolly and Baggovut commanded the others. Major-General Markov's vanguard, in which I commanded the artillery, was instructed to go through Aris, Rein, Rastenburg and Ressel to Heilsberg. The army was close behind.

There were rumours that the enemy's left flank was also moving on Prussia. Enemy cavalry soon appeared near Nikolaiken and Zeeburg, observing our movements. We also dispatched cavalry which co-operated with the locals and were very useful in a region bisected by numerous lakes. They captured several Frenchmen at Nikolaiken.

On 12 [24] January, the vanguard arrived at Elditten and learned from the residents that a French detachment lay at Liebstadt and its patrol had been inquiring about Russians just half an hour ago. We made a rather long march that day and General Markov had to call for volunteers from the less-fatigued troops. A large number volunteered but when the 5th Jager Regiment was ordered up and the others heard that Colonel Gogel himself would lead the regiment, everyone declared that they would join him and off they marched without a break. I asked for permission to take two guns and join them to witness the action. Some two verstas from Liebstadt, the enemy caught sight of us from some heights and began deploying troops on the city walls and gates, preparing for defence. We could see, however, that there were few of them. Our jagers occupied a cemetery adjacent to the town and engaged the enemy, while the line infantry went against the city gates that led to the main street. Colonel Yurkovskii with two squadrons of the Elisavetgrad Hussars rushed into the town from a side gate and the infantry made a bayonet attack. The enemy was routed and pushed into narrow and twisted streets, suffering heavy casualties. Those who fled from the town were pursued by the Cossacks of courageous Colonel Sisoev. Our guns did not fire a single shot. We captured twenty-two officers and over 300 rank and file.* The red hussar regiment, for some reason referred to simply as the Parisian, was almost destroyed here. Leaving some cavalry in the town, Markov returned to Elditten, where the exhausted troops found food and shelter. That day we had marched and fought for 16 hours.

The disposition of 13 [25] January instructed the vanguard to bivouac at Mohrungen so we marched at dawn. Colonel Yurkovskii led the way with the Elisavetgrad Hussars and two Cossack regiments and drove the enemy pickets back; as he climbed the nearby heights, that surrounded the vast Mohrungen valley, he observed large enemy forces deployed for battle. Colonel Yurkovskii made the mistake of descending into the valley and the enemy engaged him with cavalry. Moving by forced marches, the vanguard arrived on the battlefield only to find Yurkovskii hard-pressed by the enemy and falling back to a small village,

---

* According to official Russian reports, Markov captured eighteen officers, including one colonel, and 291 soldiers.

the main street of which was being bombarded by enemy artillery. I immediately brought my horse artillery company up and, taking advantage of my elevated position and numbers, I drove the enemy guns back and covered our cavalry's retreat. They took up position behind our troops while part of the Cossacks engaged the enemy. Major-General Markov deployed his troops on the nearby heights. The enemy attacked our left flank, an infantry column moving against the village. To protect itself from our artillery, it moved towards the frozen lake located on the right. Having captured the village, the infantry deployed in some gardens enclosed by high fences and ditches. Since the trees had no leaves, our skirmishers were easily detected and driven out and enemy musket fire caused us considerable harm. Colonel Vuich was ordered to attack with the 25th Jager Regiment. This unit had been formed just before the start of the campaign and was not accustomed to the dangers of war; it became disordered while crossing the ditch and could not hold its ground. Some courageous lads climbed the fence but were not supported and remained isolated. Six companies of the Ekaterinoslavskii Grenadier Regiment, led by the gallant Major Fisher, and two companies of the 5th Jagers rushed forward and, without firing a shot, broke through and exterminated virtually everyone in the gardens and the village. We captured the flag of the 9th Light Regiment, while a few survivors fled to the lake. At that moment, Lieutenant-Colonel Malakhov of the Don Cossacks brought the news that, some eight verstas away, he had detected a large body of enemy infantry and heavy artillery and discovered 1,500–2,000 men concealed three verstas away on our right flank. The latter news was particularly unpleasant because our only escape route lay in that direction.

Less than two hours later, we saw the enemy issuing from a forest on to the road to the village of Holland. Covered by cavalry, the enemy formed up for battle and advanced against our right flank. Captured flanqueurs told us that these troops belonged to Bernadotte's corps and he was in command. We could have disengaged an hour earlier, but now could not hope to escape without heavy losses. Our forces were exposed and we could not deceive the enemy in respect of our strength or force him to act cautiously. The French could see at once that they outnumbered our forces by at least three to one. The enemy advanced against the heights we occupied and, although our canister fire and bayonets defeated several columns, fresh enemy forces immediately resumed the offensive, forcing us back. Several battalions on the right, not far from the road, moved towards Georgiental, which the enemy seized with skirmishers from the infantry that Malakhov had detected earlier; we could not allow them to hold this place and General Markov led our battalions as they advanced. The enemy infantry was supported by fierce artillery fire and punished the rest of our rearguard, forcing us to retreat. Our artillery fired only canister. It was already dark when we entered the forest and the enemy ceased its pursuit, probably hoping to capture us the next day. After General Markov's departure, there were no other generals left, so Colonels Turchaninov and Vuich and I took orders from Senior Colonel Yurkovskii. Our first goal was to find an escape route, and I was concerned not to abandon some twenty artillery pieces; however, we encountered either deep snow or swamps all through the forest and could not escape. The gallant Sisoev, commander of the Don Cossack regiment, finally found a place where artillery could reach the main road, but it had to pass very close to the enemy bivouac near Georgiental. Of course, this was a very risky way of saving our guns, but we had no other choice and decided to do it. While passing the French camp, they opened up with musket fire and we had a few wounded, but we made it through. We soon found General Anrep's cavalry and returned to Liebstadt.

The commander-in-chief had sent this cavalry to our aid. Although he received this order late in the day, Anrep decided to make up for lost time and moved his cavalry at the trot. A mile and a half away from the battlefield, he met General Markov, who assured him that the battle had ended, our troops were retreating and nothing else could be done. Anrep did not accept General Markov's assurances because of the audible artillery fire and he ordered his regiments to speed up. At Georgiental, he encountered enemy infantry and his flanqueurs opened fire: just as he was climbing a nearby hill, Anrep was killed by a bullet that hit him in the head. It might still have been possible to attempt something but it would not have helped us and therefore his reconnaissance was ultimately futile.

It is remarkable that the French did not intercept us as we passed their camp, which they could have done without loss and we would have lost our entire artillery.

We found Markov at Amtmann's house at Liebstadt and he was already asleep, having enjoyed a nice dinner; his companions had devoured everything as though we were not supposed to return. To console ourselves, we could have instead admired the beautiful breasts and gorgeous eyes of Amtmann's wife, but since I was a defeated hero who had just completed a retreat, I was not granted even a glance, which, I was told, a victor would have claimed together with her heart. Well, the vanquished have no claim to any booty! Shrewd General Markov did not look surprised to see us, as though we had simply carried out his orders. We paid him back with the same indifference when an hour later Prince Bagration arrived to replace him in command of the vanguard. At Mohrungen, we suffered heavy casualties and a half company, attached to the Pskovskii Musketeer Regiment, lost one gun.* The vanguard had 5,400 men under arms, while the enemy had 19,000 men.

It must be mentioned that our troops were just three miles away from Mohrungen but still no one came to our rescue. The sound of the guns was

---

* Losses were heavy on both sides, totalling 26 officers and 670 men killed and wounded, 400 captured for the French, and 1,100 killed and wounded, 300 captured for the Russians.

heard at the main headquarters as well but only Anrep moved towards us, and only because he had orders to bivouac at Georgiental. After Golitsyn's division arrived, a few squadrons were detached to investigate the gunfire. Major-General Pahlen accompanied them and the sound of the guns brought them to Mohrungen just as the enemy attacked. Count Pahlen rushed into Mohrungen, seizing Marshal Bernadotte's headquarters and capturing his entire train, chancellery and the contribution he had levied on various Prussian cities.* A dinner ready for the victorious Marshal was even found. Count Pahlen had enough time to retreat before the enemy cavalry arrived. This event shows that had more of our troops participated in the battle, it could have ended in a brilliant victory. General Markov sent several officers to headquarters but received no response or instructions, probably because the commander-in-chief had no reliable information about the enemy.

At 9:00 a.m. on 14 [26] January, at least 50,000 men were at Liebstadt and, expecting an enemy attack, we took up strong positions on steep heights near the town; a better-informed enemy, meanwhile, abandoned Mohrungen and retreated.

Prince Bagration's vanguard was ordered to move forward and we stopped for the night at Mohrungen, now vacated by the enemy.

Marching at dawn on the 15th [27 January], we caught up with the French near the village of Zonnerwald but they did not fight, limiting their resistance to just a few artillery rounds. Later, our outposts surprised Marshal Bernadotte himself whilst dining at the village of Lubeschil and, without any Gascon bravado, he could boast of his remarkable agility. Their food was still warm. Following the enemy, we reached the town of Preusissch-Eylau, while our outposts marched towards Neimark, where the enemy destroyed a bridge and halted our advance. The vanguard established quarters here and rested with abundant supplies from the Elbing province. The army followed the vanguard along the same road.

Colonel Yurkovskii, who commanded our outposts, sent a captured courier to Bagration. Napoleon had sent him to Bernadotte with instructions to halt his retreat, the order stating that withdrawal had been necessary to lure us in the direction of Graudentz, while Napoleon planned to concentrate his entire army at Allenstein by 2 February [new style] and attack our extended forces.†

---

* Russian cavalry also captured some 300 French and rescued about 200 Russian and Prussian prisoners. The British commissioner to the Russian army, Sir Robert Wilson, claimed 12,500 ducats were found in Bernadotte's personal baggage, which he had levied for himself in Elbing, as well as a quantity of plate bearing the arms of minor German states.

† According to Napoleon's plan, the French troops would make a sweeping attack on the right from Thorn, driving Bennigsen into the angle between the Lower Vistula and the Frisches-Haff. Napoleon had approximately 115,000 men concentrated against some 50,000 Russians.

This capture was a stroke of luck because otherwise our main army would have advanced along a single road and would have been either defeated piecemeal or at least isolated and forced to retreat, abandoning its line of operations and magazines. In the latter case, only a small part of our troops would have survived; any remaining forces, isolated from Russia and pushed against the sea, would have suffered disaster and been forced to surrender.

Although it was a well-conceived plan, Napoleon's enterprise could have succeeded only because of our total carelessness. We should not have attempted our movement on Preusissch-Eylau without precise intelligence on the location of the main French army. If our goal had been the destruction of Bernadotte's corps, then we had had our chance at Mohrungen, and should not have followed him afterwards.

Prince Bagration sent the captured documents to the commander-in-chief, and, since only two days were remaining before Napoleon's offensive, he retreated on his own initiative. He divided the vanguard into two columns, with one of them moving to Bergfried, while the other, under Markov, was to proceed through Osterode. I was attached to the second column with most of our artillery and, having marched for 26 hours with two three-hour breaks, we arrived at Jankovo, near Allenstein, on 1 February [new style]. The other column joined us here and we were told to rest until further orders.

That same day, parts of the 8th Division commanded by Major-General Count Kamenski and the 3rd Division of Major-General Titov were engaged in a minor action, which turned out unsuccessfully because of the unfavourable terrain. Artillery fire was fierce on both sides.*

The morning of 22 January [3 February] revealed a large enemy force in front of us and we prepared for battle. The French were surprised by our preparedness because they had not expected us to be able to concentrate. They did not dare to attack and our commander ordered a retreat to move closer to our supply depots. The army began withdrawing to Landsberg that same evening.†

The vanguard, reinforced by Baggovut's detachment, left at dawn. It was ordered to cover the movement of our heavy artillery guns as well as the

---

* Count Nikolai Kamenski's 8th Division, supported by the 3rd Division, was deployed at Bergfried. Napoleon directed Soult and Davout against him to cut off the Russian line of retreat. The fierce fighting continued for hours and the bridge over the Alle changed hands several times.

† Bennigsen's retreat was slow because of deep snow and bad roads. On 4 February, Wilson wrote, 'At present, I can only mention that I never saw a more martial army. Their discipline is good; their marching is regular; and, considering what they have gone through, their appearance is admirable. The infantry are all equal to what you saw in England. The cavalry are excellent, with truly warlike bearing and even the infantry exult in their courage. The artillery is well appointed, and draws through fosses of snow that astonish me to look at.'

Prussian artillery. It was a surprising order since the column closest to enemy was that of the artillery; its horses were exhausted and it slowed us down considerably. The vanguard soon caught up with this column and had to take up positions to allow artillery to get clear. The enemy did not pursue until the afternoon but, although they attacked vigorously, our vanguard had managed to cover some distance. Baggovut had a fierce engagement at Warlak.

At dawn on 24 January [5 February], the enemy attacked us in superior numbers and we could hardly maintain order. At Wolfsdorf, the enemy struck our position and our left flank was only able to hold ground by charging with the bayonet, although that caused some casualties. The 7th Division of Lieutenant-General Dokhturov, whose retreat the rearguard now covered, moved in complete disorder, its transports blocking the road and causing delay. We fell back slowly, fighting until late into the night. Passing through forests in the dark, we became so confused that the only way to distinguish enemy from friend was by shouting. Major-General Count Lambert, hoping to rally our dispersed skirmishers, approached the French lines by mistake and was almost captured.*

Our artillery was under fire the entire day, and if our hussars had not captured some French horses to replace our killed animals, I would have lost a few guns. I employed my horse artillery company more than others because of its flexibility. We had to use it even in the dark forest where it fired in the direction of enemy shouts or drumbeats. The troops were extremely satisfied with it and Bagration praised it. We suffered considerable losses that day, at least equal to those of the enemy. Marshal Davout's corps was fighting against us. Marshal Soult's corps was pursuing Barclay de Tolly's detachment, but the fighting was mostly limited to skirmishing.

On 25 January [6 February] we resumed our retreat at dawn in order to beat the enemy to the junction where our rearguard and Barclay de Tolly's detachment were converging. After that rendezvous, Prince Bagration's rearguard took a narrow track towards Landsberg, while Barclay de Tolly's men headed in the same direction but along the main road through Hoff. Less than an hour later, both Davout and Soult appeared. A small force was

---

* Another participant noted: 'Often during a night march through a wood or a defile, the troops would be obliged to file past some trifling object, which blocked the way, because no one gave the order to remove the obstacle. What would I not have given to sleep on the snow for a few hours during these marches, but even that could not be . . . The weary soldier would sink instinctively to the ground, only to get up in a few minutes and do as many more paces. This went on for hours, whole nights indeed, until at last we came within sight of some broken down wagon, which had caused the jam. . . . In our regiment [the Azovskii], which has not seen the enemy and had a full complement when it marched across the frontier, the companies are reduced to 26 or 30 men. The grenadier battalion scarcely numbers 300 men, and the other two are even weaker.' The passage is cited in Lettow-Vorbeck but the author remains unknown.

dispatched to pursue Bagration but, having proceeded for some distance, it soon disappeared and the rearguard remained undisturbed for the rest of the day, which it desperately needed following recent actions. At Landsberg, we joined the main army that was deployed in battle formation.

Meanwhile, Barclay de Tolly's detachment faced a different situation. It faced a force five times its size but Barclay de Tolly opted to delay the enemy, taking up various positions and abandoning them, often in disorder and suffering heavy casualties. He finally reached Hoff and halted here but deployed his troops at a disadvantage. Hoff is in a valley surrounded by steep hills. As superior enemy cavalry engaged Barclay's exhausted cavalrymen, they would be forced to retreat through its narrow streets. His infantry, which should have occupied the town and enclosed gardens, was placed before the town and, because of the deep snow on the plain, would also have to fall back through the town. So it was – the French routed our cavalry and drove it onto our infantry and batteries. One of the batteries was captured and the commander of the second, Lieutenant Markov, fired canister against our own Olioviopol Hussars, although he also halted the enemy attack and forced it back with loss.

The Russian infantry repulsed a charge, although the enemy cavalry reached its lines. The enemy made another attempt, and this time was more successful. The Dneprovskii and Kostromskoi Musketeer Regiments withstood the charge, but they were exhausted and did not retain formation for long. They were routed and at least half of them were cut down. The flags and the regimental guns were captured. Those who escaped sought the safety of the gardens to join the jager regiments already there.

This action demonstrates how disastrous the deployment of infantry in the open can be. Barclay de Tolly had been reinforced by five battalions under Major-General Prince Dolgorukov, but this force was insufficient and the new battalions were routed as well, losing many men. Our troops, retreating through Hoff, suffered from terrible artillery fire. Fearless Barclay de Tolly paid no heed to danger and appeared everywhere. However, this battle did not flatter his skill as a commander: it would not have been difficult to find a better way!*

Night prevented the enemy disturbing our army at Landsberg. The commander-in-chief thought it prudent to abandon this position as it was not broad enough to allow the troops to deploy. The second line was separated from the first by a stream with steep banks, which, despite the frost, had not frozen and complicated communications. The right flank was adjacent to a forest which covered part of the front, and this would have placed our skirmishers,

---

* There are no official reports on the Russian losses because Barclay was wounded and many of his officers were wounded and killed at Eylau on 7 February. Estimates vary between 1,800–2,000 killed and wounded. The French losses are projected as some 1,400 men.

whom the French surpass in skill, at a disadvantage. The proximity of woods also hampered the effective use of artillery and masked enemy movements. There were two roads for retreat and both were on the extreme left flank: one of them passed over a hill, which was very difficult to ascend because its steep elevation was frozen; the second road led through narrow gates into the twisting and constricted streets of Landsberg which would cause chaos and large casualties in our troops.

On the night of 26 January [7 February], General Tuchkov (I)'s division began withdrawing over the hill in some disorder, thus delaying everyone else. The columns moving through Landsberg did not bother to maintain order and became confused in the narrow streets so, despite the long winter night, some forces remained in position because the units ahead of them had not moved. It is easy to imagine the position our rearguard was in: it faced the French but could only retreat a step at a time so that the main army could withdraw to a safe distance.

Barclay's men withdrew with the main army. Bagration's rearguard was left at Landsberg. An hour after dawn, the rearguard marched through Landsberg and took up positions near the town, having left a strong infantry detachment and several guns at the gates. Some time later, a large body of French troops approached and, diverting our attention by its artillery fire, moved against our right flank. Taking advantage of the terrain, we fought back resolutely for a considerable time before quickly traversing a field that separated us from the forest. The enemy, following us, entered Landsberg and began deploying their forces on our former positions. It was obvious that we would have to engage not only the enemy vanguard but his main body as well; fortunately for us, the region between Landsberg and Preussisch-Eylau is mostly covered by dense forest. Prince Bagration dispatched his cavalry and part of his artillery for greater freedom of movement. All the jager units were combined and the line infantry was left in reserve.

We effectively contained the French with light losses until 11:00 a.m.; however, numerous barrels of wine, abandoned by other troops in order to lighten the transports and save more valuable goods, were soon found along the road and it was impossible to restrain the troops, who were cold and hungry, from consuming alcohol. Before long, four jager regiments were so drunk it was impossible to rally them. The French noticed this confusion and made vigorous attacks, trying to cut our troops off they came from all directions. Artillery had to be committed to defend the drunkards and we were slowed down considerably. Generals Pahlen and Lambert used cavalry to protect these troops; but it was impossible to rally and withdraw these drunken soldiers and we lost plenty of them killed or captured.

Approaching Preussisch-Eylau, the rearguard came onto an open plain and was assigned positions covering the town behind which our army began deploying for battle. The rearguard was reinforced by several regiments from the 8th Division and cavalry units. We deployed on both sides of the road that ran through woods. I placed twenty-four guns on a steep plateau on the left flank. A small plain lay before this hill and the enemy would have to cross it to advance; our skirmishers were spread out there, concealed by the broken terrain. Part of the cavalry was on the right flank and the rest was moved behind our positions.

The enemy soon deployed batteries on the opposite heights and subjected us to an intense bombardment; we rarely returned fire because I did not have a single heavy artillery piece. The French columns then came down at various points but were halted by the fire of forty of our guns. Our canister fire routed some of them, inflicting considerable casualties. We maintained our position for almost two hours, but then the enemy advanced in superior numbers. Of their three columns, one marched on the main road, where we had fewer infantry, another moved against the Pskovskii and Sofivskii Musketeer Regiments and a third advanced against my 24-gun battery.* The first column moved easily and threatened to outflank our strongest point, while the other columns advanced slowly because of the deep snow and they had to endure our canister fire for a prolonged time.† Although disordered, one of them still managed to reach our position, where it was destroyed on the bayonets of the Pskovskii and Sofiskii regiments. Simultaneously, another column scattered its corpses before my battery. Meanwhile, Colonel Degtyarev led the St. Petersburgskii Dragoons against the column on the main road; to evade our cavalry, the French veered away and moved into deep snow. The haste of their action led to confusion and our cavalry regiment took full advantage, capturing one eagle and 500 men after enduring light enemy musket fire. At least another 500 were killed, including the general who commanded this column.‡

I have never witnessed a more decisive cavalry attack; I was equally surprised by how the St. Petersburgskii [Dragoon] Regiment came down a snow-covered slope without disorder. However, our success was short-lived, as the enemy brought up more troops; the French increased their batteries that now covered their columns and, being unable to contain them, we were ordered to pull back. The enemy immediately occupied our positions and followed us closely.

---

* Of the three French columns, the central one was the 46th Line, the second the 18th Line and the third, marching against the Russian left, the 24th Line.

† One of the Russian participants described this charge, 'The artillery fired canister at the masses of the attacking columns; their front ranks were mowed down in lines, but those following stepped over the corpses of their comrades and advanced forward, with remarkable heroism and impudence.' Davidov, *Recollections on the Battle of Preussisch-Eylau*, p. 211.

‡ Several Russian dragoons fought their way to the Eagle of the 2nd Battalion of the 18th Line. Dragoons Stephan Fomin, Vasilii Podvorni, Savelii Deriagin, Efim Erofeyev and trumpeter Filip Logvinov captured the Eagle and were later awarded Orders of St. George (4th class) for this exploit.

I successfully carried out my orders to cover our troops with my horse artillery as they entered Preussisch-Eylau.* As soon as I passed through the city gates, the enemy launched assaults on the town. Its defence was entrusted to Barclay de Tolly, his detachment having been reinforced by fresh troops. The unequal ratio of forces did not allow us to take full advantage of the walls and fences that ringed the town; enemy skirmishers appeared, fired in the streets and entered the nearest houses. Our infantry drove them out with bayonets on several occasions and the town was in our hands until Barclay de Tolly suffered a serious wound. Discouraged by this loss, his detachment abandoned the town to the enemy holding on to part of it. Major-General Somov, who commanded a brigade of the 4th Division, arrived with reinforcements, stormed the houses, smashed the enemy and recaptured the town.†

However, Somov made the mistake of trying to rally his troops in a remote part of town and so when the drums beat the alarm the troops retired and did not have time to organise. The appearance of the enemy spread confusion, amplified by the darkness and French canister rounds. We had to abandon the town and, in addition to considerable casualties, we also lost a few artillery pieces.‡ This incident forced the commander-in-chief to change the deployment of our army and during the night our troops shifted to different positions. Bennigsen thought this necessary because the enemy, after it captured the heights defended by our rearguard, had made a reconnaissance of our positions. [From the Russian text in A. Yermolov, *Zapiski* . . .]

Denis Davydov

I will never forget the joy that I felt as I crossed our borders for the first time in my life. Everything seemed so new and unusual to me! It was quite natural to enjoy clean, beautiful towns and villages and well-built roads, shaded by

---

* According to Bennigsen, Colonel Yermolov 'skilfully deployed his horse battery on the hill and opened effective fire against the French.' Bennigsen, 'Memoirs', *Russkaya starina* (July 1899), pp. 208–9.

† Bagration met Bennigsen behind the town and was ordered to recapture Eylau at any cost. He was given Major-General Somov's division and led the leading column in a bayonet attack. Davidov described the soldiers following him 'quietly, without noise, but, when they entered the streets, everybody howled "Hurrah", charged with bayonets – and we captured Eylau again'. In a savage combat, the Russians captured the Eagle of the 2nd Battalion of the 4th Line. Lieutenant Dmitri Kaftirev of the Polotskskii Regiment claimed the trophy but, in 1808, it was discovered that Vasilii Demchinsky of the same regiment had seized it.

‡ After Eylau was recaptured, the soldiers of the 4th Division were allowed to rest for the night and scattered looking for food and shelter. Somov had not specified the exact rallying point, and ordered the drums to beat at 9:30 p.m. in the north-east part of Eylau, close to the main Russian position.

the trees, but I was also enjoying the sights of tidy Germans with their boorish jokes [pudovye shutki] about Napoleon, whose invasion, however, made them shudder; I enjoyed local beer soup, butterbrots [sandwiches] and rude postmen who are so gentle with their horses! I travelled through Augustow and Lyck, where I spent the night at Borozdin's, Rhein, Guttstadt and, at nine o'clock in the morning on the 15th [27 January], I reached Liebstadt, just as the headquarters and the army departed for Mohrungen, where, on the 13th [25 January], Bernadotte attacked and defeated Eugene Ivanovich Markov, who commanded part of the army's vanguard.

Having received several packages in St. Petersburg and picked up a few more for the commander-in-chief [Bennigsen] along the way, I was introduced to him and had the honour of delivering these dispatches in person. I was pleased to see inside his room many of my friends and acquaintances from St. Petersburg. They all surrounded me and kept asking about friends and loved ones that stayed back at home. Many of these young men were already tired of war that was waged in such a harsh time of the year, without any decisive successes and amidst every kind of hardship. Many of them pined for the luxurious living in St. Petersburg. 'What a silly man you are,' they told me, 'What the devil has brought you here! How dearly we would pay to just get back home! You are still in a daze, just wait and we will hear what you will say in a bit.' They told me of various challenges awaiting me but I told them I knew well where I was going: I longed for fighting and not kissing, and was well aware that war would not be easy. And truly, I did not think then about the challenges and dangers: so unbounded were my hopes and so much my new status and new, varied and vivid experiences shaped my feelings. Suffice it to say that from my childhood I lived and breathed for military service and was extremely ambitious; I was then just twenty-two years old . . .

I cannot describe how delighted and intoxicated I was to observe everything around me! Preparing to move, infantry, cavalry and artillery units were still covering the nearby hillsides but at the same time the long strips of dark columns were already writhing amidst the snowy hills and plains. The sound of cannon wheels, cavalry hooves, various conversation, laughter and murmur of the infantry marching in knee-deep snow, aides-de-camp galloping in various directions, generals surrounded by their suites; the perfunctoriness and sloppiness of uniforms of the troops who had not seen any roof for two months and were sooty from the smoke of bivouacs and battles, with frozen moustaches and bullet-ridden [prostrelenye] shakos and coats – all this noble unseemliness testified to the labours and dangers experienced and all of it inexplicably electrified and elevated my soul! At last, I had found my element!

But how a person's feelings and thoughts can be shaped by different experiences! At first the art of war seemed so attractive but having travelled a few miles further on, I saw the naked hideousness of it. We approached the village of Georgenstahl, that very field where two days earlier Markov had suffered defeat. This village was dismantled for firewood for those of our troops who had been assigned to spend the night there. Some of the local residents stood outside the village, gripped by voiceless sorrow but shedding no tears and showing no resistance, which for me has always been and is more striking than wailing and crying. Inexperienced warrior that I was then, I believed that provisions were provided by special officials, who bought everything from the local residents and delivered supplies to the army on carriages hired from the same population; that bivouac bonfires were lit not from peaceful villagers' huts but rather from bushes and trees. In short, I was certain that the inhabitants of those areas, where military operations were taking place, were not subjected to any misfortune and ruin, and that they remained nothing more than calm witnesses of military events, just like the residents of Krasnoe Selo* were during the manoeuvres of the Guard. What a surprise it was to see the complete opposite! It was only then that I became witness to the hardship and misery caused by war to that class of people, which, unlike us soldiers, seeks no glory or honour, but instead loses not just its very last property, but its very last piece of bread, not only life but the honour of their wives and daughters, and dies, emaciated and stricken in everything that its holds dear and sacred, on the smouldering ruins of its homeland – and why all this misery? Just because some timeserver wants to change his red ribbon for a blue one, and a blue one for a striped one!†

But this very field offered another disgraceful sight that shattered my very soul. As I mentioned, we were on the site of the battle of Mohrungen . . . Driven by curiosity, I examined the field of battle. I first travelled along our position and then visited the enemy one. I could see where the gunfire and attacks were most intense based on the number of corpses that covered the ground in those areas. Colonel Alexsey Yermolov commanded the artillery of our advance guard and its fire had devastated, in the fullest sense of this word, infantry columns and lines of the enemy cavalry that lay in heaps near the village Pfaresfeldschen, lying stricken by cannonballs and canister in the same order as they advanced or stood during the battle. At first this valley of death, trampled as it was by us, so eagerly rushing to share the same fate, these faces and corpses, so distorted and disfigured by gunfire and cold weapons, made no particular impression on me. But as my imagination gradually took over, I must confess that I became so agitated for my future, or, to be straightforward,

---

* Founded in 1714, the village of Krasnoe Selo, near St. Petersburg, initially housed one of the first Russian paper mills established by Tsar Peter I. The village gradually expanded and beginning in 1765, the Russian army held regular military manoeuvres and reviews there.

† Davydov refers to ribbons of various orders: the red ribbon of the Order of St. Alexander, the blue one of the Order of St. Andrew and the striped (gold and black) of the Order of St. George.

I felt such timidity that upon my return to Mohrungen, I could not close my eyes all night long, dreading experiencing similar distortion and ugliness. If reason could have even the slightest involvement in my imagination, I could have easily seen that such a death was not terrible but enviable, for the deadlier the wound, the less suffering one experiences. And who cares if after death you scare the living with your appearance, you no longer feel anything anyway! Thank God, by the dawn, I came back to my senses and having recovered my earlier state of being, I laughed at myself and, as I recall, had never again experienced such a paroxysm of distorted imagination for the rest of my long military career.

I spent the day of rest [dnevka] at Mohrungen and had lunch with the commander-in-chief [Bennigsen], with whom I also dined in the evening. Despite being rather inexperienced in military service, I was very surprised by the indiscretion of Bennigsen and other generals present at the headquarters. I witnessed as Bennigsen, Knorring, Count [Osterman] Tolstoy, lying on a map, kept telling each other about their plans in the presence of various military officers and civilians, aides and foreigners!

On the 16th [28 January], early in the morning, I bought a horse and, accompanied by a Cossack, I went to Prince Bagration, who took the overall command of the advanced guards led by Markov, Barclay de Tolly and Baggovut . . . The Prince resided in the beautiful and spacious hut [izba] of a Prussian villager. He occupied a large upper room, where there was a master bed, which, on [Bagration's] orders, was covered with straw; the floor of the upper chamber was also covered with straw. His suite included Colonel Troubetzkoy of the Chevalier Guard Regiment Cavalry (who is currently adjutant-general and general of cavalry), Comte de Balmain, Count Grabowski, Afrosimov, Eichen and others. I soon met Yevgeny Ivanovich Markov and Barclay, then still a major-general, Major-General Baggovut, Colonels Yurkovskii, Ermolov, Turchaninov and others . . . I remember that at that time, although Barclay de Tolly was decorated with only [Orders of] St. George and of St. Vladimir of the 4th class, and the medal for storming Ochakov [in 1788], he already enjoyed the reputation of a brave and skilful general.

During the five years I served as Prince Bagration's adjutant, I never saw him other than properly dressed, be it day or night. His sleep was very short – three or four hours a day, and even then frequently interrupted, for anyone coming from the outposts with worthwhile news was required to wake him up. He loved living sumptuously: he always had plenty of everything, not for himself, but for others. He was personally satisfied with very little and was always completely sober. I have never seen him drink vodka or wine, except for two shots of madeira wine at lunch. [In 1807] his clothing consisted of the uniform coat with the star of [the Order of] St. George (2nd class), a cloak [burka] on his shoulders and on his side, a sword that he wore in Italy while serving with Suvorov, a grey lambskin cap on his head and a Cossack whip in his hand. Because of the rigours of the season, no one paid attention to uniforms and we all wore whatever was warmest. I initially put on a Life Guard hussar's pelisse but was persuaded to take it off so as to avoid the danger of being injured or killed by our own troops because [Marshal] Bernadotte's corps, which was deployed closest to us, included the 10th Hussars who wore similar red pelisses.

Our army was retreating from Jankovo to Preussisch-Eylau. At that time the rearguard was reorganised and was divided into two parts. One was under command of Major-General Barclay de Tolly and the other under Lieutenant-General* Prince Bagration. On 23 January [4 February] the former was engaged in a fight near Deppen, covering the retreat of the army towards Wolfsdorf. On the 24th [5 February], it was Bagration's turn to cover the retreat from Wolfsdorf to Landsberg. As far as I remember, Prince Bagration's rearguard consisted of the following regiments: the Ekaterinoslavskii and Malorossiiskii grenadiers, the Pskovskii infantry, several jager regiments, the Elisavetgradskii and Aleksandriiskii hussars, the Kurlandskii dragoons, an uhlan regiment, several Cossack regiments and up to forty cannon. The individual commanders in the rearguard were major-generals who had become famous in later years: Count Peter Petrovich Pahlen, Markov, Baggovut, Count Lambert; there were also colonels who already had a reputation: Yermolov, who commanded the entire rearguard artillery, Prince Mikhail Petrovich Dolgorukov, Gogel and Yurkovskii, who was in charge of the forward line.

The combat at Wolfsdorf was the first engagement of my long military career. I shall never forget the impatience with which I waited for the first shots, the first encounters! As if unsure of my own courage, I tried to emulate the high spirits of Prince Bagration's companions, absorbing with all my soul their gallant faces, their thoughts, observations and orders that breathed with ardour for danger and radiated a mood of carefree abandon. But it was the Prince [Bagration] himself who had the most influence over me. I had not yet witnessed his lofty spirit at its finest but deep within his outward calm I already sensed his moral strength and flashes of genius that erupted on the battlefield whenever despair of success was about to prevail and the prospects of disaster became more certain.

At dawn the enemy began to drive back our forward line near Varlak, about four verstas from Wolfsdorf. The rearguard took up arms at its bivouac beyond Wolfsdorf, parallel to the highway leading from Guttstadt to Liebstadt. This position protected a local road which led via Petersdorf to Dietrichsdorf and on to Arensdorf, Open and Kashauen, along which the rearguard was to proceed

---

* Bagration earned his promotion to lieutenant-general for his successful operations during the War of the Third Coalition, especially his defence of the Allied right flank at Austerlitz.

in the wake of the army. The edge of the woods between Wolfsdorf and Elditen was held by the men of the 5th Jager Regiment. A small cavalry detachment moved swiftly to keep the enemy under observation on our left flank.

The French advance guard, preceded by a screen of skirmishers with the whole army behind it, sporadically fired from one or two cannon at our forward line. Masses of enemy troops were moving among the snow covered hills and were streaming downhill towards Wolfsdorf. [Colonel] Yurkovskii, under cover of the Cossacks closest to the enemy, alternately halted and advanced at an angle to the battle line of the rearguard towards the right flank of the 5th Jager Regiment beyond the edge of the woods.

As aide-de-camp to Prince Bagration, and therefore without a command of my own, I asked to be sent to the front line, ostensibly to keep track of enemy movements but really to prance about on my horse, fire my pistols, flourish my sword and if circumstances allowed, to hack away at the enemy.

I galloped over to the Cossacks who were busy exchanging fire with the enemy flanquers. The enemy cavalryman closest to me, wearing a blue cape and bearskin cap, appeared to be an officer. I was at once seized by the desire to cut him off from the line and capture. But when I tried to persuade the Cossacks to support me, they simply laughed at this newly-minted knight who had appeared out of the blue with such a ridiculous proposition. None of them wanted to follow me while I, thank God, still had enough sense not to take on singlehanded an [enemy] soldier who at that very moment was joined by other fellow riders. Unfortunately, in my youthful eagerness, I let common sense desert me all too soon. I was once again filled with fighting ardour, my heart was full of fervour and, like a man possessed, I spurred my horse forward, approached the officer within pistol range and fired my pistol at him. Without altering his pace, he returned fire and soon other shots followed from the carbines of his colleagues. These were the first bullets ever to whistle past my ears. I was no Charles XII but at that moment, that enthralling split-second filled with danger, I understood the calling of that royal adventurer, felt immensely proud of myself, enveloped as I was in gunsmoke. The civilian world, in effect everything outside the confines of army life, suddenly seemed worthless.

No longer expecting any help from the Cossacks, I was supremely confident in the prowess of my steed. Filled with anger against a total stranger who, God knows, was simply carrying out his duty and obligations just like myself, I drew closer to him, brandishing my sword and swearing at him in French as loudly and expressively as possible. I challenged him to leave his line and engage me unassisted in a combat. He swore back at me and offered the same conditions; but neither of us took up the challenge and we both stayed rooted to the spot. But it must be said that I had, in fact, strayed quite a distance from the Cossacks and was within only three or four horse bounds away from the French flanquers while the [enemy] officer was within the flanquers' line itself.

To be honest, I have done everything to deserve to be patted on the head but also yanked by the ears from my horse.

At that moment a Cossack uryadnik [non-commissioned officer] galloped over to me, exclaiming: 'Why are you swearing, Your Honour? That's a sin! Fighting is a sacred business and swearing in battle is like swearing inside a church. God will punish you! You will perish and so will we. Please, better go back to where you came from!' Only then did I realise the absurdity of my pretension to be a Trojan hero and rode back to Prince Bagration.

Commanding the rearguard of an army while it is being hotly pursued is a challenging task. The basic duty of such a commander consists of two contradictory tasks: maintaining the safety of the army from enemy attacks while keeping close proximity to and constant communications with it. How does one reconcile these two seemingly contradictory functions? Should one accept battle? But every battle results in a prolonged halt that in turn opens up distance between the rearguard and the army that keep on moving. Yet, if the rearguard concentrates on keeping in close touch with the main body of troops and therefore avoids clashes with the enemy, it will easily expose the army to an attack. Bagration successfully resolved this challenge and fully comprehended the key principle of rearguard tactics, which in fourteen years were explained on the island of St. Helena by the greatest exponent of the art of war [Napoleon] himself: 'The advance guard must keep pushing relentlessly, while the rearguard must manoeuvre continually.' Bagration used this axiom as his guiding principles whenever he commanded rearguards. Under Bagration's command the rearguard never remained long in the same place and never trailed along in the wake of the army. The essence of Bagration's tactics was to keep moving from one defensive position to another without getting involved in a major battle but all the while maintaining a menacing stance by frequent counterstrikes to contain enemy attacks and sustaining a fierce and wide-ranging artillery fire. Such a vast operation requires coolness, a sharp eyes, incredible resourcefulness and savvy – qualities with which Bagration was so well endowed.

All this was quite beyond my comprehension at the time. As a hussar staff rotmistr [captain] I hungered for a fierce engagement. In my understanding of strategy, battle was absolutely necessary, and its likelihood was guaranteed by the fearless nature of the prince, who, in my opinion, was obliged to defend the Wolfsdorf position by all possible means, even at the cost of sacrificing the entire rearguard. I was so convinced of the soundness of my reasoning, so certain that everything would turn out differently if they only would listen to me, that neither Suvorov nor Napoleon would have been able to convince me otherwise! This explains the daft self-confidence which placed me in such a dangerous position and from which I was only saved by Providence.

Upon my return from the front line to the prince, I was immediately dispatched by him to the 5th Jager Regiment with orders to abandon the woods they had occupied and fall back on Dietrichsdorf, where a second position had been already chosen for the rearguard. I was puzzled and upset. 'How can it be,' I pondered, 'when so few troops have been committed to action, when not a single musket has been fired in the 5th Jager Regiment, that we are told to retreat? Where is [Bagration's] famed resoluteness that everyone sings the praises of?' Nevertheless I galloped off to the jagers and carried out my order.

Meanwhile our forward line, continuing to exchange fire with the enemy skirmishers, retreated towards the woods that the jagers were supposed to vacate. It happened that after delivering orders and returning to my post, reflecting on how I might *correct Prince Bagration's erroneous decision* [original emphasis] to give up the Wolfsdorf position without vigorous measures against the enemy attacks, I rode past the very front line where an hour earlier, I had been exchanging, so Homerically but without hexameter verses, swearwords with a French officer. As luck would have it, I spotted the same Cossack who had interrupted my epic challenge with his prosaic good sense. Yet as I approached him, an even crazier idea suddenly struck me. I had read once, Devil may know where, that in some battles previously nameless individuals had appeared and, by sheer willpower, had snatched victory from the foe despite strict orders to the contrary. How could I not tempt my own fortune? Maybe I am no less endowed with great abilities; maybe I had been chosen by Providence to accomplish just such a feat . . . My imagination ran rife! So I envisioned leading our forward line in a frontal attack on the enemy, send it reeling and then break through with the 5th Jager Regiment that was already preparing to leave the woods. Upon witnessing my success, the Prince [Bagration] would surely reinforce me with the entire rearguard and inform Bennigsen, who would promptly come up with the whole army. In short, I aimed for nothing less than to rout the entire enemy vanguard with a handful of cavalrymen and jagers and, potentially, be the main culprit in the vanquishing of Napoleon himself.

All of these ideas came to me not somewhere behind the scenes but rather on the very spot where I could see the entire area from Wolfsdorf to Varlach covered with dense columns of infantry, cavalry and countless artillery – consequently I should have realised the foolishness of my enterprise. But as it often happened to me on many other occasions, passion spoke louder than reason. Engrossed with my audacious plan, I asked the Cossack uryadnik, 'What do you say, brother, shall we have a go at them?' 'Why not, Your Honour?' he replied, pointing at the [French] flanquers who were dashing about right under our nose, and added: 'There are not many of them here so we could deal with them easily. The other time we were on our own, but now our infantry is nearby and could give us a hand.' 'Right!' I exclaimed, 'You rally the Cossacks and I will have a word with the hussars and uhlans (there were two platoons scattered in the Cossack forward line).'

Soon we were in the midst of attacking. The entire line gave a shout and hurled itself at the enemy flanquers. We got mixed up with the enemy. Swords clashed, bullets flew by and the fun began. I remember my sabre biting into live flesh and warm blood streaming from the blade. The fighting did not last very long. The French flanquers were mauled by our men and beat a hasty retreat. But in our eagerness to chase them we soon encountered their reserves that galloped to their aid. These were dragoons with horsetails streaming from their helmets. They swooped on us hungrily, fresh blows were exchanged and we in turn were beaten back towards the woods where the jagers were no longer present to support us. My grand and ludicrous plan fell apart and I, gloomy and despondent like Napoleon after Waterloo, made my way back to [Bagration], passing by Wolfsdorf towards Dietriechsdorf, where the whole rearguard was headed.

I rode alone through a valley, quite safe from the enemy because the dragoons who had thrashed us were content with their success and did not pursue us. But just as I climbed a hillock, I came suddenly face-to-face with six French horse jagers, moving from Wolfsdorf to observe the movements of our rearguard. I shuddered. Seeing them and galloping away required a split second. They fired their carbines and seriously wounded my horse, which, for the moment at any rate, did not slacken pace. I thought I had shaken them off, but no such luck! They were gaining on me from either side. I looked around to see if there was any help nearby but only caught a distant glimpse of our rearguard columns advancing on Dietrichsdorf, about three verstas away. There was not a soul in the vast field leading up to the woods. Disaster seemed imminent. I was wearing a pelisse [shinel'], buttoned with one clasp at the throat, my sword was drawn and my pistols, which I had no time to reload since firing them during the charge, were at my saddle. One of my pursuers, probably riding a better horse than his friends, caught up with me, though not quite close enough to strike me with his sword. Still he was close enough to grab the edge of my billowing pelisse and almost managed to drag me off my horse. Luckily the pelisse came undone and he was left with it in his hand. I kept galloping at full speed towards the woods, but gradually the distance between me and my pursuers shortened as my wounded horse, fast wearying, slowed down. The winter that year turned out to be short and as the result, the [thawed out] swamps turned treacherous: snow concealed impassable marshes. I no longer galloped on a road but twisted and turned at random. To my misfortune, I reached the woods at a point where, unseen by me, they bordered a swamp that was indiscernible to an eye. Galloping at full speed, my horse crashed into the water up to its belly, fell to its side and breathed its last. Moments later a sharp blade was raised above my head. Death or capture stared me in the face!

At that very moment, a patrol of about twenty Cossacks, dispatched by Yourkovskii to observe the enemy and brought here by Providence itself, burst out of the nearby woods with a mighty yell and proceeded to chase my pursuers back to Wolfsdorf. One of the Cossacks, my true saviour, mounted me behind him and delivered me to Yourkovskii, who promptly gave me the horse of a fallen hussar. And that's how I rejoined our rearguard, already in position near Dietrichsdorf.

Meanwhile, Prince Bagration, whose kindness of heart was as vast as the intrepidity of his soul, became worried about my safety and continually asked for news about me from each man returning from the front line. No one could tell him what had happened to me. At last, I appeared before him on a stranger's horse, without a pelisse, covered with mud, snow and blood, but still maintaining a somewhat triumphant appearance that stemmed from my escape from extreme danger and sense of pre-eminence in my bold exploit. Needless to say, I did not tell the Prince or even my friends about my grandiose plans which by now I had come to realise to be thoroughly quixotic. I only told them about the enemy pursuit and my salvation thanks to the Cossacks who had arrived in the nick of time. The Prince, with an approving smile, chided me a little for my reckless behaviour and gave me his own warm coat [burka] as replacement for my pelisse. Soon afterwards he nominated me for an award. [From the Russian text in Denis Davydov, *Voennye zapiski*]

4

The Bloodbath at Eylau

Eylau remains one of the bloodiest and most futile battles of the Napoleonic Wars. After a two-day bloodbath, the frozen fields were covered in tens of thousands of corpses, causing one participant to describe it as 'the bloodiest day, the most horrible butchery of men that had taken place since the beginning of the Revolutionary Wars'.

Following an indecisive combat at Jankovo, Bennigsen decided to withdraw in a north-easterly direction while Napoleon's forces vigorously pursued him. After a series of rearguard actions, the two sides met near the small town of Preussisch-Eylau, where the Russians drew up on a position stretched from the north-west to the east behind the town. Hostilities began on 7 February 1807 when the French attacked the Russian rearguard commanded by Prince Peter Bagration, who fought his way back through the streets of Eylau.

The following morning, the massed artillery of the Russians opened the battle with a bombardment that left the village of Eylau ablaze. The French artillery returned fire and several infantry assaults were launched which the Russians repelled. With these initial attacks, Napoleon ordered Marshal Pierre Augereau to charge with his 7th Corps at the Russian centre. Augereau's ill health and the atrocious weather conditions ensured that the attack ended in grisly chaos. Advancing through a blizzard, Augereau's men lost their way and ended up veering to the left and walking directly into the muzzles of the Russian grand battery. A withering bombardment ensued. In under an hour Augereau's corps had all but been destroyed, with over 5,000 killed and wounded, Augereau himself among the latter. As the Russian counter-attacked and reached the outskirts of the town, Napoleon, feeling that the battle had reached a critical phase, ordered some 10,000 men of his reserve cavalry into the fray. Led by Marshal Joachim Murat, some eighty squadrons formed into two vast columns before launching their now-legendary charge. The massed horsemen smashed through Bennigsen's infantry and, despite suffering heavy losses, brought the relief Napoleon desperately needed, allowing him to restore order among his hard-pressed formations.

In the afternoon, Davout's newly-arrived corps exerted pressure on Bennigsen's left flank, forcing it to shift its position by 45 degrees to maintain a solid front against the French forces. The steadfast Russian resistance sapped French attacks while the arrival of the Prussian corps under General Lestocq helped bolster the beleaguered Russians, who held their positions until nightfall.

Despite Napoleon's subsequent claims, the battle of Eylau was far from a great victory and is now generally viewed by historians as a costly draw at best, with losses estimated at over 25,000 Russian casualties and as many as 30,000 French, whose exhausted state rendered pursuit impossible. Both sides, severely mauled, went back into winter quarters to recover from the bloodletting, but with the certain expectation of renewed fighting in the spring.

Levin Bennigsen

Late in the evening on 8 February, Bennigsen submitted his first report on the battle of Eylau to Emperor Alexander. By then he would have had limited information on the state of the army in the wake of the bloody battle so he intentionally kept his report brief and short on details.

Sire,

I am truly happy to have it in my power to inform Your Imperial Majesty that the army, the command of which Your Majesty has deigned to confide to me, has been again victorious. The battle which has just taken place has been bloody and destructive. It began at three o'clock in the afternoon on the 26th January [7 February] and continued until six o'clock in the evening of the 27th January [8 February]. The enemy is completely defeated; over one thousand prisoners, and twelve stands of colours, which I have the honour herewith to transmit to Your Majesty, fell into the hands of the conquerors. This day Napoleon attacked my centre and both wings with his best troops, but he was repulsed and beaten on all sides. His [Imperial] Guard repeatedly attacked my centre without the smallest success. After a very brisk fire, they were repulsed at all points by the vigorous bayonets of our infantry and by the gallant charges of the cavalry. Many columns of enemy infantry, and the entire regiments of cuirassiers, which are described as the elite, have been completely destroyed.

I shall not fail to transmit to Your Imperial Majesty, as soon as possible, a detailed account of the memorable battle of Preussisch-Eylau. I think our loss may amount to some 7,000 killed; and I certainly do not exaggerate when I state the loss of the enemy at considerably more than 12,000 killed. [From the Russian text in *Zhurnal voennykh deistvii imperatorskoi Rossiiskoi armii* . . .]

After rallying his army in the wake of the battle of Eylau, Bennigsen slowly withdrew towards Königsberg where he intended to regroup. In April, with both armies settling into their quarters for a much-needed respite, Bennigsen could afford the time to prepare a detailed report on the battle for Emperor Alexander.

On 25 January [6 February] I departed from Landsberg with my army, which was only 70,000 strong, as several contingents had been detached. Napoleon, who was accompanied by Marshals Augereau, Soult, Murat and Davout, had an army that amounted to 90,000 men, and followed me very closely, continually engaging my rearguard which consisted of the detachments of Major-Generals Markov, Baggovut and Barclay de Tolly, under the overall command of Prince Bagration.

When I arrived at Preussisch-Eylau, I ordered my army to take a position at a short distance behind the town, and directed the rearguard to maintain its appointed post against the enemy, to protect my heavy artillery, which I had been obliged to dispatch by a considerable detour from Wolfsdorf, partly to avoid poor roads, and partly to facilitate the march of my columns. At the same time I caused the town of Preussisch-Eylau to be occupied by General Barclay de Tolly, and detached a few regiments of the 8th Division of Lieutenant-General Tuchkov's corps to support the rearguard. This reinforcement enabled General Markov to take a strong position, and to establish batteries on the neighbouring heights. The enemy forces soon approached and sending their light troops forward, they marched in three strong columns against the heights occupied by [General Markov]. The enemy was met by the skirmishers from the Pskovskii Musketeer Regiment and canister fire from our batteries, but neither proved sufficient to stop their progress. Therefore, Major-General Markov, upon receiving Lieutenant-General Prince Bagration's order, moved the Pskovskii and Sofiiskii Regiments in a bayonet charge against one column, which was overthrown and destroyed. At the same time, the second enemy column was attacked from the right flank by the St. Petersburgskii Dragoon Regiment, which almost annihilated the enemy and captured one colour. The third column, which hastened to support the first two, was halted by the heavy losses inflicted by the fire from our artillery batteries commanded by Colonel Yermolov.

After the defeat of these columns, the enemy next began to cannonade our line, and to march against it in four columns, while the fifth column directed its march against our left wing, with an intention to take it in flank. The Pskovskii and Sofiiskii Regiments, which had suffered losses during the enemy's first attack, were too weak to meet this charge so they received orders to fall back; and, in their stead, the Moskovskii Grenadier and the 24th Jager Regiments entered the fight; at the same time His Majesty's Life Guard Cuirassier, the Ingermanlandskii and Kargopolskii Dragoon and Elisavetgradskii Hussar Regiments charged the enemy's cavalry, which was going to outflank our right wing; they killed a large number of the enemy. On the left wing, where the enemy was initially met by the batteries of the 8th Division and by the skirmishers, the Izyumskii Hussar Regiment also charged the swarms of enemy skirmishers with great success.

The enemy, though beaten at every point, continued to receive reinforcements from all sides, and threatened to cut off our most advanced troops, I therefore ordered the latter to retreat; and consequently, the regiments of the 8th Division, and then the whole of the rearguard, retreated immediately through Preussisch-Eylau and joined the main body, which stood drawn up between the villages of Serpallen and Schloditten in the following manner: the 5th, 7th, 8th, 3nd and 2nd Divisions formed two lines, the second of which was deployed in columns; the 4th and 14th Divisions composed the reserve. The right wing was commanded by Lieutenant-General Tuchkov; the centre, by Lieutenant-General Baron Sacken, and the left wing – by Lieutenant-General Count Ostermann; and detachment of Major-General . . . [Markov] from the rearguard, commanded by Lieutenant-General Prince Bagration, was deployed on the right wing while the detachment of Major-General Baggovut occupied Serpallen. The whole of the cavalry, under the command of Lieutenant-General Prince Golitsyn, covered both wings, though parts thereof were within the lines as well. The heights, situated before my front, were occupied by strong batteries. The horse artillery of Colonel Yermolov, which had covered the retreat of the rearguard, remained with General Barclay de Tolly [in Preussisch-Eylau].

The enemy soon attacked the town [Eylau] with such force that Major-General Barclay de Tolly, notwithstanding that he performed miracles of bravery and fiercely and gallantly resisted the enemy every step of the way, was obliged to cede to superior numbers, and to retreat. As soon as I perceived this, I sent the 4th Division to support him. Major-General Somov, who commanded this division, marched in three columns towards the town. Upon approaching the town, one of the columns endured heavy enemy fire from the left but skirmishers were dispatched against the enemy, who was soon driven off. The column then entered the town and, despite the enemy's superior numbers, the ferocity of musket fire from the [enemy] skirmishers lodged inside the houses as well as the [enemy] artillery fire, our men used bayonets to clear their way in the streets and, dragging out the French who had hidden inside the houses, they captured the town and joined the detachment of Major-General Barclay de Tolly, which was also reinforced by other columns of the 4th Division. Our forces then drove out the remaining enemy forces, and, it must be noted that the Polotskii Musketeer Regiment had captured one colour. Major-General Barclay de Tolly, however, received a severe wound in the arm on this occasion.

When, at the approach of night, the enemy had entirely ceased firing, I withdrew all the troops from the town, intending to concentrate my whole force on the other side, and to prepare for a general attack to be made the next day, as well as to protect the aforementioned forces [inside Eylau] from the attack of superior enemy forces that could, during the night, cut them off from our army. To be secure from any nocturnal alarm, I placed the 4th Division,

1. Napoleon and his staff at the battle of Eylau, 8 February 1807 (by Alexander Averyanov).

2. 'Augereau's corps lost its bearings, lost contact with St. Hilaire's division and all the cavalry, and suddenly appeared, much to their and our surprise, in front of our centre battery just as the weather cleared . . . In an instant the Moscow grenadiers and the Shlusselbourg infantry, together with the Arkhangelogordskii infantry, rushed hungrily at them with lowered bayonets.' (Denis Davydov). The attack of the Moscow grenadiers at Eylau (by Alexander Averyanov).

3. The famous charge of Marshal Joachim Murat's Reserve Cavalry at Eylau (by Jean Antoine Simeon Fort).

4. The Death of General Hautpoult at Eylau. Jean-Joseph Ange d'Hautpoult commanded the famed 'iron men', the cuirassiers, and at Eylau, he led his men in the celebrated charge through the Russian position. During this attack he was hit by grapeshot and mortally wounded.

5. Prussian troops celebrating the capture of a French flag at Eylau (by Georg Buxenstein).

6. An early nineteenth-century German print of the Battle of Eylau.

7. Napoleon inspecting the field of battle in the aftermath of the carnage at Eylau. This painting by Antoine-Jean Gros is undoubtedly one of the most famous Napoleonic paintings in the world. Notice the Russian prisoners on the right.

8. Emperor Alexander of Russia (by George Dawe).

9. General Karl Baggovut.

10. General Peter Bagration.

11. General Mikhail Barclay de Tolly.

12. Alexander Benckendorff.

13. General Levin Bennigsen.

14. Faddei Bulgarin.

15. General Fedor Buxhöwden.

16. Denis Davydov, shown here at the height of his military fame in the wake of the Patriotic War of 1812, was still a young and inexperienced officer in 1807 (portrait by George Dawes).

17. General Dmitrii Dokhturov.

18. Nadezhda Durova, the famed 'Cavalry Maiden', who disguised herself as a man to enrol in a cavalry regiment.

19. The future general and commander-in-chief of the Russian forces in the Caucasus, Alexsey Yermolov commanded an artillery company during the 1807 Campaign.

20. General Dmitrii Golitsyn.

21. Field Marshal Mikhail Kamenski.

22. General Fabian von der Osten-Sacken.

23. General Alexander
Osterman-Tolstoy.

24. A close friend of Konstantin
Batyushkov, Ivan Alexandrovich Petin
(1788–1813) was a recent graduate of the
elite Page Corps and served as a lieutenant
in the elite Life Guard Jager Regiment
during the 1807 Campaign. He tragically
died at the age of twenty-six (already a
colonel) at the battle of Leipzig in 1813.

25. General Alexsey Sherbatov.

26. Infamous for his Slavophile sentiments and aversion to foreign influences, Alexander Shishkov was one of the leading Russian ideologues of the Napoleonic Wars.

27. General Peter Tolstoy.

28. A scion of an ancient aristocratic family, Sergei Volkonskii was destined for a brilliant military career. At the tender age of eight, he was enlisted in military service but began actual service in 1805 when he became a lieutenant in the Chevalier Guard Regiment. He distinguished himself during the 1806–7 campaign in Poland and served with distinction in the later Napoleonic campaigns. In 1825, however, he was one of the most active members of the failed Decembrist Uprising and was exiled to Siberia, where he spent three decades.

29. The future general of infantry and corps commander Vasilii Timofeyev was a 24-year-old captain when his regiment, the Vyborgskii Musketeers, was sent to Poland. He distinguished himself at Eylau, earning the Order of St. Vladimir. This photo shows his tombstone at the Novodevichii Monastery in Moscow.

30. Marshal Ney at Friedland, 14 June 1807 (by Alexander Averyanov).

31. The Charge of the Russian Life Guard Horse Regiment at Friedland (by Wiktor Mazurowski).

32. A early nineteenth-century French print of the battle of Friedland.

33. The Battle of Friedland (by Ernest Meissonier).

34. Napoleon celebrating his victory at Friedland (by Horace Vernet).

35. A contemporary print showing the raft in the middle of the River Nieman where Napoleon and Emperor Alexander met in June 1807.

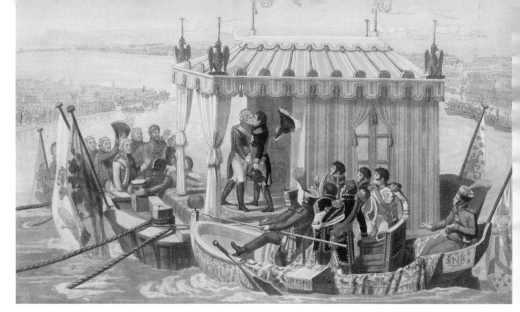

36. Emperor Alexander and Napoleon meet on the River Niemen (contemporary French print after Jean Francois Debret's painting).

37. The Meeting of Three Sovereigns: Napoleon, Alexander and Frederick William at Tilsit (contemporary German print).

reinforced by the Arkhangelogorodskii Musketeer Regiment, between the town and the army, whilst the detachment of Major-General Barclay de Tolly joined Major-General Baggovut's detachment on the left wing.

On the 27th of January [8 February], at five o'clock in the morning, I used the 7th and 4th Divisions, deployed in two columns, to form reserves in the centre of my positions, and charged Lieutenant-General Dokhturov with the command of the same; I placed another reserve, formed by the 14th Division, of Major-General Count Kamenski, on the left flank. The detachment of Major-General Markov filled the gap that was formed in my line after the 7th Division was moved to the reserves.

At break of day, when the enemy advanced through Preussisch-Eylau with his skirmishers and mounted chasseurs, I sent some jager regiments to meet them. During this fighting I observed several large enemy columns between the town and the heights to the right thereof, upon which the enemy had some batteries, which, as well as the columns, menaced my centre. Therefore I ordered my batteries to open fire at the enemy's artillery, as well as at the [French] troops defiling from the town, whereby the enemy columns were forced to halt. The French cavalry, which had attacked our right flank, was thrown back with heavy losses by the fire from the battery of Colonel Count Sievers.

The enemy endeavoured to make himself master of a village situated before our right wing, and seemed to menace our right flank with a large force; but I succeeded in dislodging him very soon from the said village, with the help of the 24th Jager Regiment and skirmishers dispatched from the other regiments. Meanwhile, several fresh columns, comprising large numbers of cavalry and infantry, moved through Preussisch-Eylau and launched an attack on my right wing, while three columns consisting of [the Imperial] Guardsmen assaulted my centre. The former columns were met, on the orders of Lieutenant-General Tuchkov, by Major-General Fock, who advanced with two columns, reinforced by the Rizhskii and Liflyandskii Dragoon Regiments, and upon deploying in line, charged with the bayonet, routed the enemy and killed a large number of them. Thereupon the enemy retreated in the greatest confusion, leaving behind him eight pieces of cannon, which we tried to remove but found impossible because the enemy had established a strong battery in front of the town that swept this area. In the centre, Major-General Zapolski, who, at the command of Lieutenant-General Dokhturov, deployed one of the reserve columns, which were placed behind the centre, and received the enemy with a well-directed fire of musketry, so that the latter was compelled to give way, and, without allowing the enemy time to rally, [Zapolski] charged them with the bayonet and overthrew them, capturing one colour and 130 prisoners.

At the same time, one part of the enemy cavalry, supported by the infantry marching behind it, advanced upon the left of our centre, and had the temerity to pass through our first line but was received with bayonets by our second line and was almost entirely annihilated by our cavalry, and especially the Cossacks. The enemy's infantry, by which this enemy cavalry was supported, was repelled by the Moskovskii Grenadier and Schlussburgskii Musketeer Regiments, which were detached from Lieutenant-General Essen III. The enemy retreated and joined the remnants of the columns that were repulsed by our Major-General Zapolski. This column was soon joined by two strong cavalry columns, and it consequently prepared to renew the attack. Major-General Somov received an order from Lieutenant-General Dokhturov to engage these enemy forces. He advanced with his division, followed by cavalry regiments, and was simultaneously supported by Major-General Zapolski, who launched a new attack on the enemy. Our attacks routed the enemy cavalry and completely destroyed the remaining enemy infantry. On this occasion, Colonel Count O'Rourke of the Pavlogradskii Hussar Regiment charged with three squadrons upon the right flank of the retreating [French] column, and pursued the same until it was sheltered by the enemy's cannon. At the same time, the St. Petersburgskii Dragoon Regiment also inflicted a severe beating on the enemy in the centre and captured one colour. During these attacks against our centre, the enemy was thus twice repelled, routed and forced to flee in disorder, leaving behind twenty pieces of cannon; yet, because these abandoned cannon remained under the protection of strong enemy batteries, we were unable to remove them.

The enemy's intended attack upon our right wing was checked by the skirmishers that Lieutenant-General Baron Sacken dispatched against the advancing enemy columns; these skirmishers became engaged in an intense firefight with the enemy side and both sides fought with equal determination.

General Baggovut, who had occupied the village of Serpallen with a detachment of the rearguard, was also attacked at daybreak. He initially defended himself with his skirmishers, but as the enemy's columns evinced an intention to move round the village, Major-General Kakhovskii, who, on the orders of Lieutenant-General Prince Golitsyn, was deployed with his own Polish Horse Regiment on the left flank [of our position] hastened to take position to the right of [Baggovut's] detachment. Supported by the Malorosiiskii Cuirassier Regiment, he charged at the advancing enemy column, routed it and forced the survivors to flee in the greatest disorder. The above-mentioned regiments then turned right and attacked other enemy columns which were moving towards our centre, supported by cavalry. Despite the enemy's fierce resistance, these columns were also routed and forced to flee; our cavalry killed more than 300 men and captured four officers and sixty-three men.

At the same time, Major-General Count Pahlen ordered the brigade of Major-General Korff to attack several French columns that were marching against Lieutenant-General Baron Sacken. These columns were also routed, and the Ordenskii Cuirassier Regiment captured one colour. On this occasion, Cornet Sacken captured one cannon but was forced to abandon it after sustaining a bayonet injury to the chest. The Izyumskii Hussar and the Kurlandskii Dragoon Regiments also made several successful attacks upon the enemy . . .

After being thus repulsed on all sides and especially by our centre and the right flank, the enemy collected, as well as he could, all his forces, and formed them into very strong columns, which were drawing towards our left wing, with an intention to march round it. General Baggovut, being too weak to withstand such a superiority, found himself obliged to abandon and set fire to the village of Serpallen in order to take a different position. His cavalry, posted before him, attacked the enemy several times, but was obliged to retreat behind our left wing. In the meanwhile, the enemy continued to reinforce himself, and proceeded in his plan to turn our left flank. General Kamenski II, who had already sent some reinforcements to General Baggovut, ordered Major-General Sherbatov, with the Uglitskii and Kostromskoi Musketeer Regiments, to proceed to the left wing to contain the enemy attack while the Ryazanskii regiment was ordered to occupy and defend the village of [Klein-]Sausgarten.

Lieutenant-General Count Ostermann, on seeing superior enemy columns advancing towards him, found it necessary to throw back his left wing, with which General Baggovut closed up soon after, upon whom those strong French columns rapidly advanced, with a considerable artillery before them, with flankers, to turn our left flank. Baggovut took position on the left of the division of Lieutenant-General Count Osterman, which continued to withstand attacks of enemy columns that sent out foot and mounted skirmishers. After prolonged and very brisk fighting between the skirmishers, Count Ostermann, just as the distance allowed for a bayonet charge, attacked with the first battalions of his regiments, whom he reinforced with the second battalions, and then advanced with the remaining reserves. The Count made numerous successful charges, inflicting heavy losses on the enemy, but notwithstanding his redoubled efforts, he was obliged to give ground to superior enemy numbers. By then the enemy were already going round our left wing, and obliged Major-General Count Kamenski to fall back. Therefore, Lieutenant-General Count Osterman retreated together with Lieutenant-General Baron Sacken and took a new position.

In the midst of such powerful attacks, when the superior enemy columns forced us back very vigorously, I ordered my horse artillery to advance. General Kutaisov and Colonel Yermolov brought three companies and established their batteries upon the heights, and fired so briskly upon the enemy that the enemy columns halted in a few moments. Our artillery fire then set fire to the manor at Auklappen and drove the enemy out of there; it also turned back mounted chasseurs and foot skirmishers that had advanced from there and were almost in our rear.

At the same time the enemy briefly captured the village of Kutschitten but were quickly driven out of there by the detachment of Major-General Czaplic, comprising three squadrons of the Pavlogradskii Hussar Regiment, the Moskovskii Dragoon Regiment and some Cossacks. Czaplic attacked the enemy in the village, drove them from it, charged another enemy column and routed it, inflicting heavy losses.

During these events, Lieutenant-General Lestocq, whom I had instructed to march as fast as he could with the corps of Prussians under his command, and the Russian Vyborgskii and Kaluzhskii Musketeer Regiments, arrived on the field of battle and hastened to reinforce our left wing. As soon as he had joined the division of Major-General Kamenski II and the detachment of Major-General Czaplic, Lestocq opened a strong cannonade at the enemy columns and a brisk musket fire against the enemy skirmishers that were scattered in the woods. He also endeavoured to flank the enemy from the left. Such an attack, which was accomplished diligently and prudently, forced the enemy, who continued to strongly resist, to fall back and, ultimately, to flee. Lestocq pursued them for a considerable distance until the fast-approaching nightfall prevented him from continuing the fight. He thus greatly contributed to ensuring our victory over the French army.

Whilst the batteries of our left wing were very briskly cannonading the enemy, the 8th Division of Lieutenant-General Essen III and the detachment of Major-General Markov took up positions on the left flank of the 2nd Division. They kept sending forward their jagers and skirmishers who maintained a brisk fire upon the enemy just as Lestocq kept up his attack on the other side [of the battlefield]. This position was also occupied by the 7th and 14th Divisions, which, upon the injury of Lieutenant-General Dokhturov, transferred to the command of Lieutenant-General Prince Bagration.

Throughout this fighting, the enemy, although he had already occupied the village of Schloditten, did not dare to attack our right wing, which consisted only of the 5th Division, because it was covered by the fire of a strong Prussian battery, which, on the order of Lieutenant-General Tuchkov, Major-General Fock set up in the centre, and by the [skilful] deployment of regiments at the most advantageous locations. At nightfall, I caused the [French] to be driven from the village of Schloditten, where they lost a considerable number of men.

The Cossacks particularly distinguished themselves during the whole of the battle, bravely pursuing the enemy troops, killing them in large numbers and capturing 470 prisoners.

Thus ended this sanguinary battle, which began at three in the afternoon on 26 January [7 February] and ended on the following day at midnight.

Although I have earlier informed Your Imperial Majesty that the enemy losses amounted to 12,000 men, I have now received more reliable reports that, together with the testimonies of the French themselves, reveal that the enemy losses amount to 30,000 killed alone, including six generals, as well as 12,000 wounded, among whom are many generals; we have captured seven officers, 909 soldiers and twelve colours. Our loss consists of 12,000 killed and 7,900 wounded.

I should think myself wanting in my first duty, if I did not place at the feet of Your Imperial Majesty, the homage due to the bravery of your troops. In covering themselves with an immortal glory, they give a memorable example to the world of what a people genuinely devoted to its Sovereign and Fatherland can accomplish. Despite his vain attempts, the enemy met certain death everywhere. The field of battle was covered with his corpses. In vain did the leader of the French [Napoleon] try, ignoring dangers, to animate his soldiers: nothing could resist the valour and intrepidity of the infuriated Russians. Only nightfall stopped their merciless arms. The French, who have become accustomed to victories, acknowledge that they have never before suffered such a severe defeat and nor have they ever endured such an utter humiliation.

After such a victorious battle I pondered which of the two options I ought to take: to remain on the field of battle or to [retreat to] defend Königsberg, whose loss I was particularly concerned about because the enemy, having gathered his forces, could have [easily] directed his efforts to capture it and deprive me of means of supplying provisions and ammunition to my army, which was already experiencing severe shortages. Thus, I chose the latter option and retreated to Königsberg. I was in hope, by thus falling back, to induce the enemy to follow me into open terrain and to give him another battle to crush his remaining forces. [From the Russian text in *Zhurnal voennykh deistvii imperatorskoi Rossiiskoi armii . . .*]

Pavel Grabbe

By February 1807, Grabbe, serving in the artillery company of Fedor Schulman, had already fought at Golymin where he barely escaped being captured. At Eylau, he witnessed the destruction of Marshal Pierre Augereau's corps.

The battle of Preussisch-Eylau was the first warning of Providence to Napoleon . . . I was then an artillery officer commanding two cannon attached to the Vladimirskii Regiment in Dokhturov's corps, almost in the centre of our positions. So it was we who faced one of the columns of Marshal Augereau, whose corps was destroyed in the carnage . . . . A strong blizzard blinded us with snow. Suddenly everything calmed down and directly in front of my cannon, no more than thirty paces away, we saw a column of Frenchmen, who were also startled by the proximity of our line. My cannon were loaded with grape-shot since I had no roundshot and only five rounds of grape shot per gun. The grape-shot had a devastating effect at such close range. The column veered right and charged the second battalion of the Vladimirskii Regiment; I stood in the interval between the 2nd and 1st Battalion. Our men received the enemy with bayonets but the [French] broke through in the middle. I was still firing the last remaining grape-shot rounds when the artillerymen behind me shouted 'Frenchmen' and made me look around. Several Frenchmen stormed into the battery from behind but they were soon followed by our men and were all stabbed with bayonets; I was able to save only a few of them from the swords of my men. Our horses were wounded and all of the ammunition used. The bayonet melee ended up with the complete destruction of this enemy column. Mounds of corpses marked the sight of the carnage.

[After this fighting] I moved [my guns] behind the [front] line, not knowing what I should do next since I lacked ammunition and had wounded horses. A large part of our artillery, especially the heavy guns, was forced to leave its positions and move to the Königsberg road for the very same reasons. To understand how it happened that our artillery suffered from the lack of ammunition in the first half of the battle, one must realise that the contemporary mobile [artillery] parks were completely inadequate. Thus, after the battles of Pultusk and Golymin, the [artillery] caissons were not replenished. Yet I did not want to follow the retreating batteries. Upon spotting [General] Rezvyi, the commander of artillery, I stopped him and asked for more ammunition. Instead, he ordered me to join the retreating batteries and pointed towards the road. But I dragged my feet, concerned what the gallant soldiers of the Vladimirskii Regiment would think. Just then I saw the Pskovskii Regiment moving to replace [the Vladimirskii Regiment] in the front line. I knew that [my comrade Artillery Captain Fedor] Anders was with this regiment and went to see him. Meeting him was always a joyous occasion for me. Upon hearing my request to share his ammunition with me, Anders pointed to a place behind the front [line] where I could find ammunition scattered on the ground and told me that I should get as much as I could since he also replenished his ammunition there. I rushed to that place and indeed found ammunition scattered all around in such quantities that I quickly filled all of my caissons and ammunition chests. I still do not know whom I should thank for this gift. Returning to my regiment I found it under a terrifying fire from the entire line of [French] batteries that concentrated against our left centre, probably to contain consequences of the destruction of Augereau's corps. [From the Russian text in P. Grabbe, *Iz Pamiatnykh zapisok* . . .]

Yakov Otroshenko

Staff Captain Otroshenko commanded a company in the 7th Jager Regiment.

On 27 January [8 February], the 7th Jager Regiment took up position on the right wing of our battle line at Preussisch-Eylau. We spread skirmishers in front of our line and immediately entered the fighting; we advanced towards the town but the French drove us back. We then received reinforcements and pushed the enemy back to the town, but were forced to retreat once more, the fighting continuing in this fashion until ten o'clock in the morning. At that time a heavy snowfall commenced. Suddenly I heard shouts to the left of me – the French columns, under cover of the falling snow, attempted to strike our right wing. But our regiments held the line and charged at these columns with the bayonet, annihilating them. I was later told that at this time the enemy cuirassiers had penetrated our lines but the survivors barely managed to return.

Meanwhile we have lost many men, even though there were over 400 men present in the morning. Now I had just two soldiers with me and one of them was already wounded. I could see no officers or non-commissioned officers around me and decided to retreat with these two jagers. Behind us we found a jager regiment which I warned that there were no longer any troops from my regiment in front of it. Just then a bullet wounded my last remaining healthy jager.

Having passed behind our lines I found only one wounded major from our regiment and no one else. I still hoped to find my men among the people who were carrying the wounded to the bivouacs. Indeed I soon found about thirty men, whom I ordered to refill their cartridge boxes and, after giving them a cup of vodka each, I led them back into the fighting. Along the way I invited a captain who had reported sick to join us. He agreed and we advanced together but just as we came under the enemy artillery fire, he suddenly developed a stomach ache so I bade farewell to him and moved forward with my jagers. At the battle line I joined some regiments who were fighting there and remained in action until the nightfall. In the evening the French pushed us hard but the Prussian cavalry, which arrived from the right, forced the enemy to halt his attacks. During the night a general retreat commenced on the road to Königsberg. I retreated along with everyone else. The area where we spent the night was completely devastated and a [nearby] barn was set on fire. I only had five jagers with me.

After marching for about five verstas [5km], I found our sick captain, accompanied by two officers and ten soldiers. They informed me that our battalion commander, Lieutenant-Colonel Drenyakin, had lost his right hand early in the morning when a cannonball sheared it off as he was standing near the brick barns that were behind our line. There was no further news about [our regiment]. During the battle the 7th Jager

Regiment was shredded [razorvan] by the French columns attacking our positions and was consequently scattered all along our battle line. By dawn [of 9 February] there had gathered about fifteen officers and the remaining healthy soldiers, totalling about 200 men. There were no staff officers and the command devolved to our sick captain, who was the most senior in rank. Thus we had become orphans, without any leaders. [From the Russian text in Y. Otroshenko, *Zapiski* . . .]

Otto Löwenstern

Having returned to London on 25 February, George Jackson was keen to hear any news about events in Poland since 'rumours of a battle with victory on the side of the allied Russian and Prussian armies, have been rife here for some days'. Unfortunately no trustworthy accounts had arrived as of yet. Jackson had to wait another week before a letter from his Russian friend, Otto Löwenstern, arrived, providing fascinating details on the bloody battle at Eylau.

March 5. A letter from my Russian friend, giving me the account of the battle fought on 8 February at Preus. Eylau, has come to hand today:

The day following the battle of Pultusk, the French took a Russian courier prisoner, who was on his way to our *corps d'armée* with an order from Kamenski to retire as far as Grodno. Intelligence of this being brought to Bonaparte, he determined not to pursue us but to take up his winter quarters between Elbing and Warsaw. Bernadotte and Ney were detached in order to station themselves in that direction, but Ney, having encountered and repulsed Lestocq at Soldau, advanced towards Heilsberg, informing Bonaparte of it, and asking for reinforcements to enable him vigorously to follow up offensive operations. Ney's letter, however, never reached Bonaparte, the officer who was the bearer of it having fallen ill on his journey, while Ney, unaware of this *contre-temps*, was waiting in vain for the arrival of the expected reinforcements.

Meanwhile, Kamenski was replaced in command of our army by Bennigsen, who was ordered to advance *coûte que coûte*. This he did, eluding observation by passing through the wooded country near Rastenberg; and Bonaparte, who believed our troops to be at Grodno, was greatly surprised when information reached him that they were closely pressing Ney and Bernadotte. Immediately he resolved to advance with his whole army to crush these Russian corps, not suspecting that the whole of the Russian army was also advancing; and nothing could exceed his astonishment when he found himself in front of it at Allenstein. Up to that moment the Russians had been everywhere successful.

These details were given by Bertrand, of whom I shall presently speak further. At Mohrungen, the Russians surprised the *equipages* of Bernadotte, and his *caisse*, containing half a million *d'écus*. His secretary barely made good his escape. At Liebstadt they took four hundred prisoners, and on the 3rd Bennigsen and his army occupied Mohrungen, Liebstadt, Guttstadt and Allenstein, while Bonaparte concentrated all his troops in the direction of Guttstadt, threatening Bennigsen's left, which was almost turned.

Being already weakened by having given the division of Sedmoratzki to Essen, and as a disastrous engagement would have deprived him of the opportunity of retreating, Bennigsen wisely determined then to withdraw his troops. His rearguard, under the brave Bagration, continually attacked but always victorious, fought for five successive days. The retreat was made in the direction of Königsberg; but when Bennigsen reached Preus. Eylau he resolved to make a stand there, and await the arrival of the enemy. He took up an excellent position behind the town, and fortified it with three hundred pieces of cannon. On the 7th his army was already ranged and ready for battle, and the town of Eylau was taken and re-taken three times that day.

On the 8th of February – an ever-memorable day – there began at daybreak the most bloody battle that has, perhaps, ever been fought. Our army, placed on a hill with a ravine before it, occupied an extremely advantageous position. Our artillery worked with good effect, making constant use of the *mitraille* [canister], which the French could not do, owing to the lowness of the ground they held.

Throughout the morning, the French attacked our centre with the bayonet, but were constantly repulsed, with immense loss. At about 2 p.m., they endeavoured to break through our left centre. They advanced in two columns, concealed from our troops by driving snow; but chance led them to the strongest part of our line, where they were exposed to a cross-fire of sixty pieces of cannon, which nearly exterminated the two columns – composed of Bonaparte's guards – the bayonet completing the work. The same fate awaited a *corps d'élite* of *grenadiers à cheval* who had passed behind our infantry, through a space in our right wing. They were surrounded, and but sixteen of the corps escaped.

Bonaparte, in despair at his want of success, detached a part of his army for the purpose of turning our left wing, and succeeded in placing a few cannon on the heights, which disquieted our troops exceedingly. An unfavourable change in the fortunes of the day seemed imminent, when Lestocq arrived with his corps – this was at about five o'clock. Lestocq had encountered a detachment of Bernadotte's division on his march, and had had to fight it; for at the commencement of the battle he was at a considerable distance from Eylau, and, therefore, had been unable to take up the position assigned to him until the very moment that it was attacked by the French. But he repulsed them, and captured their cannon.

Night put an end to this sanguinary combat, and Bennigsen, seeing that his army was worn out with fatigue, that he was destitute of ammunition, and that the strength of the enemy was unknown to him, considered it prudent to retreat. On the 9th, he fell back two miles, and on the 10th took up his position, with the whole of his army, before the walls of Königsberg, his right wing supported by the citadel. Bonaparte, on the night of the engagement, also retired to a distance of two or three miles from the battlefield, while Lestocq remained to succour the wounded; but as soon as he quitted Eylau, Bonaparte returned. The French prisoners, taken after the battle, say he was much surprised that the Russians did not pursue.

This battle may be said to be a repetition of what took place at Pultusk, but on a much larger scale, as our loss in killed and wounded amounted to eighteen thousand men, of whom nine hundred were officers. We took from the French sixteen eagles, twenty-two pieces of cannon and one thousand four hundred prisoners, nearly all of whom were taken by the Cossacks, during the action.

If reinforcements had reached us, it is probable that the whole of Bonaparte's army would have been destroyed; but the Russian troops, after a bivouac of eighteen nights, marching and fighting incessantly, were utterly exhausted, and could with difficulty move, or drag their wearied limbs from the scene of slaughter. The French were in no better condition.

It is calculated from the position of the two armies that the French could not have lost less than thirty thousand men, an incredible number, if the nature of the battle – which was one of continual assault and repulse, without any attempt to manoeuvre – did not account for it.

You will find that the letters of Hutchinson and Wilson testify fully to the bravery of our troops. They were both with Bennigsen throughout the action. Wilson's cheek was grazed, and his horse was wounded in two places by the bursting of a shell. Eight of our generals were wounded, all of them slightly, except Barclay de Tolly whose arm was fractured by a ball. All that I tell you is derived from official sources.

We have duly celebrated this victory, for it is the most fortunate event that could have happened to us. The result, especially, has proved how decisive a battle it was. For, three days later, Bonaparte sent General Bertrand to Memel to negotiate with the king, and to use every means to detach him from our side. But he has not succeeded, though his proposals were extremely advantageous to Prussia, and very different from those of the armistice at Osterode. Bonaparte offered to restore to the king all his dominions, as possessed by him before the war, without restricting him in any way as to the alliances he might wish to conclude, provided there was no question of either Russia or England in this treaty. But who could put any faith in the promises of this *grand coquin*!

The king himself is now more decided than are his ministers not to make a separate peace. You will be pleased to learn that Baron Hardenberg has, to a certain extent, lately recovered his influence, and that he and Rüchel had very little difficulty in getting Bertrand sent back on the same day that he arrived. As soon as he rejoined Bonaparte the French army began its retreat, harassed continually by our Cossacks and light troops, and so precipitate was it that they did not carry off their wounded, and they left part of their baggage and heavy artillery behind them also. The utter failure of provisions completed the *découragement* of the French army. Ours, on the contrary, with Königsberg in its rear, was abundantly supplied.

While we were negotiating, several skirmishes took place with serious consequences for the French. Bagration killed or took prisoner nearly three thousand men, and in an engagement between the French cavalry and our

Cossacks, the former lost three whole regiments, four hundred men of which were taken prisoners.

During the week that our army has been at Königsberg it has been reinforced by twenty-six thousand men, of whom five thousand are Cossacks. These troops distinguish themselves greatly on all occasions, and are the admiration of everyone. Wilson says of them, 'They are all heroes.' We expect seven thousand more in three days, and in a short time considerable reinforcements of infantry will arrive.

Bonaparte's proposals prove clearly that he is greatly embarrassed just now, and I am glad to tell you that there is every appearance of a determination to profit by it, and not to let him escape as he did at Lauban and Austerlitz. It is supposed that he is now at Thorn, as he retreated in that direction.

Deserters have been numerous; they make their way chiefly to Galicia. For the most part, they are old soldiers, who wish to enjoy there the booty they have taken; there are no less, it is computed, than twelve thousand of them in Galicia. Our troops engage very readily in this war, as they find considerable sums of money on the French prisoners.

We have received today very satisfactory news from St. Petersburg. All the Imperial Guard [regiments] . . . are to begin their march immediately. It is expected that the Emperor will come to Riga, and probably to this place. He has just sent the Order of St. Andrew to Bennigsen, and granted him a pension of twelve thousand roubles.

[English text in George Jackson, *Diaries and Letters* . . .]

Fabian von der Osten-Sacken

26th [January, 7 February 1807]. We again marched at night and, by the morning, the army reached Preussisch-Eylau. The enemy was at our heels. Bennigsen made a mistake of not occupying the town with sufficient forces. The enemy immediately rushed into the town but was later driven out. Yet, Somov soon got scared, retreated and the enemy recaptured the town.

27 [January, 8 February] Sunday. The battle of Preussisch-Eylau. Due to Bennigsen's negligence, we did not occupy the town [of Eylau] and failed to reinforce the hill on our left flank though it dominated the entire position. We remained in our position from 7 in the morning to three o'clock in the afternoon. Our artillery, having exhausted its ammunition, had to withdraw. Bennigsen could not be found anywhere on the battlefield. At 3:00 p.m. the left flank [was forced] to change its position [by the French advance]. The army remained on the battlefield until night and, as expected, it then retreated.

5th [12 February]. I visited hospitals, which are in the most miserable condition. We have over 8,000 wounded, many of whom still have not been treated. Some 100 [wounded] are dying every day.

6th [18 February]. Prince Bagration, commanding our advance guard, left for St. Petersburg. He despises the way of life many pursue here – everyone is involved in intrigue of some kind. [From the Russian text in F. Sacken, *Iz zapisok feldmarshala Sackena . . .*]

Eduard von Löwenstern

After taking part in the battle at Mohrungen and the subsequent retreat, the cold and hungry Löwenstern finally approached the town of Eylau.

Toward evening, we halted before the little town of Preussisch-Eylau. [My brother] Theodor was hit by gunshot in the back; it passed through his pelisse and stopped under the skin. The enemy forced us into the town. Our infantry held until late in the night and resisted them every step of the way in the streets of that unhappy town. It nevertheless fell into enemy hands, and we set up a bivouac on the other side.

The following dawn had barely broken when the thunder of cannon awakened all of us. A heavy fall of snow quickly covered both battle-ready armies. Soon small-arms fire was boiling like water in a kettle and was often interspersed with the crack of heavy ordnance and the cheers of the attacking cavalry. Our brave hussars attacked several times and even dared to stand up against the feared Grenadiers à Cheval. In the middle of the turmoil of the battle, Colonel Ushakov ordered me to take several wounded officers and Captain of Cavalry Shishkin to Königsberg.* I found the necessary sleds and horses in the next village, packed my wounded in them and hurried to Königsberg. The whole way there was filled with badly and lightly wounded; many of whom for the lack of carts had to be left lying there in their misery. Poltroons and marauders deserting the battle were plundering the villages; and only with difficulty could I find a place for my casualties in a noble's desolate estate. After completing my business of bringing the wounded to the infirmary and eating something nourishing at the head commissioners of the infirmary, I mounted my neighing grey again and rode out of the city the same evening. But before leaving Königsberg, I bought a large quantity of gingerbread and sweets at the nearest confectioner's shop and rode, seemingly strengthened, whistling my little song, out of the town gate.

I could still hear the thunder of cannon in the area of Preussisch-Eylau and hurried toward it. To give my horse some rest, I spent the night in a plundered village filled with men from the Polish Light Horse Regiment. Those fellows bedded down in the warm peasant parlour and I retired to a barn. The vermin in the hay left me no peace. The itching all over my body

---

* The former Königsberg, now Kaliningrad, is some 43km from Eylau (now Bagrationovsk).

was made even more unbearable because of the warmth. I lay down in the snow and fell asleep. The Polish Horse [Regiment] broke into the barn in the night and stole my saddlebags and everything I had in them. In the morning, I discovered the theft, but there was nothing left for me to do but to wear what I had on, a ragged shirt, half-rotted breeches and boots and not even a red *heller*★ of wealth. I cried like a child but what had happened had happened; good or bad, I had to make the best of my miserable fate; moaning and lamenting would not help any, since no one was looking after me. Most of all I regretted losing the sweets and gingerbread that I wanted to treat Theodor with.

Only late in the evening, after searching for a long time, was I able to find the Regiment. Everyone was still talking about the battle we had survived near Preussisch-Eylau, each one boasting of deeds he had done or not done. For my part, I kept silent and was nevertheless no less vain. They praised me for my proven bravery in all of the events, and I was allowed to believe in the truthfulness of the praise. [From the German text in Eduard von Löwenstern, *Mit Graf Pahlens Reiterei gegen Napoleon . . .*]

Mikhail Petrov

The day after the battle of Pultusk, our army retreated to Ostrolenka and, after 17 [29] December, hastened to anticipate the enemy movement to Königsberg, proceeding by forced marshes through Willenberg, Ortelsburg, Bischofsburg, Seeburg, Jankowo and Landsberg towards Preussisch-Eylau, where on 26 January [7 February] Bennigsen's army took up positions blocking the French from our supply depots that were set up in Königsberg, Pillau and Memel. That same day, in the afternoon, the enemy advanced through the woods, from the direction of Landsberg, in pursuit of the Russian rearguard commanded by Prince Bagration and attacked Bennigsen with large forces. The purpose of this enemy attack was to reconnoitre our entire position and capture the town of Eylau which was defended by the detachment of Major-General Barclay de Tolly. Much French blood was shed on the streets of this town by the already distinguished General Barclay. Three times the French rushed into the town and each time layers of their corpses, covered in snow that fell heavily that day, built up in front of the menacing lines of the Russian infantry that engaged the enemy with skilfully directed crossfire and bayonet charges that valiantly repelled each enemy attack. But while repelling the last enemy attack and pursuing the enemy beyond the city, General Barclay de Tolly, who was notable for so

---

★ A small German coin (oftentimes spelled as häller) produced in red, white and black versions. Minted since the thirteenth century, the coin became a symbol of low worth.

many qualities, collapsed from the loss of blood due to his serious injury. He was replaced by Major-General Somov, who was next in seniority but, unlike Barclay, could not defend or hold on to this most crucial point in our position. Thus, around two o'clock in the morning, the town was lost to the enemy due to disorders allowed by our regimental commanders.

By dawn on 27 January [8 February] our commander-in-chief had changed his dispositions in the centre in response to the French capture of Eylau. As the sun rose that morning, the French troops, deployed in thick columns, attacked . . . our forward outposts and then assaulted the entire battle line in the centre and the right flank of the Russian army that was deployed in three lines in zigzag formation [zigzagami]. But the heavy snow that began to fall soon thereafter had concealed all our positions and in this twilight Augereau's corps deviated from the path that Napoleon had given it and, as it is now well known, veered to the left and wandered straight into the corner of our three-line deep zigzag position, coming out of the snowy shroud directly in front of our main forty-gun battery that erupted with grapeshot fire. The French tried to fall back but it was too late, since our regiments from Osterman's and other divisions flanked the two forward battalions of each regiment, surrounded them and began to destroy them, applying the good old Russian bayonet! We were reinforced by considerable forces of infantry and cavalry and horrifying piles of enemy corpses soon filled up the valley in front of the town. Together with my company, I was also involved in enacting the vengeance of the hardened heart amidst the horrors of war never before seen amidst the snowdrifts of the northern realms but my martial fury soon subsided and was replaced by a heartfelt sorrow when our enraged soldiers, having crushed and destroyed everything in front of them, began to tear apart with bayonets the corpses of the fallen enemy seeking the still-living Frenchmen underneath them. Oh Lord, I have witnessed that, but, alas, 'Hear them not, thou avenger in heaven! How can I avert it?'*

In the evening General Lestocq's Prussian corps arrived to our succour from the direction of Bronsberg and the French were driven back in the direction of Osterode, covered with thick woods. Our regiment, as all others, suffered heavy casualties in this battle: our earnest and fearless chef was shot in his right leg, above the calf; regimental commander Lieutenant-Colonel Tankachev was shot dead; all battalion commanders were wounded and only six officers out of 43 attended 370 rank-and-file that survived out of the almost full-strength three-battalion regiment that was now under the command of Captain Tikhonov I. In my company, I only had forty-seven men surviving. I was wounded in the right cheek by a bullet while my brother – just nineteen – was injured in the head.

---

* A quote from Friedrich Schiller's famous *The Robbers*.

During the night after the battle, many seriously and lightly wounded officers gathered around bonfires that were set up some five verstas behind the battle line, in the village occupied by the army and corps headquarters. I found my brother, [Staff Captain] Shenshin and other officers from our regiment lying with bandaged wounds on the straw scattered around a bonfire and joined their company. Looking back at the terrible whirlwind of bloodshed, I told my comrades, 'I do not think one can envision any worse massacre between the offspring of Adam than the one that occurred today.' Staff Captain Shenshin, who was lying next to me, raised his head and leaning on his good hand, he said, 'If anyone had tried to surpass today's butchery, Satan himself would never allow him for he had exhausted all of his devilish skills today, and what a job he did!' 'That's truc,' added Staff Captain Scheffler, 'today's battle is the greatest undertaking of the infernal academy and we would not lie if we say that the imps themselves did not dare to stay in between the fighting columns but preferred to admire the sight from the distant hills and applaud the [murderous] play that they had prepared for us to perform. We are lucky that winter days are short, for they would have added another two-act play for us to perform.' [From the Russian text in M. Petrov, *Rasskazy . . .*]

Alexsey Yermolov

It was 27 January [8 February] and the battle of Preussisch-Eylau was one of the bloodiest battles in recent times. Details of this battle can be read in various histories. I will briefly describe the advantages and disadvantages of our deployment. The main flaw was that our entire left flank faced heights on which the enemy had concentrated their artillery. The proximity of the forest to our rear further inhibited us. Preussisch-Eylau would protect the enemy if he chose to approach our centre and we now had to defend it with a large battery and keep these guns constantly in position. The right flank was completely to our advantage because a vast marshy plain in front of our positions did not favour large actions there and the French pushed out only a few skirmishers in this direction. It is incredible that our quartermaster-general was unaware of these swamps and committed 12,000 men here without purpose. These troops were limited to futile exchange of fire with distant enemy batteries while we were in dire need of forces at other places. I was deployed here with my two horse artillery companies and fired without any purpose until the afternoon.

The French made several futile attacks against our centre and suffered from sixty guns that were concentrated here. Their attack on our left was more successful. Neither could General Baron Sacken's reasonable orders, nor the intrepid Major-General Count Osterman-Tolstoy's resistance halt the French. The left flank moved back and was virtually at right-angles to the rest of army. At around 11:00 a.m., dense snowfall obscured everything and action was delayed for 15 minutes. Just then, two squadrons of French guard cuirassiers lost their way and found themselves between our infantry and cavalry; only a few of them managed to escape.* The resumption of light revealed a column of French infantry less than 100 paces away from our 7th Division. The French stopped in bewilderment at the sudden appearance of our regiments. With a loud cheer, the Vladimirskii Musketeers attacked and left nobody alive in the French column to mourn the death of their comrades.†

Our troops met variable success but held their ground everywhere except on the left flank. Between the centre and left, seven cavalry regiments made a rapid attack and overwhelmed everything that opposed them; the enemy infantry abandoned its muskets and fled to the forest; our cavalry almost captured an enemy battery but failed in the ensuing confusion. It was shameful that it fled from inferior enemy cavalry that could have been halted by the Alexandriiskii Hussars alone.‡

Soon after the battle began, a distant cannonade was heard on our right flank. We learned that Marshal Ney was pursuing the Prussians of General Lestocq, who was ordered to join our army as soon as possible but failed to accomplish it.§ When the enemy resumed their attacks around 2:00 p.m.,

---

* This is how Yermolov describes Murat's famous cavalry charge, when, at around 11:40 a.m., eighty French squadrons advanced in one of the greatest cavalry charges in history. Davidov recalled, 'The field was engulfed in a roar and the snow, ploughed over by some 12,000 riders lifted and swirled from under them like a storm. Brilliant Murat followed by a large cavalry mass, was ablaze ahead of the onslaught with a naked sabre and flew directly into the thick of the fight. Musket and cannon fire and levelled bayonets were unable to stem the deadly tide.' The French overwhelmed the Russian cavalry, broke through the infantry line and then charged back again through the Russian positions.
† At around 10:00 a.m., Napoleon ordered Marshal Augereau to take his 9,000 men against the Russian left. A blinding snowstorm and dark clouds of artillery smoke obscured the view of the marching Frenchmen. So, the French divisions strayed from their path and went straight towards the massed Russian batteries in the centre. Over sixty Russian guns suddenly opened fire with canister at point-blank range.
‡ Yermolov describes the Russian counter-attack following the destruction of Augereau's corps, when some Russian units advanced as far as the cemetery at Eylau and threatened Napoleon's command post. However, Napoleon's personal guard was sufficient to drive the Russians back.
§ Yermolov is unfair in his criticism of Lestocq. The Prussian general succeeded in eluding Marshal Ney's superior corps and fought a series of delaying actions to prevent the French from reaching the battlefield. The arrival of fresh Prussian forces (5,583 men with two horse artillery batteries) turned the tide on the Russian left flank.

the commander-in-chief sent a dispatch requesting Lestocq to join us as soon as possible. Meanwhile, it was necessary to contain the enemy success on our left. The 8th Division was recalled to the centre; our reserves were fully committed so I was ordered to move my two horse artillery companies. Lieutenant-General Count Tolstoy simply pointed to the left and I followed this direction. I did not know what my objectives were, nor under whose command I would operate. Taking another horse artillery company, I arrived at the vast plain on the extreme left flank, where the remnants of our forces were barely holding their ground against a superior enemy who had captured the nearby heights as well as a village close to the rear of our troops. I opened fire and set this village on fire, driving out the enemy infantry that harassed my guns. Then, I directed my fire against the enemy batteries and held my ground for two hours.*

It was then that General Lestocq's corps began to arrive, with our Kaluzhskii and Vyborgskii Regiments leading its column against the enemy flank. The enemy fire, directed against me, became infrequent and I observed large numbers of enemy guns being diverted against Lestocq. I moved my battery every time it was obscured by smoke and moved all the horses, including my own, and equipment to the rear, declaring to my troops that retreat would be unacceptable. I directed all my efforts on the road at the bottom of the hill by which the enemy was trying to move its infantry as it was impossible to move through the deep snow on either side. I caused heavy casualties with the canister fire of my thirty guns. In short, the enemy failed to pass and it was late to look for a different path since Lestocq, encountering inferior enemy forces, routed them, falling on the heights and batteries which the enemy abandoned. Gloomy night descended on the battlefield. The commander-in-chief, wanting to see Lestocq's actions, arrived on the left flank and was surprised to see my horses and equipment but not a single gun. Hearing my explanation, he was very pleased by my action.

Marshal Ney's corps pursued Lestocq's troops along the road to Königsberg, passing behind our rear and occupying a village with a strong detachment. Prince Dolgoruky was ordered to attack them with the Tavrida Grenadiers. When, after two failed attacks, Dolgoruky persisted, the enemy withdrew unnoticed, probably because of the general retreat of the French. [From the Russian text in A. Yermolov, *Zapiski* . . .]

---

* General Alexander Kutaisov is usually credited for bringing these artillery companies to the left flank but Yermolov was first to arrive with thirty-six guns. Kutaisov followed him with twelve more. However, after the battle Kutaisov received the prestigious Order of St. George (3rd class) for his actions; the fact that he was a cousin of the chief of the Russian artillery probably played a role in the receipt of this award.

Vasilii Timofeyev

The future general of infantry and corps commander Vasilii Timofeyev was a 24-year-old captain when his regiment, the Vyborgskii Musketeers, was sent to Poland. At Eylau, he distinguished himself leading a squad of skirmishers that surprised and defeated French troops near the village of Kutschitten, garnering him the Order of St. Vladimir (4th class). After Eylau, Timofeyev transferred to Count Arakcheyev's Grenadier Regiment and spent two years training new recruits. His success in this position was recognised with promotion to lieutenant-colonel and the command of a battalion in the newly established Life Guard Litovskii Regiment. Leading this battalion, Timofeyev took part in the Patriotic War of 1812 and distinguished himself at Borodino, where he demonstrated the utmost gallantry fighting the French cuirassiers but was seriously wounded in action. His exploits earned him the rank of colonel and the Order of St. George (4th class). He spent over a year convalescing and returned to the army at the end of the Napoleonic Wars, when he was given command of the Guard Reserve Division in Warsaw.

In 1807, following the battle of Pultusk, the Vyborgskii Infantry Regiment, where I served as a captain, was attached to the Prussian forces under General Lestocq for the duration of the entire war. When this corps arrived to the left flank of our army located at Preussisch-Eylau on 27 January [8 February], Lestocq initially dispatched only the Vyborgskii Regiment to fight in the battle. The regiment deployed in front of Kutschitten which was occupied by the French. Our regimental commander Colonel Piller, present with the regiment, asked for volunteers [okhotniki] and about 1,000 rank-and-file stepped forward, but not a single officer. As this was taking place in front of the Prussian forces, I found it rather embarrassing to let only rank-and-file, without any officers, volunteer for this service. So even though I was a company commander, I stepped forward and my entire company followed me. As we approached the village of Kutschitten, the French, hiding behind the fence covered with snow, opened musket fire at us. Noticing that our return fire could not harm the enemy who was behind the fence and snow, I strictly prohibited firing and advanced with the bayonet against them. Faced by our fortitude, the French, already cut off, fell into disorder, dropped their muskets and appealed for mercy. I cannot say how many of them were there and I certainly did not have time to determine it because a French infantry column appeared to the left of the village's centre.

Our volunteers were surprised by this early success but I exploited it and, pointing to the enemy column that threatened us, I led the men in another bayonet charge, which routed the enemy and forced him to flee towards the street that was crossing the village in the direction of the enemy position. To further exploit this success, I led my men in pursuit of the enemy column, which, moving in mass, could not outrun us. In the middle of the street, the column split up to reveal four cannon, deployed en échiquier order, with the two guns in front firing canister at us. But I was not stopped by this salvo and instead charged forward. Three Russian cannon and one French licorne or howitzer, whose crews departed with the fleeing column, were captured on the spot. Although losing twelve men in this attack, I decided not to waste a minute and continued my pursuit of the French, who were no more than 50 or 60 paces away from us by the end of the village. A large enemy column advanced towards the village to support the retreating column but I could not see it yet because the street was full of fleeing Frenchmen. Had I seen it in time, I certainly would not have dared to pursue any further, especially since our regiment could not be seen behind us and could not have arrived in time to rescue us because from the very beginning of the attack my volunteers advanced by running, which the circumstances required; the success which I gained could not have been achieved otherwise. So I desired to catch up with the fleeing enemy column and force it to drop its weapons as did their skirmishers earlier in the fight. But this column, as it fled from our bayonets in great fright and disorder, encountered the rescue column some 60 paces from the village, smashed into it and spread disorder in its leading ranks. But the rear platoons [vzvody] already began to deploy to the right and left and two of them had already opened fire on us.

This was the moment when I could have perished. The French had about 1,000 men in both columns while I had up to then 250 volunteers, and, frankly, I doubt I had even that many. The enemy, whose rear platoons were not disordered and began to deploy, could have rallied at any moment and I would have been annihilated at once. This was the most decisive and critical moment.

To prevent the enemy from seeing the numerical inferiority of our troops as they were running out [of the village] and to exploit the enemy's disorder and panic, I ordered the volunteers to shout 'hurrah' and rushed with them directly against the French, spreading indescribable fear and confusion amongst them. The enemy dropped their weapons, begging for mercy. I prohibited bayoneting the enemy and instructed my men to take weapons from those holding them and to break their butts. The French in the rear platoons ran back across the field. Because we had fewer troops than the enemy, I could not prevent them from escaping. Fortunately, a Cossack officer reached us at that moment and twenty or thirty Cossacks who accompanied him, rushed to plunder the French. I threatened the officer to have his Cossacks beaten with the butts of our muskets if he did not put an end to it and follow my order which required him to split his command into two groups and charge the retreating French from the flanks with the hope that they would be forced to retreat to their column. The Cossack officer, understanding the importance and necessity of my intention, skilfully accomplished it and drove almost all the fleeing Frenchmen back to the column.* Some time later our regiment caught up with us. All of its officers came to see me and expressed their sentiments in such expressions that a humble man like me cannot describe.

The rank-and-file of our regiment became mixed with the French, taking away their watches, money and other possessions; during this disorder, two enemy jager battalions appeared at the edge of the woods, about half of a versta away from us, deployed with their front turned to us and rapidly advanced towards our mob. We were not deployed in any manner whatsoever. The enemy battalions could have exploited our disarray and the two columns that had already surrendered to us would have only helped them in this. To prevent this adversity, I exploited the influence I wielded over my soldiers.

Running into the field, I addressed the regiment with the following words: 'Volunteers [okhotniki]! These are ours (I said pointing towards the captured Frenchmen) and those (I pointed toward the advancing enemy battalion) are about to become ours too. Follow me, advance!' I had to take measures to contain the regiment's eagerness since almost all the lower ranks rushed after me. I firmly insisted that only those who had volunteered earlier should follow me but it was in vain and the number of soldiers [willing to follow me] was much greater; this time two officers, Lieutenant Nekrasov and Sub-lieutenant Seleznev, stepped forward as well. After hastily deploying the volunteers into a line and prohibiting them from firing, I led them into a bayonet attack against the enemy. In front of the entire regiment, my men routed the French and drove them back into the woods, pursuing them to the grove that preceded the meadow between the grove and the main forest. There, we had to stop upon observing a French cavalry column deployed on the edge of the woods and expecting to charge us in the flank as soon as we entered the field. The Prussian cavalrymen promptly attacked this cavalry column and forced it to fall back. Meanwhile, our regiment, lacking two grenadier battalions, reached the grove where my volunteers were located, the Prussian infantry on its right and left wings while I commanded the volunteers in the front.

The forest in front of us was strongly defended by French batteries and infantry columns and our troops, as they approached to close range of the enemy, initially engaged them with battalion fire. After Prussian artillery arrived and fired several very successful rounds, the Vyborgskii Regiment

---

* Author's comment: Aside from these prisoners, the [Prussian] corps captured no more prisoners during the rest of the battle, or, to be precise, if captured, only in very few numbers since the Prussians entered the battle in the evening when they engaged in the vast forest where the French retreated without waiting for our bayonet attack. I do not know where the Prussian cavalry operated but, as I understand, it only engaged the French cavalry column in the same vast forest but remained idle by the end of the battle. It was said that they picked up a French standard that had fallen to the ground.

charged with the bayonet, and was followed by the Prussians. The enemy was dislodged from the woods and pursued, although this pursuit did not last long since General Lestocq, concerned about encountering French batteries behind the woods, ordered the troops to stop and take up their previous position within the forest. By then, it was already getting dark.

General Count Kamenski, having deployed his men in a line behind us, repeatedly visited our regiment with persistent demands for us to advance, repeating that the enemy was retreating in disarray and our courageous regiment, which so far had been successful in the fighting, should take advantage of it . . . The Count was very displeased to see that, despite his requests, the Vyborgskii Regiment remained in place and demanded to see the regimental commander, who, despite the successful turn of events, was not present. Our regimental commander Colonel Piller had a habit of leading men from afar, delivering only reports about the regiment's trophies about which he learned from our wounded men. Upon hearing this, Count Kamenski demanded to see the commanding officer, then Major Ermolin, and told him that 'if the regiment did not advance at once, even though Lestocq had ordered to remain in place, it would receive no rewards and instead would be subject to punishment.'

[. . .]

Ermolin called for volunteers but no one stepped forward without me. I could not volunteer because of severe stomach pains that struck me after I, covered in hot sweat, made a mistake of drinking cold spring water. Only after desperate appeals from Major Ermolin and feeling slightly better, did I step in front of the troops and was followed by up to sixty men from the lower ranks. It was already dark when we passed through the wood and we could barely see two paces ahead of us. I advanced straight while the regiment moved on my right which I could discern from the noise it was making in the wood. After encountering a French [skirmish] line and realising it was quite strong, I chose to fall back with my volunteers to the woods. The night was so impenetrable that we could see individual men only after stumbling upon them. At this time a French battery fired several illumination rounds and it was clear that they were aiming their cannon at the right side of the woods where our regiment was located. The battery then opened canister fire which caused heavy losses in our regiment which was forced to hastily withdraw to its assigned location. After crossing the woods with my volunteers, I rejoined the regiment when it was already in its place. [From the Russian text in V. Timofeyev, *Iz Vospominanii* . . .]

Denis Davydov

The battle of Eylau has almost disappeared from contemporary memory after the bloodbath that was the battle of Borodino, and because many now feel that it was not an equally significant event. For a Russian, the issue that was debated by forces of arms at Borodino was nobler, more involving and more emotional than the contest at Eylau because what was at stake [at Borodino] was Russia's very survival. The object of dispute at Eylau was on quite a different level. Certainly, it served as a bloody prelude to Napoleon's invasion of Russia, but at the time no one could have foreseen this. It appeared rather as a struggle for military prestige by both armies, in the spirit, say, of card players fighting it out with their wallets still crammed with cash, not obliged to wager their last morsel of bread or contemplate shooting themselves through the head in the event that they lost.

It is not really fair to compare the two battles just based on the number of participants or casualties. At Eylau, different weapons and fighting methods prevailed. At Borodino, the main weapon was firepower, while at Eylau it was hand-to-hand combat that took the principal role. Bayonet and sword held sway, drinking their fill of blood. No other battle had seen clashes of infantry and cavalry and exchanges of musket fire on such a scale; cannon fire merely played a supporting role here. As in other battles, the artillery produced more noise than destruction and made a greater impression on the minds and morale of the troops, speeding up the destruction of the enemy by other means.

I was only about twenty years old, full of verve, looking forward to any sort of adventure and eager to confront every sort of danger. I must have been immune to the rain of cannonballs that hummed overhead, crashed around me and ploughed through the ranks beside me, or the hail of shells that exploded above my head and at my feet. It was a vast hurricane of death that seemed to smash and erase from the face of the earth everything in its path . . . .

The disposition of our army, comprising between 70,000 to 80,000 men, was as follows: its right flank was anchored on the main Königsberg highway near the village of Schloditten and extended at an angle towards the town but about half a mile from its walls made an angle and rested its left flank on Klein-Sausgarten. The village of Serpallen, just ahead of Sausgarten, was occupied by a weak detachment under Major-General Baggovut. Five infantry divisions: the 2nd, 3rd, 5th, 7th and 8th, were arranged in two lines; two battalions of each regiment were deployed in front and the third behind them in column; with them were arrayed over 200 guns. The reserve, consisting of two divisions, the 4th and the 14th were disposed in two dense columns and had sixty pieces of horse artillery. At sunrise it was moved closer to the centre of the army. All the cavalry was divided in three groups and placed on the flanks and in the centre of the army where there was no more than twenty-eight squadrons; as for the Cossack regiments they were positioned on the approaches to both flanks.

Independently of the artillery which was deployed along the line and kept with the reserve, the first battery of forty heavy pieces and twenty light pieces was initially on the right flank of the army, next to the Königsberg highway, but when the town was occupied by the enemy it was moved 700 paces away from it; the second battery of seventy heavy pieces was arrayed almost in the centre of the army, about a mile from the town and finally the third battery of forty heavy pieces stood between our centre and Sausgarten. All three batteries were linked by the troops of our first line as if they were bastions protruding from fortifications.

The Prussian corps under Lestocq, strengthened by the Vyborgskii Musketeer Regiment and numbering up to 8,000 men, was still quite far away, but was moving towards Althof, that is towards our right flank. One of its brigades, under General Plotz, was to lure Ney towards Kreitzburg and away from the coming battle. Our right flank was under the command of Lt. General Tuchkov I, the centre under Lt. General Sacken, the left flank under Lt. General Osterman-Tolstoy; the reserve under Lt. General Dokhturov, all the cavalry under Lt. General Golitsyn, and the artillery under Lt. General Rezvoy. Bagration, who was the youngest of the generals, had no independent command and was assigned to Dokhturov's reserve.

On the eve of battle the French army was disposed as follows: on the approaches to the town and inside it – General Legrand's infantry division; on the right side of the town – Vivienne's infantry brigade; and on the left Fere's infantry brigade (they were both part of Lewal's infantry division). St. Hilaire's infantry division was on the right flank of Vivienne's brigade. All three divisions were part of Marshal Soult's corps. To the right of St. Hilaire's division was the dragoon division under Milhaud. Behind the town, on either side of the Landsberg road, were to be found Klein and Grouchy's dragoon division, and on their left, behind Fere's brigade, was the Guard cavalry division. Further to the left were the light cavalry brigades of Colbert, Guyot and Bruyere and the cuirassier division under Hautpoult. The light cavalry brigade of Durosnel was at the very end of the left flank of the whole army, next to the village of Althof. Behind Hautpoult's cuirassiers, on the road leading from Eylau to the village of Stroben, was the infantry corps of [Marshal] Augereau. The Imperial Guard and its own bivouac was on the hill between Eylau and Grunhofchen. Davout's infantry corps was on the road to Bartenstein, about 20 miles away from the main body of the army. Ney's corps was about 25 miles from the army, on the road to Zinten. The infantry corps commanded by [Marshal] Bernadotte was several days' march behind the main army.

The surrounding area, occupied by our positions, was a slightly rolling plain which adjoined on the left side several hills overlooking our left flank which were very dangerous from the strategic point of view. Snow covered the ground and this made it difficult to move the artillery while various ponds, also frozen and covered in snow, were scattered around the field of battle and were very treacherous as they offered flat surfaces that appeared firm but were quite dangerous when moving artillery pieces. Swamps made movement impossible even for infantry! A forest of brambles stretched between the villages of Sausgarten, Auklappen and Kutschitten. The weather was clear on the whole, although marred by passing snow flurries. Only a light frost, no more than 3 or 4 degrees.

In the half-light of the early morning, the army awoke and got their weapons ready. The camp fires where the men had slept were still smouldering between the dark lines of the formations crisscrossing the pristine snow-covered fields of the coming battle; nowhere had a shot been fired yet; you could only see a certain commotion in the lines and columns which were coming into final battle order. The 4th Infantry Division and the Arkhangelogorodskii [Musketeer] Regiment returned to their place as part of the general army reserve.

Daylight suddenly broke and with it the sixty-piece battery of our right flank opened up with a roar. Part of the enemy artillery which was at rest behind the first buildings of the town came out from behind them and answered the challenge – and Napoleon saw with his own eyes that it was no longer a question of a fight with the rearguard, as he had first thought, but with our whole army. It is impossible that at that moment the great army commander did not reproach himself for allowing the corps of Ney and Davout to be such a distance from the army as they were and that did not become annoyed that fate had left him without Bernadotte's corps on such a decisive day. Staff officers immediately rushed to Davout and Ney with orders to hurry to Eylau. In the meantime a severe cannonade roared around the city, and the main French forces began to redeploy. The light cavalry brigades of Durosnel, Bruyere, Guyot and Colbert remained on the left of Eylau. The infantry division of Lewal, concentrating all three brigades, presented its left flank to these light cavalry brigades and their right towards the city. Legrand's infantry division moved forward from there and linked up with Lewal's right flank. Augereau's corps formed two lines: Desjardin's division was the first and Hudelet's division made up the second. Both of them anchored their left to the church which was at the end of the town where Napoleon remained for the duration of the battle.

Behind Augereau was deployed Hautpoult's cuirassier division which was next to the Guard infantry behind the church on a rise. Behind Hautpoult was the cavalry of the Guard, and to the right, lined up with them were Grouchy's dragoons. St. Hilaire (from Soult's corps) was on the right flank of Augereau's first line, screening Klein's dragoon division.

The cannonade from both sides increased with the deployment of the French army parallel to ours. It became generalised but still appeared stronger near the town than elsewhere. This was due to the fact that there we were trying to stop Legrand and Lewal from attacking our right flank and the French were attempting to draw our attention away from our left and facilitate Davout's effort at that point, whose arrival was meant to decide the outcome of the battle.

The fire from several hundred guns had already lasted for about three hours straight but nothing remarkable had happened neither on the enemy's nor our side. Having received the news of the impending arrival of Davout's corps, which was under orders to move from the Heilsberg road to the Bartenstein road, Napoleon ordered the centre of his army to move to the right and combine their operations with those of Davout. The armies moved forward but at that instant a heavy snowstorm hit and you couldn't see anything two paces away.

Augereau's corps lost its bearings, lost contact with St. Hilaire's division and all the cavalry, and suddenly appeared, much to their and our surprise, in front of our centre battery just as the weather cleared. Seventy cannons belched total hell and a hail of grapeshot started to ring against their musket barrels and hammer at the live mass of flesh and bone. In an instant the Moscow grenadiers and the Shlusselbourg infantry, together with the Arkhangelogordskii infantry, rushed hungrily at them with lowered bayonets. The French wavered, but recovered and stood their ground, meeting bayonet with bayonet.

There then took place an engagement the likes of which had never been seen before. Over 20,000 men from both sides were plunging three-faceted blades into each other. Men fell in droves. I was a personal witness of this Homeric slaughter and I must say truly that over the course of the sixteen campaigns in my service record and through all the Napoleonic campaigns, justly referred to as the legend of our century, I have never seen the likes of it! For about half an hour you couldn't hear a cannon or a musket shot neither in the midst of this struggle nor around it – you could only hear this inexpressible roar of thousands of brave soldiers in hand-to-hand combat, mixing and cutting each other up. Mounds of dead bodies were covered over with new mounds; men were falling on top of each other by the hundreds, so that this whole part of the battlefield resembled the high parapet of a suddenly-erected fortification. Finally, our side got the upper hand!

Augereau's corps was overthrown and hotly pursued by our infantry and Prince Golitsyn, who had galloped with the cavalry of the centre to support them. The pitch of their fervour reached improbable heights: in hot pursuit, one of our battalions went right through the enemy position and appeared at the church a hundred paces away from Napoleon himself, which is mentioned by all Frenchmen in their war diaries of that time. It was a critical moment. Napoleon, whose resolve grew incrementally with multiplying dangers, ordered Murat and Bessières together with the three Hautpoult divisions, Klein, Grouchy and the Guard cavalry to strike at our troops rushing in with shouts of HURRAH. This movement was necessary to save even part of Augereau's corps and to forestall our general onslaught. More than sixty squadrons galloped around to the right of the fleeing corps and rushed against us, waving their swords. The field was engulfed in a roar and the snow, ploughed up by 12,000 united riders, lifted and swirled from under them like a storm. The brilliant Murat with his carnival-like costume followed by a large suite, was ablaze ahead of the onslaught with a naked sabre and flew directly into the thick of the fight. Musket and cannon fire and levelled bayonets were unable to stem the deadly tide. The French cavalry crushed and stomped on everything, breaking through the first line of the army and its impetuous rush had reached the second line and our reserve, but here it broke against the cliff of a stronger will. The second line and the reserve stood their ground, did not waver and turned back the awesome tidal wave with heavy artillery and musketry fire.

Then, pursued by our own horsemen, they broke back through our re-formed first line, which had got back on its feet and was firing back again, and was chased even beyond the position they had occupied at the beginning of the day. The pursuit of the cavalry was breathtakingly successful and followed through to the hilt. The enemy batteries left on that line were seized by several of our squadrons and the gun crews together with the carriage wheels were hacked to pieces while the draught horses and their drivers had fled in panic.

In this hand-to-hand engagement and the flowing back and forth of the cavalry, the following generals – Hautpoult of the cavalry, Daleman of the Guard, Desjardin of the infantry and Corbineau – all fell on the field of battle. Marshal Augereau himself, along with General of Division Hudelet and Brigadier-General Lochet, were wounded; several other brigadier-generals and staff officers such as Lacuyet, Marois, Bouvier and others shared the same fate. Two squadrons of the Horse Grenadiers of the Guard, at the rear of the retreating enemy cavalry, were intercepted by ours and laid down their lives between the church and the second line. The 14th Regiment of the Line lost all its officers and the 24th of the Line had only five left alive. Only fragments remained of Augereau's entire corps, three cavalry divisions and the Cavalry of the Guard. The whole corps of Augereau, three cavalry divisions and the mounted guard represented only fragments of their former selves. We captured six eagles.

What an opportunity for a forceful and combined thrust by all our forces at the division of St. Hilaire, left without support and any hope of help! All around this division had been destroyed or overthrown and what was more important left without the spirit to come to its aid or the will to fight back. Moreover, it wasn't quite eleven o'clock in the morning, therefore there were still two hours left before Davout's arrival on the battlefield. But to put such moments to good use, it is not enough to have a thorough knowledge of one's craft, and to have a determined spirit or a sharp mind: all this is nothing without the inspiration, without this incomprehensive, inexpressible impulse which is instantaneous, like an electric spark, which is just as necessary to the poet as it is to a military commander; it was innate to Napoleon and to Suvorov – it belonged to poets and men that made things happen such as Pindar and Mirabeau – who had a command over words.

The propitious moment, which promised such advantage to our arms, passed. Our troops pursuing the enemy were forced to return to the main body of the army from which not a single battalion was sent forward to help us and the enemy, who had been in disarray, rallied and taking advantage of this lull got back in order and took heart. Then the opposing armies resumed the same positions they were in before the onslaught and bloodshed which had devoured uselessly such numbers of men, and all these miracles of prowess, all the selflessness and heroism of these soldiers who had heaped their bodies in piles over the disputed ground, turned to naught as if it never happened!

The fighting limited itself to a severe cannonade which again engulfed the entire length of both armies and the slaughter of new thousands, just like that, to while the time away, until the arrival of Davout's corps to the French and the Prussian corps of Lestocq to our side.

Now came the second phase of the battle. Around one o'clock in the afternoon, on the crest of the hills which rose to the left of us and where our left flank was anchored, a few isolated men on horseback appeared. Behind them came masses of cavalry and then masses of infantry and artillery as well. The horizon grew dark and rippled with motion. The hills of Sausgarten, silent until then, flashed, belched smoke and roared.

Davout answered them with forty field pieces and flowed in mass over the battlefield at about the same time as St. Hilaire's division, reinforced by Milhaud's cavalry division, moved to meet him. To the left of St. Hilaire came the cavalry divisions of Klein, Grouchy and Hautpoult, which had already been mauled in battle and were now arrayed in three lines. Further to the left of this cavalry advanced the remains of Augereau's corps in two lines. Behind them marched the Guard infantry and bringing up the rear of Hautpoult, no less mauled than the other cavalry, came the Guard cavalry. However, the divisions of Legrand and Lewal, as well as four light cavalry brigades, remained where they were.

All attention on both sides was now riveted on Davout and our left wing. Adjutants were galloping up the Althof road with orders for Lestocq to speed up his arrival not on our right flank anymore, but through Schmoditten to our threatened left wing. A portion of the cavalry and artillery situated on our right and in the centre moved to the left as well, which the enemy forces were forcing to fall back towards the centre, already suffering from the fire of batteries deployed behind the stone walls of the town. These batteries were firing all along the length of our army from Eylau to Auklappen and the woods between Sausgarten, Auklappen and Kutschitten.

The situation did not appear very rosy. Davout, having pushed back our left flank behind the woods, now occupied the area between Kutschitten and Sausgarten, deployed an enormous battery on the heights of Sausgarten and was hitting the whole length of our army with the same sweeping enfilade fire which we were getting from Eylau. The village of Kutschitten was full of Davout's infantry as well as the infantry of St. Hilaire which had captured Auklappen (where Bennigsen had his headquarters the night before). The fearless and unflappable Count Osterman and Count Palen were attempting to fend off the strengthening assault, but to no avail! Disorder was beginning to affect our troops. The whole field of battle from Kutschitten to Schmoditten was covered with scattered soldiers: they were stretched towards the Königsberg highway under the protection of those comrades in arms who had not lost spirit or order and were shedding their blood for every step of ground they fought for. The crossfire of the ever-increasing enemy batteries ploughed and blew up everything that was to be seen on the battlefield. Pieces of muskets, chunks of gun- carriages, headgear, helmets were flying everywhere, everything was cracking and falling apart.

Amidst the storm of screaming shot and exploding shells, among the fallen and the falling men and horses, surrounded by the hustle and bustle of the fight and clouds of smoke, there towered the huge figure of Bennigsen like a flag of honour. To him and from him streamed adjutants: messages and orders were followed by news and further orders, the race was without end and the activity unflagging. But the situation of the army did not improve because all thoughts, intentions, dispositions of our leader were influenced by carefulness, calculation, the product of an exact and sound mind, equal to the task of grappling with minds of the same type, but not up to dealing with flashes of genius, sudden events which escape foresight and clever guesses grounded in classic rules. All that Bennigsen ordered and all that was carried out as a result tended only to oppose systematically the attacks of Davout and St. Hilaire, opposing bayonet to bayonet and firearm to firearm, but did not address any unexpected move which came out of the ordinary, and did not forestall a bolt out of the blue on some point which was deemed safe from the enemy.

And actually, how were things going? Davout continued to press on, capturing more and more of our left flank, while the centre and right, not moving at all, were shedding small portions of infantry, cavalry and artillery to help out the retreating left wing, not undertaking anything that might suddenly surprise the enemy. But even the fact that we were opposing the enemy right flank was bringing us no small advantage: by postponing a decisive defeat, it gave time for Lestocq's corps to arrive on the battlefield. But to do this properly we should have been propping up this flank with large masses and not just small units.

Bagration, who in moments of danger found his proper place through willpower and inborn talents, moved the reserve towards Auklappen and had it facing Davout and St. Hilaire. Yermolov galloped to the same spot with thirty-six horse guns from the reserve, peppered Auklappen with incendiary shells, set it immediately on fire and forced the enemy infantry to leave it;

Major-General Kutaisov also arrived there with twelve guns but some time later. Then, not losing a moment, he rushed to the stream crossing the woods and attacked the batteries which had been stationed there and preventing the infantry columns from either moving into the woods or Auklappen or Kutschitten and reinforcing the troops pouring into this last village. But these successes, or rather the postponement of the threatened disaster, could not last. To snatch decisive victory from the enemy it was vital not only to stop but to defeat Davout by bearing down on his right flank and simultaneously to threaten his rear by a general offensive against Augereau's corps and the cavalry which were contiguous to his forces.

Finally the adjutants rode up with the news of Lestocq's approach, which we had awaited so long and so patiently. Having occupied the greater part of Ney's corps with battling the brigade of General Plotz and pursuing him to Kreizburg, Lestocq turned to Leisen, Graventen and Althof with his main forces, consisting of nine battalions and twenty-nine squadrons. It was already around 4:00 p.m.; the road to Althof was black with troops and Bennigsen galloped to meet them – to speed them up and so that he could direct them according to his own intentions. It was noticeable that with the arrival of the commander-in-chief the entire corps began to move faster. Lestocq was directed towards Schmoditten; he moved past this village and just short of Kutschitten arranged his troops in battle order. The right column was composed of the Vyborgskii Musketeer Regiment, the left was Ruchel's regiment and the reserve behind them, the grenadier battalion of Fobetsky deployed in one line. The infantry regiment of Shoning, marching in column, bypassed the village on the left and slammed into the enemy infantry facing them, overthrew it and chased it into the woods. General Kal, with cavalry and one Cossack regiment which joined him from the main body of the army, leaving Kutschitten to the right, fell on the enemy cavalry adjoining this village, throwing their ranks into disorder and turned on the infantry fleeing in disarray from the village, trampled them and destroyed the greater part of them, preventing their escape into the woods where the first elements had found refuge.

In this engagement the Vyborgskii [Musketeer] Regiment won back three guns that the French had captured from our forces on our left flank during their retreat. Having taken possession of Kutschitten, Lestocq turned his troops to the right and arranged them facing the woods. The regiment of Shoning composed his right flank, the grenadier battalion of Fobetsky and the Vyborgskii [Regiment] the centre, and the Ruchel regiment was the left. A second line of defence was made up of the Wagenfeld cuirassier regiment and the dragoon regiments of Auer and Batchko. A light cavalry regiment composed of various elements was arranged to the left of the infantry. Our left flank which had been retreating came to a halt and order was restored, and its reserve under the command of Major-General Kamenski and the reserve cavalry under Major-General Czaplic came to reinforce the Prussian corps.

The attack on the woods was carried out with great courage and in impeccable order. The woods were cleared partly by firepower, partly by cold steel. The moment was ripe for a combined effort by the centre and the reserve of our army against the remains of Augereau's corps (mauled that morning), the cavalry of the Guard and the three cavalry divisions of Klein, Grouchy and Hautpoult which connected the left flank of the French army with the right. Such a combination had given victory to Napoleon at Austerlitz. But our army remained on the spot, limiting its response to a cannonade. The pressure Lestocq was exerting was added to by his own artillery hammering the troops of Davout and St. Hilaire, and also Yermolov's artillery, sweeping the enemy's entire line from left to right.

Despite this general inactivity on our side, which relied solely on the efforts of Lestocq and Yermolov's artillery, the enemy was not able to stand up to them. Their retreat, which at first began with some semblance of order, turned into inexcusable disorder, so much in fact that twenty-eight guns, some damaged and some not, were abandoned by them on the battlefield. The gathering darkness and poor intelligence did not allow the Prussian general to crown this day with these important trophies. Having left the field of battle, Davout and St. Hilaire arranged their troops on either side of Sausgarten; the front line and sentries were placed a few yards ahead. The whole enemy line divided the battlefield from Sausgarten to Eylau. At Eylau the divisions of Lewal and Legrand remained in their previous positions; but four light cavalry brigades moved forward to the Althof stream to keep open the lines of communication with Ney who was approaching Althof.

On our side, the troops were disposed as follows: the forward line rested its left flank against the road, going from Kutschitten to Domnau following the line of the stream which flowed from Auklappen and cut the woods in two. From there the line continued in front of Auklappen and rested against our central battery, which had played such an important role in the first phase of the battle. The troops of the right flank were also closed-up to this battery, as they were in their original deployment prior to the battle. This defensive battle order of the opposing forces at the end of the battle proves the absence of a decisive superiority of one side over the other. The French and our army as well remained in the positions they originally occupied with essentially small changes on our left flank, giving way a few yards to Davout's corps and St. Hilaire's division because the coming darkness made fighting more difficult. If we had had one more hour of daylight, Lestocq would have inevitably taken possession of the artillery abandoned by the French and would have compelled Davout and St. Hilaire to retreat behind Sausgarten and beyond. Late night darkened further and further over the blood-soaked field of Eylau. All the surrounding villages were now the prey of flames and the reflection of the fires shone over the exhausted troops, still standing under arms and awaiting further orders. Here and there you could see camp fires being lit, around which gathered or beckoned to thousands of crawling wounded soldiers. The torn bodies of men and horses, broken wagons, powder cases and gun carriages, outfit and arms – all this scattered here, piled up there gave the plain a look of terror and destruction worthy of the brush of the inspired creator of THE LAST DAYS OF POMPEII.

The engagement had ended but the uncertainty: 'Should we renew the battle or retreat to Königsberg?' and for the French, 'Should we pull back to the Vistula?' gripped the minds of the commanders of both armies. The most obstinate of the two finally triumphed not because he renewed the offensive but because he remained on the battlefield until dawn.

Bennigsen left the field around midnight, posting several squadrons to keep watch on the enemy and to provide a screen for the army heading for Königsberg. Lestocq retired through Allenburg to Byelo. There was no pursuit. The French, like a disabled man-of-war with torn sails and broken masts, were bobbing about menacingly, but were unable to make any headway to fight or to pursue.

Suddenly we heard musketry in Schmoditten. We were astonished. Our first thought was that it was Ney, who we had forgotten about. And sure enough, Ney arrived with part of his corps at Althof around 9 o'clock in the evening, finding there the Prussian battalion of Captain Kurowsky, who realising he was seriously outnumbered, left the village and joined the rest of the army. General Liger-Belair, with the 6th and 39th Regiments pursued him and entered Schmoditten village, which was filled with wounded and troops that had got there to protect them. They opened fire on the French and a firefight ensued. To assist them we sent the Voronezhskii Musketeer Regiment and a few cannons; but the enemy did not choose to await their arrival and retreated to Althof, and thus the alarm was over.

On the 9th our army, having rested at Muhlhausen, continued its march to Königsberg around which it stopped, having left Prince Bagration with the rearguard in Ludwigswald. The French army, fearing a new battle up ahead, chose to remain near Eylau. Only twenty-four squadrons moved forward to keep the banks of the Frisching [Świeża] under observation, and then towards Mansfeld and Ludwigswald and that only two days later when Napoleon was assured that our army had arrived at Pregel. On 17 February Napoleon decided to retreat behind the Passarge River to take up his winter quarters and left Eylau, pursued by our advance guard and all the Cossack regiments under the command of their leader Platoff, who from that day forward acquired his European reputation.

The retrograde march of the enemy was no less costly in many respects than the retreat suffered five years later from Moscow to the Niemen, in spite of the moderate cold. The later losses were ascribed to the cold weather by the French but today, however, few people give it credence. Being in the advance guard myself, I was witness to the bloody trail from Eylau to Gutstadt. The whole road was littered with unending debris. We met everywhere hundreds of horses dying or obstructing our path, and ambulances filled with dying or dead soldiers and men of rank mutilated in the Eylau battle. The rush to evacuate had become such that besides the sufferers left in the carriages we found many that had been simply dumped on the snow without cover or clothes, bleeding to death. On each mile of road there weren't two, but tens and hundreds. Moreover, all the villages along the way were filled with sick and wounded, without doctors or food or the least care. In this pursuit the Cossacks captured many exhausted men, marauders and eight artillery pieces, stuck in the snow without harnesses.

Our losses in this battle reached almost half of the number of the fighting men, that is to say 37,000 men killed or wounded. According to the army registers it appears that our army was composed of 46,800 men (regular army) and 2,500 Cossacks. There was no equal to such losses in the annals of military history since the invention of gunpowder. The reader can imagine what the losses of the French army were, since they possessed less artillery than us and had been beaten back in two hot assaults in the centre and the left flank of our army. Our trophies consisted of nine eagles torn from the ranks of the enemy and 2,000 prisoners. The Prussian king took two eagles.

I was involved in a touching episode after the battle. A year and two months before, our army had been defeated at Austerlitz. The Horse Guard Regiment shared the defeat along with the others. My own brother, then a 20-year-old youth who served in this regiment, was grievously wounded: he received five sabre cuts, one bullet wound and a bayonet thrust and had been left for dead in a mound of corpses on the battlefield. There he lay until late at night. He regained consciousness in the dark, got up and somehow hobbled towards a fire which could be seen in a nearby village which he found overflowing with Russian wounded, among whom he found a spot.

After three days two men from his regiment who had sustained much lighter wounds – Arapov and Barkovsky – persuaded him to walk in the direction of our retreating army, and he, not really knowing what direction it had taken, made his way with them, wandering about the way people exhausted by suffering and hunger are apt to do. Their journey did not last very long. A squadron of Grenadiers à Cheval of [the Imperial] Guard, detached from the French army to gather the wounded from both sides caught up with them and informed them of their fate. There was nothing to be done – they had to obey. The squadron continued on, but their commanding officer entrusted my brother and his two comrades to one of the officers of the squadron with orders to convey them to Brünn where Napoleon's headquarters were located. But as our proverb says, the poor folk get lost but God looks after them. This particular officer was Second-Lieutenant Serugues, a nephew of Minister Maret (the Duke of Bassano) and to his mercy was left the life and death of my brother. I say life and death because the hatred of the French towards the Russians and vice-versa had originated from about that time. In both armies they got into the habit of stripping prisoners of their last clothes, their boots and leaving them to die, overcome by hunger and exhaustion, of cold or wounds.

This was not part of a system ordered from above, but such acts were never questioned by superiors. A humane and compassionate man, however, Serugues had not yet been infected by these loathsome examples. Taking a heartfelt interest in the misfortune of his prisoner, he extended his indulgence and even forbade him to walk on foot, put him on a horse and, seeing how weak he was from hunger, shared with him his last morsel of bread. Thus he conveyed him to the pastor of the nearest village, saw to it that he was fed until full, got a cart ready for him and sent him on to Brünn, cheering him on with a friendly, almost brotherly concern. Moreover, he gave his word to my brother that he would look for him and find him again in Brünn where he hoped to return soon, but failing that got him to promise he would apply for assistance from his uncle, Minister Maret, and insist that every necessary help be given him. All this I heard from my brother upon his return from captivity and a few weeks before I myself left to join the army. Having arrived with the rearguard into Ludwigswald on 29 January, I begged permission from Bagration to visit Königsberg on personal affairs, and having gotten there quartered myself with General Czaplic who was assigned the duty of commander of the city. Czaplic told me that there was some French officer, wounded in the last engagement who was making inquiries about me and asking whether there was a lieutenant of the guard Davidov? I was the only guard officer by that name in the whole army and in my curiosity to find out the name of this French officer I asked to see the list of prisoners of rank. You can imagine my surprise when the name of Second Lieutenant Serugues jumped out at me the moment I opened the enormous folio! To spot this name, to run and find him was all one motion. I was still running, not having seen his face yet, but I was already his brother, a friend for life and the most devoted relative.

It must be mentioned here that the inhabitants of Königsberg, having learned of the arrival of our army under their walls, feared its further retreat and the eventual occupation of the city by the French. Therefore to earn the good graces of Napoleon beforehand, they made every effort to beg Bennigsen for the permission to divide among themselves the wounded French officers in order to quarter them and keep them in their homes at their own expense.

It goes without saying that fortune was even more favourable to the nephew of the Minister than to others. Serugues enjoyed the hospitality of one of the wealthiest citizens of Königsberg. I found him in a tall, luxuriously appointed house, whose entire first floor had been put at his disposal. A bed with a large canopy, choice linens, screens, small tables and sofas, comfortable armchairs near the bed, semi-darkness and fragrant incense, a doctor and medicines, surely nothing was lacking. But he lay there pale, worn out and in great pain. Several sword slashes on his head and arms did not incommode him as much as a deep and eventually mortal wound to the groin.

I approached quietly and carefully towards the bed of the wretched sufferer and told him my name. We embraced as true blood-brothers. He asked about mine with genuine concern; I thanked him for having preserved him and offered my services with deep emotion. He answered me: 'You see I am in the care of a good person and don't lack for anything. However, you can do me a great service. Undoubtedly among the prisoners there are some wounded from my outfit; could you possibly appeal to the authorities and arrange for two or perhaps even one of my horse grenadiers to remain by my side. Let me die, still keeping to the end my eyes on the uniform of my regiment and the guard of a great man.' It goes without saying that I rushed to see Bennigsen and Czaplic and obtained their permission to choose from the crowd of prisoners two horse grenadiers from Serugues' own squad and in two hours' time I returned to him, accompanied by two moustachioed fellows, crowned with bearskin hats and in full uniform. It is impossible to express the joy of my ill-fated friend at the sight of his comrades-in-arms. Expressions of gratitude would have been endless without my begging him to restrain these outbursts of the heart, so exhausting in his state. For two days I did not leave Serugues' side, day or night; on the third everything came to an end: he died in my arms and was buried in the Königsberg cemetery. Behind the casket walked the two aforementioned French horse-grenadiers and I, a second lieutenant of the Russian guard. A strange juxtaposition of uniforms! A deep sorrow was clearly evident on the faces of the old veterans, my companions in the procession – I was young – I was crying. [From the Russian text in Denis Davydov, *Voennye zapiski*]

Yakov Otroshenko

Staff Captain Otroshenko commanded a company in the 7th Jager Regiment. After fighting at Eylau, his men retreated to Königsberg but were then attached to a detachment that attacked the French outposts and reached the outskirts of Eylau.

[After Eylau] we retreated to the vicinity of Königsberg, where we were joined by our newly appointed regimental chef [Major-General Nikolay Korf],* who . . . welcomed us like a good father. We thanked God for giving us such a chef.

---

* The 45-year-old Korf had earlier commanded the Staroningermandlandskii Musketeer Regiment and served as chef of the Uglitskii Musketeer Regiment. He was

Several days later a special detachment was formed with orders to attack a French cavalry detachment that had come too close to our positions. We attacked and routed it. Two days later we were told to advance further so our detachment moved through Landberg, which the French had passed on their retreat from Preussisch-Eylau and left behind a vast hospital with the wounded and the sick. A few days later we reached the village of Peterswalde.

By then, the thaw had begun, turning the roads muddy; our men were utterly exhausted. Our general [Korf], wanting to rest us, ordered our men to [the new] lodgings. Officers of the 7th Regiment were all billeted in one house in front of the church. Our host revealed to us that there were French in the woods not far from us. These woods were no more than three-fourths of a versta [750m] away along the road to the village of Altkirch. I advised our senior captain, who acted as our regiment's commanding officer, to inform the general about this development and inquire whether he would like us to deploy outposts at the entrances into the village. He had indeed informed the general, who consented to this suggestion. So we sent out outposts: about eighty men from the 25th Jager Regiment were deployed on the road leading to the woods, while other entrances were guarded by 25-man strong outposts detailed from various regiments. Having deployed these outposts, everyone went calmly to bed.

I woke up around four o'clock in the morning and asked my senior captain if he was asleep. He was not and asked me to go to relieve our outpost. I woke up an adjutant and ordered him to assemble men, I mounted my horse and led the soldiers to the outpost, where I personally deployed sentries and instructed them individually on the importance of being vigilant and explained how to recognise the enemy. This was a necessary measure because our regiment had few veterans and most of our men were new recruits. Afterwards I returned to my lodging, but just as I approached it, a shot was fired in front of the village, followed by another one. I jumped off my horse and rushed into the houses where my company was billeted. Bullets were already whizzing through the village. My men, caught unprepared, rushed outside not fully dressed, just grabbing their muskets. I stopped in front of my lodgings, halting and rallying anyone running by me. I soon saw the outpost of the 25th Jager Regiment, previously deployed on the road leading to the woods, calmly marching past me and asked the officer [leading it] to stop it here, explaining that all the troops would then rally to us. But he paid no attention to me and simply kept walking. Behind him was a small group of people whom I took for another outpost because it was difficult to identify them in the darkness. Thus I did not worry about them and continued arranging my men. But suddenly this group lit up with

---

appointed the chef of the 7th Jagers in late December 1806 and remained at this post until March 1807, when he was replaced by Major-General Peter Bestuzhev-Ryumin.

flashes of fire and bullets started hitting my men. Several men fell to the ground while the rest scattered around. I ran with them and saw as the commander of the 25th [Jager] Regiment* was shouting to the soldiers, 'Save yourselves, lads!'

At dawn we got out of the village. The regiments were all mixed up at first but the men soon deployed by companies. Still, neither our general [Korf] nor any staff officers from other regiments could be found. Our regimental physician, who was billeted with our general, claimed that [Korf] had probably been captured [by the French]. It was too late for us to do anything about it, especially since the French were already attacking our right flank.

I took two companies of our regiment and advanced against the enemy, who halted and opened fire at my front. I ordered one of my companies to disperse into a skirmish line and deployed the other one in a hollow to protect it from the enemy fire. Meanwhile our cavalry appeared from the village of Zechern and the French withdrew into the woods, allowing us to return to the village [of Peterswalde].

The cavalry was led by Count Pavel Petrovich von der Pahlen. The colonel who had been shouting 'Save yourselves, lads!', appeared in front of him to accuse our unfortunate 7th Jager Regiment of losing its regimental chef [Korf], even though we did not know where precisely the chef had been lodged. Four captains, except for our senior captain, decided to go to Count Pahlen to defend ourselves. When the villainous [colonel of the 25th Jagers] continued besmirching our regiment, I told him bluntly, 'Sir, were you not the one shouting "Save yourselves, lads!" to the soldiers?' For this we were quickly expelled and threatened with being reported to the Emperor himself.

[Otroshenko's regiment spent the next few days engaged in continued fighting with the French around the villages of Zechern and Peterswalde.]

Any time the French skirmishers approached us, I dispatched our own skirmishers against them. And whenever I observed that they were clearing the area for their artillery, which I could observe, I ordered my men to stand behind trees and thus shielded them from grapeshot and cannonballs. I was soon joined by some 250 soldiers from other regiments, yet there were not enough officers. I placed these troops under the command of non-commissioned officers, who remained by my side throughout the fighting. The more soldiers admire an officer who shares their dangers and protects them, the more they hate an officer who leads them from behind. Upon observing that their officer was far behind them, some soldiers even told me, 'We will

---

* Otroshenko makes no mention of this individual's name. The regimental files show that Lieutenant-Colonel Markov (promoted to colonel after the campaign was over) commanded this regiment until December 1807. Colonel Nikolay Vuich served as the regimental chef.

shoot him in the head.' But I urged them, 'Leave him alone, cannot you see that he is ashamed to approach us?'

By now we had already run out of bread and biscuits. One soldier took two biscuits out of his coat and gave them to me, saying, 'If you please, Your Honour, eat these. We know that you do not have anything to eat.' 'What about you,' I replied. 'Well, I will get by somehow. When one of those heathens [Frenchmen] will approach us, I will shoot him and he will [probably] have some bread or biscuits.'

[After another day of fighting, the French withdrew and Otroshenko's men could rest in the vicinity of Peterswalde and Altkirch.]

We occupied the village of Altkirch with our outposts and kept the regiments in the woods. Thick pine forest protected us from the wind while the fluffy snow served for our beds. I was the first to build a small hut out of branches and covered it with snow; inside, around the fire, I fashioned a bed out of pine branches. My comrades followed my example and built similar huts, so we were well set. Soldiers built square huts . . . and everything would have been fine if we had a sufficient amount of bread. Soldiers slept near the fire so they were hot on one side and cold on another, forcing them to toss and turn constantly as if roasting on a spit. Occasionally a spark fell into our cartridge boxes, causing the cartridges to ignite. But no harm was done to the jagers, only frightening them and causing to roll around . . . .

Our senior captain was a dim-witted imbecile, who cared nothing for the regiment and spent his time inside his hut. We lost patience with him and asked General [Peter] Passek★ to give us a new staff officer to command our regiment. Our request was soon fulfilled and a new staff officer arrived. Alas, he turned out to be a lamebrain as well, so we complained once more to receive a more effective commander. By now, it was already late March – extreme hunger was all around us and our soldiers were swelling and dying from starvation; soldiers ate all the [ox] hides that had earlier covered our tents, and were surviving on various roots picked in the woods. The commander-in-chief was informed that soldiers were [frequently] consuming unsafe roots and an order had been issued informing troops of safe and unsafe plants. [From the Russian text in Y. Otroshenko, *Zapiski* . . .]

Sergei Volkonskii

During the battle of Eylau, Volkonskii, who served in General Alexander Ostermann-Tolstoy's staff, was wounded and sent to Königsberg, where

---

★ Otroshenko refers to Major-General Peter Passek, who commanded the Kievskii Grenadier Regiment until 1803, retired in 1804–5 and was appointed to the Russian headquarters in 1806. In January 1807, he was given command of a brigade in the 5th Division.

thousands of other Russian wounded were sent as well. Fortunately for Volkonskii, he met his relative, Major-General Sergey Kozhin, who was also convalescing in Königsberg. Kozhin was concerned that in the wake of Eylau, the French might be able to reach Königsberg so he decided to move to Tilsit and took Volkonskii with him. After fully recovering from the wound, Volkonskii returned to the Russian army that was on its winter quarters in the Polish countryside.

During our stay in [winter] quarters, the army's supply system had utterly failed both people and horses, who sustained themselves largely through foraging with a rather small number of transports; the advance guard, commanded by Prince Bagration and bivouacked in huts near Launau, was however better provided because it had to be constantly prepared to repeal a French attack.

The supply problems were so great that supply transports moving to the advance guard had to be sent under protection of a [military] escort so they were not halted by the troops of the corps deployed along the road to Launau.

The disorders in the supply system were the result of numerous illegal financial machinations that the regimental chefs had made with the supply commissary. These chefs received monies from the commissary, put them into their pockets and then provided for their troops through forceful requisitioning of the local population. After the war ended all the receipts had been sent to a specially-established commission in Memel but it failed to unravel this mess and the illegitimately-acquired money thus remained in the pockets of these [miscreants]. [From the Russian text in S. Volkonskii, *Zapiski* . . .]

5

The Spring Campaign

After the battle of Eylau, both the French and Russian armies spent several weeks regrouping and preparing for a new campaign. Napoleon remained on the battlefield for over a week, realising it was necessary to convince Europe of his victory at Eylau. However, his army was in disarray and needed reinforcements and supplies. So, in late February, Napoleon ordered his forces to take up positions behind the Passarge River. From 16 to 19 February, the French army was arranged along a line between Braunsberg, Liebstadt and Allestein. The French withdrawal was conducted in such secrecy that the Russian patrols detected it only a couple of days later. Bennigsen immediately dispatched Ataman Platov to pursue the French. The Cossacks occupied Eylau late on 19 February and two days later they were in Landsberg while Bennigsen moved his main forces to Eylau and Kreutzberg.

In March, Bennigsen deployed his army in two lines and had his main headquarters established at Bartenstein. The Prussian corps was around Zinten and Plauten with advance guards on the Lower Passarge. The French and Russian forces spent two months (March and April) in winter quarters receiving supplies and reinforcements. Both sides avoided any major actions, but minor outpost skirmishes occurred daily. In late March, Emperor Alexander personally visited the army to encourage his troops in the oncoming campaign. He held parades of the main army and negotiated with Prussia and Britain about the joint operations against Napoleon. In April, strong reinforcements joined the Russian army, including some 17,000 men of the Imperial Guard. Alexander and Frederick William III of Prussia visited Heilsberg, where Bennigsen had constructed strong defensive positions. Bennigsen was concerned about the French dispositions and was already considering an attack on Marshal Ney's corps that was 'boldly' deployed at Guttstadt. So Bennigsen decided to anticipate the French concentration and destroy the isolated 6th Corps. By the middle of May, he had concentrated his army around Heilsberg and Migehnen. The Russian army remained at these positions for the next two weeks. The supply system was poorly maintained and the troops suffered from the lack of provisions. On some occasions, the regiments even attacked supply trains to get food.

On 30 May, Russian headquarters received news of the surrender of Danzig which allowed Napoleon to divert his forces from the fortress to the Passarge River.

Bennigsen reacted by launching an offensive against Marshal Ney before the main French forces arrived. He issued a disposition for offensive that considered attacking in six columns along a fifteen-mile wide front. Marshal Ney anticipated the Russo-Prussian moves. Although dense forests prevented him from seeing the Russian advance, his cavalry patrols had intercepted Allied correspondence that revealed the impending offensive.

On the morning of 5 June, the Prussian corps made a series of attacks on the French positions at Spanden but could not progress further. Simultaneously, General Dokhturov marched during the night of 5 June to Wormditt and attacked the French positions at the bridge at Lomitten. Over the next several hours, a ferocious combat took place in the vicinity of the bridge, which changed hands several times before the French claimed it for good. The remaining Russian columns were no more successful. Late on 6 June, Bennigsen received intelligence of Napoleon concentrating his forces at Saalfeld. So, after a brief stay between Guttstadt and the Passarge, he led the Russian army to positions along the banks of the Alle River in front of Heilsberg. During the previous weeks, various fortifications and ramparts were constructed there. On 10 June, the French army attacked the Russians in these fortified positions but suffered heavy losses. During the night, the Russian command, apprehensive of possible flanking manoeuvres, decided to abandon the battlefield and retreat to Friedland.

Nikolai Levshin

Nikolai Levshin served in the Life Guard Jager Regiment and despite his youth (just eighteen years old), he was already a veteran of the Austerlitz campaign, where his regiment suffered considerable losses and spent the next year recovering from them. In the early spring of 1807, Emperor Alexander decided to send his guard units to reinforce Bennigsen's fatigued forces and Levshin and his comrades were thus ordered to start preparations. As he aptly described it, 'Russian preparations do not last long: knapsack behind the shoulders, backsword on the thigh and musket in hand – and you are ready'. In March 1807, the entire Guard left St. Petersburg.

Our march [to Riga] was quite unpleasant because of the challenges posed by the springtime, and it was also clear that we were in a hurry; our marches were thirty or more verists long, and our rest days were few and far between. Even flooded rivers could not delay us – rather fine crossings had been prepared in advance everywhere and not a single incident occurred during the entire march. The Guard entered Riga with a large parade on 15 [27] March. Here we learned about Napoleon's victories and the devastation that the Prussian kingdom had suffered. We only briefly rested in Riga and proceeded to Mitau, where we also rested.

Our Colonel [Emmanuel] St. Priest ordered several officers, namely Count Rastignac, Chevalier Delagarde, Prince Khilkov and me, to come in full uniform to him. He then took us to a château located near the town [Mitau] and declared that we were going to meet the King of France. The old, completely dilapidated château soon appeared in front of us. Climbing a dusty staircase, we entered rooms that surprised us with their obsoleteness and untidiness. Old, tattered and worn furniture revealed how impoverished their owners were. Even though wallpaper covered the walls, it was so tattered that pieces of it were hanging off walls while gilded frames had all faded and gilt glistened only in places. In the presence chamber we encountered five members of the royal suite, among whom was [Louis Antoine] Duc de Angoulême.★ They were all wearing casual clothes [partikulyarnye platya] and well-worn coats. After the usual pleasantries we were lead to the king's cabinet, which was not any better decorated or furnished than the rooms that we had already passed through. King Louis XVIII, although he was not old, was a fat man, with a large pot belly and suffering from gout. Sitting motionlessly in the Voltaire chair, he greeted us with a pleasant smile. He seated Count St. Priest next to him and spoke to him with great pleasure. We were introduced individually to him and then stood aside. At this time I could indeed affirm that I was looking at the genuine descendant of the Bourbon family – noses of a particular shape, which members of this dynasty all possess, are their tell-tale signs. We were preoccupied in conversation with the members of the royal suite and the Duc de Angoulême. The Duchess of Angoulême,† the daughter of the unfortunate king Louis XVI, sat, with the most forlorn expression on her face, next to the king. She was a woman of greater than average height and thin as a skeleton. The king's clothing included a blue cotton coat and the star of the Order of the Holy Spirit. Our meeting lasted no more than an hour and as he was bidding us farewell, the king told us, 'Messieurs, battez bien les Français, mais epargnez les après, car ce sont mes infants.'‡

The following day the members of the royal suite paid us a visit in Mitau and the Colonel [St. Priest] and the officers of our regiment treated them to a splendid dinner at a tavern, which pleased these marquises greatly. These émigrés came to admire us and even shared their secrets with us, showing us the signs of their loyalty [to the cause] – the Order of St. Louis that they had sewn between the cloth and the lining of their coats and which they had never removed since fleeing from their Fatherland. One wonders if the king knew that in the shortest time he would lose this shelter as well. After the

---

★ Nephew of Louis XVIII and the eldest son of the future Charles X.
† Princess Marie-Thérèse-Charlotte, daughter of Louis XVI of France and his wife Queen Marie Antoinette. She was imprisoned during the French Revolution but survived, even though her parents and brother perished. She married her first cousin, the Duc de Angoulême, in 1799 in Mitau.
‡ 'Gentlemen! Give the French a good beating but then show compassion to them, for they are all my children.'

disastrous battle at Friedland, the distressed king hastily departed with his entire suite for England. Could he have foreseen that just six years later he would be back on the throne of his ancestors? Everything is in the hands of the Lord, who works in miraculous ways!

Here is an amusing incident that transpired with me. What do people do in taverns? Drink, eat and play billiards. I never liked playing but [on this one occasion] I was playfully rolling balls. A German dandy [frant] soon approached me and very tactfully offered to play a game with him. Without explaining, I began to play with him for a glass of water and soon won the game. So my opponent drank a glass of water and then offered me to play once more. I replied with an offer to play for money. The German agreed at once, adding 'Should we play for 5 thalers [silver coins]?' I responded, 'I cannot accept it but am ready to play for 5 chervonets [gold coins]' and took my money out of my pocket. Just then our officers had entered the room and two of them, upon overhearing my conversation with the German, took me aside and told me with a laugh, 'What are you doing? Do you know who you are playing with this? He is a billiard marker and he owns this game. He beat us all yesterday while you cannot even play and are only rolling balls around.' 'I will try my luck,' I replied and put down my five chervonets. The German did the same and we began to compete. My comrades went to another room, where they laughed and made noise. My battle with the German ended in my victory – I put the money in my pocket and went to my deriders announcing my victory. So we all began to laugh and rollick. I told them, 'How did you not think that I will win the first game with the marker – seeing a wallet full of money, men like him usually intentionally lose first and even the second game to a novice. The question now is whether I will play any more games with him.' Without wasting any more time, I ordered a dinner with wine for five persons and spent the game money to treat all of my friends. Thus, we had a rather enjoyable dinner, and we did not eat as much as we laughed. As this boisterous dinner ended, I took my hat and sword and began walking across the billiard room to get back to my post. I was truly in a hurry not to be late for my tour of duty since I was a battalion adjutant. Just then the German loser jumped in front of me, offering to play another game. I apologised saying that I was hurrying to my post and added, 'Besides, you yourself asked me to play a game, and yet I played two games with you.' Everyone witnessing this scene began to laugh heartily and left the room while the German remained standing with a bewildered look and sighing heavily as he watched me leave. The following day almost the entire city knew about these two lost billiard games.

The march soon resumed and we hurried despite the bad weather. By 1 [13] April the entire corps was already at Jurburg, where we crossed the Niemen on ferries. On the Prussian side we were greeted by King Frederick William III and his family.

[. . .]

Upon our entry into Prussia, the Prussian King took over the responsibility of providing our troops with provisions and forage under the receipts. So our troops lacked nothing. But I cannot keep silent about certain consequences of such an arrangement. We have committed many shameful acts. Many quartermasters and other ranks tasked with receiving provisions and forage, gave foremen and local officials in the villages receipts containing imbecilic texts, such as 'somebody was here, somebody received, somebody issued receipt' and numerous other examples like this. And how was this entire mess resolved? Upon his return to St. Petersburg, the Prussian king personally delivered these receipts to [Emperor] Alexander I, who ordered the establishment of a special commission to analyse them and issue proper compensation; but since the receipts could not be analysed or counted, we ended up paying the Prussians three times more than they were entitled to.

We had rather comfortable lodgings. Two weeks later the guard approached the main army and took up positions not far from Eylau. Before reaching our quarters, we were tasked with the crossing of the Passarge River. The Life Guard Jager regiment was in the advance guard so it had to cross the river first. But because of the springtime and unusual swiftness of the river flow, it was impossible to even think of crossing the river on ferries or any other way. Since this news had to be immediately delivered to the commander-in-chief, our corps commander, Kologrivov, dispatched me with a strict order to immediately deliver this message to Grand Duke Constantine Pavlovich who was already on the opposite bank, about fifteen miles from the crossing.

Military service does not tolerate any suppositions, claims of impossibility or slowness. So I seized a fishing boat and, accompanied by two Prussian oarsmen and one non-commissioned officer, I set off across the river. As soon as we reached the middle, where the flow was the strongest, we were no longer sailing but rather spinning around. My head spun around as well and I fell and lost consciousness in the boat. The oarsmen no longer guide the boat but rather prayed to God for salvation and bid good bye to their lives. I regained my senses when we were already at the shore. I could not understand where I was. My comrades suffered from the same condition but recovered before me and did not know what to do with me. So they poured water on my face and were preparing to drag me on the shore, thinking that I had died. After resting for no more than hour, we moved along the bank and, standing opposite to our corps deployed on the riverbank, we decided to send a signal that we had safely crossed the river and raised a long pole with my coat and kiwer. No one could believe that we had survived!

On the third day of my trip to headquarters, I encountered the Grand Duke's adjutant Shulhin, who was going to see our corps. I gave him relevant papers and, upon receiving verbal instructions and written orders, I returned to my regiment which I found already across the river which it had crossed on the large boats that were delivered from Königsberg by the Prussian government.

At the completion of this rather dangerous crossing, I was dispatched with a report from the entire Guard corps to Grand Duke Constantine and with instructions to receive further orders on where the corps was supposed to proceed, lodge or camp, since upon crossing the river, the corps moved forward for five miles, concentrated and halted at a small village not knowing where it should go next.

I was given strict orders to hasten back with the response. Changing horses at stations, I managed, in just half a day, to reach the headquarters of the Grand Duke. Unfortunately, on my return trip, I had to travel during the night and by dawn, my postman guide and I both fell asleep. Although I took the precaution of tying my horse with a rope [arkan] to the postman's mount, the rope loosened and I suddenly found myself up to my knees in water. Startled by the sudden sensation of cold, I looked around and saw a vast expanse of water while my companion was gone. So what had happened? As the rope loosened, my slumbering guide kept riding on the road while my horse, feeling free, turned off the road towards the lake and started to drink water on the bank. I got out of the water with some difficulty but got completely wet up to my waist and, catching up with the postman, scolded him in both Russian and German.

By 9 o'clock in the morning I arrived at, or rather dragged myself through the worst imaginable mud to, a magnificent château. Upon entering its wide courtyard, I saw that the Grand Duke was sitting on a chair, next to the staircase and under the colonnade, at the very entrance to the château. I immediately dismounted and approached the Grand Duke's entourage. I was soaking wet and my face was barely visible because of the mud. Everyone laughed and felt sorry for me while the Grand Duke ordered me to approach and asked whether everything was fine in the corps. He then laughed and joked about me, exclaiming, 'How well you have disguised yourself, your uniform cannot be recognised at all.' He asked for a post horn [truba] that hung around my companion's neck, and began blowing it, playing some cavalry signal. He then turned to his adjutant [Nikolay] Olsufiev and told him, 'Feed this Levshin and let him go back as soon as you can.'

In half an hour the papers were ready. I was given no food (and by the way, it was the Great Sabbath) and there was no time to rest, so I immediately embarked on the return trip, hurrying as much as I could. Half-way there I met an old acquaintance whom I knew from my childhood years – Lieutenant Nikolai Fedoseevich Bykov of the Starooskolskii Musketeer Regiment, who also served as an adjutant and was travelling to receive orders. We had not seen each other in over twelve years but immediately recognised each other and, after conversing for about ten minutes, bid farewell to never encounter each other for the rest of the campaign. On the very day of the Holy Easter, I got back to my regiment and our men barely had time to break their fast when a general march was sounded and the entire corps embarked on another march.

In the last days of April, our regiment deployed in the villages not far from the town of Friedland. Count St. Priest's headquarters was at the Kloster Springborn, the former Catholic monastery. I had never seen such a variety of beautiful flowers, especially daffodils. The monastery's entire grounds were covered in daffodils, as if someone had poured milk all over them. Upon the approach of our reinforcements, an armistice was supposedly negotiated. Napoleon had suffered a major blow at the hands of the Russian forces and General Baron Bennigsen won a decisive battle [at Pultusk], where Napoleon himself was in command but was forced to retreat and consider an armistice. These negotiations were conducted secretly for over five weeks but led, as it was customary, to another war. Napoleon, as a keen inciter of quarrels and fights, rejected [our] peaceful offers.

By 9 [21] May, on the day of St. Nicholas, everyone already knew that we would soon face the French on the field of battle. This day was my name-day so many of my comrades gathered at my lodging and organised a rather earnest feast. We ate and drank to the full and behaved boisterously because in those days a larger share of officers were young men who behaved like madcaps. In the heat of our feasting it was noticed that the host himself was in fact missing – seeing that things were taking a dangerous turn, I actually hid in the attic but was soon discovered and dragged back to the yard, where I was put into a coat and swung back and forth to the shouts of 'hurrah!' Seeing that I still did not pull myself together, but in fact became even more disturbed, my comrades decided to bathe me in the pond. To the rumbling music of our regimental band, they carried me on a coat towards the pond. Fortunately Colonel Potemkin, my former battalion commander, came across this entire ceremony – he turned back and dispersed everyone, otherwise I might have been drowned in that pond.

A few days later, a secret order was received to start preparing for a march since military operations were about to resume. After celebrating Pentecost at the Kloster Springborn, the entire Guard advanced on the main road towards the town of Guttstadt. I remember vividly as on the eve of Pentecost I visited the headquarters of Count St. Priest and long admired the daffodils and tulips that covered the entire monastery grounds and its frontage. The following day, not a single flower could be seen as they had been made into bouquets and garlands to beautifully decorate the interior of the church.

On the third day after our departure, our entire Guard corps camped not far from the towns of Liebstadt and Guttstadt. The new campaign was offensive in nature. Towns and villages along the Passarge River were all suddenly attacked on 24 May [5 June] and the French were driven off at all points.

The Life Guard Jager Regiment, consisting of only two battalions, was assigned to General Dokhturov's division, on the right flank of the army, about three miles from Guttstadt. Around 2 o'clock in the afternoon our regiment had reached the village of Lomitten, where we halted and rested a bit. During this halt Count St. Priest dispatched me to find a village where our wounded were treated. About one and a half verists to the right from our line, I had to travel across a rye field, close to the enemy outposts. Although the rye was quite tall, the French continually fired on me since I was still visible above the waist and my gilded embroidery and kiwer were glistening from afar. With the Lord's blessing, I safely reached the village, where I witnessed a veritable hell. Legs being sawed off in one place, hands cut off in another and men being buried out in the fields or in the gardens. The incessant moans and cries drove me out there and, inquiring the name of the village, I returned the same way to the colonel and informed him that his order had been fulfilled; I also showed him the spot where the French fired at me.

Shortly after my return, an order was issued to deploy to the front and our regiment was supposed, by lot, to join a battalion of the Life Guard Semeyonovskii Regiment, commanded by Colonel Kriedner, to form a single unit. But Colonel Kriedner claimed some excuse and avoided this responsibility. Just half an hour later, our wounded were already being carried away to get medical treatment or, in the case of those who had died, to be buried.

In front of the fortified village of Lomitten, there was a tall pine forest that was intersected by a deep ravine. On the opposite side of this ravine the French voltigeurs had felled large pines trees and turned their roots upwards in such a manner that branches and trunks made a direct assault almost impossible while the roots shielded them from shots. But our jagers did not ponder this for too long. Leading his 1st Battalion, Count St. Priest veered to the left to move around the ravine but came under heavy canister fire and was quickly seriously injured to the leg, while his brother, Count Louis St. Priest, was wounded in the chest. Captain Wolf, who assumed command, was soon killed. Despite such challenges, our battalion still reached the Passarge River and drove the enemy column beyond the bridge and [artillery] batteries.

Meanwhile, the 2nd Battalion, under the command of Colonel Potemkin, took the ravine by storm. Demonstrating incredible gallantry, our jagers climbed over the pine branches. But we suffered heavy losses – many had been killed by bullets striking vertically on the tops of their heads. After dislodging the French from the woods, the 2nd Battalion rejoined the 1st, crossed the Passarge River and stormed the [French] earthworks and climbed into the batteries. The jagers stuck their muskets and bayonets into the earthworks and climbed on top of them as if on ladders. The enemy managed to remove their guns from these batteries and abandoned this fortified position and the village of Lomitten.

The village was captured so rapidly that when our troops entered the local manor, they found the table set [for over twenty people and] laden with various dishes and bottles, hastily abandoned by the [French] generals and their companions who had left behind their entire baggage. Those who have first-hand knowledge of Bonaparte's warriors know that this is true.

The French [often] bragged that 'those Russian rascals would never get through to us, it is impossible,'* but they were frequently wrong. Many of our officers were wounded, including Engelhardt who had lost his leg and Ogon'-Doganovskii who was killed.†

[. . .]

After the capture of the village of Lomitten, the Life Guard Jager Regiment was ordered to move to Liebstadt to join the main forces that stood in between this town and Guttstadt. Everyone spoke of the gallantry of the Guard jagers. When the regiment approached the army, all regiments shouted, 'Glorious, glorious! Well done the Guard Jagers!' and [regular] soldiers shared their provisions with the jagers since our regiment had eaten almost nothing in three days. After the capture of Lomitten we were given just three or four hours to rest.

During the fighting I suffered a strong blow to the chest from a shell splinter. So I was taken to the town of Wormditt and then to Heilsberg, where I received some medical treatment. A few hours after my arrival at Heilsberg, we learned that the entire army was in retreat and that the advance guard was already in the fortified camp at Heilsberg. Soon thereafter we heard a cannonade, followed by a musket fire. The Cossacks began to clear the town of transports.

The Guard approached the town and I decided to visit my brethren. But it proved to be impossible since the battle was already raging. Upon encountering a new wave of wounded, among whom was General Verderevskii, I was compelled to obey the Cossacks and depart for Gumbinnen. At Gumbinnen, an order was issued for all transports and the wounded to move hastily to the border town of Jurburg. So the transports and those who could endure such rapid travel proceeded there and, on the road, we learned about the defeat at Friedland. [From the Russian text in N. Levshin, *Domashnii pamyatnik* . . .]

Alexander Eyler

Eyler commanded two artillery companies in the Life Guard Artillery Battalion.

---

* Levshin cites 'Ma foi il est impossible, pour que le gredins de ruses parviennent jusqu'a nous'.

† Levshin's note: [During the assault on French battery,] Ensign Alexander Lavlovich Levshin was the first to climb on to the fortification. General Dokhturov, observing the actions of the guard from a hill and acting as a commander-in-chief in this location, dispatched his adjutant to learn the name of the officer who climbed first onto the battery and waved his sword to rally his jagers. For this exploit, Ensign Levshin were given a golden sword 'for gallantry'.

In January 1807, due to the illness of Major-General [Ivan] Kasperski,★ I assumed [temporary] command of the Life Guard Artillery Battalion while remaining the commander of my two companies. In February, an immediate campaign to Prussia was announced and on the 16th [28 February] I already departed with the entire battalion. There was unusually deep snow and I was allowed to halt at Tsarskoe Selo in order to transfer the guns and supplies onto sledges. This was done in the morning of the 17th [1 March] and, by noon, Count [Alexsey] Arakcheyev arrived to examine my arrangements. He was very content with what he had seen, for which he thanked me and drank tea with my family before returning to St. Petersburg in the evening.

On the 18th [2 March] we arrived at Gatchina where I tearfully bid farewell to my wife . . . We were required to ride draught [obyvatelskie] horses and lead our own horses by reins and for this very purpose, orders had been made to prepare some 900 carts [podvoda] at each station. But in reality none of these stations had more than 500 carts and even those were unsuitable for heavy loads such as artillery. Consequently only Count Arakcheyev's company spared its horses and travelled on carts while other companies had to harness their own horses to carts while I distributed the remaining carts among the quartermasters and officers, who received two carts each. I was ordered to march 1,000 verists [1,070 km] to Jurburg in just 30 days, making marches 30–40 verists long. I was allowed to halt for rest only in Pskov so the battalion could confess and receive communion (the Holy Synod† having issued a permission for a [special] one-day service) which meant that this halt brought no rest to my men. In Bauska, Major-General Kasperski caught up with us and assumed command of the battalion while I, with my two companies, separated from him and, moving by forced marches, made two additional marches in order to reach the road running through Telsiai and follow in the wake of the Grand Duke [Constantine's] column. I arrived in Jurburg within the allotted time and spent two weeks there, resting and recovering [from the long march]. In early April, the Guard [crossed the border] and entered Prussia. The complete thaw greatly complicated the movement of the heavy artillery in the muddy chernozem [black earth], which is why, as well as in order to improve our supplying, we were ordered to halt at Insterburg; Count Arakcheyev's company only managed to reach Gumbinnen. We spent two weeks in Insterburg, where there were virtually no men while ladies refused to see in me a 28-year-old colonel, which caused many amusing disputes. On 1 [13] May the Guard was placed in positions at Heilsberg, but was then moved the following day and the artillery were assigned billets in a small village about ten verists [10km] away from the town.

★ Kasperski graduated from the Artillery and Engineer Cadet Corps in 1786 and was promoted to major-general in 1803, when he also assumed command of the Life Guard Artillery Battalion.

† The governing body of the Russian Orthodox Church.

One evening I was returning from my comrades and had to walk on round logs laid across a stream. The water had risen and the logs suddenly moved and I found myself straddling one of them. I struggled to get back to the bank and lost my engagement ring in the process. But early next morning my soldiers, upon learning of this incident, dispersed along the bank and found the ring at a depth of over one arshin [70cm]; I rewarded the lucky finder with a chervonets [gold coin]. [From the Russian text in A. Eyler, *Zapiski* . . .]

Vasilii Grigoryev

The son of a minor government official, Vasilii Grigoryev followed in his father's footsteps, starting work as a clerk in the Governing Senate and earning the civil rank of college assessor at the age of twenty-two in 1803. But this young and intelligent man was rather indifferent to his dull work and preferred spending time in the company of drinking buddies and women, which resulted in frequent reprimands from his superiors. Irked and eager for change, Grigoryev jumped at the opportunity that arrived in late 1806. On 30 November, Emperor Alexander issued a manifesto on the creation of regional militia forces (see Chapter 1). The decree created seven new military administrative districts, with St. Petersburg province, where Grigoryev lived, placed in the 1st District. In February 1807, the 1st District began forming the St. Petersburg Militia Battalion of Skirmishers (Sankt-Peterburgskii militsionnyi battalion strelkov) under command of Lieutenant-Colonel N. Verevkin of the Life Guard Grenadier Regiment. Just two weeks later, the unit was ordered to join the Life Guard Jager regiment and proceed to the theatre of war in Poland. Training as they went, the militiamen reached the Russian army just in time to participate in the spring offensive.

1 [14] April. I woke up at 6 o'clock in the morning and, reading the regimental order on the crossing [of the Niemen], I realised that I had to find [hair] powder. So I dressed and went to a local tavern [korchma] to get some from the Jews, who instead gave me wheat flour which I, out of necessity, had to use to powder my hair.

The regiment assembled and deployed on the bank of the Niemen at seven o'clock in the morning and at nine, the crossing had started using transport vessels. Since [Lieutenant Mikhail] Matsnev was absent that day, as the most senior in rank I was tasked with taking my company on the first boat to the Prussian bank, where, upon landing and deploying, I ordered it to deploy in the front just as His Majesty the Emperor himself was reviewing troops in the company of his Adjutant-General Prince Peter Mikhailovich Volkonskii. Upon hearing me shouting orders, His Majesty approached me and deigned to inquire about the quality of my men. I responded that the men behaved well on the march and were quickly getting used to active service. Just then

Frederick William III, the King of Prussia, approached and the Emperor told him, 'these are my still-inexperienced [skorospelyi] troops, who are getting trained and equipped on the march'.

Meanwhile other vessels had crossed the river and the entire regiment deployed near the dock. So the Emperor issued an order 'by section to the right and quick march', and then moved ahead accompanied by the [Prussian] king.

Having marched no more than a versta [1km] from the dock, I came across a rather attractive building that might have been a manor or a pastor's home since there was a [Protestant] church nearby. I assumed that the [Prussian] king was staying there since a Prussian outpost, commanded by an officer, was standing near the house. As I was very thirsty, I asked for a glass of water from an old woman standing near this home. She brought it on a clean plate and upon drinking water, I decided to thank her for her help by giving her a chervonets [a gold coin] that I had won [in a card game]. As I put the coin on the plate, the Prussian sentry officer could not conceal his amazement, exclaiming in German, 'Oh, my Lord, a Russian officer is paying a chervonets for a simple glass of water!'

Marching for another four verstas [4km], we stopped to rest and, after eating breakfast, we gathered our songsters and began singing songs. But upon seeing the Emperor and the Prussian king riding towards us, we immediately commanded 'to your places' and 'attention' but as he approached us His Majesty told the regimental commander to continue singing and to ensure that the men were resting and having fun.

By nightfall we reached the village of Romaniski while our regimental supply train was still at Jurbug because of deep mud [on the road].

2 [14 April] We had a day of rest at the village [Romaniski] and I took advantage of this respite to write my eighth letter to my loved ones.

3 [15 April] Continued marching, spent the night at a village where our officer Vasilii Trusov excelled in his knowledge of the German language by using some words and gestures to ask our hostess to bring him eggs for dinner, but instead she brought him a latrine chair.

4–5 [16–17 April] Marching on a rather bad road that kept firm by the morning frost alone, but larks – the heralds of the spring – are already in the fields.

6 [18 April] We halted at a village, where we for the first time encountered captured French officers who were escorted by the brash Prussian hussars. Prince Golitsyn and I invited these prisoners to drink tea with us and, after spending an hour with us, they cheered up and told us about military operations and shared their grievances about the rudeness and abuses of their escorts.

7 [19 April] Marching again, spent the night at a village.

8 [20 April] Same as above. The village was located near the sea coastline and because of the high tide, the water had spilled into various parts of the roads, rising up to the waist deep. So we had to take at least two verstas [2km] long roundabout to get around these places, but cold and dampness would

have almost certainly made me sick if not for a tavern that we encountered; I ordered to halt there and, taking a strong liquor, I rubbed with it all the parts of my body that had got wet and then drank a sizable cup of it. I also ordered a pail of this veritable nectar, which locals call Branntwein,* to be distributed to the jagers and skirmishers who claimed that they could make no other use of it but to consume it since this way it would truly reach all parts of the body. With the Lord's blessing, all of them were healthy. Truly, the Russian people can endure anything! Marching about ten verstas [10km] from this tavern, we stopped for the night at a village.

9 [21 April] Marching again. By noon we arrived at Insterburg,† which is a small town but does have several stone buildings as well as an apothecary and a small market. We rested here.

10 [22 April] On the road, spent the night at a village.

11 [23 April] Around 2 o'clock in the afternoon we arrived at the village of Imsdorf, located not far from the town of Allenburg,‡ and stopped there.

12 [24 April] In the morning I travelled to the town [Allenburg] to find a decent lunch there. The town is even better than Insterburg, and features buildings made of wood covered with clay plaster, although there are stone buildings as well. The town has a central square and a main street, where two churches and city hall are located. At a local tavern I indulged myself in German dishes that seemed delicious only because I was famished, and returned to my quarters around 3 o'clock in the afternoon.

At five o'clock in the afternoon, at a suitable place near the village, we held training drills for two jager companies, involving deployment and firing. The training continued for two hours and as we later learned, it frightened a quartermaster of the Life Guard Cossack Regiment, who was sent to Allenburg to get billets. Upon hearing gunfire and observing standing and lying skirmishers, he became convinced, out of fear and cajolery of a German fuhrmann [coachman], that these were the French and those on the ground were killed in action. So he turned around and rushed back to inform his commander Colonel [Peter] Chernozubov of this discovery. This news caused alarm in the regiment and a half-squadron led by Staff Rotmistr Ivan Efremov§ was dispatched to reconnoitre this imaginary enemy. Efremov arrived at our village late in the day and had to spend the night there. We learned about this the following day and laughed heartily about it.

---

*   Branntwein or brännvin is a strong liquor distilled from potatoes, grain or, in some instances, wood cellulose. The term literally means 'burn-wine', indicating its high alcohol content.
†   Today Chernyakhovsk in the Kaliningrad region of Russia.
‡   Nowadays Druzhba in the Kaliningrad region of Russia.
§   Future lieutenant-general (1829) and commander of the Life Guard Cossack Regiment.

13 [25 April] It is the Holy Saturday, so we remained in the same village. I was suffering from extreme boredom and had not a single penny [ni grosha] in my pocket while our treasure chest, where I could borrow money from, was still stuck in Insterburg because of muddy road. Our regiment's Lieutenant Prince N. M. Golitsyn was sent to ensure its timely delivery to us and upon his departure the prince split in twain the remaining money, namely two chervonets [gold coins] and six silver rubles – that is all I had to celebrate this holiday, wishing for a brighter future.

14 [26 April] Easter Sunday. Because of a strange order issued last evening, we gathered at a designated place at 6 o'clock in the morning and marched to the town of Allenburg, where we halted for some time, allowing the officers to gather in the billet of the battalion commander Lieutenant-Colonel Nikolay Nikitich Verevkin, listen to the prayers read by a priest and celebrate the day. We then resumed our march and, passing through the town and covering some fifteen verstas [15km], we halted at the village of Wensschnuren[?], located near the town of Friedland. Matsnev and I got a billet with a rather affluent peasant and, after resting and eating, spent time coming up with different kinds of mischief. We sent our host to Friedland to bring us some wenches [devki] and he returned with three so late in the evening we all gathered at the lodging of the battalion commander, Verevkin, and merrily spent the night in cordial and frank conversations. A battalion training exercise was scheduled for the morning.

15 [27 April] After the training exercise, I had lunch at home and spent another merry evening with the wenches, with each of us showing off in his own manner. Even our virtuous Matsnev decided to participate but his mischievous servant Nikanorka restrained him from this sinful behaviour by preaching him a sermon on the consequences that can be particularly appreciable during a campaign.* But this morality, as is usually the case with all preachers, did not stem from a genuine concern but rather came out of the desire to exploit the circumstances.

16–17 [28–29 April] We remain in the same place. The time is passed in usual affairs, training, card games, and so on.

18 [30 April] After learning from the passing officers that my cousin-in-law [Lieutenant-Colonel] Stepan Leontievich Osipov was in command of two companies in an artillery brigade stationed not far from us, I saddled my horse after lunch and went to find him. I travelled through Friedland, which, as is the custom with all small towns, has one main street. I rode along this street and, following directions, moved left across the vast field† and wandering in the vast pine forest, I somehow found the manor where Osipov was billeted;

---

* Grigoryev implies that Nikanorka spoke about sexually-transmitted diseases and the dangers they posed.

† Grigoryev's later insertion: 'where a fierce battle raged on 2 [14] June'.

fortunately, he was in and our meeting proved to be pleasant and enjoyable for both of us. I shared news about his family which he had not seen in a long time, since during the winter campaign he was wounded in the hand at the battle of Preussisch-Eylau. We got so preoccupied with conversation that we did not even notice how the time flew by. In the evening, officers, who were lodged with him, were joined by others from various companies, and [among others] I was introduced to Colonel Count [Jacob] Sievers and Captain [Fedor] Begunov.

After eating a very late dinner, I travelled back in the company of those who came from the town since I would not have found the road in the dark. Since it was very dark in the woods, the oilcloth covering [kleenchatyi' chekhol] of Count Sievers' kiwer served as a signpost for us. Upon reaching the town, we all went off in various directions. I turned right off the main road and went to that bridge over the Alle River that is located near a mill. [As I travelled] a night sentry, standing at the corner of the central square, was shouting wholeheartedly, as is required here, that it was already midnight and was accompanying his cries with the sound of a rattle, which so frightened my horse that she bolted past the bridge towards the river and I barely managed to halt her. I had to turn around and cross the bridge, safely reaching my lodgings, where I found my comrades sleeping in the sweet embrace of the hetaerae,★ and followed their example.

19 [April; 1 May] At five o'clock in the morning I was woken up by a drum beating 'assembly'. I hastily dressed and joined the company. At seven o'clock, we departed. The road ran past the town of Bartenstein [Bartoszyce] where the [Russian] Emperor's headquarters was located. Near the city we saw Grand Duke Constantine and our regiment, deploying by platoons, passed by him in a ceremonial march; His Excellency was visibly pleased by the order and organisation of the skirmisher battalion and announced his gratitude to us. Because of the distance to the [nearest] village, tonight we are bivouacked in an open field.

20 [April; 2 May] On the march, we spent the night in the village that was almost completely uninhabited, and had been plundered by the French. We could not find a morsel of food here except for rotten potatoes.

21 [April; 3 May] We spent the night in the same place and after exploring villages in a fifteen-versta [15km] wide area, we only found a few eggs and one sheep.

22 [April; 4 May] On the march; stopped for the night at the village that was no better than the previous one.

23 [April; 5 May] On the march; spent the night at a rather affluent village, at least we were able to eat well and this was quite something.

★ Hetaera (pl. hetaerae), from ancient Greek hetairai, a female companion, or courtesan.

24 [April; 6 May] On the march again; we stopped for the night at the village of Ostroviken [?], one of the devastated villages in the area. Whatever provisions survived the plunder have been buried by the peasants in the woods. My comrades and I were billeted at the affluent home of Schultz, whose abode was especially appealing because he had a seventeen-year-old daughter Katerina, a very pretty and kind girl who has already had the first experience of physical [sexual] encounter, courtesy of the French who had been here shortly before our arrival.

25 [April; 7 May] At the same place; we spent the time in pointless card games and other dealings. After acquainting with us, our host was very helpful and showed us receipts for the delivery of oats, potato, peas and other provisions issued by the Russian officers of various regiments, who, in fact, wrote every sort of nonsense that one can think of.

26 [April; 8 May] Upon learning that Peter Aleksandrovich Ogon'Doganov-skii has returned from Mittau and is lodging with Aleksey Kologrivov in the village about three verstas [3km] from ours, I rode over there in the evening. I found them in the company of some of our officers. This unexpected meeting of the long-lost friends offered an occasion for a proper carousal [popoika] which so excited Kologrivov that he decided to go hunting jack-snipes and great snipes, even though it was already nine o'clock in the evening and therefore quite dark. Since Doganovskii joined him in this enterprise, I involuntarily followed them as well. We took muskets and left the lodgings, but after travelling for some distance, Kologrivov encountered his company's drummer, with a drum on his back, and came up with an idea to beat the alarm to see how quickly his company would assemble, forgetting that shortly before that an order was issued to sound the alarm [only] if the enemy unexpectedly attacked and, in that case, [the troops were] to assemble at the Main Headquarters. So Kologrivov ordered his drummer to beat the drum and sound alarm, upon which his company indeed assembled in no more than five minutes and deployed in full fighting gear. Furthermore, we soon heard the other units deployed in the vicinity responding to our sounding of the alarm.

Realising that this prank had already gone too far, I [immediately] left the hunt and the hunters, running back to Kologrivov's lodging, returned the weapon and, mounting my horse, I rushed to my company, which was already deployed and ready to march. I barely convinced Matsnev and other officers that all of this transpired because of Kologrivov's prank and we then dispatched messengers to the neighbouring posts to inform them.

27 [April; 9 May] We remained in the same place. We learned that Kologrivov's prank resulted in him spending a week under arrest and receiving a severe reprimand from the commander-in-chief.

28 [April; 10 May] We are on the march; spent the night in a village.

29 [April; 11 May] On the road again; we spent the night near Heilsberg, at an abandoned village that had been so devastated by the French that there

was not a single soul living there and most windows were missing glass. Consequently, we could not find any provisions and had to be content with whatever supplies we had with us.

30 [April; 12 May] Another day at the same depopulated village. I shared my boredom with Prince Nikolay M. Golitsyn, who was completely distressed by a letter he has received from his father,* who, in rather humiliating terms, spoke of his feeling and the sense of honour; this letter was especially upsetting for him because it was written due to the intrigues of his stepmother. As I was a close friend of the prince, I tried various means to dispel his grief and humiliation, and had some success in this.

1 [13] May We departed at five o'clock in the morning and, having marched through the town of Heilsberg, we halted behind it, at the bivouacs already prepared in the field. Not knowing whose successors we have become, we immediately began improving the bivouacs as best we could. I got a hut in a rather nice location, not far from the Alle River.

This day reminded us of the St. Petersburg festivities at Ekaterinhof so after resting, we turned to playing various games that were entirely in Russian fashion, such as svaika† and gorodki.‡ In the former the best player was the junior colonel of our regiment, Jacob Alekseyevich Potemkin, while in the latter – Captain Nikita Ivanovich Wolf.

2–3 [14–15 May] I explored the neighbourhood of our camp, which is very suitable for military operations; the position is advantageous because the centre of our camp features an open field. On the left side from the town there are some hills where, as well as in hollows adjacent to the woods, are deployed batteries of 18- and 24-pounder cannon, with six or eight pieces in each battery. On the right side flows the Alle River while behind [the camp] is the town of Heilsberg, which is quite large and includes many buildings and a large public garden in the English fashion. We received various provisions from this town, but most often we simply dine at the local tavern called 'Sem sester' [Seven Sisters], the name being given to it by the Russians.

4 [16 May] I woke up very early, around 3 a.m., and when I left my hut to swim in the river, I witnessed the following magnificent view: the rising sun illuminated a vast expanse of the plain and the tops of hills occupied by the troops, and in just an hour's time, all of this came to life and began to move; some were improving their huts, others training and still others

---

* In 1807, Prince Mikhail Golitsyn was the governor of Yaroslav and was married to his third wife, Natalya Tolstoy.

† A popular throwing game in Russia up to the twentieth century. The game involved throwing a marlinspike-like spear into the middle of a metal ring lying on the ground some distance away.

‡ A popular Russian folk game that involved throwing a bat from a predetermined distance at the 'gorodki', a group of skittles arranged in various patterns. A variation of this game was played all across the Baltic region.

cooking – such was the morning. By sunset, this picture transformed with the approaching twilight, the coolness of the air [seemingly] calls for indulgence and everywhere joyous songs and music can be heard; and once the sunset call is sounded, a complete stillness descends, now and then interrupted by the signals of sentries.

5 [17 May] I was thrilled by the arrival of my old friend and former comrade-in-arms in the Horse Guards, Rotmistr Alexander Andreevich Pogrebov of the Life Guard Hussar Regiment. He dined with me and we spent the evening in pleasant remembrance of the past.

6 [18 May] Spent the day in usual training exercises; in the evening, while walking in the camp, I got acquainted with Staff Captain Peter Ivanovich Borozdin of the Kexholmskii Infantry Regiment. I like him a lot as a man to keep pleasant company with.

7 [19 May] Following the orders I, for the first time, left my battalion to join a sentry post in the forward line that covers our troops and a six-gun battery. Soon I had to place in the hauptwachhe [guardhouse] a soldier of the Olonetskii battalion who had deserted his unit but, not knowing the road, walked straight into our advance posts. I asked him who prompted him to desert. He responded that he is slow-witted but despite this, the following day, on the commander-in-chief [Bennigsen's] order, he was run six times through a battalion gauntlet* as an example to others and to prevent similar attempts.

8 [20 May] At the training exercises in the morning and, in the company of my comrades and routine exercises – card games, smoking, drinking – in the evening.

9 [21 May] I travelled to Heilsberg and for the first time since our departure from Russia I was able to listen to the liturgy to St. Nicholas performed at our regiment's field church. I had a lunch at a tavern and after a walk in the city garden, I came across some gentlewomen from St. Petersburg: Madame Khrapovitskii† and Madame Uvarov,‡ who was previously married to Count Valerian Zubov,§ accompanied by her two companions. Around eight o'clock in the evening I returned to the same tavern to drink tea and found there a large gathering of officers from various regiments. While drinking tea I got acquainted with Staff Captain Pavel Lvovich Yezefovich of the Rostovskii Regiment. By then a rather lucrative card game was underway and the

---

* A form of corporal punishment where a captive was run between two rows of soldiers who repeatedly struck him. The Russian army used spießruten, long and flexible rods that soldiers used to strike the captive's back.

† Sofia Alekseevna Khrapoviotskii was married to Colonel Matvei Khrapovitskii of the Life Guard Izmailovskii Regiment.

‡ Maria Fedorovna Uvarov was married to General Fedor Uvarov.

§ General-en-Chef Valerian Zubov (1771–1804) was a powerful favourite under Empress Catherine II. He commanded the Persian Expedition of 1796 but was recalled and disgraced by Emperor Paul.

glistening of gold coins tempted me to try my luck. Alas, fortune rarely smiled on my family name and this effort ended with the loss of a dozen gold coins. Around midnight I decided to return to the camp but as I passed through the town, I resolved to stop by the three little houses that stood on the edge of a pond at the end of the vorstadt [suburb] and to find the soubrettes who frequently came to our camp to sell various provisions. Since there was no light inside the room and the shutters were closed, I had to look for them by touch and thus came across sleeping Germans, whom I woke up with my whip [nagaika] in order to see who they were. They ran away, leaving me all alone. It was rather fortunate that German cowardice caused them, despite numbering some five men, to flee because otherwise I could have fared badly struggling with them in the dark and would have ended up in the pond. So I resumed my trip and safely returned to my bivouac.

10 [22 May] I was at the training exercises in the morning and later ate with my comrades Major Andrey Adamovich Lefner of the Pernovskii Regiment and Staff Captain Peter Ivanovich Borozdin. Later I invited them as well as Staff Captain Semen Pavlovich Chernoviech of the Pernovskii Regiment and Ivan Matveevich Stassel of the Kexholmskii Regiment, to come over to my hut to drink tea. Soon after their arrival, we were visited by the two soubrettes whom I looked for yesterday. They brought fruit, sugar and rum, all of which was quickly bought from them. But since they were rather pleasant-looking and had nothing else to sell, we started bartering with them for their own goods. I was first to initiate it and some of my guests followed my example. Fortunately, I suffered none of the undesirable consequences that usually happen in such circumstances, probably because right after the incident I bathed in the Alle River.

11 [23 May] Around twelve o'clock, having eaten with my officers, we all travelled to the city garden and afterwards went to see the [memorial] monuments of Lieutenant-General [Roman] Anrep who was killed by a [French] tirailleur after the battle of Preussisch-Eylau,* and of Major-General [Alexander] Siedmioraczki.† The former had a simple wooden cross, painted black with a white inscription indicating who he was and where and how he lost his life; the latter was commemorated with a white pointed stone pyramid, with a bronze plate revealing that it was built by the Belozerskii Regiment in memory and gratitude to its chef. Honour and praise to such a commander and his subordinates. The sight of these monuments brought sadness and reminded me how fleeting life actually is and how insignificant all the great earthly endeavours are, especially when every one of us was so close to losing his life. We dined at the well-frequented tavern in the town and returned to our bivouacs in the evening.

---

* Anrep was killed at Mohrungen on 25 January 1807.
† Siedmioraczki was killed on 28 April 1807.

12 [24 May] [I was] on guard duty at the battery, in the field, when an unexpected event alarmed me: it was already an evening and was time for rundes* to issue the password but the non-commissioned officer, who was dispatched for this purpose to the army's duty general, did not return. So another two messengers were sent but neither of them returned before retreat was sounded. In fact, they all returned only at midnight – I learned that the reason for their delay was simple: Duty General Nikolay Ivanovich Verderevskii,† Major-General Nikolay Nikolayevich Mazovskoi‡ and our battalion commander Nikolay [Nikitovich] Verevkin were together celebrating their name-day. The password was – Pskov; reply – St. George; signal – invincible.

13 [25 May] I was replaced on guard duty and spent the day as usual.

14 [26 May] I was in Heilsberg, had a joyous and pleasant time with my comrades.

15 [27 May] Training exercises [during the day]. At night, as the result of frequent and powerful lightning strikes, accompanied with thunder, an alarm was sounded in the entire camp – the light of beacons had been earlier set as the signal for assembly in case of the appearance of enemy forces and the lightning strikes were mistaken for such a signal.

16 [28 May] Orders have been issued to prepare to march. Our battalion was detached from the Life Guard Jager Regiment and assigned to the division of Count [Peter] Tolstoy.§ Consequently, we spent most of the day in Heilsberg bidding farewell to our comrades and, I must admit, it proved be a rather emotional experience for me.

17 [29 May] At seven o'clock we formed up and half an hour later we despondently marched away, leaving behind our good and kind comrades. Having marched for three miles¶ and about one versta [1km] away from Seeburg, we halted in an open field and built bivouacs.

18 [30 May] I was in Seeburg, which burned to the ground just a few days before our arrival and some of the ruins were still smouldering. Two regiments – the Belozerskii and Nizovskii Musketeers – had been foraging here before. The surroundings are fine and we are in an open plain that is surrounded by a vast pine forest which provides plenty of material for our bivouacs.

19 [31 May] In the morning and afternoon we held company training exercises, so I was rather bored all day long.

---

* A runde was an officer appointed to assist the duty officer in supervising sentries.
† Verderevskii was also chef of the Kexholmskii Musketeer Regiment and later commanded the Life Guard Semeyonovskii Regiment (1807–9)
‡ Mazovskoi was chef of the Pavlovskii Grenadier Regiment and killed at Friedland on 14 June.
§ Lieutenant-General Peter Tolstoy temporarily commanded the 6th Division.
¶ Grigoryev does not specify the type of mile he is referring to. A Russian mile (milya) is 7.46km while a German meile, which is often mentioned in the contemporary Russian writings, is 7.53km.

20 [May; 1 June] Battalion exercises held in the morning and afternoon, the rest of time I spent in the company of my officer [friends].

21 [May; 2 June] Orders have been issued that the 2nd Division, on the occasion of Lieutenant-General [Nikolay] Tuchkov's illness, should transfer under command of Count Tolstoy while our division, which Tolstoy commanded until now, is given to Prince Aleksey Ivanovich Gorchakov.

22 [May; 3 June] We are ordered to prepare to march but because such orders have become commonplace, we all remained preoccupied with our usual matters. [From the Russian text in V. Grigoryev, Podennyj zhurnal . . .]

Faddei Bulgarin

Newly enlisted in a cavalry regiment, Bulgarin spent most of April and May marching to the theatre of war. Upon arriving in Heilsberg, he decided to visit the headquarters hoping to use his connections to secure a comfortable position close to the commander-in-chief.

On 21 May [2 June], the headquarters was at Heilsberg and I asked Colonel [Anton] Chalikov [of the Sumskii Hussars] to grant me permission to go to the town to deliver letters to the commander-in-chief and the duty general. Glancing at the names of letter recipients, Colonel Chalikov exclaimed, 'Fancy-pancy [frontery-pontery]! Go ahead, lad, and instead of patronage, bring us some bread and vodka from headquarters.' So I left, escorted by an uhlan, and, by nine o'clock in the morning, had already reached Heilsberg.

The headquarters, even if the ruler himself is not present, serves for the army the same role that a court does in the state. The headquarters is the source of all the graces and rewards and consequently all desires are directed there and all fortune-seekers flock there. The small town of Heilsberg was seething with life and people. Troops were marching through the town along the main street while numerous officers from various branches were staying behind to eat or grab some provisions. Almost all the local ladies were preoccupied with renting their apartments, whether legally or illegally. Staff officers received lodgings from the municipal authorities and their hosts were responsible for provisioning. Everyone else, however, stayed at the homes as they wished, oftentimes asking nothing but the space and the residents rarely refused this.

Residents traded anything they could. All streets were full of sellers offering alcohol, bread and various provisions; in the two or three existing taverns there was such crowding of the Russian and Prussian officers that one could hardly squeeze into the room. There was a deafening noise everywhere. Card games were played in the taverns and in homes and fistfuls of gold coins instantly changed hands. In these battles on green fields the supply commissioners, who were entrusted enormous sums of money to procure food for the troops, particularly distinguished themselves.

There was a shocking level of abuse in the commissary. The army was supplied, as well as it could be, at the expense of the population and we had never seen a state supply transport delivering provisions, even though the treasury spent millions for that exact purpose. Afterwards many supply commissioners were court-martialled, many of them were demoted and the entire staff of the supply service lost its military uniforms as punishment for their abuses. But [back in June 1807], the supply commissioners could not foresee this storm and lived luxuriously, riding in rich carriages, entertaining their mistresses, losing tens and even hundreds of thousands of rubles and recklessly squandering away. I knew one commissioner who bet one thousand chervonets [gold coins] per game, gave one hundred chervonets to local beauties, refused to drink anything but champagne and wore nothing but cambric underwear – and yet he ended his life in utter poverty, court-martialled, imprisoned, and begging for paper rubles in the streets of St. Petersburg! And there were many other examples like that.

Wine flowed freely in the taverns. I still do not understand how merchants of such small towns could procure sufficient champagne, which the Russian officers consumed as if it was water. As a result of card games and frequent binge drinking, there were many instances of duels as well as fistfights with cardsharpers, for whom there was plenty of bounty.

Although the Prussians were our allies, the Russian officers had strained relations with them while the French were, on the contrary, honoured and well treated whenever we met them. The Prussian officers refused to give us precedence, acted haughtily and arrogantly, occasionally even bragging; with their customary German frugality, they drank beer when champagne flowed freely on the Russian tables, and bet a gulden when we threw down piles of gold. This served as the cause for our ridicule, which, naturally, caused quarrels and fights. Russian hussars were most likely to fight with the Prussians because the Prussians, true to their traditions of the Seven Years War, considered their cavalry the best in the world. Whenever our hussars encountered Prussian cavalry officers, their meeting inevitably led to a duel. The army was full of stories about these incidents . . . [From the Russian text in F. Bulgarin, *Vospominaniya*]

Eduard von Löwenstern

After successfully carrying out his mission to Königsberg but getting robbed on the way back, Löwenstern rejoined his Sumskii Hussar Regiment as the battle of Eylau was ending.

After several marches, we arrived at Borchersdorf. All of us, officers as well as common soldiers, had gotten more used to the enemy and no longer feared him as before but rested, even though we knew that he was very near. In Fuchsberg, we sought forage and plundered all united together, especially Lieutenant Henkel who became the scourge of the inhabitants of that unhappy village. One morning six enemy dragoon regiments were deployed on the plains near Borchersdorf. Our squadrons very calmly went into formation. The French at first seemed to want to fight us but took flight at our first shouts of 'Hurrah!' The greatest confusion ruled in their line and never had a victory been so easy. As nasty as Lieutenant Obosenko otherwise was, he distinguished himself exceedingly in this affair. With our squadron he surrounded the village, attacked the enemy in the rear with the loud shout, 'Hurrah Sumskii! Hurrah Sumskii!' and decided the victory. We did not give the enemy even a moment to consider his next move but followed the fleeing dragoons to Ludwigsdorf [?]. Most of them were cut down, and over 300 taken prisoner including many officers of higher ranks. I also mingled with the pursuing hussars and let many a fleeing Frenchman feel the cruelty of my arm and the sharpness of my sabre. Colonel Ushakov sent me to lead Captain Kremenetski and Lieutenant Shakhmatov, who were holding an outpost two [Prussian] meiles* from there, into the action; however, the squadrons arrived in Borchersdorf too late. The village churchyard soon turned into a marketplace. Hussars were selling watches, rings, tobacco boxes, sabres, books, horses, pipes, saddles, pistols, in a word all kinds of plundered booty, for almost nothing. I did not buy anything since no one was probably poorer than I. Even though I had had the opportunity, I had taken no booty. My faithful Koptschik, who had taken a musket ball in the jaw, became ill there; despite that, I continued to ride him.

After the more amusing than bloody chase, we went to Kreuzburg and from there I went with Captain Shishkin to Königsberg where we stayed for a couple of days. After a week of crossing back and forth in East Prussia, after several smaller and now and then important skirmishes and duels around Königsberg, we set up camp near Launau on the orders of Prince Bagration. Seven or eight light cavalry regiments under General [Fedor] Korff were taken by surprise in Peterswalde, cut down and several men were taken prisoner. The Sumskii and Izumskii Hussar Regiments had to mount their horses and hurriedly go at a full trot to help the light cavalry. When they saw them coming, the French retreated into the woods near Guttstadt and took along General Korff as prisoner with many other staff and senior officers. While chasing the enemy, my horse and I fell, but I did not do myself any further damage. Near Launau, a [Prussian] meile [7.5km] from Heilsberg, the Izumskii, Sumskii, Olviopolskii, Yelisavetgradskii and Alexandriiskii Hussar Regiments, and several light cavalry units bivouacked.

For the first few days, because of inexcusable thefts, the authorities in charge of supply could not procure sufficient provisions and forage. That

---

* About 15 km or 9 miles.

scarcity increased day by day without their trying in Königsberg or in the main headquarters in Bartenstein to alleviate our misery. I still find it incomprehensible how Meirovitch, Arbuzov and Konsorten could steal the army's provisions in such an outrageous manner. If anyone deserved the gallows, those unworthy scoundrels do in full measure, who revelled together with the likes of them and filled their pockets in Königsberg while we unhappy soldiers in camp were dying of hunger.

[My brother] Georges was with the Izumskii Hussars very close to us. We built barracks, hauled straw and wood, and the larger the camp became, the smaller that unhappy village of Launau got until it finally disappeared. Only one house, the one in which Prince Bagration lived, remained. Since the storehouse in Königsberg did not send us any provisions or forage, we soon had to get everything by force. The plain around Heilsberg, Bischofstein, etc. was soon looted by our foragers. That unbridled band, plundering from hunger and need, committed the greatest excesses without anyone daring to put a stop to it. During such expeditions, I often witnessed outrageous injustices and cruelty. The time of the rule of force and barbarity seemed to have returned worse than ever. Daily, horses in the camp died of hunger and cold. The rest stood there more like skeletons than cavalry horses and awaited their inescapable deaths. For a long time, even the thought of giving them oats had not been possible, and the poor animals ate ravenously the small amount of hay stolen with the greatest of effort in the countryside. I too was in a completely abject situation. I had lost my good [comrade] Salei since I was sent to the First Peloton after Theodor had become an officer.

Lieutenant Obosenko, a peasant himself, mistreated every nobleman as much as he could and was as strict as he could be with me. In particular, he had forbade the hussars to give me any help. It went so far that I was forced to look after the horse of the hussar who plaited my long hussar braid every morning, and I had to beg a lot around the camp until I found someone who would put my dishevelled hair in order. Anyone who has not worn a hussar braid himself, has no idea about the discomfort that very pretty-looking braid can cause. The hair on each side of the head is tied tight against the temple with a lead ring and made into a braid. From the temple a braid is made across the head. The hair of the back of the head is braided into eight to ten smaller braids and end, mixed with fake hair, in a braid that reaches more than half-way down the back. You had to have it done every day if you did not want to be tortured by the pulling and irritation of the fake hair, of the many lead rings and the thickly-smeared pomade. The hussars did each other's hair with the greatest of speed. Since I, however, was not used to doing it at all, I could neither help myself nor anyone else.

I had no money. The few ducats from the Mohrungen booty had been long since spent. The Polish Light Horse had stolen my saddlebags after the battle at Eylau. I simply had nothing. My coat was half-way a robbery of the bivouac fire; my boots torn; the leather buttons on my breeches had completely shrunk from unbuttoning, a means of getting at the vermin, and were barely held together by torn and rotten rags. My only shirt had turned into lint. Only the collar and the sleeves clung to my body, emaciated by hunger and worry. But even thinner and more miserable was my brave Koptschik. The long unaccustomed fasting had totally changed his otherwise cheerful nature. He stood quietly for days before his empty manger and patiently awaited a terrible undeserved death from hunger. I saw an unavoidable end to my first cavalry campaign because what could I have done on that poor animal that could barely stand?

Often I wished to be taken prisoner, since my helpless position could never have become worse. Kovtun, the private in the peloton and the factotum of my lieutenant, bullied and offended me where and whenever he could. I promised each one, him and his lieutenant, a ball through the head in the first battle and would have kept my God-given word. That threat that I repeated loudly and often in camp finally got me some peace and quiet, for I was known in the squadron as quite determined. On a nightly patrol between Zechern and Peterswalde, I had my pistol ready, only my good heart that was against assassination saved Obosenko from certain death.

One evening – if I am not mistaken, the beginning of March – I returned to camp tired and weak from foraging. Once again we had had to seek hay at a great distance and had spent the whole day riding around in a quagmire. I could barely stand straight from exhaustion – wrapped in my coat, I threw myself on the ground and fell asleep. Soon I was quite rudely shaken awake. 'Get going to the captain.' A hussar yelled at me, 'He has called for you several times and has something important to tell you.'

'May the Devil take you and the captain!' I thought, rubbed the sleep out of my eyes, buckled my sabre around me and went. Full punch glasses and congratulations greeted me. I had become – consider my endless joy – an officer! I stopped as if turned to stone. I did not know what was happening to me. Was it a dream? Was it reality? Everything that had happened was forgotten! My anger toward my officers who had treated me so roughly was drowned in punch and wine, leaving behind a friendly feeling for my former superiors. The continually drunk Shishkin, the strict but brave Obosenko, the dumb Emelyanov, the no-good but foolhardy Borodovski threw themselves into my arms and were happy from the depths of their hearts. The dark, murky horizon of my life seemingly began to clear up. At least several warm rays of sun shone through the black clouds. I could take solace in a more pleasant future. If on that joy-filled evening an unbidden prophet had murmured in my ear: 'Don't believe anything. It is only a bluff. You are not yet an officer.' I think that I would have lost my mind.

I reported to First Lieutenant Delyanov, who greeted me with open arms. Both of these brothers,* excellent young men, took me into their nice warm bivouac. Now there was no private waking me with a rough voice before sunrise to water [my horse]. My horse was in the care of a soldier. And after such a long time, I could eat my fill to my heart's content at the First Lieutenant's well-filled table. I nevertheless dared not cut off my hussar braid since I had only become an officer on Bennigsen's order and still needed the imperial confirmation. I used the time while I was living at Delyanov's to put my very damaged uniform back in order. My linens were increased by a nice white shirt that I had taken off a dead French cuirassier officer.

On 24 March, I was given a command of fifty men to forage as far as possible into the countryside. Just after Heilsberg, my Koptschik collapsed under me. My faithful companion in war lay there and stretched all of his legs out. After all attempts to get the animal on its feet again failed, I petted that poor good horse and gently took my leave. A hussar had to dismount. We exchanged horses, and I left him behind in the village. After several days of marching, that whinnying brave Rehar, whom I now rode, carried me into pretty Rastenburg.† The entire town trembled before that horrible command [detachment] that immediately settled down in the market square and began to plunder a brandy inn. The reigning mayor and the high council humbly requested my protection. I, tattered fellow, was called Sir, Lieutenant, and treated royally in the city hall. Everyone fawned. I had myself given quarters, ate and drank as much as I wanted, generously spared the city from the foraging and rested on my laurels together with my people for several days. From here I foraged in the plain; and after I had foraged a large quantity and was just finished bringing the booty into camp, I received the order not to go further but to wait for the regiment.

Prince Bagration had finally succeeded in getting the Emperor to let the [exhausted and] almost useless cavalry rest for some time. The Sumskii [Regiment] went to Rhein, the Izumskii to Goldap, and the Olviopolskii to Lötzen. We marched from Rastenburg to Rhein by way of Rössel and Heiligelinde. In First Lieutenant Delyanov's absence, Captain Khvostov commanded the squadron, which set up its cantonment in Gross-Notiz. I was part of the Third Column in Klein-Notiz. Potapov, having recovered from his wounds, was in Schimonken where [my brother] Theodor also was.

In Schimonken my hussar braid was properly braided with fake hair, since I had earlier only used twine or a dirty ribbon. Here we had everything we needed. Food and drink were present in abundance. That part of Lithuania is richer and better cultivated than the remaining part of East Prussia or

---

* Löwenstern's note: The younger Delyanov was shot and killed in a battle near Smolensk in 1812. The older one was badly wounded in 1813 near Altenburg.

† Today Kętrzyn, Poland.

Ermeland. The peasants are well off and the country is pretty. My landlady in Klein-Notiz, a good peasant woman, cared for me like a son and strengthened me with strong meat broths. I had got back my beloved Koptschik – happily, that jolly comrade had escaped death on the road to Heilsberg and came back healthy and fat.

But soon forage again began to be in short supply. The elder Delyanov and I had to mount [our horses] once again with fifty men to rustle up forage for the squadron in the interior of Lithuania. I reluctantly left my little village where I had come to feel so comfortable. The good inhabitants accompanied me in tears. I too could not prevent a feeling of melancholy overcoming me when my landlady true-heartedly shook my hand and her daughters wiped their eyes and noses with their aprons.

The time of year was wonderful. Our horses were fresh once again and in good condition. We headed to Lötzen and Angerburg and foraged in the countryside to our heart's delight. We treated the Poles as enemies. Everything was taken from them by force. If someone resisted, for the outrage of defending his property, he was mistreated in the cruellest of ways. Villages and towns were plundered. Individual houses set on fire. Women and girls were treated violently. I was too young and too inexperienced to restrain hussars addicted to spoils. We went through Lötzen, Angerburg, Goldap, Philippowo, Augustowo as far as Lyck. I traversed the countryside with fire and sword. The Lithuanians will long remember me and my lively band and will tell their children and children's children for hundreds of years how the Sumskii [Hussars] dwelled here. We were called 'Pahlen's wild hunt' and did not disgrace that name. We boldly rode through the countryside, straight through the crops, through the yellow grain; [from then on] 'they know the Sumskii hunting horn'. I rode through Oletzko.* My reputation had preceded me. Whole villages fled with their valuables into the nearest forest as soon as they saw the sky-blue pelisses from afar, leaving behind me and my band snorting for booty in empty houses and desolate huts.

I had delivered several transports of oats, flour, grits, leather, iron, etc. to the squadron upon my arrival in Rastenburg. Just imagine my astonishment when I found the entire regiment passing through. The cavalry was changing quarters and the Sumskii Regiment was sent to Lablaken, not far from Königsberg. I turned over the forage to the captain and dismissed my command, glad to be rid of those infamous fellows who had become much too much for me.

We marched by way of Wehlau and Tapiau and set up our quarters near Lablaken. Both Delyanovs and I lived together at a noble estate belonging to the wine merchant Scheeres from Königsberg. We were treated like princes. The finest wines and port flowed on our table well-set with delicacies. At noon

---

* Today Olecko or Marggrabowa, Poland.

we usually ate in a cool arbour, walked with the ladies in a beautiful expansive park. Toward evening the party gathered on the banks of a lovely river on the soft grass and enjoyed the pleasant evening air. We were given rooms in the manor house, the soft beds, so clean, so white, so beautiful, the silk covers, the china washbowls, all of it new to me; the contrast with the dirty bivouacs or the dark peasant rooms on my march through Lithuania was so great that my head was dizzy with joy at being allowed to relish all of this.

I barely dared to touch the soft pillows with the tips of my fingers and blessed the good lady of the house who made it possible for me to forget my earlier misery for a while. But how could I, as dirty as I was, defile the pristine bedding. Since it had become dark and everyone, so I thought, was asleep, I threw my hussar coat around my shoulders, slipped through the garden gate into the park and hurried to the little river flowing through it. Here I took off my shirt – my only one – and washed it after bathing in the cool water. To my great consternation the ladies in the meantime had decided to take a walk in the moonlight. I saw them coming and hid in a thicket. In my hurry my wet torn shirt was still on the bank. The ladies sat down on benches not too far from me. Mademoiselle Scheeres had brought a guitar along and sang tender songs in a very lovely voice accompanied by her brother on his flute. I listened, barely breathing in my hiding place, and trembled for fear that the children playing on the shore would take my last shirt for a useless rag and throw it into the water. They talked about us, and it made me very happy to hear the ladies calling me the 'handsome amiable Livonian'. The young lady of the house, who could barely find sufficient words to praise me, was especially interested in me. I lay quiet as a mouse in the bushes, took in every word, and now and again peered through the rose bushes at my abandoned property at the river. It became cool and the party finally, to my great joy, left their seats, not suspecting that I had eavesdropped on them. I hurriedly pulled on my damp shirt and followed the ladies into the manor. Scheeres' son, a young man, amused us very much by shooting six or seven large carp in the pond with his musket – a completely new way to fish for me.

After about eight quiet days, we got the order to march again. The squadron assembled in the courtyard. My horse was led in; but how great was my astonishment upon seeing my saddlebags, which were usually very small and tiny, now packed full on my Koptschik. I checked him out; and how great was my surprise to find a half-dozen batiste shirts, just as many pairs of socks, two vests, a silk neckscarf and several other things very neatly packed in them, a very engaging note from the good woman lying on top – she had seen my lack of linens and took it as her pleasant duty to help me with the tokens. Twelve ducats were in the pocket of the saddle sack.

I was filled with gratitude, but God knows, how false my idea of honour back then was. I was ashamed to accept such a well-intentioned gift. My pride was offended – in short, I did not want to take anything. Despite all their entreaties, I gave back all of the packages, kissed the hands of that amiable admirable woman, assured her I would find my equipage in Wehlau and that I then would not suffer any more deprivation. She caressed me like a child, kissed me several times on the forehead, took the things back *bon gré mal gré* and cried bitter tears as I waved to her a last farewell from my horse.

In Tapiau we had a day of rest. From there we went to Wehlau. Now I was silently sorry that I had not accepted that well-meant gift, since I had no prospect of getting some linen. I called myself a dumb donkey, thought about that amicable woman, and fell asleep. Look here, upon awakening, I find the same packages on the table next to my bed, but neither a note from her nor the slightest trace of how or in what way the things had been sent and brought into my room. Only the twelve ducats were missing, which had not been sent from delicacy or perhaps the messenger had pocketed them as his reward. Quickly, I threw my ragged shirt behind the stove and dressed for the first time in several months in clean whites.

In the meantime the battles of Guttstadt and Heilsberg had been fought, in which we had not been able to take part. During our renewed march through Wehlau – I do not know the cause – the part of the city on the other side of the Alle was designated for our soldiers to plunder. Thus many a demure beauty will remember our bearded Hussars. With several comrades I sacked a butcher's shop taking along as many uncooked sausages as we could carry. [From the German text in Eduard von Löwenstern, *Mit Graf Pahlens Reiterei gegen Napoleon . . .*]

Mikhail Petrov

Mikhail Petrov was a staff captain and commander of the 1st Company in the Yeletskii Musketeer Regiment.

The battle of Preussisch-Eylau was followed by a four-month pause in military operations. The Russian corps were deployed near Heilsberg, with the advance guard, commanded by Prince Bagration, at Launau and Stolzenhagen while the French were across the Passarge River, amidst the thick woods in front of Osterode, where they were regrouping, just as we were. During this interval our [regimental] chef had recovered from his wound and rejoined his brigade and regiment. He placed 230 of the finest skirmishers under my command with four officers from the St. Petersburgskii Grenadier and Yeletskii Musketeer Regiments of his brigade, and entrusted me with the entire line of advance outposts in front of Guttstadt, inside the thick forest, between the village of Stolzenhagen to the brick workshop where the left flank of my line of outposts was anchored. I maintained this position, remaining under the overall command of Colonel [George] Emmanuel, until the battle of Guttstadt, during which I commanded my skirmishers in front of Count

Osterman's division and distinguished myself clearing French ambushes [zasady] out of the villages of Szarnik and Lingnau [Lingenauer] . . . In late May [June] we launched a new campaign and attacked [Marshal Michel] Ney's corps at Guttstadt and, having defeated it, drove it across the Passarge River. We then fought in a ferocious battle at Heilsberg – although we retained the field of battle, we were then compelled to abandon it to anticipate the enemy at Friedland . . . [From the Russian text in M. Petrov, *Rasskazy* . . .]

Andrey Engelhardt

Born in 1785, Andrey Engelhardt belonged to a prominent Russian noble family and was a grand-nephew of the powerful Prince Gregory Potemkin. After spending his childhood at the family estate in the village of Chizhovo, Engelhardt enlisted in March 1802 as a non-commissioned officer in the St. Peterburgskii Dragoon Regiment, which was led by his uncle Major-General Pavel Engelhardt. By then he was already a dashing and well-educated young man, who, as his official record of service notes, could 'speak the Russian, German and French languages, and [was] well versed in general history, geography, geometry, and a larger part of mathematics'. Two years later, Prince Peter Bagration, who was related to Engelhardt's family by marriage, helped him transfer to the Life Guard Jager Battalion and then to the 20th Jager Regiment. Young, ambitious and reckless, Engelhardt was, in his own words, 'equally loved and hated by Bagration for my skills, knowledge, and agility as well as for my antics and various reckless exploits, for which he had me arrested four times'. During the War of the Third Coalition in 1805, Sub-Lieutenant Engelhardt took part in the expedition to Hannover, during which he distinguished himself for his romantic escapades in every town he visited. ★*After returning to Russia, he transferred back to the Life Guard Jager Regiment and therefore missed the opening months of the new campaign in Poland, arriving there only in the aftermath of the battle of Eylau. Promoted to lieutenant of the Guard in March 1807, he was eager to experience battle at long last.*

[We finally arrived at] Allenburg where the headquarters of the Guard commander Grand Duke Constantine was located. Our regiment was given canton-quarters ahead of everyone else and I was tasked with surveying the environs occupied by our battalion, which I successfully accomplished in two days.

★ Engelhardt left brief memoirs focusing on the 1805–7 campaigns. The memoirs were first published in 1895 but without attribution. The authorship of this memoir was established by A. Yurganov in his article 'Posylaem byl v opasneishie mesta...' ('Ustanovlenie avtorstva vospominanii russkogo ofitsera o voine 1805-1807 gg.' *Sovetskie arkhivy* 6 (1987), pp. 74–6.

[In June we took] positions in front of Heilsberg, in the wake of some unimportant movements of the enemy's advance guard, which deliberately tried to attract our attention so as to divert us from Danzig, which the enemy was vigorously trying to capture. Our commander-in-chief [Bennigsen] believed these diversions and gathered his entire army at these prepared positions as if hoping that the enemy would be so foolish as to attack him in such a place.

Our regiment occupied earthworks [shantsy] in front of the main battery on the left flank of the woods where a company of our jagers was deployed as an advance outpost; meanwhile, in anticipation of the enemy, we [officers] gathered with our comrades from other regiments in a small hut where we indulged ourselves to careless tippling and huzzahing [urakalis'] each other's health in the open air.

When the enemy movements did not materialise and both sides' advance guards remained in their original locations around Launau, the commander-in-chief, whose only goal was to lure the enemy onto the position at Heilsberg, did not think it necessary to exhaust the army by moving it to campaign bivouacs and, as before, kept it at canton-quarters. The entire Guard was deployed in quarters behind the army, about one mile from Bartenstein to Heilsberg, in order to guard the Imperial headquarters that was located at Bartenstein. My inability for a parade front service saved me from guard duty but I did not idle in the meanwhile. Ardent card games with like-minded comrades provided plenty of diversion in my leisure time. The vast multitudes of common snipe that populated the area proved to be a source of considerable anxiety [in the army]. One of my comrades, who was partial to hunting, gathered a few jagers known for their particularly sharpshooting skills and one evening they hunted snipe with such intensity that the nearby companies assumed the war had broken out and sounded the alarm, with their drumbeats causing the rest of the regiment to rally until it was finally established that it was just a few of us hunting snipe. Colonel St. Priest severely reprimanded each of those responsible.

After Bennigsen's defensive preparations had given all the advantages and time to Napoleon to capture the [strategically] important fortress of Danzig and seize its 16,000-strong garrison under Kalckreuth and our gallant Prince Sherbatov, our commander-in-chief finally decided, in order to compensate for such an important loss, to take advantage of the main enemy forces being deployed far away at Danzig to contain and surround the forward corps of Marshals Ney and Soult and, once this first line of the French army was pierced, to fall onto the weakened forces of Napoleon at Osterode, thereby successfully transforming his defensive preparations into a decisive offensive. Such an excellent plan, potentially capable of compensating for the loss of Danzig with continued victories over the Napoleonic hordes [Napoleonovy polchischa], would have had a decisive impact on the already critical circumstances of

Europe oppressed by Napoleon, if only its execution corresponded with the breadth of the Russian commander's thinking and if Napoleon's shrewdness had not frustrated all these efforts. Ordered to surround and destroy Ney's advance guard, our army proceeded in multiple directions towards its goal. The Russian Guard, as usual in such operations, comprised the reserve that was to support the overall movement of the army and proceed to those units that required reinforcements to overcome the enemy's steadfast defence. The entire Guard was deployed on [a vast] plain and could see as Bagration's advance guard came out of woods and, moving with considerable agility, overwhelmed the enemy outposts, and turned on Guttstadt. The sight of the town on fire marked the start of the fierce fighting at Guttstadt.

The first battle took place at the village of Lomitten on the Passarge river. As our main army, together with Bagration's advance guard and Count Platov's Don Cossacks, rushed to Guttstadt with the intention not just to attack Marshal Ney's corps but to surround it and force its surrender, General Dokhturov's corps was supposed to attack from the front, the French having strengthened their position with abatis. Marshal Soult's advance guard was at the village of Lomitten, which protected the crossing over the Passarge River. Sacken's corps was ordered to cross the Passarge and move into the enemy's rear, attacking Marshal Soult simultaneously [with Dokhturov]. According to his orders, at 10 a.m., General Dokhturov launched his attack on the fortified positions of the enemy, who courageously defended them and continued to receive reinforcements from across the Passarge, frustrating all our efforts. Dokhturov soon committed thirteen battalions that drove the French from positions adjacent to the fortification but they were unable to capture it due to heavy casualties. Marshal Soult's success was facilitated by Sacken's failure to arrive in time which allowed the enemy to continually replenish his forces. General Dokhturov was forced to ask for immediate succour from Grand Duke Constantine, who dispatched two battalions of our Life Guard Jager Regiment and five squadrons of uhlans under overall command of his adjutant General Khitrovo. We reached the battlefield around 4 p.m. and joined the fight half an hour later. Capable leadership on the part of our Colonel Count St. Priest turned the tide of battle within an hour. He ordered the first battalion to pass through our exhausted troops that had been engaged in pointless gunfire with the enemy and storm the abatis; once the fighting was underway, St. Priest himself intended to lead the [other battalion] in a flanking manoeuvre and, through a rapid attack, to get the enemy in a crossfire and sow confusion and disorder in his ranks. This plan was successfully carried out. The first battalion, where I served, fearlessly engaged the enemy and although it was unable to dislodge him on the first try, we at least forced him to commit all of his troops to contain our assaults. Upon seeing this, the intelligent Count St. Priest quickly launched a flanking manoeuvre and, with rare gallantry, charged into the enemy's rear. Finding themselves surrounded, the enemy troops became disordered and, thinking only of their salvation, hastily and in great confusion abandoned their positions. Our jagers pursued the fleeing enemy troops, who received reinforcements in the village of Lomitten but were still routed by the triumphant jagers. Count St. Priest's successful attack and the belated appearance of Sacken's corps in the rear forced Marshal Soult's corps to quickly fall back to Osterode, where Napoleon himself was located. [At Lomitten] the enemy had about 6,000 men and lost up to 1,500 killed and wounded, as well as 100 prisoners captured during the pursuit along the Passarge River.

Our forces numbered over 9,000 troops and our losses in killed and wounded, if not exceeding the enemy's was certainly equal to them. Our Life Guard Jager Regiment alone lost more than 250 killed and wounded, and, in fact, we lost some of our best officers here. Our worthy leader Count St. Priest was wounded in the left foot (tibia), which left him lame for the rest of his life. His brother Lieutenant St. Priest was wounded in the chest; the gallant Captain Rüdinger, who commanded the first battalion under Potemkin, was injured with a ramrod in the stomach; our kind Captain Wolf was killed on the spot; the enlightened and brave Delagarde was wounded in the side; my comrade Doganovskii, fearless and fun-loving, was shot through the throat and died an hour later. As for me, this baptism by fire cost me a leg . . .

When our regiment approached the battlefield, I felt delighted to finally see my long-time desire to find myself under enemy bullets fulfilled. When the first battalion prepared to enter the woods, I, commanding half of the 4th Company, advanced with my soldiers and upon seeing old Colonel Bernarbos [Benardos*], asked him about the enemy's whereabouts; he replied that I should not get hot-headed since bullets were whizzing all around. I countered that his long service probably made him weary of them but for me they were rather delightful because as an inexperienced young lad I was excited by all these new things, especially when it came to an actual battle. Moving ahead of his regiment, I ordered my troops to take cover behind large trees while I myself went forward to reconnoitre the enemy position and determine best ways of attacking it. With bullets whizzing around me I made some 60 paces towards the enemy and was separated by just a ravine when a ricocheting bullet shattered the heel of my foot. Excited as I was, I initially did not think that I was wounded but feeling the increasing heaviness of my leg and seeing blood gushing, I shouted to my soldiers; upon seeing me injured and out of particular love for me, about ten of them rushed to help me despite the danger to their own lives. Their devotion to me cost two lives while one more soldier was wounded. I was taken to the front of the second battalion. Seeing

---

* Colonel Panteleimon Benardos, who was forty-six years old in 1807, served as the chef of the Vladimirskii Musketeer Regiment and distinguished himself during the campaign in Poland, earning promotion to major-general in December 1807.

me wounded, Count St. Priest felt genuinely sorry for me and immediately ordered the second battalion to start a flanking manoeuvre. Meanwhile I was taken to our physician who, using a cursed lancet, tried in vain to remove the bullet, until a cannonball struck the tree next to which he was practising his quackery and forced him to abandon me with a hasty speech that medicine would be of no use if a cannonball were to smash his head.

In this battle I was the first one in the entire regiment, counting not just officers but the rank-and-file, who was wounded. I was placed in a cart [brichka] and taken to the nearby town where I was incidentally billeted in the apartment of a physician at whose house I stayed during my return from the campaign in Hannover [in 1805]. We recognised each other and he did his best to attend to my wound, bandaged it and treated me to a coffee. Two hours later [soldiers] brought severely wounded younger St. Priest who sustained an injury to his chest. The wounded from my company gradually gathered around my quarters; there were twenty-nine of them. I gave a chervonetz to each of them and stayed with a dozen of them.

The alarm was sounded some time later. Rumours spread that the French, having repelled our troops at Lomitten, were advancing directly here. This news astonished me. I had no desire to become a prisoner of war and [instructed] my lightly-wounded soldiers to fetch a local municipal official so he could promptly provide me with horses. This rascal demurred for a long time but a few beating-up lessons from my eager comrade-in-arms resulted in me on top of a horse, without a saddle or stirrups despite my wounded leg. Soldier Stepan, who carried me out of the battle, pledged to accompany me and, as we proceeded on the road to Launau, he held the reigns of my flighty Bucephalus. The alarm, as we later discovered, was false.

At Launau. At dusk I arrived at this former headquarters of Prince Bagration's advance guard. I was soon lodged in the same apartment with Count St. Priest, who was in a very weak condition and was not allowed to speak to avoid further aggravation of his chest wound. This was first and last night when I could catch some sleep despite my injury.

At Heilsberg. I was lodged in the same house as my wounded comrades Rüdinger and Delagarde. I will forever remember how difficult it was to climb to the third floor of that tall house. Enduring unbearable pain caused by the broken bones in my leg and unable to calm down for even a moment, I suffered greatly while my companions, especially Rüdinger, relaxed with the help of punch and were getting irritated that my moaning would not let them sleep. At one point our disagreement reached such a pitch that we even crawled towards each other to engage in a fistfight but our batmen intervened to put an end to our frail heroism. Since my heel bone was completely smashed and the bullet still remained inside the wound, I continued to endure indescribable pain every minute. My leg was swollen well above the knee. Every time an irresistible yearning to sleep came over me, I was woken up by the most agonising pain that spread through my entire body. I became so apprehensive of it that despite all the desire to close my eyes, I tried my best to stay awake and avoid this soothing temptation and yet every time nature took its course, I suffered from excruciating pain that struck all my joints. At last, on the third day since my injury, I developed a severe fever and begged the Lord to send me death [to escape further suffering]. However, the fever soon passed and I once again suffered that torturous pain. Furthermore, I soon developed gangrene in my heel and toes which began to turn blue. Amidst this unbearable agony, I, together with my comrades, intended to spend three more days at Heilsberg to recuperate when an alarm was sounded throughout the city: the French were approaching. Without any further delay I instructed my soldier to bring my jittery Bucephalus to the porch, enduring agonising pain as I climbed down the stairs and, just as everyone was fearful that the French were supposedly already entering the city, I mounted the horse and departed in the company of my soldier, who, in order to disguise himself, had put on my warm half-coat and was therefore profusely sweating [under the June sun].

I hurried to the main sentry post, which rallied under my orders and comprised a single company; I ordered its captain to have his men load muskets and prepare to meet the attacking Frenchmen with a volley but this worthless coward clutched his stomach and pretended to be sick, in front of his entire unit. Having cursed him for what he was worth, I ordered a senior lieutenant to take over command and, after giving proper instructions, I was on my way to Bartenstein, which I found already crammed with soldiers fleeing from Heilsberg; among them were civilians and even the wounded, some running, others crawling away in order to avoid French captivity. My comrades, travelling in an ambulance carriage [lazaretnaya kareta], caught up with me half-way [to Bartenstein]. This alarm was caused by the following circumstances: when Napoleon advanced to attack our army from various directions, our forces retreated too hastily [exposing the town], which was then threatened by the appearance on its outskirts of the enemy's cavalry scouts, who, however, did not dare to enter it.

At Bartenstein. I was again lodged in the same apartment as my comrades. My injury would not let me even for a moment indulge in slumber that continually overpowered me only to be awakened by continued bouts of agonising pain. By now my heel and toes had already gone blue-black. Here one Russian physician congratulated me that due to the brisk French offensive I would be unable to undergo proper surgery and he assured me that in a week's time I would be discussing this war with Charon* on the Elysian Fields.

---

* In Greek mythology, Charon or Kharon is the ferryman of Hades who carries souls of the newly deceased across the rivers Styx and Acheron that divided the worlds of the living and dead.

The rumours about the retreat of our army made us feel unsafe at Bartenstein and compelled us to leave. To further safeguard ourselves, we decided to move to the right to reach Schlippenbeil.

My comrades Rüdinger and de Lagarde lay calmly on pillows inside the ambulance carriage while I, with my wounded leg undressed, rode the jittery horse without a saddle and stirrups so that I learned, out of dire necessity, to stay on top of him like Centauri. I rode behind my companions with the appearance of a defeated and wounded knight who was being dragged to an iron cage. Throughout our journey, we heard a heavy cannonade from the direction of Heilsberg.

At Schlippenbeil. After lodging together once again in the same room, we barely spent the night here as we received confirmed news that part of the French army was advancing in the direction of Königsberg. Not knowing where we could find shelter from the French, whose advance outposts we feared the most, we decided, on my suggestion, to return to the [Russian army's] line of communications, thinking that if the enemy captured us, we would not be alone but with many other [Russian] troops. And so that same morning we hurried toward Friedland. Slush, mud, torrential rain and cold only further exacerbated my injury and made me experience all the horrors of my condition. Because we were intent on reaching Friedland as soon as possible, especially since we encountered few others along the road, we kept moving well after nightfall which could have been equally disastrous for me: my skittish horse kept bouncing off every tree. My companion soldier's timely support and diligence saved me from several falls, which, in light of my condition and weakness, could have been fatal. We reached Friedland around 9 o'clock in the evening. [From the Russian text in A. Engelhardt, 'Zhurnal biograficheskoi moei zhizni']

Lev Bode

Born into a German baronial family, Bode was the son of Karl August Bode, who had served in the French army during the Seven Years War (1756–63), married an Englishwoman and settled in Alsace. During the French Revolution, Bode's family was persecuted for its royalist sentiments and had to flee to Russia, where Emperor Paul I granted it large estates and hundreds of serfs. The young Bode studied at the Cadet Corps in Shklov (Škloŭ) until 1801 when his mother insisted on returning to France where she hoped to benefit from the amnesty that First Consul Napoleon Bonaparte had declared. Bode's efforts, however, proved futile and the family had to settle in Hesse-Kassel, where Lev Bode began serving in the Guards. In late 1806, already an ensign in the Hessian service, Bode returned to Russia and was appointed as a non-commissioned officer (portepee-ensign) in the elite Life Guard Jager Regiment. Just days later he was on his way to the regiment that was already in Poland . . .

I caught up with my regiment at Bartenstein a few days before the battle of Guttstadt. From the very first day my colonel – Count [Emmanuel] St. Priest whom I knew from St. Petersburg – treated me genially, even though I was just a non-commissioned officer, and introduced me to his private circle. Our little circle included Colonel [Jacob] Potemkin, Count [Carl] Rastignac, Count Louis de St. Priest, Prince [Gregory] Khilkov of the Horse Guards,★ [Staff] Captain [Fedor] Vlasov and me. In such private circles awkwardness was never felt and politeness, amiability and courtesy were central. Even though we all were military men, some occasionally appeared without ties and in civilian clothing, as if we were in a salon in St. Petersburg.

I was assigned to the company commanded by Rastignac. He was from Gascony, a man of lively and original mind, oftentimes humorous but always a man of honour and a model of gallantry. I was a line officer and in my free time I enjoyed being with him, considering him an older friend. He supported my passion for reading and I loved listening to him read; in addition, he passionately loved playing a violin which always accompanied him. Like all southerners, he slept very little and we oftentimes felt sick from the screeching sound of the old violin which he played for hours without a break.

Finally, the day had come when I would receive my baptism of fire. As drums beat a general assembly, our regiment gathered at the parade ground and we went through an inspection of muskets and ammunition. We also received biscuits and our regiment, led by our commander, marched forward. After a rather long march, we were ordered to halt. We could already hear the sound of a cannonade in the distance. We then received the order to load our muskets. A young soldier inadvertently fired his musket and hit his neighbour in the stomach. This unfortunate incident provided us with the sight of terrible convulsions resulting in death.

The fighting, meanwhile, turned serious. Our battalion commanders called for volunteers [okhotniki] to form skirmishers. I stepped forward and was brought in front of my commander, who entrusted me with the command of our battalion's skirmishers. The regiment's skirmishers were under the overall command of Lieutenant [Peter Ogon'-]Doganovskii.

The regiment then advanced. Just as we crossed the field, our military songs were replaced by a profound silence. We passed by the field hospital of [Dmitri] Dokhturov's corps that was engaged with the enemy. Along the fence that ran the length of the road, numerous wounded were being bandaged and [we could see] those dying, groaning, with terrible faces, disfigured from pain and in deadly convulsions. Complaints, curses, desperate shouts could be all heard from this place of suffering and they tore our hearts. The further we advanced, the louder the rumble of gunfire was becoming; we could even

---

★ Lieutenant Khilkov used to serve in the Life Guard Horse Regiment but transferred to the Life Guard Jager Regiment in 1806.

distinguish human cries. Our colonel ordered us to turn left so we could not see this miserable scene.

As for myself, I felt tired. Marching on an empty stomach and deeply depressed by the scenes of death that I had witnessed in its worst manifestations, I felt that the ground was slipping from under me. I was so anxious that my physical weakness would forever stain my honour that I almost passed out.

Meanwhile, our regiment deployed into line. Count St. Priest dispatched Colonel Potemkin to flank the enemy, who was lodged inside abatis and was fiercely fighting off the detachment of Dokhturov, which we were supposed to replace. Count [Louis] St. Priest, who led my company, suddenly noticed that I was on the verge of passing out. He took out of his pocket a flask with vinegar-water and sprinkled it on my face, smilingly telling me, 'My dear baron, you look like scrambled eggs, but bear in mind that you are commanding skirmishers and therefore carry this responsibility. But look there, the troops are carrying the officer who commanded the [regimental] skirmishers. Oh, poor Doganovskii!' In reality I could not imagine such a misfortune as getting shot in the throat and being carried dead on a coat. But the count's words and vinegar-water quickly revived me. I returned to my squad and assumed command. Having revived my physical and spiritual strength, I now dreamt of just one thing – to get rid of that instinctive feeling of indecision.

Our regiment charged with the bayonet and momentarily routed the enemy. But in the heat of the action it moved away from the direction indicated by Colonel Count St. Priest, who specifically pointed towards the abatis on the right. The colonel rushed to the skirmishers and was soon next to me. The cries of 'hurrah' and the artillery and musket fire made it very difficult to hear his voice. He thought that the soldiers were following him but amidst heavy clouds of smoke and dust our regiment did not even notice him and marched forward, passing by the abatis. Count St. Priest suddenly fell down right next to me. We were alone since I was next to him during the attack on the abatis. The colonel was hit by a musket bullet that injured his leg. I refused to leave my gallant commander and thus we were all alone amidst the ancient and gloomy wood that was occupied by the enemy.

As the smoke began to dissipate, we found ourselves in front of a group of [French General Nicolas Charles] Oudinot's soldiers in bearskin caps, who had not fled yet. The count, lying on the ground, ordered me to shoot at them at once. I loaded a musket and, standing by the tree, I aimed at the bewildered grenadiers and fired a shot. Over the next twenty minutes or so I spent sixty cartridges and was pleased to see how these haughty warriors turned and fled. Firing the last farewell bullet at them, I felt proud of my agility and continued to aim in the enemy's direction until I was alone in my dark jager uniform. As I was standing by the tree and loading my musket, I still did not fully realise that we could suffer considerable losses. The fighting was still continuing along the entire line and one could assume that there were plenty of soldiers around. While I finally turned around to give the good news to Count St. Priest, I found him with great difficulty as I had to remove plenty of branches that the enemy bullets broke off the trees. They probably were aiming at this location when the troops were deployed here.

Count St. Priest asked me to drag him through the abatis to the field hospital. He was concerned about being captured. Yet I was so young and weak. His suffering was becoming unbearable. At last, several soldiers from Dokhturov's detachment, who were freed by our jagers, happened to pass by us in search of a way out of the woods. I requested their help and they picked up the unfortunate colonel and carried him as I showed the way to the field hospital. As we moved, St. Priest suffered greatly from excruciating pain so I offered to stay with him. But he assured me that he was now safe and in good hands and that my company was no longer required. I asked for his permission to return to him [later]. He told me to embrace him and bade farewell to me.

I returned from the battlefield walking along the road, encountering numerous stragglers and soldiers carrying the wounded to the field hospital; all of them were from Dokhturov's corps. I ordered them to rally and follow me. The Russian soldiers obeyed as if they were children who were treated with dignity and who therefore respond worthily. And what about me? I burned with a desire to distinguish myself in front of the regiment.

I soon reached the place where the fighting was still raging. Exactly 300 men followed me. The fighting was mainly at close quarters [vrukopashnuyu]. I inquired about the whereabouts of my company, or to be precise, Rastignac's company. I was pointed towards the village of Lomitten located on the hill that extended almost to the island that the Passage River surrounded and that, together with the hillsides, represented a long dam seemingly constructed by Nature itself. There, on the top of the hill, was part of our troops while the entire dam was occupied by the enemy. Rastignac was cut off from the rest of [the regiment] and probably would have been captured together with his company. As soon as I learned of this, I ordered my detachment to follow me and prepared to launch an assault on the dam in front of the company commanded by Captain U. [Andrey Ivanovich Uvarov] who did not even stir on the pretence that he could not dare to advance without a proper order from his superior.

My detachment stood firmly by me during the attack and swept everything from the top of the dam. And all of this unfolded in front of the company in which I served. To my great joy, we saved our men. Just as I intended to move toward Count Rastignac, who was running towards me, a French infantryman, accompanied by several other reckless daredevils, began climbing back on to the dam. I wanted to smack him but missed and so had, in a frenzy, to push him on to the ground just two steps away from me. Earlier, when I was dragging Colonel St. Priest to the hospital, I had to discard my musket and so now I simply grabbed another one from the ground so I could be prepared to fight. I loaded but did not realise that the bayonet was bent. Back then our muskets were far from perfection . . . [so when I fired] I sustained such a strong recoil to my shoulders that I fell to the ground. My soldiers assumed that I was dead and came to my senses only when four jagers were already holding me and Count Rastignac was sprinkling my face with vinegar-water. I felt nothing but [a severe] headache. I was brought back to the company that continued to defend the farm and the dam until a battalion of regular infantry came to its succour.

In the evening we returned from the battlefield. Count Rastignac embraced me heartily and told everyone about my exploits that saved him and his company. Colonel Potemkin replaced Count St. Priest in charge of the regiment . . . [which] suffered very heavy losses. One-third of the officers were killed and wounded; the latter included Count St. Priest, his brother Louis and Chevalier [Augustin Marie] Delagarde.* But our regiment covered itself with glory. As for myself, I already felt a different person . . .

The following day Grand Duke Constantine highly praised the splendid actions of the Guard jagers – our regiment fought alone against an entire enemy division, but still managed to defend its position, fighting to the last, and to force the enemy to retreat – and sent forty St. George Crosses for distribution among the most gallant rank-and-file. So the new soldiers, who had been recruited just recently, saved the Guard. We were chosen from each company, placed in a circle and, to universal approval, I received from the hands of a soldier the Medal of Distinction of the Military Order,† which brought me the greatest joy of all the rewards that I eventually received. Barely had I fixed this medal on my uniform when Colonel Potemkin received Count St. Priest's letter describing his unfortunate incident and giving high praise to the young portepee-ensign who had gallantly fought and stood by him; he finished his letter with the request for Colonel Potemkin to nominate me, as the most distinguished man in the regiment, for a high reward. So I received a St. George's Cross from the soldiers' hands and was then nominated to officer rank, although I was not approved at that time and received this promotion only after the war.‡ [From the Russian text in L. Bode, 'Moim dorogim detyam . . . ']

---

* Born into a French noble family, Delagarde fled France during the Revolution and enlisted in the Russian service, joining the Life Guard Jager Regiment in 1806.
† This medal was the highest military award for the rank-and-file and was popularly referred to as the St. George Cross or soldiers' St. George.
‡ Bode was promoted to ensign in September 1807.

Prince Alexander Obolenskii

Born into a prominent and wealthy noble family, Obolenskii was still a teenager when he begged his parents to allow him to enlist. The example of his brother-in-law Prince Sherbatov, who at twenty years old was already a colonel of the Guard, was certainly enthralling. Yet his father decided otherwise and chose a diplomatic career for his son. Fortunately for the young man, Emperor Paul decreed the transfer of young noblemen from the College of Foreign Affairs to the Horse Guards and Obolenskii found himself among them. He served as a non-commissioned officer for over a year before earning promotion to cornet in 1801. Yet just a year later Obolenskii decided to retire. He spent the next four years at his rural estate ...

Having to spend more than half of the year in the village, without much to do, I preoccupied myself with plenty of reading. Yet the choice of books proved to be harmful for me. I voraciously consumed the works of the *philosophes* of the eighteenth century, whose tyranny of thought had such an impact on me that I spent the rest of my life trying to eradicate its effects and subordinate my mind to the faith ...

In 1805 a new war broke out in support of Austria against France but it ended with the infamous defeat at Austerlitz and the truce that was so humiliating for Russia. A year later Russia once more came to the aid of Prussia. My blood was boiling in my veins and I was itching to fight. My parents at first managed to restrain me but by the end of 1806 gave me their blessing to [return to military service]. My brother Prince Andrey Petrovich gave me money and I travelled to St. Petersburg to request reinstatement in the army. I retired with the rank of lieutenant of the Imperial Guard so I was accepted back to the service as a captain in the [regular] army. Upon my request, I was assigned to the corps of my brother-in-law Dokhturov and was placed in the Ingermandlandskii Dragoon Regiment which I chose because it had the fewest number of staff officers and I could, therefore, become a squadron commander.*

In March 1807 I travelled to [East] Prussia to get to our main headquarters that had been established at Wartenstein.† After travelling for six days straight on a cart, with hardly any sleep, I was completely exhausted. I remember finding at last a small room in an attic, where three elderly German women had their coffee room, and passing out on an old couch despite the women's best efforts to dislodge me. The following day I learned that the women, out of concern for their modesty, managed to drag me out of the house but then took pity on me and hauled me back in. I was so deeply asleep that I felt none of this commotion.

---

* Obolenskii was officially appointed as captain in the Ingermanlandskii Dragoon Regiment on 14 April 1807.

† Today Przyrzecze in west Poland.

In the morning I arrived in front of the duty general who sent me to General Dokhturov who was with the advance guard. General Dokhturov and my brother, Prince Vasily, who served as his aide-de-camp, were thrilled to see me. The general decided to keep me with him not just because we were related but also because the regiment in which I served was disordered in many regards. It was then that I discovered the full scale of devastation that had been produced. The troops had remained in the same region for two months. There were no inhabitants in many villages, which were completely plundered. Our advance guard troops suffered terrible shortages of provisions, even though there were considerable stockpiles 80 verstas from us at Weninberg. But the highway was not built yet and the existing roads were impassable and were covered in watery mud an arshin [more than 2 feet] deep. Transports sent to fetch bread were stuck in the middle of the road while the horses, already weakened, could no longer pull them and simply died of exhaustion on the spot. This was happening throughout March and April . . .

Our corps was soon ordered to move to Lomitten, which was on the Passarge River, and to drive the enemy out of the position it held there. Having occupied Lomitten, we encountered woods in between this town and the river that were occupied by the enemy who had constructed abatis in it. And we were supposed to attack them the following day!? As I prepared for my first battle, I could not sleep all night. I was not as concerned about the danger that lay ahead of me but was rather apprehensive that having not tested the steadfastness of my spirit or bravery I might not live up to expectations, while my mind imagined combats in the most horrible way.

The fighting began at dawn on 24 May [5 June]. I found myself under heavy enemy fire but I did not find it intimidating, especially after all that I had imagined [the day before]. The enemy had fortified the woods to such a degree that our regiments, repeatedly sent to capture it, had lost many men but still could not accomplish their mission. General Dokhturov sent me to the commander-in-chief [Bennigsen] to inform him of the circumstances and request reinforcements.

I found Bennigsen directing the assault on the enemy's fortified camp. After hearing my report he replied, 'What a pity that you became involved in a major combat, we only needed a diversion in that direction.' His response surprised me very much because if we were only expected to divert the enemy's attention, instead of engaging him in a full-blown battle, we would not have had to lose up to 1,000 killed and wounded; yet the order precisely instructed us to attack the enemy and clear the banks of the Passarge River. The commander-in-chief ordered me to stay with him to await further instructions and reinforced Dokhturov with the Life Guard Jager Regiment which joined the battle and turned the tide in our favour; the enemy was driven out of the woods and beyond the Passarge River while we rejoined the main forces.

This offensive was well conceived but poorly carried out. The French corps [of Marshal Michel Ney] was not concentrated and an unexpected attack could have destroyed it piecemeal. Alas, the commander-in-chief's plan was not followed. General Sacken did not arrive at his designated spot, allowing the French, who lost few men, to escape. General Sacken, the future field marshal, was later court-martialled for his actions.

Soon thereafter the French themselves went on the offensive and we had to retreat. We occupied a strong position near the town of Heilsberg. Napoleon, although having no need for it, sacrificed several thousand of his best troops in order to capture this town but had his army moved against our flank, we would have abandoned it anyway. As it was, on 29 May [10 June] the columns of [French] grenadiers advanced one after the other, in remarkable order, onto our positions. Our twenty-four cannon first met them with roundshot and then canister. Losing up to half of their men, the enemy columns reached our batteries only to be counter-attacked by our infantry. Both sides converged to point-blank range and halted, firing volleys at each other but not daring to charge with bayonets. The French could not endure such a ferocious fire and were forced to retreat, which they did in good order but lost many men. We retained the field of battle.

I spent the entire day tasked with a difficult assignment, sorting out the wounded and taking only those who could be helped. There were so many wounded, especially the French, that despite having men and carriages, I still could not take all of them to the hospitals located in the town about one versta [1km] from the battlefield. As a result I became acquainted with the horrors and hardships that wars bring to both military participants and civilians who have their homes burned and their last piece of bread requisitioned. After my exploits, I could not sleep all night; after getting my full share of the torments of the wounded men and witnessing death in its various manifestations, I spent the night crying.

The following day we retreated to Friedland . . . [From the Russian text in A. Obolenskii, *Voposminaniya* . . .]

Yakov Otroshenko

Staff Captain Otroshenko commanded a company in the 7th Jager Regiment. After fighting at Eylau, his men spent several weeks around Königsberg before moving to Peterswalde, where they occasionally clashed with the French outposts.

On 24 May [5 June] our entire army advanced. Our advance guard left its camp and, to the right of the Peterswalde woods, it attacked the French camp at the village of Altkirch. We found the enemy bivouacs very well arranged and supplied with bread and all the necessities. The following day we forced the

French to retreat across the river but during their withdrawal, they did cause considerable harm to our regiment with their grapeshot after we unexpectedly stumbled into the area fired upon by a concealed [French] battery. Our skirmishers crossed the river but were soon ordered to return, and the crossing of the river on the smouldering remnants of the bridge was strictly prohibited. We scattered through the brushwoods and [sat] behind large trees growing along the river bank. We were furious to watch how the French hauled flour from a stone building across the river. We kept firing at them with our two-pounder cannon but these moppets [malyutki] only scratched the limestone and could not penetrate the walls of the house, while the grapeshot [could not reach the opposite bank] and instead grazed our own men. The French did the same from the opposite bank.

Captain Drenyakin went to order our gun crew to cease fire but along the way he came across our villain* who rudely asked him, 'Which regiment do you belong to?' 'The 7th Jagers,' replied Drenyakin. The man then began speaking impertinently about our regiment so Drenyakin grabbed him with his powerful arm and told him, 'Come with me, I will show you my regiment.' Taken aback by this audacity, the rascal replied, 'I was just joking, lad. Do you have any tobacco?' Drenyakin let him go and returned to tell our officers about what had happened. We all decided to greet this scoundrel.

Meanwhile the gunfire subsided. We sat together around a fire in a hollow. At a short distance from us we could see a group of generals, with our villain standing next to them. He approached us, asking to smoke a pipe and we surrounded him at once. He tried to leave but we would not let him go. He got frightened and asked, 'What do you want from me, gentlemen?'

'We are the men of the 7th Jager Regiment, and we have decided to punish you for your turpitude. How dare you slander our regiment?'

'What? Me? I have never done any of that,' replied he.

'Do you remember Peterswalde?'

'I must have been deranged that day.'

Upon hearing this, I told my comrades, 'Gentlemen, do not dirty your hands with this lunatic,' and we let him go. He never complained about our audacious behaviour to anyone.

[. . .] During the night we heard brief gunfire in the distance. This was a daring attack by our Cossacks, who, in the evening, went on the prowl and attacked an enemy [supply] convoy that was left unprotected, seized the horses and burned the ammunition.

At dawn on the 26th [7 June] we began to retreat. The enemy quickly caught up with us and the fighting commenced. The enemy vigorously pursued us with all of his forces . . . During this fighting I noticed that the French, who were

---

* See Chapter 4. Otroshenko refers to the colonel of the 25th Jager Regiment who slandered the 7th Jagers during an earlier action.

advancing in squares, had no artillery inside them. The 7th Jager Regiment was ordered to deploy in the gardens [on the approaches to] Guttstadt to delay the enemy but we were soon instructed to get out into an open field and hasten to our artillery which was under attack by enemy cavalry. We rushed to it at once, saved the artillery and then commenced our withdrawal. My company was dispersed to the left of the road and the enemy cavalry [soon] cut me off from the other companies. My men gathered together and retreated, fighting off the enemy cavalrymen. Approaching the town of Guttstadt we observed that the road had been already occupied by the enemy cavalry so we moved closer to the river, stopped in a boggy area and opened volley fire to force these cavalrymen to move beyond the hill. The gardens were not far from me and I thought that the worst was finally behind me, unaware that the bridge over the river had already been destroyed. Unfortunately, the enemy cavalry was soon replaced by infantry which cut me off from the gardens. I had no other recourse but to swim across the river. I grabbed a branch, intending to slowly lower myself into the water but the ground gave way, snapping the branch and plunging me to the bottom of the river. The river was not wide but it was deep. I could not swim and was wearing my coat and knapsack. I do not remember how I managed to cross to the opposite bank but just as I reached it and tried to climb up, two jagers from my company grabbed me by the coat and dragged me back into the river. I redoubled my efforts and managed to climb up and helped the jagers as well; some did drown in the river, though. The French showered us with bullets but we escaped their captivity, though all of our muskets lay at the bottom of the river.

I hastened to leave the place where bullets were still causing us harm. We still had to cross sluices that were bombarded by both our and the enemy's artillery. Our artillery took us for the enemy and fired cannonballs that shattered the logs underneath us and sent splinters flying all around us. But with the Lord's help, we managed to pass this place without much harm and rejoined our troops as they were moving through the woods.

The enemy could not pursue us on this road because the bridge had been destroyed so he proceeded with all of his forces along the left bank of the Alle towards Zechern and Launau, and then pursued our combined forces. We moved through the boggy areas inside the woods and halted near the earthworks that had been built on the right bank of the Alle [near Heilsberg]. [From the Russian text in Y. Otroshenko, *Zapiski* . . .]

Nadezhda Durova

The famed 'Cavalry Maiden', Nadezhda Durova had a difficult childhood. Her mother 'passionately desired a son' and was greatly disappointed by the birth of a daughter, whom she mistreated. Her father, a hussar officer, raised her steeped in military traditions. In her memoirs Durova describes her fascination with the Cossacks passing through her town that led to her decision to run away from home at age sixteen. In reality, her account does not correspond to the truth and her memoirs intentionally omit seven years of her life when she got married and gave birth to a son in 1803. She suffered further mistreatment at the hands of her dissolute husband and eventually decided to leave him, seeking a more exciting life in the Russian army. In 1806, she disguised herself as a man and joined the Polish Uhlan Regiment under the alias 'Alexander Sokolov' (in her memoirs, she described her alias as Durov). Just weeks later she was on her way to fight the French ...

May 22, 1807. Guttstadt. For the first time I have seen a battle and taken part in it. What a lot of absurd things I have been told about the first battle, about the fear, timidity, and, not least of, about desperate courage! What nonsense! Our regiment went on the attack several times, not all at once but by squadrons. I was reprimanded for joining the attack with each squadron but this was honestly not from any excess of bravery but simply from ignorance; I thought that was how it was done, and I was amazed when the wachtmeister [sergeant] of another squadron, alongside which I was galloping like a whirlwind, shouted at me, 'Get the hell out of here! What are you galloping here for?' I returned to my squadron, but, instead of taking my place in formation, I went on riding around nearby. The novelty of the scene absorbed all my attention: the menacing and majestic thundering of cannon fire, the roar or kind of rumble of the flying cannonballs, the charging cavalry, the glittering bayonets of the infantry, the roll of drums, and the firm pace and calm appearance with which our infantry regiments advanced on the enemy – all this filled my soul with sensations that I have no words to express.

I came close to losing my priceless horse Alcides. While I was riding around, as I said before, near my squadron and looking over the curious scene of battle, I observed several enemy dragoons surrounding a Russian officer and knocking him off his horse with a pistol shot. He fell down, and they prepared to hack at him as he lay. I rushed at once toward them with my lance lowered. I can only suppose that this madcap bravery frightened them, because in a flash they abandoned the officer and scattered. I galloped over to the wounded man and stopped above him; for a couple of minutes I watched him in silence. He lay with his eyes closed and gave no sign of life; he obviously thought that it was the enemy standing over him. At last he risked a glance, and I at once asked him if he wanted to get on my horse.

'Oh, be so kind, my friend!' he said in a barely audible voice. At once I dismounted from my horse and with great effort managed to raise the wounded man, but here the aid I could render him came to an end: he fell chest-down across my arm and I, barely able to remain on my feet, had no idea what to do and how to get him onto Alcides, whom I was also holding by the reins with my other hand. This situation would have ended very disadvantageously for us both – that is, for the officer and for me – except that a soldier from his regiment rode over to us and helped me to seat the wounded man on my horse. I told the soldier to send the horse to Recruit Durov in the Polish Horse Regiment, and the dragoon told me that the officer I had saved was Lieutenant Panin of the Finlyandskii Dragoon Regiment and they would return my horse immediately.

The officer was carried off to his regiment and I set out for mine. I felt at a complete disadvantage, left on foot among charges, gunfire, and swordfights. Seeing everywhere men either flying by like lightning or quietly galloping in various directions with complete confidence in their good steeds, I exclaimed, 'Alas, my Alcides! Where is he now?' I deeply repented having so rashly given up my horse – and even more when my captain, after first asking me with concern, 'Did they kill your horse, Durov? Are you wounded?' shouted at me in vexation, 'Get away from the front, you scamp!' when he heard how I happened to be wandering about on foot. Quickly, albeit sadly, I headed for the spot where I saw lances with the pennons of the Polish Horse. The men I passed said with compassion, 'Oh, my God! Look, what a young boy has been wounded!' Nobody who saw an uhlan on foot in a uniform covered with blood could think anything else. As I mentioned, the wounded officer had lain chest-down across my arm, and I have to assume that his was a chest wound, because my sleeve was all bloody.

To my inexpressible joy, Alcides was returned to me – not quite the way I hoped, but at least returned. I was walking pensively through the fields to my regiment, when suddenly I saw our Lieutenant Podwyszacki riding away from the enemy position on my horse. I was beside myself with joy and, without stopping to wonder how my horse had turned up under Podwyszacki, ran over to stroke and caress Alcides, who also expressed his joy by frisking and neighing loudly.

'Is this really your horse?' asked the astonished Podwyszacki.

I recounted my adventure to him. He too had no praise for my rashness. He said that he had bought my horse from Cossacks for two gold pieces. I begged him to return Alcides and take from me the money he had paid for him.

'Very well, but let me keep him today. My horse was killed, and I have nothing to ride in action!' And with this he spurred Alcides and galloped off on him. I was close to weeping as I saw my comrade in arms in strange hands, and I swore with all my heart never again to give up my horse as long as I lived! At last this agonising day came to an end. Podwyszacki returned Alcides to me, and our army is now pursuing the retreating enemy.

May 24. On the banks of the Passarge. What a strange affair! We made so little haste to pursue the enemy that he managed to cross this little river, on the banks of which we are now standing, and met us with gunfire. Perhaps I do not understand anything about it, but it seems to me we should have stayed on the enemy's heels and crushed him at the crossing.

The same spot, on the banks of the Passarge. We have been standing here doing nothing for two days now – and there is nothing to be done. In front of us jagers are exchanging fire with enemy skirmishers across the river. Our regiment is stationed directly behind the jagers but, since we have absolutely nothing to do, we have been ordered to dismount. I am perishing from hunger! I do not have even a single biscuit. The Cossacks who captured my Alcides took from him the saddlebags with biscuits, coat and valise. I got my horse back with only a saddle, and everything else was gone. I try sleeping to forget how hungry I am, but it does not help.

At last the uhlan who was assigned to supervise me and still holds a mentor's authority, noticed that my saddle was missing its bags and that my face was pale. He offered me three large mouldy biscuits. I took them eagerly and laid them in a hole filled with rainwater to soften them a bit. Although I had not eaten for nearly two days, the biscuits were so large, bitter, and green that I could eat only one of them.

We are still remaining in the same place. The skirmishers are exchanging fire, while the uhlans are lying on the grass. Out of boredom I went for a walk around the hills where the Cossack vedettes are posted. Coming down off a knoll, I saw a horrible scene: two jagers, who had evidently wanted to take shelter from the gunfire or simply to drink their liquor at leisure, both lay dead. Death had found them in their refuge; they were both killed by a single cannonball which tore away the chest of the one sitting higher up, pierced the side of his comrade, who was sitting somewhat lower, ripped out his intestines, and lay there with him. Beside them also lay their canteen of vodka. Shuddering, I left the dreadful sight of the two bodies. I returned to the regiment, lay down in the bushes, and went to sleep, only to be roused very quickly and disagreeably; a cannonball fell close to me, and a few more came flying after it. I jumped up and ran ten paces away from the spot, but I did not have time to snatch up my cap and left it behind. It lay on the ground, and against the dark green grass its bright crimson colour made it look like a huge flower. The wachtmeister [sergeant] ordered me to go and pick it up and I went, albeit rather reluctantly, because balls were falling thick and fast into the shrubbery. The reason for this sudden rain of fire onto us was our pennons: we had driven our lances into the ground by our horses. The multi-coloured pennons playing in the wind and fluttering in the air attracted the attention of the enemy, who, suspecting that we were in the woods, directed his cannon fire there. So we have been led farther away and ordered to lay the lances on the ground.

In the evening our regiment was ordered to mount. Until late at night we sat on our steeds and waited for orders to move out. We have become the rearguard and will cover the army's retreat. At least that's what our captain tells us. Since I was deathly tired from sitting on my horse so long, I asked Wyszemirski if he did not want to get down. He said that he would have dismounted long ago if he was not expecting the regiment to leave at any minute.

'We will hear it and can be back on our horses in a flash,' I saw, ' but now let's lead them across the ditch and lie down on the grass there.' Wyszemirski followed my advice. We led our horses across the ditch and lay down in the bushes. I wound the reins around my arm and instantly fell asleep. I heard my name repeated twice, I felt Alcides nudging me with his head, snorting and pawing the ground, I felt the earth trembling under me, and then everything became quiet. My heart sank. I understood the danger and made an effort to wake up, but I could not. Although Alcides, my priceless steed, was left alone, hearing his comrades in the distance and free because the reins had slackened and fallen off my arm, he did not leave me, but kept on incessantly pawing the ground and snorting, bending his muzzle to me. At last with difficulty I opened my eyes and got up. I saw that Wyszemirski was gone. I looked at the spot where the regiment had stood – it was gone, too! I was surrounded by a nocturnal darkness and quiet that under the circumstances was quite dreadful. The hollow reverberation of horses' hooves convinced me that the regiment was riding away at a trot. I made haste to mount Alcides, and justice demands that I admit that my foot was slow to find the stirrup. Seated, I loosened the reins, and my steed, my excellent, trusty steed, jumped the ditch and carried me right through the shrubbery at an easy, rapid canter right to the regiment; in a quarter of an hour he caught up with it and took his place in the ranks. Wyszemirski said he thought it was the end of me. He said that he himself was very alarmed when he heard the regiment departing and, therefore, after calling me twice, he had left my fate in God's hands.

May 29 and 30. Heilsberg. The French fought furiously here. Oh, man is horrible in his frenzy! All the qualities of the wild are then combined in him! No, this is no longer bravery! I do not know what to call this wild, bestial daring but it is unworthy of being called fearlessness! Our regiment could take only a small active part in this battle: it was the artillery which pounded [the positions], and the victorious bayonets of our infantry which struck [the enemy]. But we took some punishment anyway; we were covering the artillery, which is a most disadvantageous situation, because the insult is taken without response – that is, no matter what happens, you must stand your ground without moving.

Even now I do not see anything frightening in battle, but I see many men as white as sheets, I see them duck when a shell flies over as if they could evade it. Evidently in these men, fear has more force than reason. I have already seen a great many killed and severely wounded. It is pitiful to watch the latter moaning and crawling over the so-called field of honour. What can mitigate the horror of a position like that for a common soldier? A recruit? For an educated man it is a completely different matter: the lofty feeling of honour, heroism, devotion to the emperor, and sacred duty to his native land compel him to face death fearlessly, endure suffering courageously, and part with life calmly.

For the first time danger was so close to me that it could not have been closer. A shell landed under the belly of my horse and at once exploded. Whistling fragments flew in all directions. Stunned and showered with dirt, I barely kept my seat on Alcides, who gave such a leap to the side that I thought he was possessed by the devil. Poor Wyszemirski, who screws up his eyes at every bullet, says that such a violent caper would have thrown him. But the most astonishing thing is that not a single fragment struck either me or Alcides! This is so extraordinary that my comrades cannot stop marvelling at it. Oh, it is clear that my father's prayers and my old grandmother's blessing are preserving my life amid these terrible, bloody scenes.

It has been raining heavily ever since morning. I am shivering; nothing I have on is dry. Rain streams unimpeded onto my helmet, across my helmet onto my head, down my face, under my collar, over my entire body, and into my boots. It fills them and runs in several streams onto the ground. I am shivering in every limb like an aspen leaf. At last we have been ordered to pull back; another cavalry regiment is going to take our place. And it is long overdue! We have been standing here almost the entire day. We are soaked to the bone and stiff with cold, we no longer look at all human, and, moreover, we have lost many men.

When our regiment took up position beyond the range of enemy bullets, I asked the captain for permission to make a quick trip into Heilsberg, which is a versta away from us. I needed to get Alcides shod – he had lost a shoe – and, besides, I wanted to buy something to eat. I was so hungry that I even looked with envy at a chunk of bread one of our officers was holding. The captain permitted me to go, ordering me to return as quickly as possible since night was falling and the regiment might change position. Alcides and I, both of us shivering from cold and hunger, raced like a whirlwind to Heilsberg. I put my horse into the first wayside tavern I came across and, seeing blacksmiths there shoeing Cossack horses, asked them to shoe mine as well. I went inside. In the parlour a large fire was burning in a kind of hearth or fireplace of unusual construction. I sat down at once in the large leather armchair standing beside it and barely had time to give the Jewess money to buy some bread before falling instantly into a deep sleep. Fatigue, cold from horseback, and my tender age not yet conditioned to endure many combined rigours – all this exhausted my strength and betrayed me defencelessly into the power of a sleep as untimely as it was dangerous. I was awakened by someone shaking my shoulder with great force. I opened my eyes and looked around dumbfounded. I could not understand where l was, what I was doing there, or even what I myself had become. Although my eyes were open, sleep was still stupefying my mental faculties. At last I came to my senses, alarmed beyond measure. It was already the dead of night, and everything around me was cloaked in darkness. There was barely enough fire left in the hearth to illuminate the room. By the light of the flickering flame, I saw that the creature shaking my shoulder was a soldier, a jager, who from my elegant epaulets took me for an officer and kept saying, 'Wake up, wake up, your honour! The cannon fire is getting stronger. Cannonballs are falling on the town!'

I dashed headlong to the spot where I had left my horse. I saw that he was still standing there and looked at his hoof – unshod! There was not a soul in the tavern. The Jew and Jewess had run away – there was no point even thinking of bread. I led Alcides outside and saw that it was not as late as I thought. The sun had just set, and it was a fine evening, the rain had stopped, and the sky was clear. I mounted my poor, hungry, unshod Alcides. As I approached the gates, I was horrified by the numbers of wounded crowding around them. I was forced to a halt. There was no way I could get through that throng of men on foot and horseback, women and children. Disabled cannons and pontoons were being carried through also, and everything was so crowded and crushed in the gates that I was driven to complete despair. Time was flying, and I could not even begin to stir, surrounded as I was on all sides by a throng incessantly streaming toward me with no sign of letting up.

At last it became completely dark. The cannon fire died down, and everything around fell silent, except for the spot where I stood. There the groaning, whining, screeching, swearing and shouting nearly drove me and my steed out of our wits. Had there been any space at all, he would have reared, but since there was not, he snorted and kicked at whomever he could. God, how was I going to break out of this? Where would I find the regiment now? The night was not just dark, but pitch black. What was I going to do?

To my great good fortune, I caught sight of some Cossacks forcing a path in some unfathomable way through that compressed mass of people, horses and artillery. I saw them dashing adroitly through the gates and in a flash joined them and dashed through also, but only by badly bruising my knee and almost breaking my shoulder. Escaping into the open, I stroked Alcides' arched neck: I am sorry for you, trusty comrade, but there is nothing to be done for it; on your way at the gallop! A light touch of my foot, and my steed took off at a run. I put all my faith in Alcides' instinct. I had no way at all of ascertaining the correct route; the night was so dark that it was impossible to see objects twenty paces away. I loosed the reins. Alcides soon stopped galloping and went at a walk, continually snorting and flicking his ears. I guessed that he was seeing or smelling something dreadful, but since I could not, as the saying goes, see my nose before my face, I had no way of avoiding any misfortune that might lie before me. It was evident that the army had changed position and I was left alone to blunder through unfamiliar fields surrounded by darkness and the hush of death.

At last Alcides began to climb such an extraordinarily steep slope that I had to clutch his mane with all my might to keep from rolling off the saddle. The darkness had gotten so thick that I could not see anything before me. I had no idea where I was going and how this journey might end. While I went on thinking and changing my mind about what I should do, Alcides suddenly began heading downhill at the same horrible steep angle at which he had gone up. Now there was no more time for reflection. To save my neck, I leaped hastily off my horse and led him on foot, stooping close to the ground to see where to put my feet and taking all the precautions necessary during such a perilous descent.

When Alcides and I stood at last on a level spot, I saw a dreadful and at the same time lamentable sight: countless numbers of dead bodies covered the field. They were quite visible: they were either totally stripped or wore only their shirts and lay like white shadows on the black earth. At a distance a number of fires could be seen, and the highway was right beside me. Behind me was the redoubt which Alcides had clambered up and I had descended in such fear. Having found out at last where I was and taking it for granted that the fires I saw were those lit by our army, I remounted my horse and began heading down the road toward the fires directly ahead of me; but Alcides turned left and took off at a gallop. The route he chose was horrifying to me: he was racing among the dead bodies, jumping over them, stepping on them, leaping aside, or stopping and bending his muzzle to sniff a corpse and snort over it. I could no longer bear it and turned him back to the road. My steed obeyed me with marked reluctance and went at a walk, continually trying, however, to head leftward.

After a few minutes I heard the hooves of many horses and male voices, and at last caught sight of a group of mounted men riding directly toward me; they were talking about something or other and kept repeating, 'Your Excellency!' I was delighted, taking it for granted that His Excellency would know which were the fires of the Polish Horse or, if he did not, would allow me to join his suite. When they came close to me, the man in front – I assume it was the general himself – asked me, 'Who goes there?'

'A Polish Horse soldier," I answered.

'And where are you going?'

'To the regiment!'

'But your regiment is standing over there,' said the general gesturing in the direction that my trusty Alcides had so insistently tried to take, 'and you are heading toward the enemy.'

The general and his suite galloped off to Heilsberg, and, after kissing my priceless Alcides' ears several times, I left him at liberty to choose the way. Finding himself free, my trusty steed reared to express his delight, neighed, and galloped directly toward the fires glimmering to the left side of the road. There were no dead bodies on my route, and, thanks to Alcides' speed, in a quarter of an hour I was at home – that is, with the regiment. The Polish Horse soldiers were already mounted. Alcides took his place in the ranks with a sort of quiet, amicable neigh. He had no sooner settled down than the command rang out: 'To the right by threes, march!' The regiment moved out. Wyszemirski and our other comrades in my unit were delighted at my return, but the sergeant-major felt obliged to scold me: 'You do foolish things, Durov! You won't keep your head on your shoulders. At Guttstadt, in the heat of battle, you decided to give up your horse to some wounded man or other. Are you really too half-witted to realise that a cavalryman on foot in the midst of combat is bound to perish? At the Passarge you dismounted and went to sleep in the bushes when the entire regiment was expecting orders at any minute to depart and go at a trot. Whatever would have become of you if you didn't have a horse who, no offence meant, is a great deal smarter than you are? They let you go into Heilsberg for half an hour, and you settled down by the fireplace and went to sleep, at a time when even to think about sleeping was impossible – that is, impermissible. A soldier has to be more than human. In this calling there is no question of age: he has to carry out his duties the same way at seventeen and at thirty and at eighty. I advise you to die on your horse and in the ranks, or else I warn you that you will either be taken prisoner in disgrace or killed by marauders, or, worst of all, considered a coward.' The sergeant-major fell silent, but his last phrase stung me cruelly. Blood rushed to my face.

There are, however, limits to human endurance . . . Despite our sergeant-major's philosophising about a soldier's obligations, I was dropping from lack of sleep and fatigue. My clothing was soaked. For two days I had neither slept nor eaten. I had been constantly on the march, and, even when we stopped, I was on horseback with only my uniform to wear, exposed without protection to the cold wind and rain. I could feel my strength slipping away by the hour. We were riding three abreast, but whenever we happened upon a narrow bridge or some other obstacle that we could not cross as a unit, we went two at a time or sometimes even by single file. At such times the fourth platoon was forced to stand motionless for several minutes in one spot. I was in the fourth platoon, and at each beneficent stop I would dismount in a flash, lie down on the ground, and instantly fall asleep. The platoon began moving, my comrades shouted and called me and, since a frequently-interrupted sleep cannot be a deep one, I awoke at once, got up, and scrambled back onto Alcides, dragging my heavy oak lance behind me. These episodes were repeated at even the briefest of halts. My sergeant was losing patience, and my comrades were angry with me. They all told me that they would abandon me on the road if I dismounted even once more: 'After all, you can see that we doze, but at least we do not get off our horses and lie down on the ground. Do it our way.' The sergeant-major grumbled in a low voice, 'Why do these whelps wriggle their way into the army? They should stay in the nest.'

I spent the rest of the night on horseback, dozing, sleeping, bending to Alcides' mane, and rousing in fright, feeling as if I were falling. I seemed to be losing my mind. My eyes were open, but objects kept altering in a dreamlike way. I took uhlans for forest, and forest for uhlans. My head was burning, but the rest of me was shivering; I was very cold. Everything I had on was wet to the skin . . .

Dawn broke. We halted and were permitted to kindle a fire and cook porridge. Oh, thank God, now I could lie down and sleep by the fire; I could warm up and dry out. 'You cannot do that,' said the sergeant-major, as he saw me sitting down by the fire and rolling grass into a clump to put under my head. 'You cannot. The captain has ordered the horses fed on grass. Take the curb-bit out of your horse's mouth and lead him to pasture.' I joined the others and walked Alcides around the fields. He grazed the dewy grass while I stood sadly beside him.

'You're as pale as a corpse,' said Wyszemirski, approaching me with his horse. 'What is wrong with you? Are you sick?'

'I am not sick, just severely chilled. The rain has soaked clear through me, my blood has turned to ice, and now I have to go walking around on the damp grass!'

'It seems that the rain soaked us all equally; why are we dry then?'

'You're all wearing greatcoats.'

'And where is yours then?'

'The Cossacks took it, along with my saddlebags and valise.'

'What miracle brought that about?'

'Have you forgotten already that I put a wounded dragoon officer on my horse and let it be used to return him to his regiment?'

'Well, yes, I remember. What about it?'

'This is what: when I found my horse again, he was already in Podwyszacki's hands. He bought it from Cossacks with just the saddle, and everything else had disappeared!'

'That is bad, you are the youngest of us all. You will not last long during these cold nights without a greatcoat. Tell the sergeant-major; he will give you a coat left from those killed. They are sending huge piles of them back to the supply train.'

We talked for a while longer. At last the sun rose quite high, the day warmed up, my uniform dried out, and my fatigue passed. I would have been very cheerful if I could have hoped for something to eat. But there was no use even thinking of it; I had no share in the porridge that was on the fire. And so I began diligently searching the grass for berries. As the captain rode past the uhlans walking around the fields with their horses, he noticed my pursuit.

'What are you looking for, Durov?' he asked, riding up to me. I replied that I was looking for berries. The captain must have guessed the reason, because he turned to the platoon sergeant and said to him in a low voice, 'See that Durov and Wyszemirski get enough to eat.'

He rode away, and the old soldiers said to his back, 'If we have enough to eat, they should, too. They always think more about these whelps than about seasoned old soldiers.'

'What fools you are, seasoned old soldiers!' said the sergeant-major, approaching us. 'Who should we worry about if not children? I think you can see for yourselves that both of these recruits are scarcely out of their childhood. Come with me, children,' said the sergeant-major jovially, taking us both by the arm. 'The captain ordered us to feed you.' We were given soup, roast meat and white bread.

Seeing the horses grazing quietly and the uhlans sleeping in the meadow, I decided there was no need for me to be the only one standing vigil. It was afternoon already, and the heat had become unbearable. I climbed down to the banks of the little river which flowed by our camp and lay down in the tall grass to sleep. Alcides was roaming around not far from me. My sound sleep was bloke by a shout of 'Curb your horse! . . . Mount!' and the tramp of uhlans running to their horses and wither horses into the ranks. I jumped up precipitately. The sergeant-major was already on his steed and hurrying the uhlans into formation; I looked around for Alcides and, to my horror, saw him swimming across the river, heading directly for the far bank. Just then the sergeant-major galloped up to me, 'Why are you standing there without your horse?'

There was no time to hesitate! I plunged after my Alcides, and we came out together on the opposite bank. In a minute I curbed him, mounted, and swam back. I saw standing in place before the troops had finished forming ranks. 'Well, at least that was a plucky recovery,' said the sergeant-major, looking pleased.

Schippenbeil. Great God, what horror! This little village was almost completely incinerated. How many people were burned alive here! Oh, the poor wretches! [From the Russian text in N. Durova, 'Kavalerist-devitsa']

Vasilii Grigoryev

Having spent the last week of May training with his St. Petersburg Militia Battalion of Skirmishers, Vasilii Gregoryev found himself on the frontline at Guttstadt.

23 [May; 4 June] The Feast of the Ascension. I woke up at six o'clock in the morning and learned that a rogation would be held; as the result the entire camp came into motion within two hours and the rogation was held, first by companies, then by battalions. Here one can clearly see the greatness of God and the insignificance of human beings, and one may assume that the prayer of each of the faithful was sincere and performed with tender emotion, for with a battle with the enemy already set, each of us considered it as the last one in his life. At one o'clock in the afternoon we ate lunch and, at five o'clock, the entire division formed a huge square on the plain, the flags of all regiments were gathered in the middle of it and the regimental priests began a general service

with the blessing of the waters and both the flags and warriors were blessed with the holy water. Our corps commander [korpusnyj nachalnik] Prince Gorchakov addressed the soldiers with a short speech about the impending battle and reminded each of us of our responsibility to the Fatherland and Russian honour. Afterwards, the infantry regiments marched as they were standing, one after another by sections [odin za drugim otdeleniyami], while the cavalry moved on the flanks.

We marched on the road leading to the town of Guttstadt and it was noteworthy that, in each village we passed, local churches rang bells as soon as our troops appeared as if they were giving a signal of our approach. Around one o'clock in the afternoon, about one and a half verstas [1.5km] away from the [Passarge] River, which we were supposed to cross at Guttstadt, we halted near a hill and rested for two hours.

24 [May; 5 June]. We advanced and reached the river, where a pontoon bridge was already completed. Our battalion was ordered to leave its knapsacks and coats behind, check and load our muskets, holding them at the ready, to run across the bridge and provide cover to the columns of the Kexholmskii and Pernovskii Regiments that were following us. Upon crossing we were met by the shots of the enemy batteries established on the nearby heights but these quickly subsided after our light cavalry dislodged them. About one-and-a-half hours later the French retreated and we occupied Guttstadt, capturing some 4,000 men while the commander of the enemy forces, Marshal Ney, with the largest part of his troops, which, people say, amounted to 15,000 before the battle, barely escaped capture because of our swift and unexpected attack that surprised the enemy. We halted at the bivouacs that the French had built for themselves – these were well built and clean, everything was made of wooden boards, in two lines, with a distance of about 15 sazhens in between them. These huts are painted in lead-coloured [svintsovyi] paint and the number of the regiment or a company is indicated above each entrance; part of the provisions, various items and clothing became the victor's trophies – my prize included a geographic map of Prussia where military operations have taken place.

Around two o'clock in the afternoon we ate soldiers' porridge and whatever we could get from Guttstadt through the Jewish merchants, who, on this occasion, did not shy away from deceiving my soldier who was sent to buy a bottle of rum – he paid two silver rubles for a bottle labelled 'Rum' but upon opening it we discovered that it contained a potato siwucha.*

We spent rather a disagreeable evening and night because of the considerable cold and, lacking our coats, we had to sleep on the bare ground, which in turn meant that the shoddy Jewish 'rum' was quickly put to use.

25 [May; 6 June]. At sunrise we heard heavy artillery fire and learned that a battle had begun with the enemy crossing the Passarge River at Liebstadt.

---

* Moonshine, an incompletely-rectified vodka made from potatoes or grain.

Soon thereafter our battalion and two companies of skirmishers from the Kexholmskii and Pernovskii Regiments were ordered to drive off one part of the enemy forces that had hunkered down in the woods. Consequently, we veered slightly to the left, leaving the main battle to our right, and proceeded through the woods, which, fortunately, were not too thick but did have many marshy areas that complicated our advance. Our cavalry outposts encountered a small number of enemy troops, who had two field guns that were captured without a fight. After marching through the woods, we came out on a flat plain and deployed into the second line behind a hill near the Passarge River since the enemy had already managed to cross it. The subsequent pursuit was rather feeble [since] our first line comprised of just the 24th and 26th Jager Regiments, which amounted to 600 men scattered amidst the bulrushes on the riverbank, and an artillery company under the command of Staff Captain Nikolay Petrovich Buch. The French waged a rather intensive cannonade from the opposite bank, directing plunging fire [navesnye vystrely] from their two batteries. Although we returned fire with five cannon of the battery commanded by Colonel Count Sievers, the French still caused considerable harm to us, injuring a considerable number of men in the second line and damaging three artillery limbers, not to mention horses. Unfortunately, [among the wounded] was an old cannonier who was hit by a grapeshot that tore off his manhood and injured his leg, and in a fit of temper, he came running to the second line, complaining of his injury. As the enemy fire subsided, I came across a number of my old acquaintances, namely [Colonel Peter] Yershov, commander of the Tenginskii Regiment, and Colonel* Ivan Grigorievich Heidenreich and Major Lev Fedorovich Maksimov of the same regiment.

The meeting was pleasant but after a prolonged forced march we were all starving and had nothing to eat. Fortunately, my non-commissioned officer Dmitriev revealed his virtuous side by giving me a small flask of branntwein which he had kept inside his kiwer and which my dear friends and I quickly consumed. This revived us better than the mythical nectar† might have done. Exhausted as we were, sleep soon overpowered us and we fell asleep between stacked muskets within an hour. By then the gunfire, which the enemy still maintained, completely subsided. Around five o'clock in the morning I and fifteen other officers, conversing as we were, decided to descend to the riverbank to better observe the enemy position. But as we came down, an enemy battery, deployed on the opposite bank, suddenly fired up to ten shots which caused us to disperse. [Fortunately] we suffered

---

* Heidenreich was still a lieutenant-colonel and earned his promotion to colonel only in 1811.
† Grigoryev is referring to nectar (Latin) or ambrosia (Greek), the favoured drink of the Olympian gods that was believed to confer immortality upon whoever consumed it.

no losses, although Major Maksimov was hit by a clump of soil, thrown up by a cannonball, in his right cheek. At six o'clock in the morning our division adjutant Lieutenant Borovskii of the Kexholmskii Regiment arrived with orders from the corps commander, Prince Gorchakov, to retreat, which were carried out [at once]. After withdrawing one and a half verstas [1.5km] from the bridge, we halted in an open field.

Here, the Cossacks, under the command of General [Matvei] Platov, established a cordon, the infantry took up position in the middle and we joined those regiments that were kept in reserve. I learned that among these units was the Belozerskii Regiment and that after the death of Major-General Siedmioraczki, the brigade was under command of my acquaintance, Colonel Afanasii Demidovich Gordeyev.* So I went to see him. This meeting proved to be very pleasant and we spent several hours without noticing how quickly time passed in remembering the past and discussing the present. He told me that during the fighting for Guttstadt and the subsequent pursuit to the Passarge River the enemy lost 7,000–8,000 killed, wounded and captured; and that near Guttstadt, while pursuing Marshal Ney, Platov's Cossacks captured the Marshal's entire supply train, including his personal silverware. As befits wartime, he treated me to plenty of punch, good rum and Dutch cheese. We bade each other farewell well after midnight.

26 [May; 7 June]. Our camp remained in the same place until noon, when we received orders to retreat to the town of Guttstadt. We arrived there around 4 o'clock, taking position in the same field as before. Rumours spread that the enemy intended to turn our flank, so consequently . . . [text is missing].

27 [May; 8 June]. At noon we received orders to return to our earlier position at Heilsberg. Since our circumstances did not require major preparations, around 4 o'clock in the afternoon we departed and spent [the rest of the day and] almost all night marching on backcountry roads, frequently through the woods, without any guides. Because the area is rather marshy, we became exhausted and many people fell behind as stragglers along the road. By sunrise, we somehow managed to get to Heilsberg, where we took up our earlier bivouacs. Exhausted as I was, I was excited by this opportunity to rest.

28 [May; 9 June]. Upon waking up this morning I found our soldiers preoccupied – some, in order to clean and refresh themselves, were bathing in the waters of the Alle, other were cooking food. The latter got up my appetite and I was thrilled to learn that my batman had acquired twenty eggs and white bread in the city. I ordered him to prepare breakfast while I took a bath [in the river]. I was about to plunge into the waters when an alarm was sounded and the entire corps immediately took up arms. So my half-prepared eggs were quickly wrapped into a napkin while I dressed without bathing and took my position [in the unit]. Two hours later we learned that this alarm was the result

---

* Gordeyev also commanded the Belozerskii Regiment.

of the looting of Heilsberg by the Cossacks and the cowardice of the Germans whom the former [Cossacks] convinced that the French were approaching the city and thereby caused them to flee.

Around six o'clock we were once again ordered to deploy but there was no alarm, instead we simply changed our position. We were assigned to the right side of the Alle River, near Launau. The evening was splendid and time flew by pleasantly in the company of friends; only [Lieutenant] Nikolay Svechin was so unusually sombre and pensive that he bored others by his complaints that he was suffering from unusual dolefulness.

29 [May; 10 June]. I woke up at 4 o'clock, the morning was splendid. Frequent artillery fire could be heard in the distance but since this had become a common occurrence since the 23rd, no one paid particular attention to it. Around seven o'clock I went to the colonel to ask for permission to go for an hour or two to the city. Upon receiving permission, I was quickly on my way there, first going to the vorstadt [suburb] where General of Cavalry Andrey Semenovich Kologrivov was lodging so I could meet his regimental adjutant A.A. Pogrebov, who was billeted with him. The latter was already gone but the general was in very good spirits and upon seeing me, called me inside and made me drink a large glass of tea with rum. He then went to the camp for the Guard regiments – Life Guard Semenovskii, Izmailovskii, Life Guard Jager, Life Guard Grenadier and Pavlovskii Regiments and the Finlyandskii Militia Battalion commanded by Lieutenant-Colonel Andrey Andreevich Troshinskii – to visit Lieutenant-General Peter Fedorovich Malyutin and took me with him.

Upon arriving there we found Malyutin in the company of numerous officers enjoying a splendid luncheon. Here I became acquainted with [Sub-Lieutenant] Fedor Vasilievich Kryukovskii of the Izmailovskii Regiment and, since I had already eaten, I returned to our bivouacs around noon. After learning that the colonel was still in the town, I decided to make the most of it and travelled to the Kexholmskii regiment which was located about one and a half verstas [1.5km] from our battalion. I visited Peter Ivanovich Borozdin★ where I met Lefner, who was cooking a beefsteak. They invited me to share their meal and just as we finished it, we heard the command to take up arms. I immediately rushed back to my battalion, which I found already deployed to the front and joined it after giving my horse to the batman. The sound of gun fire could be heard nearby and after marching about one versta [1km] towards Launau, we came under enemy [artillery] fire that killed about a dozen privates and Lieutenant Nikolay Svechin. We were first ordered to deploy in a skirmish line [tsep'] to cover the infantry regiments of the left wing, and then redeployed into dense columns [gustye kolony]; and so we moved forward in such a manner, changing [skirmish] lines. Around 5 o'clock in the afternoon, a major movement was observed on the heights directly in front of us where the French

---

★ Borozdin was a staff captain in the Kexholmskii Regiment.

army was deployed. The French chasseurs [schesyury], who were covering their troops, suddenly shouted 'En avant, Vive L'Empereur!' and launched a fierce assault on the left wing of our column. Our troops discharged a volley and then charged with bayonets but were repelled; so we began to retreat to Heilsberg so as to lead the enemy onto our [fortified] batteries established there. During this disorderly [besporyadochnyj] retreat, which stretched over a distance of two verstas [2 km], I suffered an injury (a concussion to the head) while our non-commissioned officer Dmitriev had both of his legs torn off by a cannonball and was, therefore, left behind. By seven o'clock in the evening our battered line was already on the other side of Heilsberg, on the road to Bartenstein. Here I encountered other wounded men: Brigadier-General Verderevskii, and our officers Alexander Lomanskii and Petelin – Verderevskii had been wounded by a bullet below his knee while both officers had sustained injuries to their arms.

Our batteries maintained a strong cannonade. The rumbling thunder of gunfire, screams of warriors and groaning of the wounded – all of this combined to create a terrifying picture of death and destruction, which was, on top of it, illuminated by the glow of burning Schippenbeil, where, it is said, the French prisoners set fire to an infirmary.

On the road I came across our colonel, Count St. Priest, wounded by a bullet in the left leg and travelling in a carriage. He invited me into the carriage and together we arrived at Bartenstein around midnight since the road was extremely congested by the wagons of the artillery park and the large number of wounded soldiers and officers.

The Count lodged in the house of the local mayor and was so kind to me that upon bidding farewell he reassured me that he would include me in his nominations for awards to His Majesty King of Prussia. I was billeted in the apartment of a certain tradesman, who had a large family and was, seemingly, not very affluent. I drank plenty of tea but still could not get rid of headaches. At last, the health-some sleep overpowered me, tired and fatigued as I was, and soothed my pain.

30 [May; 11 June]. I woke up at 4 o'clock [in the morning] and feeling refreshed and revived, I decided to search for my comrades. A terrifying spectacle unfolded in front of me: over 800 wounded staff and junior officers gathered at Bartenstein and among them were several of my acquaintances: Major Stassel of the Kexholmskii Regiment, who [during the battle] was wounded in the chest in front of me as he was accompanying our skirmishers; Captain Neterfeldt [of the Kexholmskii Regiment] – wounded by a grapeshot to the right thigh; Lieutenant Zenin [of the Kexholmskii Regiment] had his right leg torn off [by a cannonball]; Golovin [of the Kexholmskii Regiment] – wounded in the mouth by a bullet; [Colonel Carl] Leble* of the 2nd Jager Regiment – wounded in the left leg by a bullet. There were numerous other horribly disfigured officers from

---

* Leble commanded the 2nd Jager Regiment.

various regiments. And to cap off this dreadful scene, there was almost no food in the city and whatever was available fetched exorbitant prices. I had no money whatsoever since only God knew where our supply wagons were. Fortunately, this morning, the Emperor [Alexander I], accompanied by Prince Volkonskii, arrived here and, upon seeing our disastrous conditions, he ordered to provide all possible means to the wounded; so the supply officials, including the military counsellor [Alexander] Howe, distributed chervontsy [gold coins], but mainly to those who could come and pick them up. I received forty chervontsy that, considering [the exorbitant] prices, were unlikely to last long.

31 [May; 12 June]. We remained at the same place but in the afternoon received orders to proceed on the right bank of the Alle River in the direction of the town of Friedland, where we need to anticipate the enemy who is marching on a shorter route. I could have stayed behind because of my injury but, out of my devotion to the service and unwilling to leave the few remaining comrades, I embarked on this march and, after covering about four miles that day, I bivouacked in an open field. We had no food and could not find anything in the vicinity; only late at night did our foragers return with a few handfuls of rye, which we [quickly] cooked in water and ate using our flask caps. The night was cold and I suffered badly through it all. [From the Russian text in V. Grigoryev, Podennyj zhurnal . . .]

Alexsey Yermolov

Our army marched to Königsberg that same night. Ataman Platov, who arrived with the Don Cossack Host a day before, was ordered to remain on the battlefield.

The enemy also retreated and during the night, their rearguard withdrew to Landsberg. On the next day, seeing that our army had abandoned Preussisch-Eylau, the French returned to gather their guns and transports. We soon learned that special orders had been issued directing the evacuation of hospitals, the commissariat and the army treasury. And after this, Napoleon had the impertinence to claim the battle as a victory!

The commander-in-chief initially wanted to pursue the enemy and he even told his senior commanders of his intent; however, it proved impossible to rally our troops, dispersed over such a vast area. The soldiers were exhausted and weakened by heavy losses. It was known that Napoleon still had Bernadotte's corps and with such superiority of forces, our success seemed doubtful. Besides, the lack of supplies further restricted us.* The commander-in-chief

---

* Robert Wilson described, 'The Prussians had provisions, but the Russians had no other sustenance than the frozen snow. Their wants had induced numbers during the battle to search for food in the adjoining villages and the plain was covered by foraging parties passing and repassing.' Wilson, *Brief Remarks*, p. 109.

did not escape criticism; and since detractors often have no understanding of the subjects they are discussing, so it was with the critics of Bennigsen.

Approaching Königsberg, the army bivouacked in the vicinity of the town, while the vanguard was some 12 verstas [12km] ahead of it.* A small number of enemy cavalry appeared on the last march to Königsberg, and, as their number rapidly increased, the French took up positions some distance from us.

Early in February, a detachment from our vanguard had destroyed some enemy troops at Mansfeld and Bochersdorf. General Lambert distinguished himself in these actions. It was obvious that the French cavalry was so exhausted that on one occasion two squadrons, forced to withdraw across a lake, fell off their horses and were captured lying on the ground. Both squadrons numbered only sixty men.

The commander-in-chief dispatched Bagration to St. Petersburg with a detailed description of Preussisch-Eylau, which had been unjustly described to the Tsar because of various court intrigues. There was talk that Count Tolstoy used his brother, who was close to the Tsar, to spread malicious rumours against the commander-in-chief. The general opinion was in favour of the latter.

Less than two weeks after arriving at Königsberg, the army advanced again. Two marches later, the vanguard under Major-General Markov arrived at Preussisch-Eylau. He was supported by General Prince Golitsyn's cavalry.

I surveyed the battlefield with intense curiosity. I was horrified to see so many corpses lying where our lines had been. I found even more bodies where the enemy troops had been, especially where their columns massed before attacks. Local residents (who informed for us) were ordered several days ago to throw the French corpses into the nearby lakes, since it was impossible to dig graves in the frozen soil. As an artillery officer I noticed evidence of our artillery fire and was pleased. There was not a single undamaged building in town; a suburb had burnt to the ground, and here, according to the locals, the French wounded had been gathered and consequently many of them died.

The French abandoned Preussisch-Eylau upon our approach. Numerous abandoned transports, caissons and ambulances with wounded and sick indicated a hasty retreat. Soon, a thaw made the roads impassable and, because the retreating side always suffers more in such conditions, the French had to abandon all their ambulances at various towns and villages.

Arriving at Landsberg, we found a hospital for French officers; these were surprised to receive better care from us. Some of them had had no bandages

---

* The Russian army arrived on 10 February 1807. Juliette de Krüdener wrote in her diary, 'The town was overflowing with wounded; it was impossible to find shelter for everybody, nor to dress the wounds immediately.' Juliette de Krüdener, 'Journal 1806-1808', cited in Francis Ley, *Madame de Krüdener et son temps 1764-1824* (Paris, 1964), pp. 273–4.

for several days. The landlord of my apartment spoke poor French and told me that he overheard the officers discussing the terrible conditions in their army when it arrived at Landsberg after the battle; they mentioned that if it had not been for Bernadotte's corps which did not participate in the battle and was left as the rearguard, there would have been no one else to cover the French retreat since the troops were in complete disorder and the number of pillagers was impossible. Many corps lacked ammunition. The French rearguard had reached Landsberg that same evening.

Our vanguard quickly marched on Arensdorf and some troops seized Guttstadt. Ataman Platov, with his Cossacks, a battalion of hussars and a battalion of Jagers, was deployed at Benern. General Count Pahlen was at one of the crossings over the Passarge, maintaining communications with Colonel Vuich's detachment at Wormsdit. Baron Sacken's division, the closest to the vanguard, occupied Launau. The remaining forces were approaching Heilsberg and the main headquarters was at Bartenstein.

The enemy was on the other side of the Passarge and Napoleon's head-quarters was at Osterode. On 18 February [2 March], the enemy concentrated his forces on the right and crossed the Passarge, while other forces appeared near Guttstadt and Arensdorf. We hastily abandoned the latter place but could join neither Ataman Platov nor General Count Pahlen. Major-General Baggovut could not defend Guttstadt and the enemy drove back his 5th Jager Regiment, capturing the village of Zechern as well. During this unexpected attack, we almost lost our guns. General Baggovut joined General Baron Sacken at Launau, where Adjutant General Uvarov also arrived with his cavalry.

The vanguard had no other way to retreat other than to pass close by to the French camp at Peterswalde; all the other roads were too far off and the enemy had outposts there. To avoid confusion and disorder, the French hated to do anything important during the night so we were able to freely pass their bivouacs.

The vanguard passed through Launau and joined General Baron Sacken. Other detachments, previously isolated from each other, soon concentrated here as well.

On the 19th [3 March], our forces concentrated around Launau. Marshal Ney's corps opposed us, with its headquarters at Guttstadt. Enemy skirmishers, deployed in the direction of Peterswalde, covered the forest in front of our camp. Well-positioned and defended French batteries harassed us from Zechern. General Baron Sacken also deployed skirmishers, but the French were more experienced and inflicted considerable casualties on us for two days. Therefore, General Sacken decided to launch a night attack on Zechern, hoping that the enemy would be driven from there and forced to abandon Peterswalde, leaving us better off. During the attack, the infantry began to shout 'Hurrah' some way from the batteries, and awoke the French, who immediately prepared themselves. We exchanged canister and musket fire; the men at the head of our column grew timid and threw themselves down, while the rear ranks continued to advance and it all became so confused that it was impossible to move them out of harm's way for a long time. We lost several officers and many rank-and-file during the fighting. It was here that I observed for the first time how cavalry covered retreating infantry in darkness. I do not know why the disordered troops were not rallied by the drummers but, instead, General Count Pahlen and his Sumskii Hussars had to round the soldiers up.

The following day, the French commander at Zechern sent a message that he would allow us to bury our corpses and mockingly noted how far these were from his guns. We had to keep our mouths shut; however, everyone criticised Sacken for restarting his old night-time excursions! The vanguard was reinforced by several units and Sacken was given a different assignment. Major-General Markov ordered the establishment of a battery in front of Zechern, and I set to willingly since my company had suffered a lot at that spot. Having reconnoitred part of the forest defended by the enemy, I deployed six guns close to the edge of the woods and masked them with fir branches; I then waited for dawn when the enemy usually moved its infantry from the camp near Peterswalde. Early in the morning, a large enemy column left the camp and proceeded in a carefree manner towards the woods where a small contingent was always deployed for the night. During its march, the column exposed its flank to my battery and the canister fire of my six guns at close range caused such confusion that, having abandoned many corpses, it fled towards the camp pursued by our fire. We occupied the remaining part of the forest and the enemy did not dare challenge us. We now had some six infantry regiments here. The batteries near Zechern often exchanged fire, mostly ineffective, with the French. Marshal Ney's courier was captured delivering a message to Prince Berthier with information that the Russians indeed planned to defend their position since they had constructed batteries at various points. The enemy soon abandoned Zechern and Peterswalde, and dug trenches along the edge of the forest.

General Markov occupied Zechern with two jager regiments, while two hussar squadrons and some rotating infantry units were at Peterswalde. There were frequent skirmishes with the French, who searched for dry wood in the village. My horse artillery company had already suffered enough and was replaced by another unit and moved back for repairs and reinforcement. However, due to the whims of the senior artillery colonels, neither of whom had held such a distinguished command, I was ordered to join my company.*
The commander-in-chief was told that this change was made to give me some

---

* Yermolov is suggesting that the senior officers envied him his role in the vanguard and tried to remove him from command.

rest, and he later said the same to Bagration. Having just returned from St. Petersburg, Bagration requested that he keep me and so I remained with this commander, whom we all completely trusted.

An unpleasant incident took place prior to Bagration's return. Four Jäger regiments at Peterswalde, commanded by Major-General Korff, lost their commander in bizarre circumstances. Billeted in the best house in the village, which belonged to a priest, Korff was busy with his usual exercise, sipping punch, and did not trouble himself about security. He kept a hussar officer in charge of the outposts with him. Meanwhile, a few French voltigeurs, guided by the priest, entered the house via the garden and, under cover of darkness, captured the general. In the ensuing noisy struggle, our regiments were called to arms but, following a skirmish, the French escaped with their prize.*

Napoleon did not miss the chance of portraying this skirmish as a victorious battle in his bulletin. They had captured a corps commander and, to exaggerate this victory, Korff's gallantry and noble character were emphasised. But I would have been surprised if the French had been able to identify their prisoner right away as the general was too drunk to even use his tongue. The French can only have thought Baron Korff a general due to the darkness and wouldn't have guessed such from his condition and appearance. Then we would not have had to learn about his merits by reading foreign newspapers.

Following this incident, there was complete inactivity on both sides for almost three months; there were no skirmish lines and not a single shot was fired, although no armistice was concluded. A general commanding the French advance troops offered to make Peterswalde neutral because otherwise it would be a source of constant strife and the French would have to capture it. Bagration responded that he agreed with the latter contention but warned that it was easier for the French to demand this than to actually carry it out. So, French threats remained words and we retained control of Peterswalde.

The French deployed against us suffered greatly from the lack of supplies and their cavalry was sent back to refit. The 27th Dragoons was exhausted by hunger and deserted to us in large numbers. Our vanguard endured similar hardships; there was no bread or salt; biscuits were completely rotten and very scarce. The soldiers ate ox hides which had earlier covered our tents for two or three weeks. In the 23rd and 24th Jager Regiments the soldiers began slaughtering horses and the latter unit had many deserters.

Prince Bagration sent me to describe our hardships to the commander-in-chief. Despite stern orders, the situation remained the same. The duty officer, Major-General Foch, was upset by my report and I also found myself the subject of his enmity because I did not admire his mediocre abilities

---

* It is unclear when Korff was released from captivity because his record of service shows him fighting at Heilsberg and Friedland, for which he received a golden sword with diamonds and the Prussian Order of the Red Eagle (1st class).

whilst others praised them. We were both in the artillery and had known each other for a long time.

The Tsar soon joined the army and the Guard, commanded by the Grand Duke, also arrived. Imperial headquarters was at Bartenstein, while the Grand Duke remained at Schipenbeil.* Parades and foppishness took over and, despite our hungry bellies, we had to turn to arranging ammunition.

Grand Duke Constantine visited us first as, after Suvorov's campaign in Italy, he had established friendly relations with Bagration. Observing our lack of provisions, he took care to improve our supplies. The first supply train that he insisted on sending to the vanguard was diverted *en route* to other troops. However, he assigned escorts to the subsequent trains, which reached us safely. Instead of a shortage, we soon found ourselves in abundance.

Among other officials introduced to him, the Grand Duke honoured me following Prince Bagration's commendation of my service. Until then, he had not known me because I had never served at the capital. We were soon ordered to prepare to meet the Tsar and the King of Prussia.

Having arranged our huts uniformly and made them look smart, we organised the rest of our camp. Picked men were chosen from various regiments, given the uniforms of others and armed. The troops thus deprived of their clothing were hidden in the woods or sent to man an outpost on a distant hill. Here, I saw how the Tsar was shown his troops in the best light and assured that they lacked nothing. He introduced each commander to the King of Prussia, and, among others, he mentioned me and that he was satisfied with my service in the previous campaign. The Tsar's attention and benevolence fascinated everyone. Without any flattery, I must admit that he had the ability to encourage everyone. The Prussian king awarded the *Pour le Mérite* to three staff officers,† and I was one of them. These were the first Prussian orders awarded and were not yet rendered worthless by their subsequent multiplicity.

Medals for Preussisch-Eylau were soon issued. Instead of the Order of St. George (3rd class), for which the commander-in-chief had nominated me, I received the St. Vladimir. Major-General Count Kutaisov was portrayed as having assisted me in battle. Yet, it was only curiosity that had brought him to my company and since I was not subordinated to him, he did not interfere with my orders. However, he was awarded the St. George (3rd class), even though he did not yet have the 4th class. They intended to describe him as my superior in the official report but Baron Steingel knew the facts and opposed this. Bagration explained this injustice to the commander-in-chief,

---

* In late March, Alexander personally visited the army to encourage his troops for the oncoming campaign.

† Yermolov's note: Awards were given to the chef of the 5th Jager Regiment (Colonel Gogel), myself and the commander of the Pskov Musketeers, Lieutenant-Colonel Loshkarev.

who acknowledged that I was mistreated but did not do anything about it. So, this was one of those many pleasant events that I experienced in my career.

It was beneficial to Napoleon to prolong this inactivity because he could send a large corps to reinforce the troops besieging Danzig. The corps of Davout, deployed at Allenstein, and of Ney, at Guttstadt, were small and parts of their cavalry and artillery had been detached for foraging. So it was decided to attack Ney's corps on 1 [13] May. A day before, the Guard had arrived at Launau, the rest of the army had concentrated and everything was ready. The vanguard took up a position in the woods with the intention of occupying the Altkirch plain and cutting the French line of retreat towards Guttstadt.

The Tsar reviewed the vanguard and, in the company of the commander-in-chief, he visited those outposts deployed before Zechern and Peterswalde which screened the movement of the vanguard. I do not know why the offensive was called off. The Tsar returned to headquarters, the troops returned to their bivouacs and the vanguard returned to Launau.*

The enemy, meanwhile, continued besieging Danzig. Although Major-General Count Kamenski was dispatched with a strong detachment to reinforce the garrison,† the enemy had superior forces and he was prevented from reaching the fortress and was repulsed with loss. Had it been undertaken earlier, this operation would have succeeded. Soon thereafter, the fortress had to surrender because of lack of ammunition, especially after an English ship carrying munitions was captured by the French. It was unpleasant to hear about the capitulation of Danzig and there was no doubt Napoleon would recall most of the besieging force.

I do not know why we, after cancelling our offensive on 1 May, hesitated until the 24th when the enemy army had already been reinforced. The operation was so well planned that the entire corps of Ney should have been in our hands. The direction of the main parts of our army was as follows:

The vanguard moved to Altkirch to cut the French off in the woods extending from Peterswalde to Guttstadt while two Jager regiments attacked them. The vanguard's action was to be cautious so as to allow other parts of the army to outflank the enemy.

On the right, Lieutenant-General Baron von der Osten-Sacken was to outflank the enemy and prevent him from reaching the Passarge. On the left, Lieutenant-General Prince Gorchakov was to cross the Alle and surround

---

* French scouts had detected the Russian movement and Ney was warned of the possible attack. The rumour also spread that Napoleon was marching to reinforce Ney. So, Bennigsen postponed his offensive but the troops were exasperated by these movements, calling them 'the 1st of May ramble'.

† Yermolov's note: Danzig was defended by the Prussians, three garrison battalions and two Cossack regiments under Major-General Prince Sherbatov. After the surrender, these troops were allowed to leave the fortress on condition that they did not serve against the French. Sherbatov rejected this and rejoined the army.

Guttstadt. Lieutenant-General Dokhturov was to drive off an enemy outpost on our right and rejoin the main army. General Prince Golitsyn was to support Baron Sacken with his cavalry. The Guard was left in reserve. Ataman General Platov was to observe the movement of Davout's corps towards Allenstein.

The vanguard marched to Altkirch early on the morning of 24 May. To the left of the woods, we observed French sentries, calmly changing guard. Soon, a few artillery rounds signalled the start of the offensive and we observed the hasty movement of troops towards Altkirch. An intense cannonade ensued but we did not do anything much. Considering the amount of time which had elapsed, Bagration believed that Sacken should have outflanked the enemy by now but not a single shot was heard in that direction and the inaction of the French troops in front of us also raised doubts. Officers were dispatched to gather intelligence but no troops were observed except General Prince Golitsyn's cavalry moving in the distance.

Meanwhile, the French managed to concentrate at Altkirch and our vanguard was ordered to attack them. Bitter fighting followed. The enemy resisted for a long time before retreating. The left wing of the vanguard, led by General Baggovut, came under ferocious fire. Baggovut moved through Amt-Guttstadt (a suburb of Guttstadt), leaving troops to contain 600 Frenchmen. We did not receive support from Gorchakov, as he encountered the enemy at the crossing of the Alle, took his time crossing it and then spent time seizing Guttstadt, thereby failing to arrive on time. It should be noted that this town had no fortifications, was defended by a mere 600 men and, had we marched on, it would have surrendered without having committed an entire corps to its capture. But, because of the hiatus in May, headquarters had heard rumours that the French had fortified the town and that they considered it important. So Gorchakov thought its capture would be considered a great exploit. Had Gorchakov left a small detachment there and moved forward, Ney would have suffered heavy casualties.

The vanguard pursued the enemy until nightfall and bivouacked near Quetz. We had captured many prisoners during the day; some of the French had been unable to reach a rallying point at Altkirch and had found themselves cut off.

It was Sacken's fault that the plan did not work. He was late arriving at his objective, excusing himself by claiming he had taken a long detour and needed further instructions. But rumour had it that, irritated by the commander-in-chief, Sacken had deliberately sabotaged the enterprise, preventing Bennigsen from succeeding. Many were furious that a favourable chance to annihilate an entire enemy corps was so wasted.*

---

* The main reasons for failure lay in the quality of the French troops as well as in the flawed campaign plan itself. But Sacken's delay was crucial too. In a letter to Alexander, Bennigsen accused Sacken of insubordination and held him responsible for the failure.

The commander-in-chief saw how fewer than 600 French infantry had fearlessly opposed our cavalry. The infantry had deployed near the village. Our three cavalry regiments charged one after another but were repulsed, each time the French commander courageously appeared in front of his troops to close ranks. Only after our two guns were deployed and opened canister fire did the French withdraw. Otherwise, we would have had to give up and look for other means to prevail. The French infantry escaped us.

General Dokhturov found the enemy weak but in strong positions and exchanged fire with them committing a battalion at a time. Two battalions of the Guard Jager Regiment then made a swift bayonet attack and drove the enemy back at once.

By 25 May, our forces were facing an enemy fortified in strong positions so our artillery went into action. The vanguard's Jager regiments under Major-General Rayevskii were ordered to encircle the enemy's right. The French withdrew when our skirmishers approached their batteries and, having occupied some gardens near Quetz, they deployed some infantry supported by several artillery pieces. The vanguard hastily advanced along the main road. I opened canister fire and drove the enemy out of Quetz; however, when the Grodno Hussars attacked the French in the open, two enemy canister rounds routed them.* Although it was hot, our jager regiments ran forwards. Despite their tenacious defence, the French could not hold their ground as their troops were in great confusion. The woods prevented us from coordinating our actions and helped the French rescue their artillery. Nevertheless, they sacrificed their rearguard, had many captured or killed and abandoned their wounded and transports.† Only two guns were captured; one by the Cossacks, another by the courageous Major Kulnev, who led two weak squadrons of the Grodno Hussars and caught up with an enemy artillery park on the Passarge, seizing a few artillery pieces. Informed by prisoners that the rest of the artillery was trying to escape nearby, he rushed to capture it but took the wrong road and encountered superior enemy cavalry which forced him to retreat. Returning, he came across the artillery park he took earlier. The enemy did not risk attacking him and Kulnev crossed the river. He captured many officers in this action.

The Cossacks, meanwhile, captured some French wagons, including Marshal Ney's personal carriage with his silver dinner service and other

---

Sacken was under court-martial for over three years. The court found him guilty of insubordination but did not impose a punishment due to his distinguished record.

* Yermolov's note: This regiment was assembled from squadrons of different units which had never fought together. Its officers were excellent. Colonel Shepelev often hosted lavish breakfasts and lunches, bragging that he would make a gaping hole in the enemy at the very first engagement.

† Russian sources claim 1,500 French killed and wounded and two guns captured in two days of combat; Russian losses were unknown but may have been as many as 2,000 killed and wounded.

belongings.* Earrings and bracelets were found and it would have been a mystery as to where the Marshal had acquired these trinkets if it was not for the coats of arms of various Polish families etched on the silver.

The vanguard bivouacked near Deppen on the Passarge. On the opposite bank, the enemy occupied Kallisten and the adjacent heights. Our outposts stretched along the bank towards Elditten, where the enemy had a detachment with a few guns. General Dokhturov, despite having his corps nearby, thought it unnecessary to capture it and so the French detachment remained alone on our bank, protecting the best crossing site. The army soon followed and bivouacked close by.

On 26 May [7 June], the enemy, taking advantage of the heights, harassed us with an artillery bombardment which lasted all day. We responded and a line of Jagers was engaged in a fierce fire fight along the riverbank. We noticed that the enemy received reinforcements. The Cossack outposts kept us informed that the enemy had been observed near Elditten on the right flank. The day ended without incident.

At daybreak, movement was observed among the enemy deployed against our vanguard. Troops, artillery parks and transports were gradually concentrating. At 10:00 a.m. outposts were reinforced and intense fighting began. Two enemy infantry columns and one of cavalry moved towards Kallisten. Having routed the 7th Jagers under the command of the timid Lieutenant-Colonel Laptev,† one enemy column advanced quickly to the artillery battery where I chanced to be. I initially thought these were our troops; and I only perceived they were French after seeing their white shoulder belts (only our jagers were deployed here). The enemy column was shaken by our canister. The jagers, the 5th under Colonel Gogel and the 20th of Colonel Bistrom, engaged the French near the crossing, killed many of them and, pursuing the rest, they rushed into Kallisten and exterminated everyone.

Meanwhile, another enemy column, observing our reinforcements, turned back. Despite our fire, the French cavalry plunged into the river, but the 26th Jagers threw it into confusion with its battalion fire and then attacked with bayonets. The horses were stuck in the swampy river and the French suffered accordingly. We were not attacked for a few hours after this combat. Prince Bagration ordered the entire vanguard to be ready for battle‡ and this

---

* Yermolov's note: It must be noted that Cossacks capture wagons not because they are always ahead of the troops, but because they stay with the wagons while everyone else pursues the enemy.

† Yermolov's note: He should not be mistaken for the gallant Colonel Laptev, under whose command the 8th Jager Regiment was renowned for fearlessness and discipline.

‡ Yermolov's note: On my request, several heavy (batareinikh) guns were sent to me because I often suffered from the enemy's larger calibre artillery. At Königsberg, I experienced first-hand what three-pounder licornes could do against good artillery and I am sure the enemy was surprised that they did not rout us with their very first shot.

precaution would prove very useful! At 6:00 pm the enemy opened artillery fire against Kallisten but we held on. The French advanced in large numbers against us in order to drive our Jagers back. They fought back tenaciously and the village changed hands several times before superior French forces finally captured it. We moved across the river and the combat ended with darkness. Just then, Major-General Ilovaisky (IV) informed us that Soult's corps had crossed the river at Elditten and had advanced at least three verstas [3km]. This could have cut off our line of retreat. So at dawn, the vanguard retreated in two columns; the first of them was commanded by General Markov, who was accompanied by Bagration. General Baggovut led the second column along the main road and I was attached to it with most of our artillery. The enemy caught up with us half-way to Guttstadt; cavalry and Cossacks engaged in combat; several cavalry units were sent to our support. The army was, meanwhile, passing through Guttstadt.* Roads through forests are inconvenient and we moved slowly. Besides, the main army had started marching four hours later than it should have done; the headquarters was burdened by numerous creatures useless to the army, who, while we were fighting against the French, were calmly enjoying themselves. To protect such people an order was delivered to Prince Bagration instructing him to hold his ground as long as possible and a few cavalry regiments were sent as well.

Some of the French attacks went entirely to our advantage. One Italian dragoon regiment was pushed into the swamp, where it was forced to dismount. Surrounded, most of its soldiers were captured. But when the enemy infantry arrived in large numbers, we could barely hold our ground on the heights near Guttstadt. That day, I was under such ferocious fire that I destroyed one enemy battery using nothing but canister. The St. Petersburg Dragoons screening my company held their ground under fire with incredible restraint. We were last to retreat following the vanguard and burning a bridge over the Alle. The enemy had occupied the town. Its infantry filled the houses along the bank and I suffered from musket fire and retreated only after setting fire to the town in several places. This was my revenge on the rascals who lived there, those supporters of the French, who back in February, when the 5th Jagers were driven out, had expressed their joy with applause and jeering.

Having retreated to Heilsberg in the wake of our army, the vanguard stopped near the river.

On 29 May [10 June], the vanguard was dispatched to Launau, where another detachment was already deployed to delay any enemy move in this

---

* Napoleon launched the offensive towards Elditen and Deppen. Murat's cavalry, supported by Ney, was ordered to cross the Passarge at Deppen. Lannes and the Imperial Guard followed them closely. On the right, Davout moved his corps across the river at Hasenburg.

direction.* There was no doubt that the French would advance this way because this road was much better than the others passing through the forest; besides the other roads led to a plain too narrow to deploy an entire army.

The enemy, having beaten us to Launau, encountered the vanguard at Bewernick.† Meanwhile, our army took up positions in the trenches constructed at Heilsberg but it again acted so slowly that the vanguard had to delay the enemy forces for two additional hours, suffering heavy casualties in the process. The terrain sloped down from Bewernick to Heilsberg and was to the enemy's advantage. The vanguard deployed its line infantry on the left straddling the main road; the jager regiments were on the right, supported by cavalry that was sent from the main army. My company was attached to the cavalry.

We held our ground for a long time and our cavalry made several dazzling charges. However, the enemy soon came up in strength and attacked our trenches, having 150 guns against our 40 pieces. Its cavalry extended beyond our extreme right and we found ourselves in a very dangerous position. They broke our lines and some of my guns were captured from the rear. One of these cavalry attacks was so formidable that most of our cavalry was scattered behind Langwiese. However, General Rayevskii's jagers limited the enemy's success and our cavalry, having rallied, returned to the battlefield, recapturing our guns. I escaped only thanks to my swift horse, as part of the enemy attacked us from the rear and several French cuirassiers rushed toward me. Meanwhile, our infantry, having endured horrendous fire and suffered heavy casualties, began to withdraw. At this moment, duty officer Major-General Foch arrived and demanded to know why Bagration was retreating without orders when the army was not yet deployed. Prince Peter was infuriated by Foch's question – he was known as a brave officer but was relatively junior. Prince Bagration took him into the very heart of the action to demonstrate why the troops were retreating. Five minutes later, Foch was seriously wounded and we were pursued back to our trenches. The vanguard lost at least half of its strength; no regiment returned with its commander unscathed, and very few staff officers survived.

Grand Duke Constantine witnessed the battle, the commander-in-chief having ordered him to move the vanguard's infantry and artillery across the Alle while its unscathed cavalry was to rejoin the army for further actions. Among those distinguished that day were Baggovut, Rayevskii (who commanded the

---

* A new vanguard under Mikhail Borozdin was at Launau, some six miles from Heilsberg, while Bagration with his detachment remained at Reichenberg.

† On 10 June, Murat's cavalry attacked Borozdin, driving him to Bewernick. Bennigsen reinforced Borozdin and ordered Bagration from Reichenberg to Bewernick. He crossed the Alle at Amt-Heilsberg and joined Borozdin as he was retreating. Bagration rallied his forces in the valley between Bewernick and Langwiese.

Jagers) and Liven, head of the Liven Dragoons. The commander-in-chief thanked me for my service and the Grand Duke showed me his particular benevolence.*

Pursuing the vanguard, the enemy columns descended on our trenches. The French tried hardest from the direction from Langwiese; repulsed, they always resumed their attacks and fresh forces replaced their routed units. In the evening, a vicious attack was made and some of our batteries on the right flank were captured.† However, the French could not hold them because of the proximity of some fortifications, which brought fire to bear on them, especially a redoubt constructed on the heights that dominated the vicinity. Without taking this fortification the French could not hope to succeed and so a strong column of French grenadiers advanced against it. A wide ravine protected them for some distance from our fire, but as they came out of it, they were caught in a crossfire from our batteries and canister rounds from the redoubt. Despite some confusion, this column still reached the ditch in front of the redoubt but our units, defending this fortification, made a bayonet attack and routed them. The entire valley was covered with bodies. It was difficult to repulse an attack by such a good army, but they simply could not withstand the crossfire. Other attacks fared no better and the enemy was pursued far beyond the fortifications. There were no trenches on our right flank and our cavalry was deployed to cover this direction. The French did not manage to bring sufficient cavalry to bear at this point and the commander-in-chief ordered a counter-attack; the French could not resist our cavalry and were driven back to the forest, where the French infantry opened fire to cover their survivors and turned our cavalry back. Two Prussian cavalry units distinguished themselves in this action. In some places, the infantry clambered out of the fortifications and in one particular place entire lines fired by battalions. The darkness ended the battle and our joyous troops returned to their forts.

According to information we later received, the enemy lost some 12,000 men and our losses were considerably lower.‡ Napoleon was not present and his marshals fought the battle.

---

* Yermolov's note: He enjoyed my response to an adjutant he had sent to me with a message that the French column was too close to my battery: 'I will fire when I can distinguish blondes from brunettes.' He saw that column routed!

† Wilson recalled, 'About 11:00 p.m., the [French] shouted arrêtez le combat along their line of tirailleurs . . . and the massacre, for no other term can be so properly applied, terminated.'

‡ Heilsberg is often overshadowed by other Napoleonic battles, although it was a bloody fight and both sides suffered enormous casualties. Soult lost 8,286 men while Lannes' attack cost his troops 2,284 dead and wounded. Russian losses were 2,000–3,000 killed and over 5,000 wounded, including eight generals. Bennigsen himself was so exhausted physically and mentally that he collapsed on the battlefield and regained consciousness some time later.

On 30 May [11 June], the enemy, occupying Bewernick and Langwiese, dispatched its main body towards Königsberg.* Our army stayed in trenches but during the night of 31st, it retreated to Bartenstein because the enemy movement threatened our lines of operation.† Napoleon, by forcing us to abandon our fortified positions, showed how imprudent his marshals had been when they decided to attack in view of our advantages and how useless was the battle itself.

The rearguard retreated at dawn. The enemy cavalry caught up with it around 10:00 am but only observed its movement from a distance. The rearguard spent the night near Bartenstein.

In the evening of 1 [13] June the rearguard passed Schippenbeil. The enemy cavalry was present in numbers, but the day ended with only a futile exchange of fire. At Schippenbeil, Bagration received the order to quickly proceed to Friedland.

Many were surprised by the direction of our army, but we soon learned that squadrons of the Tatar Uhlans had captured some French cavalry‡ that imprudently entered Friedland and the prisoners revealed that the French army was advancing on Königsberg and only one corps was deployed nearby. It was therefore assumed that the commander-in-chief wanted to destroy this corps before it was reinforced and so he concentrated the entire army to ensure complete success. [From the Russian text in A. Yermolov, *Zapiski . . .*]

Pavel Grabbe

Our offensive of 24 May [5 June] woke the slumbering [French] lion. I witnessed the battle at Guttstadt but took almost no part in it. Retreating to Heilsberg, I received an order to see [General] Rezvyi, commander of all the artillery, and was assigned to him. The army occupied the already prepared fortified position. This bloody battle, during which the French, through their reckless assaults, filled the ditches of our redoubts with their corpses, was presented in Napoleon's bulletins as a minor mistake. Being frequently dispatched by Rezvyi, I was able to witness the most important developments at the most crucial points of this battle. Thus, I witnessed a little-known incident that probably had impact on the course of the battle

---

* During the night of 10 June, Napoleon arrived on the battlefield with the Imperial Guard and Ney's 6th Corps.

† The morning mist prevented Bennigsen from observing Napoleon's movements, but, around 10:00 a.m., he noted large masses of the French troops marching against his left and ordered the retreat.

‡ Bennigsen dispatched Prince Golitsyn's detachment to beat the French to Friedland. As he approached Friedland, Golitsyn found the town already occupied by Lannes.

but could have produced rather dire consequences. Towards the end of the battle that proved successful for us at all points, our commander-in-chief General Bennigsen passed out due to exhaustion and the army, thus, found itself without leadership, but remained unaware of this. General Kologrivov, the next most senior [general], refused to take command, which was then assumed by General Gorchakov. [From the Russian text in P. Grabbe, *Iz Pamiatnykh zapisok . . .*]

6

The Disaster at Friedland

Napoleon's decisive victory at Friedland ended the two-year war against the Fourth Coalition and effectively forced Emperor Alexander I to negotiate. The battle showed to the full Napoleon's ability to quickly size up a situation and exploit the enemy's mistakes, tailoring his tactics according to circumstances. After unsuccessful fighting at Guttstadt and Heilsberg, Bennigsen feared a flanking manoeuvre by Napoleon and ordered further retreat toward the Russian frontier. Late on the afternoon of 13 June, the Russian advance guard approached Friedland and found it already occupied by the advance guard of Marshal Jean Lannes' corps. After a cavalry skirmish, the Russians carried the town and established a cavalry screen on the left bank of the Alle. The French prisoners indicated that only Lannes's advance guard was in the vicinity of Friedland so Bennigsen decided to move part of his army to the left bank. During the night, the rest of the army concentrated on the right bank. Bennigsen initially did not intend to give battle around Friedland but wanted to secure his march northward to Wehlau, whence he planned to attack Napoleon's flank and rear if the French advanced to Königsberg.

By now Bennigsen was exhausted and in poor health, so on the evening of 13 June he left the army to spend the night in a house in Friedland. He had barely had any rest when, at 11:00 p.m., he was informed that General Nicolas Oudinot's troops were deployed near Postehnen. Concerned about his positions, Bennigsen moved additional troops across the river and took up positions near the forest of Sortlach. By late evening there were some 25,000 Russians on the left bank of the Alle. Furthermore, that same evening two pontoon bridges were constructed, and additional forces moved to the left bank to secure the flanks. Thus, the Russian troops were deployed in a half-circle around Friedland. This position was extremely unfavourable for several reasons. First, a deep ravine in the centre divided the Russian forces into two parts and complicated communications between them. Second, the troops were deployed on marshy terrain with their backs to the Alle. In case of defeat, the Russians could escape only through the narrow streets and across one small wooden bridge and three pontoon bridges at Friedland. No attempt was made to reconnoitre the river for fords or to examine the terrain on the flanks.

The fighting began shortly after midnight when the French skirmishers engaged the Russian outposts in the woods of Sortlach, and rapidly intensified as both sides committed additional forces. By dawn, the battle was already raging in earnest, especially on the Russian left flank where Prince Bagration launched several attacks against Oudinot's men. The fighting continued throughout the morning and early afternoon. Napoleon, meanwhile, received news of the battle and rapidly concentrated his army at Friedland. He personally arrived near the town around noon, declaring to his troops 'Today is a happy day – it is the anniversary of Marengo.' Examining the Russian positions, he realised that he had a chance of destroying the Russian army in a single battle. He made quick adjustments to the French dispositions and designated two corps for a flanking attack. Ney was ordered to move to the right flank, passing Postehnen toward the woods of Sortlach. Lannes would form the centre in front of Postehnen, while Oudinot's troops were to turn to the left in order to draw upon themselves the attention of the enemy. Napoleon's planned manoeuvre was aimed at destroying the bridges at Friedland and cutting the Russian line of retreat.

Around 5:30 p.m. a salvo of twenty French guns signalled the renewal of battle. The French attack against the Russian left flank proved to be irresistible and Bagration's men were forced to retreat. The advancing French skilfully deployed their artillery, commanded by General Alexandre Antoine Senarmont, chief of artillery of Victor's corps, who made a daring decision to move his cannon ahead of the infantry and open devastating fire at the tightly packed masses of the Russian infantry. By 8:00 p.m. the Russian army had begun to withdraw through Friedland and had the houses in the southern suburbs set on fire to slow down the French.

The battle of Friedland was the final engagement of a long campaign. The Russian army had suffered a crushing defeat and struggled to field another army. The casualties were staggering, as the Russians lost some 20,000 killed and wounded; the French lost only 7,000–8,000.

Alexsey Yermolov

Yermolov was in command of a horse artillery battery.

The rearguard marched without rest during the night and reached Friedland at dawn; artillery fire could occasionally be heard. Prince Bagration dispatched General Rayevskii and his jagers on ahead and ordered me to advance with the horse artillery. Having crossed the river at Friedland,* we

---

* Wilson described Friedland as 'a considerable town situated on the left bank of the Alle; a long wooden bridge connects the town with the right bank – west of the town is a capacious lake – the country for a mile in the direction of Heilsberg forms a semicircle of apparent plain, but is cut by a deep and narrow ravine full of water, and scarcely fordable, which runs from Domnau into the lakes. Near the town, on the left

were assigned a place on the left, where we found grenadiers of the Life Guard Izmailovsk Regiment already engaged in a skirmish. Our troops were gradually concentrating but there were still only a few of them. We replaced the Guards and their regiment moved back. The enemy, as we later learned, had 10,000 grenadiers under Marshal Oudinot, who masked his weakness by deploying his troops in the forest opposite our position. Soon most of our troops had come up while the enemy remained the same. Unfortunately, the commander-in-chief was not feeling well that day;* Quartermaster-General Baron Steingeil and the new duty officer Lieutenant-General Essen (I) were bruised during a reconnaissance of the position at Friedland and so we received no orders for quite some time.

We should have attacked the French corps, which was dispersed and could not have properly defended itself or made an easy retreat. The French army was also extended on its march to Königsberg and could not have arrived in time to support this corps; even if it managed to, the troops would have arrived piecemeal and could not have resisted the combined forces of our entire army. Perhaps our commander-in-chief did not plan to intercept the French on their march but he should at least have taken the opportunity of destroying an isolated corps. Instead, we were occupied in a prolonged and useless exchange of fire and wasted so much time that some French cavalry arrived on our right and some infantry filled the forest in front of our rearguard. Our cavalry was routed and was only able to rally behind our infantry. However, taking advantage of the confusion engendered by their pursuit, the courageous General Count Lambert counter-attacked with the Alexandria Hussars and, with the support of our other units, the enemy was driven back to the edge of the woods. The French remained there for the rest of the day, occasionally appearing at the edge of the forest. On the left, the rearguard, reinforced by many other units, captured the forest several times but was finally forced to relinquish it to superior enemy forces. The Life Guard Jager Regiment fought with remarkable fearlessness. We made many successful attacks along our front; however, our actions were uncoordinated and nothing decisive was achieved.†

---

of the plain, the ground abruptly descends and woods border down the Alle – a deep wood fringed the plain from the Alle to the village of Heinricksdorf [*sic*], where there was a little interruption, but woods again closed round to the Alle, the banks of which were very steep, the fords, subsequently used, were yet unknown.'

* Bennigsen was exhausted by constant campaigning and late on 13 June, he left the army to spend the night in a house in Friedland. According to Alexander Mikhailovskii-Danilevskii, some Russian officers and participants later asserted, 'Had Bennigsen found proper lodgings to rest on the right bank . . . the battle of Friedland would have never taken place.'

† By now it was becoming clear that the Russian army had failed to annihilate Lannes' corps. Bennigsen could still have safely retreated across the Alle before the arrival of

Around 6:00 p.m. Napoleon arrived and the entire French army too. With a forest concealing their movements, masses of French gathered against our left; a battery of forty guns was deployed★ on the edge of the forest and a fierce cannonade began.† Because of the close range, the artillery fire was direct and our rearguard's cavalry greatly suffered from it.‡ The rearguard was soon retreating as well. The army soon began withdrawing to the bridges. The only way to reach the main bridge was through the city itself. Chaos reigned in the narrow streets and this was further increased by the enemy artillery. Based on the direction of the enemy columns, it was obvious that they intended to cut us off from the crossing; to delay them, the Life Guard Izmailovskii and Pavlovskii Grenadier regiments made an attack, but that same ghastly battery halted their gallant assault and the regiments turned back.

The cavalry of the [Russian Imperial] Guard no longer showed their usual gallantry. I managed to cross the river via the nearest pontoon bridge with the rearguard's artillery but it was already under enemy fire and part of it was damaged. The bridge in the city (the main bridge) was prematurely set on fire for unknown reasons and without any orders. Only one bridge remained and a number of troops and artillery had not yet crossed. The enemy pressed them against the bank and every minute was extremely precious.§ The artillery, which we would have had to abandon, was saved when a ford was discovered nearby.¶ Thus, our total loss in guns, either damaged, abandoned or sunk during the chaotic retreat, amounted to thirteen pieces. Lieutenant-General Dokhturov's 7th Division was among

---

the main French army but the initiative swung away from the Russians with the arrival of Napoleon.

★ According to Mikhailovskii-Danilevskii, 'The Russian gunners were surprised by the sudden appearance of the French 36-gun battery' and failed to react in time.

† General Alexandre Antoine Senarmont, chief of artillery of Victor's corps, recalled, 'The Russian batteries, deployed on the opposite side of the Alle, fired on our flanks; some of them were at very close range, including one battery, on the hill near the river turn, which decimated our ranks.'

‡ During the battle, General Senarmont organised two companies of fifteen guns, with six pieces in reserve, and placed them on both flanks of General Dupont's division. As the French advanced, Senarmont outpaced the infantry and opened fire at Bagration's troops from close range.

§ Lord Hutchinson later declared, 'The Russians would have rendered their success undoubted if courage alone could ensure victory, but whatever may be the end, the officers and men of the Russian army have done their duty in the noblest manner and are justly entitled to the praise and admiration of every person.'

¶ Yermolov's note: This ford was discovered by Artillery Colonel Begunov, who had lived at Friedland whist refitting his company, he often hunted in the vicinity and knew the local residents who told him about the ford.

the last to cross the river, but it was now commanded by Colonel Benardos, chef of the Vladimir Infantry, an intrepid Greek.*

By nightfall two artillery companies failed to cross the river and the road to the ford was already in enemy hands. Major-General Count Lambert escorted them with the Alexandria Hussars, marching two miles along the enemy bank towards Allenburg and, having crossed the Alle at dawn, rejoined the army.

Thus, instead of defeating and annihilating a weak enemy corps, which could not have been reinforced in time, we lost a general battle. I cannot but repeat that had our commander-in-chief not been ill at the beginning, our situation would have been dramatically different. Lieutenant-General Prince Gorchakov actually commanded the army during the battle, but he failed to rise to the occasion and the troops had no confidence in him.

On the morning of 3 [15] June, the rearguard arrived at Allenburg, finding there what remained of the retreating main army; everything was in complete disarray. The enemy was occupied constructing bridges and failed to take advantage of our disorder. Enemy cavalry detachments were observed on both sides of the river, but they had no communication with each other.

We reached Wehlau without difficulty. I do not know if the rumours that the commander-in-chief planned to give another battle here were true, but it was clear that the construction of redoubts was started; however, the approach of the enemy did not permit their completion.

As the rearguard retreated, our outposts discovered General Kamenski's detachment marching from Königsberg pursued by large enemy forces.† There was a junction ahead and Count Kamenski would lead the enemy there, potentially cutting our line of retreat. Prince Bagration kindly listened to my observations and allowed me to propose the dispatch of our entire cavalry to the left, bringing it against the pursuing enemy, halting this threat and allowing our infantry to pass the crossroads and wait for Kamenski. Bagration ordered the plan carried out immediately and we just beat Kamenski there whilst our cavalry arrived with his last troops. Kamenski marched to join the army and the rearguard was left alone.

At the village of Taplaken, we awaited the enemy and a brutal combat with the enemy's vanguard was crowned with success.

Some 12 verstas [12km] from Tilsit, we came across some cavalry who had been ordered to delay the enemy by the commander-in-chief while the army got across the Niemen. This wide river flows by Tilsit and there was only one bridge across it. It was impossible to establish a *tête du pont* there and everyone recognised the difficulty of the mission assigned to Bagration and what danger

---

* Yermolov's note: We should be relieved by the fact that all the divisional generals were alive. They probably wanted to be first to test the crossings.

† Soult occupied Königsberg on 16 June, capturing 3,600 sick and wounded Russians and 4,000 Prussians.

the rearguard was exposed to. The rearguard was deployed for battle and ordered to hold its ground at all costs until nightfall. Bagration retained only his cavalry and Cossacks and, to everyone's delight, returned the rest of the cavalry so that it did not hinder his crossing. We prepared for this last battle on the territory of our ally! Our outposts were driven back with gunfire and the enemy closed in. But it is possible that the resolution with which we faced the French filled them with respect and they shared our opinion that it would be impossible to defeat us without bringing large numbers against us as they remained inactive the entire day. They awaited their army while we eagerly looked forward to nightfall.

The rearguard, and our cavalry, reached Tilsit at dawn. The Cossacks and artillery had been first to cross the Niemen, followed by the line infantry. Only the jagers remained in the town and prepared the bridge for destruction. Around 9:00 a.m. large enemy forces approached and began reconnoitring. We abandoned the town and the jagers had hardly crossed the bridge when Murat rushed it with his cavalry and the bridge was set on fire virtually under his horse.

The enemy occupied the town and deployed its artillery along the bank that was considerably higher than ours. During the rest of the day, the French army gathered and began to spread out. We did not try to guess what might happen next but simply awaited the future without anxiety.

Our army was weak and in disarray. It had been weakened by the many stragglers who had fallen behind during the retreat. Gathering in bands, they wandered along the roads, pillaged food and thousands of them crossed the Niemen at Jurburg, Alytus, Merech and some as far away as Grodno. As proof of the disorder I can cite the following. The Izumskii Hussars were forgotten in Prussia, where they had been quartered to rest their horses; hearing about Friedland from local residents, they marched to join us but ran into French marauders who told them that we were in retreat. So they marched to the Niemen and successfully crossed over. Similarly, Colonel Sisoev was forgotten with his Don Cossack regiment, and they were even deeper into Prussia. He encountered enemy forces, fought them, passed their quarters, captured prisoners and finally rejoined us. Part of our artillery did not receive orders in time and had itself to select the direction of its retreat, crossing the Niemen at Jurburg, where it found a previously unknown ford.*

The army bivouacked some distance from the river; the wooded surroundings shielding its vulnerability. The vanguard was ordered to remain on the bank. Bagration was ordered to send his adjutant with a proposal

---

* Yermolov's note: Naturally, one wonders who was issuing the orders? It was Colonel Aderkass. And of course who would have dared dispute them with a German? Since ancient times, we have been unable to find a Russian for the position of general quartermaster.

for a truce. He was introduced to Murat and then to Berthier and told that Napoleon sought peace, not an armistice! The following day, Berthier arrived at our headquarters with the details and a message was sent to the Tsar at Siauliai. Two days later, the Tsar reached the army and Prince Lobanov-Rostovskii* was sent to Napoleon. An armistice was concluded and soon peace negotiations began.† [From the Russian text in A. Yermolov, *Zapiski* . . .]

Sergei Volkonskii

Volkonskii served on General Bennigsen's staff.

Bennigsen had correctly anticipated the French intention to cut our lines of communication. Prince Golitsyn, moving by forced marches, had soon arrived at Friedland and found it already occupied by an enemy light cavalry detachment consisting of two regiments. Using his superior numbers, Golitsyn drove the French out of the town, inflicting heavy casualties on them. Yet Prince Golitsyn then made a grave mistake of limiting himself to occupying the town, located on the opposite side of the river, and the plains extending to the woods in front of it. He should have sent our outposts to reconnoitre the woods and thereby he would have protected our movement from a sudden and concealed attack of the French army. Our entire army reached Friedland the following day and a proposal had been made to spend the night at the position in front of the city and then to resume our movement to, as I recall, Preusissch-Eylau, whereas Bennigsen, who had widely read about the Seven Years War, knew Frederick the Great had fought a battle at a very advantageous position. This was a major mistake: neither Suvorov nor Napoleon followed the trotted paths but instead designed plans of campaign themselves and therefore always prevailed. Bennigsen's proposal, however, could not be carried out: at dawn the French attacked us and were continually strengthened by the arriving reinforcements, whose movements and exit onto the above mentioned plain was always concealed by the woods.

Thus Bennigsen was compelled to accept battle and, to our great chagrin, his condition‡ so worsened that he could not sit his horse and instead lay on the ground on top of a hill near the city; he could partly observe the general movements of the army and was partly guided by reports delivered to him by Essen and Steinheil. Until four o'clock in the afternoon, the French efforts to dislodge us from our positions had all failed. They were repelled everywhere and

---

* Dmitry Lobanov-Rostovskii (1758–1838) conducted the peace negotiations at Tilsit in 1807.
† The armistice was signed on 21 June 1807.
‡ Bennigsen suffered from kidney stones.

in many places the Russian troops had prevailed splendidly over their opponent. But, as I said, everything had changed at four o'clock in the afternoon . . .

Shortly after three o'clock in the afternoon a large cloud of dust had been observed along the entire extent of the road running through the above-mentioned woods, behind the position occupied by the French on the plain. Bennigsen, desiring to learn the cause of this cloud, asked General [Christopher Hely-]Hutchinson, the English commissioner to our army, to go to the town, climb the town hall tower and try to determine its cause. The English general agreed to do this and Flügel Adjutant Prince Lopukhin, who had been on Bennigsen's staff, and I accompanied him to translate and convey messages. Upon arriving at the town hall, I encountered a scene that was very unexpected and shameful for Russian honour, especially in the presence of a foreigner: the room was full of two generals and numerous staff and junior officers, who had not been wounded but were away from their positions on the battlefield. This sight shocked me. I will conceal the names of these two generals while the rest of the people who were present there were unknown to me. But I must note that these two generals belonged to that group of people whom we used to call 'the Gatchina Rareripes from [Emperor] Paul's Time'. Without stopping, we climbed to the top of the tower, where General Hutchinson could observe that the dust cloud was occasioned by the movement of the French troops that were on their way to reinforce the units already fighting us.

I was sent to deliver this news to General Bennigsen. Just as I reached him, thick enemy columns began to pour out of the woods in front of the left flank of our army. Shortly thereafter Napoleon, who personally led these new troops, established a strong battery and began to bombard our left flank which became greatly disordered. Exploiting this, Napoleon forced our troops to fall back, despite the excellent performance of the Life Guard Hussar Regiment, the Life Guard Jager Regiment, and the battalions of the [Life Guard] Finlyandskii and Pavlovskii Grenadier Regiments; the left flank [of the Russian army] was completely dislodged from its position while the our right flank had not only held its ground but even successfully attacked the enemy. This circumstance compelled Bennigsen, who feared being cut off from his line of retreat through the town and across the river, to order a general withdrawal of the entire army. But another incident further complicated the situation: the pontoon bridges had been already built but an officer in charge of one of these bridges dismantled it for still-unknown reasons. This only further intensified the confusion caused by the withdrawal, so that the troops from the left wing and some from the centre packed the permanent bridge in the city, increasing the disorder, while the remaining part of the centre and the right wing were deprived of the opportunity to move across the bridges and had been compelled to attempt to ford the river. The French pursuit of our troops was sluggish and the enemy had failed to take full advantage of this fortuitous circumstance. Maybe this was caused by the appearance of a column of several thousand convalescing soldiers who were moving from their hospitals to join our army, and whom Napoleon probably took for a strong reinforcement. The French pursuit ended at nightfall. [From the Russian text in S. Volkonskii, *Zapisiki* . . .]

Prince Alexander Obolenskii

Obolenskii served as a captain in the Ingermandlandskii Dragoon Regiment.

At dawn on 2 [14] June the battle began and it initially seemed turning to our favour. My troops were on the right flank of the army. Our infantry, together with the cavalry, overwhelmed the attacking enemy forces and we even captured a French eagle, which I personally presented to the commander-in-chief. At the same time, on [General Dokhturov's] request, I asked [Bennigsen] for further instructions, explaining that our current position was untenable since we had approached the woods where the enemy, having brought up his artillery, was inflicting heavy casualties on us. Bennigsen replied, 'Tell General Dokhturov that he should not provoke the enemy since I am certain that the enemy does not intend to engage us in a [major] battle.'

Just as I was about leave him, I saw the British Colonel [Robert] Wilson, who was nicknamed 'the Beacon' for always choosing the highest spot so he could conveniently observe the field of battle, arrive with a report that dense enemy columns, accompanied by a vast amount of artillery, were attacking the centre of our army.

The commander-in-chief dispatched me to inform General Dokhturov about this development and ordered him to do his best to concentrate his forces to prevent the enemy from breaking through our line. The general entrusted this mission to me but it was already too late. The enemy was attacking with such superior forces that he was able, despite our fierce resistance, to break through our centre and set fire to the town of Friedland and the pontoon bridges across the Alle River in our rear, which made our retreat impossible. Fortunately, the fast-approaching darkness saved us from certain destruction. Having located fords, our troops spent the night moving across the waist-deep river, completing the crossing by dawn. The consequences and losses that we had suffered in this battle are well known. Several thousand wounded, who had been [left] in the town, died in the flames while the army was completely disordered.

I developed a fever after being utterly exhausted and unable to dry myself after swimming across the river and spending the night under a heavy rain. I barely held onto my horse to arrive at the first town, where I was moved to a supply wagon and came back to my senses only two weeks later when I was already in Jurburg. [From the Russian text in A. Obolenskii, *Vozpominaniya* . . .]

Nadezhda Durova

14 June 1807. Friedland. Over half of our brave regiment fell in this fierce and unsuccessful battle. Several times we attacked, several times we repulsed the enemy, and in turn we ourselves were driven back more than once. We were showered with grapeshot and smashed by cannonballs, and the shrill whine of the hellish bullets has completely deafened me. Oh, I cannot bear them! The cannonball is a different matter. It roars so majestically at least, and there are always brief intervals in between. After some hours of heated battle, the remnants of our regiment were ordered to pull back a little to rest. I took advantage of this to go watch the operations of our artillery, without stopping to think that I might get my head torn off for no good reason. Bullets were showering me and my horse, but what do bullets matter beside the savage, unceasing roar of the cannons?

An uhlan from our regiment, covered in blood, with a bandaged head and bloodied face, was riding aimlessly around the field in one direction or another. The poor fellow could not remember where he was going and was having trouble keeping his seat in the saddle. I rode up to him and asked him which squadron he was from. He muttered something and swayed so violently that I had to support him to keep him from falling. Seeing that he was out of his senses, I tied his horse's reins to Alcides' neck and, supporting the wounded man with one hand, rode with him to the river to refresh him with water. At the river he came to his wits somewhat, slipped off his horse, and fell at my feet from weakness. What could I do? I could not abandon him – he would perish! There was no way of getting him to a safe place, and what place here was safe anyway? There was gun and cannon fire all around us, cannonballs were skipping in all directions, shells were bursting in the air and on the ground; the cavalry was rushing forward and falling back like a stormy sea, and amid this terrible upheaval I could no longer see the pennons of our regiment anywhere. Meanwhile, there was no time to lose. I scooped up water in my helmet and poured it over the head and face of the wounded man. He opened his eyes. 'For God's sake, don't abandon me here,' he said, making an effort to rise. 'I will get on my horse somehow; walk me back behind the lines of our army. God will reward your human kindness.' I helped him to mount his horse, got onto Alcides, picked up the reins of the wounded man's horse again, and we rode toward Friedland.

The city's inhabitants were fleeing, and regiments were retreating. Scoundrelly soldiers in large numbers, who had run away from the field of battle without being wounded, were spreading terror among the retreating crowds, shouting, 'All is lost!' 'We are beaten to the last man!' 'The enemy is at our heels.' 'Flee! Save yourselves!' Although I did not completely trust these cowards, I could not keep from worrying as I saw entire platoons of dragoons riding at the trot through the city. I regretted wholeheartedly the curiosity that had lured me to watch the cannon fire and the evil destiny that had sent me the wounded man. To leave him to the whims of fate seemed to me base and inhuman in the extreme – I could not do it! The unfortunate uhlan, his face numb with fear, turned his alarmed gaze to me. I understood his apprehensions.

'Can you go a little faster?' I asked.

'No, I cannot,' answered the unfortunate man and sighed deeply.

We continued at a walk. Men were running and galloping past us, shouting to us, 'Step it up! The enemy is not far off!' At last we came into a forest. I turned off the highway and rode through the thickets without letting go of the reins of the wounded uhlan's horse. The shade and coolness of the forest revived my comrade's strength somewhat, but, to his woe, he put that strength to the worst possible use. He decided to smoke his pipe, stopped, struck a light, and took a puff of his repulsive tobacco. A moment later his eyes rolled up, the pipe fell from his hands, and he fell lifeless onto the neck of his horse. I stopped, dragged him to the ground, laid him flat and, since I had no way of bringing him to his senses, stood beside him with both horses, waiting for him to recover. In a quarter of an hour he opened his eyes, raised himself, and sat up, looking at me with a crazed air. I saw that he was out of his wits. His head was covered with sabre cuts, and the tobacco smoke had acted on him like liquor. 'Mount your horse,' I said. 'Otherwise we will get there too late. Get up, I will help you.'

He didn't answer me, but he did try to stand up. I helped him to his feet. Holding the horses' reins in one hand and using the other to help him up into the stirrup, I came close to falling, because, instead of clutching the mane, the half-crazed uhlan put all his weight on my shoulder. We rode off again. The crowds were still fleeing with the same shout, 'Save yourselves!' At last I saw some passing artillery pieces. I asked my protégé whether he would not like to stay with them: it would be easier for him lying on a caisson than riding on horseback. He was obviously delighted by my proposal, and I at once asked the sergeant of artillery if he would take the wounded uhlan and his horse under his care. He agreed willingly and ordered his men at once to take my comrade off his horse, spread a few saddle blankets on the caisson, and lay him on it.

I quivered with joy at finding myself free and would have gone immediately to look for the regiment, if I could have found out from anyone where it was. I rode alone until nightfall, asking those who passed me if they knew where the Polish Uhlan regiment was. Some said that it was up ahead; others, that one part of the army had gone off somewhere to the flank and my regiment was in that detachment. I was in despair! Night had fallen, and I had to give Alcides a chance to rest. I caught sight of a group of Cossacks who had kindled a fire and were cooking their supper.

I dismounted and went over to them, 'Hello, friends! Are you planning to spend the night here?'

'We are,' they replied.

'And how about the horses? Do you put them out to grass?'

They looked at me in astonishment. 'Where else then? Of course we do.'

'And they do not stray too far from you?'

'What do you want to know that for?' asked one old Cossack, staring intently into my eyes.

'I would like to let my horse graze with yours, but I'm afraid he will get too far away.'

'Well, take care of him then: hobble him with a tether and wrap it around your arm. Then the horse cannot wander off without waking you. We keep ours on a tether.'

And with this, the old Cossack invited me to share their porridge with them. Afterwards they hobbled their horses, tying them on tethers and wrapping the ends around their arms, and went to sleep. I walked around after Alcides in perplexity: I too wanted to lie down, but how could I leave my horse free to roam all night? I had no tether. At last I got the idea of tying a handkerchief around Alcides' forefeet. It was a delicate batiste handkerchief from a dozen that my grandmother had given me back in Little Russia. Only one of the dozen was left intact, and it went everywhere with me. I was very fond of it and washed it myself every day wherever I had a chance – in a brook, a river, a lake, or a puddle. I used this handkerchief to bind Alcides' legs, allowed him to graze, and went to sleep not far from the Cossacks.

Dawn had already broken when I awoke. The Cossacks and the horses were gone, and Alcides as well. Mortally alarmed and saddened beyond expression, I got up from the grass on which I had slept so peacefully. The saddled horses of dragoons were roaming the fields all around me. With a heart full of bitter regret, I began searching among them at random for Alcides. I had been walking about in one direction or another for half an hour when I caught sight of a scrap of my handkerchief gleaming white in the distance. I ran over to it, and, to my indescribable joy, Alcides came running up to me, frisking; he neighed and rested his head on my shoulder. One end of the white handkerchief was still trailing from his right leg, but the rest was ripped to shreds and scattered about the field. His curb, snaffle, and reins, had been taken. It was useless to ask the dragoons about them: who could make them tell me or, more to the point, give them back? It was a horrible situation! How could I appear in the regiment looking like that? This was an excellent opportunity to learn egotism: to make a firm resolution, always and in every case, to think more of myself than of others. Twice I had yielded to feelings of compassion, and both times I had been very badly rewarded. Moreover, the first time the captain had called me a scamp, and what would he think of me now? The battle was still in progress when I decided to go watch the cannons and suddenly disappeared. What a horrible thought! I was afraid to dwell on it. . . .

When the dragoons heard the reason for my distress, they gave me a long strap to use for reins and said that my regiment could not be very far ahead; it had spent the night where they did, and I could catch it still on the spot. As I tied the repulsive strap to the halter Alcides was still wearing, I felt extremely vexed with myself. Oh, my fine steed, I was thinking, you are in the hands of such a capricious fool of a girl! But neither repentance nor regret nor vexation saved me from woe!

I reached the regiment, and this time it was not the captain, but Kakhovskii, our general, who told me that my bravery was scatterbrained and my compassion witless; I rushed into the heat of battle when I was not supposed to, went on the attack with other squadrons, rescued anyone and everyone I came across in the midst of combat, and, giving up my horse to anyone who decided to ask for him, was left on foot among the fiercest clashes; he was out of patience with my pranks and was ordering me to go at once to the supply train. Me, in the supply! Every last drop of blood drained from my face. In my worst nightmare I never imagined anything so horrible as this punishment. Kazimirski, who loved me like a father, looked with pity at the change in my face. He said something under his breath to the commander, but the other answered, 'No! No, we have to protect him.' Then he turned to me, speaking now in a much kinder tone, 'I am sending you to the supply train in order to preserve a brave officer for our native land in times to come. In a few years you will be able to make better use of that daring which now threatens to cost you your life with no benefit to anyone.'

Oh, how little those hollow words of consolation meant to me! They were mere words, and the truth of the matter was that I was going to the supply train. I went over to Alcides to get him ready for the shameful journey. Embracing my trusty comrade-in-arms, I wept with shame and sorrow. My hot tears fell on his black mane and skipped and rolled down the saddle-frame. Wyszemirski was also being sent to the wagons, and why should that be? He was always in the proper spot, and he cannot be reproached for either witless daring or misplaced compassion: he has all the common sense and equanimity of an adult.

Everything was ready, and our funereal procession began: wounded horses, wounded men, and we two, in the prime of life and completely healthy, moving slowly, step by step, to our final resting place, to the damned supply train. There is nothing in the world I desire so fiercely as that Kakhovski shall see no action for the rest of the campaign! [From the Russian text in N. Durova, 'Kavalerist-devitsa']

Mikhail Petrov

Mikhail Petrov was a staff captain and commander of the 1st Company in the Yeletskii Musketeer Regiment.

[In June], we fought in a ferocious battle at Heilsberg – although we retained the field of battle, we were then compelled to abandon it to anticipate the enemy at Friedland, where Bennigsen, in order to protect the magazines in Königsberg, was forced to accept another battle on disadvantageous positions on the left bank of the Alle. We lost the battle, having suffered many thousands killed and wounded but without losing flags or cannon. Our division, commanded by Osterman, was in the centre of the general position. [At Friedland] our regiment lost its chef, General Sukin II, who had his left foot torn off by a cannon ball; [we also lost] Major Turgenev who was wounded and captured during the enemy attack on the brushwood that we were holding on the left flank. Because of the loss of [so many] senior officers, I, despite being just a staff captain, had to assume command of the entire regiment. When our army retreated through Friedland to the right bank of the Alle River and burned the bridge, I was still on the enemy side of the river in order to defend the village of Sortlach on the left flank of our position, about one versta upstream from the city. I ordered soldiers who could not swim to collect boards and logs and cross the river holding on to them and carrying the wounded [on them], while I myself stayed behind with officers and soldiers who could swim to cover our withdrawal. Once my men were across the river, I ordered the rest of my troops to throw their muskets, backswords [tesak] and knapsacks into the river and follow me to the right bank. I swam across wearing my uniform, but without boots, and with my unsheathed sword on my back. Once across the river, I gathered my surviving men around our standard-bearers, who were already there, and, the following day, we rejoined our division as it was retreating to Tilsit, where peace was [soon] signed.

[As mentioned above,] during the battle at Friedland, a cannonball tore off our regimental chef Major-General Sukin II's foot up to his ankle. He underwent a first amputation by the division's staff physician Dehio behind the battle line but, amidst the tumult and commotion, the surgery was not performed sufficiently well and the wound [quickly] deteriorated because some flesh was left on the tip of the sawed off tibia bone and the remaining skin was not sufficient to fully cover it. Two weeks after the battle, at the town of Jurburg on the [Russo-]Prussian border, [Sukin] was examined by Leib-Physician James Wylie, who upon his arrival from England to Russia had served as a junior physician in our Yeletskii regiment . . . * Upon seeing gangrene already developed on the exposed tip of the bone, Wylie understood that Death was raising her scythe to claim our hero . . . Wylie asked Sukin if

---

* Born in Scotland, James Wylie graduated from the famed University of Edinburgh in 1790 and travelled to Russia where he entered Russian service and was appointed as a physician in the Yeletskii Infantry Regiment in December 1790. For more details see Mary McGrigor, *The Tsar's Doctor: The Life and Times of Sir James Wylie* (Edinburgh, 2010).

he could undergo another operation, this time performed by his experienced and diligent hand. Sukin replied, 'I know how to stomach pain, so do whatever you can, I will just lie quietly.' Wylie immediately took off his coat, vest and tie, and with his hefty shoulders wrapped in a red shirt and strapped with suspenders, he rolled up his sleeves and without a minute's delay, he cut off [Sukin's] tibia bone up to his knee. Thus, the life of our general continued on one original leg and another one made of wood. But our regiment, and especially the officers, lost its affable leader, who was [always] discerning and attentive to their service and private life. The new commander of the regiment was the next surviving senior officer, Turgenev, who got out of the [French] captivity and was promoted to lieutenant-colonel, He knew a lot about putting the regimental chest to use but had not learn anything from Sukin about ensuring the well-being of officers, who became disheartened and, for a variety of reasons, chose divergent paths of life. [From the Russian text in M. Petrov, *Rasskazy* . . .]

Yakov Otroshenko

Staff Captain Otroshenko commanded a company in the 7th Jager Regiment. After fighting at Guttstadt and Heilsberg, Otroshenko retreated with his men to Bartenstein on the road to Friedland.

In the morning we passed by Barstenstein, where we found our supply depots already burning. The soldiers rushed [to save whatever they could] but found only rotting bread inside. As the proverb goes, they used fire to hide their misdeeds, and our supply commissioners did exactly that. We marched hastily through Schippenbeil and at dawn [of 13 June] we approached the town of Friedland. After crossing to the left bank of the Alle River on the newly built bridge, the 7th Jager Regiment stopped near the river, under the high riverbank, and we all quickly fell asleep out of sheer exhaustion. At dawn [on 14 June] we heard the sound of gunfire and the enemy cannonballs began to fly above us and land into the river; several companies, including mine, were sent from our regiment to engage the enemy. We approached the woods but were met with a battalion fire. So we charged with bayonets and drove the French into the swamp, capturing some 200 Guardsmen and one colonel. However, the French soon rallied and overwhelmed us, driving out of the woods. We then received reinforcements and entered the woods once more but was to yield to the superior numbers of the enemy. We came out of the woods and scattered in a skirmisher chain in an open field, where we remained for a while. Our cavalrymen occasionally rode in front of us . . .

Around seven o'clock, the French deployed artillery at the edge of the woods which were adjacent to their right flank, and opened a vigorous fire at our left flank which abutted to the Alle River and formed a curved angle because several jager regiments were deployed forward along the riverbank and were close to the woods held by the French. All other forces in the valley moved behind protection of the tall riverbank to the edge of the river while the jager regiments, still deployed at the edge of the woods, upon perceiving the enemy's vigorous attack, became concerned that the enemy would cut their line of retreat, which the French could have easily accomplished. Therefore, these regiments began hastily retreating while our forces were still crowding on the riverbank.

Observing the direction of the French artillery fire, I realised that the French columns would soon advance to intercept the retreating jager regiments. By then I found myself alone in the field and decided not to go to the bank but rather walk along the valley back to our line, convinced that I might be killed here but no one will dare to capture me on this blood-drenched path. In front of me was the [Life Guard] Ismailovskii Regiment, deployed in full front and firing battalion volleys at the French while [regimental artillery, deployed] in intervals between battalions, fired grapeshot. The French showered the regiment with grape-shot, cannonballs and shells. I moved amidst the hail of grapeshot and bullets that threw dirt into the air and [even] passed between my legs. In the Pavlovskii Grenadier Regiment whole files fell to the ground, but its line did not waver, despite the large gaps in it because of the loss of men. After passing through our front line, I turned to the riverbank and saw that the jager regiments marching along the bank greatly suffered from the enemy. The French infantry managed to reach that bank together with [our] retreating forces and mercilessly slaughtered our jagers as they crowded near the river.

Prince Bagration rode behind the [Pavlovskii] Grenadiers and encouraged the soldiers, while General Sabaneev sat on a rock, with a brand-kugel* burning in front of him. I noticed my men walking along with soldiers from other regiments. After stopping both groups, I led them to the left flank of the [Pavlovskii] Grenadier Regiment while the jager regiment was moving across the bridge that was built over the Alle River.

As darkness fell, a general retreat commenced but I suffered a severe contusion to my right foot. I fell to the ground but then managed to get up with the help of a musket and went [limping] back. A Cossack noticed me and offered me a general's beautiful horse to ride but just as I tried to mount it, an enemy cannonball shattered the cornice of a nearby house, frightening the horse which broke free and ran away. I then noticed that fuhrleiters† had

---

* A hollow cast-iron ball filled with flammable material and with four holes to allow the ignition of the internal charge and subsequent jetting of the flaming material into the target.

† Soldiers attached to the supply transports.

set up bonfires in the garden and were calmly cooking porridge even though cannonballs were flying above them. These men were truly made of rock.

On the bridge, there was indescribable crowding as the retreating men and the wounded carried [to safety] were jostling for passage. Straw was already scattered on top of the bridge in preparation for its burning. I somehow managed to get across and rejoined my regiment.

I thought that if a strong battery had been deployed on the right bank behind the left flank of the [Pavlovskii] Grenadier Regiment, the enemy would not have dared to undertake such an audacious attack without suffering heavy casualties. Our artillery, meanwhile, would have been safe because it would have been on the other side of the river. [From the Russian text in Y. Otroshenko, *Zapiski* . . .]

Alexander Eyler

Eyler commanded two artillery companies in the Life Guard Artillery Battalion. After spending several days at Heilsberg, he took part in the June offensive against Ney but was soon ordered to fall back to Friedland.

At dawn Napoleon attacked our left flank with his superior forces and our soldiers retreated in disarray. Deployed slightly to the right of them, I crossed the already-burning bridge at Friedland and, after ascending the opposite bank, I was stopped by General Rezvyi in order to prevent the French from crossing the river. The French had, by then, already occupied the town and my battery came under musket fire from the windows of [nearby] houses; the enemy wounded eleven of my men so I immediately opened artillery fire and set fire to Friedland; thereafter I remained quietly in this position. Five volunteers [from my company] managed to drag an abandoned cannon from Count Sievers' company across the burning pontoon bridge and were all rewarded with the St. George Cross while I was awarded the Order of St. Vladimir with a ribbon. [By the end of the battle] I had been left without any protection or supervision and I still marvel that the French did not capture us. At midnight I finally decided myself to withdraw my battery and, by dawn, I caught up with our army that was in complete disorder. [From the Russian text in A. Eyler, *Zapiski* . . .]

Eduard von Löwenstern

During the battle at Friedland, Löwenstern's regiment was deployed at Allenburg and therefore observed the entire battle from afar. In the wake of the battle he witnessed the disarray that reigned in the Russian army.

General Baron Pahlen* was stabbed to death in front of his [Liflyandskii Dragoon] Regiment and carried by his dragoons to us. Our officers buried him here. From all sides came the news that the battle was totally lost. Soldiers with all kinds of weapons fled past us. Grenadiers on hussar horses, sluggish Cuirassiers on foot, soldiers of the Russian Guard, and Prussian foot soldiers fled mixed all together and formed a leaderless mob that no one attempted to rally or stop.

Count [Peter von der] Pahlen with his still fresh cavalry formed the rearguard. We let the completely beaten army run past us and early in the morning met the enemy army, drunk with victory, pushing quickly forward. After numerous skirmishes, always strongly pressed, we reached the Niemen near Tilsit on June 7.

Together with ten hussars, I was ordered to have all of the bread available in the depots in Tilsit loaded up and take it along. The gentlemen provision commissioners had luckily already taken care of emptying all the depots, even a quarter of an hour longer stay and the retreat over the burning Memel bridge would have been impossible for me; and without the possibility of being saved, I would have been taken prisoner by the French, whose trumpets I could hear at the other end of the city. I galloped across the burning bridge with my hussars behind me. I was barely over the river when the King of Naples [Joachim] Murat, with his cavalry, appeared on the other shore. The enemy sappers tried to extinguish the fire, but without success. We set up camp on the flats. Officers with a flag of truce went back and forth . . . [From the German text in Eduard von Löwenstern, *Mit Graf Pahlens Reiterei gegen Napoleon . . .*]

Andrey Engelhardt

By 14 June, Engelhardt, who had been badly wounded in the leg at the combat at Lomitten, was in agonising pain. Gathering his last strength, he continued riding his horse Bucephalus but his leg had already swollen well above his knee and was gradually turning black. Unable to get proper medical help, he was forced to start cutting rotting flesh from his foot himself.

At Friedland. We lodged in a nice apartment and learned from its owner that earlier that day, around 3 p.m., French quartermasters had visited him, leaving a notice that tomorrow, at seven o'clock in the morning, French troops, which were deployed less than ten verists away, would enter the city. [I suffered from] anxiety, exhaustion and rotting flesh in the wound, which festered in

---

* Dmitrii Fedorovich von der Pahlen was chef of the Liflyandskii Dragoon Regiment and was promoted to major-general on 5 June 1807. He was officially struck from the roster as 'killed in action' on 9 July 1807.

the terrible rain and wind and turned my entire heel black; I could no longer feel my leg in many places and since agonising pain still prevented me from sleeping, I decided to make better use of time by taking a knife and cutting large slices of dead and rotting flesh from the sole of my foot, becoming thrilled when, upon slicing, I could find still-living flesh. I kept at this exercise until I removed all that had to be cut; my sole was drenched with blood. As the result of this procedure my foot resembled a hawk's beak because it was cut at the heel but had a crimson tumour on top. Unable to get any sleep, I was no longer capable of staying on my horse. A Prussian-style long carriage was brought and I was laid down on straw that was scattered inside it. At dawn, in order to escape the French, we promptly left Friedland in the direction of Allenburg. The violent shaking of the springless carriage caused me such agonising pain that just half a mile after our departure I was forced to get back on my Bucephalus, who, despite my complete exhaustion, kept leaping to the side. I cursed the war, the horse and myself.

At Allenburg. It was late in the evening when we reached this city, which was occupied by the numerous wounded and the entire reserve artillery park. We were thus unable to find an apartment for ourselves . . . [Just as we settled at a small shelter] a fiery glow that appeared over the entire town announced the start of a conflagration. The ensuring disorder and clamour prompted us to get out of there as soon as we could. As we were deciding where to go, the reserve artillery rushed, at full speed [vo ves' dukh], along the narrow main street. My comrades' ambulance carriage was bumped by artillery but they barely felt it. Sitting on a horse, I tried to press as tightly against the house wall as I could but my wounded leg still suffered from the passing artillery carriages, while my horse was banged by almost every passing piece of ordnance and it was only through the Divine Providence that it was not dragged away and crushed by some rushing cannon; the following dawn I saw for myself how mutilated were his back legs. Just as the artillery passed by, the flames, driven by a strong wind, began to spread in our direction so we immediately departed, illuminated by this devastating sight. About two verists away from the town, we noticed a fire at short distance from the road and discovered a village, where we spent the night.

All these adventures, sleeplessness, exhaustion, the still-spreading gangrene as well as two blackened bruises that I got on the thigh and calf of my wounded leg from the passing artillery limbers, deprived me of the very last strengths. I was preparing myself to die and bemoaned that the gangrene was spreading so slowly.

The following day my comrades Rüdinger and de Lagarde left me in the village, where I, with the utmost help of my escorting soldier, left my fatigued Bucephalus with the local villagers and departed on a heavy and creaky Prussian-style cart to Insterburg.

[. . .]

At Insterburg. The City Hall gave me a billet with a local carpenter. The unbearable burning pain caused me to shout at the host to bring me a tub of cold water, with which I hoped to cool my inflammation. The carpenter, thinking that I was not so severely wounded, sternly uttered a few harsh words but as soon as he saw the condition of my leg, his sternness was immediately replaced by forbearance and from that time he afforded me every assistance, bringing two physicians who, upon examining my leg, refused to operate on it. The carpenter kept encouraging me that he would find another one who, he assured me, would certainly help me. Indeed, some time later, a young man of no more than 22 years of age, a recent graduate of the Berlin Academy, examined my leg and assured me that if could not save it, he would at least preserve my life; as he spoke, he sliced and probed my flesh in order to find still-healthy tissue, which he found in a few places.

In the evening I was visited by many comrades from the 20th Jager Regiment, who informed me that our army was in retreat. I bade them an emotional farewell.

On the third day Marshal Ney's corps approached the town. I wrote him to procure a billet but the municipal authorities informed me that Napoleon had ordered all the wounded to be conveyed to Königsberg by river. After discussing with my physician and sensing that I would be unable to endure this transportation, I wrote to Marshal Ney, describing my condition, in which I could pose no threat [to the French troops] and asking for his benevolence. The Marshal initially refused but, after verifying my condition, he finally agreed with me. At the same time eight of my seriously-wounded comrades were transported in rather miserable conditions and hardly any of them survived this experience.★ [From the Russian text in A. Engelhardt, 'Zhurnal biograficheskoi moei zhizni']

★ Engelhardt's memoir ends at this point and one only wishes he had continued writing. His leg was soon amputated but this physical disability only encouraged him to test himself on the field of battle. For seven more years he fought valiantly in the ranks of the Russian army. After recovering from his wound, he returned to the army and was sent to the Army of Moldavia in 1811. He took part in military operations against the Turks, distinguishing himself at Ruse (where Mikhail Kutuzov annihilated an Ottoman army) where he commanded a special detachment in at least four combats, earning promotion to lieutenant-colonel and a golden sword for gallantry. In 1812, when Napoleon invaded Russia, Engelhardt transferred to the 2nd Western Army, where Prince Bagration chose him as one of his senior aides-de-camp. Engelhardt then took part in the battles of Smolensk, Shevardino and Borodino, where he distinguished himself once more. After Bagration's mortal wound at Borodino, Engelhardt became senior aide-de-camp to his successor General Peter Konovnitsyn and took part in the battles at Tarutino and Maloyaroslavets, where he earned his promotion to colonel. In November, he served in General Winzigerode's flying corps, where he commanded a detachment of seven battalions and twelve guns. In 1813, he was assigned to General Barclay de Tolly and participated in more than a dozen battles, including Dresden,

Vasilii Grigoryev

Officer in the St. Petersburg Militia Battalion.

1 [13] June. At four o'clock in the morning, without eating any food, we embarked on another exhausting march and arrived at Friedland by half past eight.

2 [14 June]. We learned that the French army was deployed in battle order on the other side of the city, concealed by the vast pine forest. Having marched across the bridge near the mill and crossed the city, our troops occupied the valley in front of the woods. Our grenadier and musketeer regiments were deployed in columns while the cavalry was on the flanks to protect the artillery.

Around midnight light skirmishing erupted between our jagers and the enemy chasseurs. When the enemy opened artillery fire on our columns, our batteries responded with almost continuous fire. Around five o'clock in the morning I was wounded once more, this time by a grapeshot to the left side, but the shot seemed already spent because, aside from a severe impact, it [initially] caused no other injury to me. But a few minutes later I felt excruciating pain in my side and the spot, where the grapeshot hit me, became swollen and turned dark. So, assisted by two jagers, I had to leave the front line and walking for one and half verists, I stopped at the same village where I was quartered [back in April]. Fortunately, my batman was able to find our regimental physician Renz, who hastily prepared and applied some kind of embrocation.

The gunfire continued without interruption and, as I later learned, lasted until [almost] all ammunition, including musket cartridges, had been exhausted. Around seven o'clock [in the evening], the enemy advanced out of the woods, launched an attack that dislodged our troops from their positions and pursued them rather forcefully. As I heard from the arriving officers, our men withdrew in disarray and just as some of them ran across the bridge on the Alle River, the bridge was set on fire; those cut off on the other side had to cross the river through the discovered ford and had to use their cold weapons and butts of their muskets to fight off the attacking [French]. By nightfall, out of our entire army, just thirteen thousand troops gathered around the village where I was located, They set up bonfires but still lacked food of any kind. Meanwhile the French halted on the opposite banks and did not pursue us any further, out of concerns for our fresh reinforcements which, in reality, could not be found anywhere nearby. Around 11 p.m., I was evacuated, together with the other wounded officers, to the town of Allenburg. [From the Russian text in V. Grigoryev, Podennyj zhurnal . . .]

Kulm and Leipzig, during the War of German Liberation. He finished the war in Paris. Returning to Russia, he retired from the military and spent the rest of his life at his prosperous estates in the Smolensk, Mogilev and Chernigov provinces. For details see A. Yurganov, 'Posylaem byl v opasneishie mesta... Ustanovlenie avtorstva vospominanii russkogo ofitsera o voine 1805-1807 gg.', *Sovetskie arkhivy* 6 (1987), pp. 74–6.

7

The Aftermath of the Campaign

After the battle of Friedland, the battered Russian army retreated towards the Niemen River that marked the boundary of the Russian Empire. On 19 June, Prince Bagration received Bennigsen's letter instructing him to offer an armistice to the French. The message, which Bagration conveyed to Marshal Murat, stated, 'After the torrents of blood which have lately flowed in battles as sanguinary as frequent, [Russians] should desire to assuage the evils of this destructive war, by proposing an armistice before we enter upon a conflict, a fresh war, perhaps more terrible than the first.'

On 25 June, Emperor Alexander met Napoleon on a raft in the middle of the Niemen to discuss peace. On 7 July, the two emperors concluded a peace treaty, which was ratified two days later. Russia agreed to join the Continental System and to give up the Ionian Islands and some other Mediterranean islands in its possession. In return, France agreed to support Russia in its war against the Ottoman Empire if the Sultan did not make peace within three months. In addition, with French support, Russia gained a free hand in north-eastern Europe where it had long had designs on Finland, which was then a province of Sweden. Although Russia had gotten off lightly by the Treaty of Tilsit, the Russian army had suffered terribly during the campaign and desperately needed time to recover.

Denis Davydov

I shall never forget the hardships that we experienced during the night that followed this bloody day. Our rearguard, worn out by the ten-day fighting [withdrawal] and reeling from the latest blow which fell harder on it than any other troops, had covered the disorderly retreat of an army that only a few hours before had been so imposing, orderly and beautiful. Our physical strength buckled under the strain of duties entailed in front-line guard service. Ever cheerful, vigilant and heedless of any dangers and disasters, Bagration was in command of this part of the army. But like his subordinates, he was worn out from lack of sleep and food. His close associates, who were just setting out on the road to fame – Count Pahlen, Rayevskii, Yermolov and Kulnev – were carrying out their duties by sheer willpower; the soldiers barely dragged their feet while the cavalrymen kept dozing off and swaying in their saddles.

At sunrise the army arrived at Wehlau and during the day crossed the Pregel; after joining the rest of the army, the rearguard destroyed the bridge. The whole army regrouped, as much as time allowed it, and proceeded towards Taplaken, Klein-Schirau and Papelken, heading for Tilsit. Our marching order was as follows: ahead were the Guard and the heavy artillery, followed by two regiments of light cavalry of the right flank (the remaining cavalry of this flank Bennigsen used to reinforce the rearguard), then came the heavy cavalry gathered from both flanks and finally the whole of our infantry and light artillery, together with the main headquarters. The rearguard formed the tail end of the troops.

[...]

During the course of 3 [15] June, the pursuit was conducted without the notable enthusiasm and confidence that the French normally displayed at the least success. On the 4th [16 June], however, we noticed that the numbers of the forces pursuing our troops had increased, reflecting the iron will of their commander-in-chief. Our rearguard was mercilessly attacked at Klein-Schirau, Bitemen and Papelken. We were still far from the trisection of the roads with the main road to Tilsit, and even father from the main forces. We had received no news from Lestocq's corps, nor any intelligence from the parties that had been dispatched to keep an eye on [Marshal] Ney's movements [around Guttstadt] and direction. It was enough to make us despair.

On that day, as if to offer us distraction from dire events, several Bashkir regiments arrived to join our rearguard. Armed with bows and arrows, wearing caps with long ear-flaps and dressed in weird-looking caftans, riding on short, bulky mounts that lacked any elegance, they seemed to represent caricatures of bold Circassian horsemen. We were supposed to believe that their appearance was intended to impress Napoleon with the notion that all the peoples and nations under Russia's rule were ready to rise up against him and give him real cause for concern.

What might have given him concern was not the spectacle of a handful of barbarous tribesmen, but the prospect of 300,000 reserve soldiers of the regular army standing battle-ready at the frontiers of the empire, under the command of a determined general well-skilled in the art of war. But as it was, Napoleon was hardly likely to be deluded by such fantasies. Had the situation been reversed and our victorious army invaded a European nation, it is just possible that a multitude of natives from the Urals, Kalmyks and Bashkirs, sent as a diversion in the enemy's rear, might have induced a state of panic. Their numbers, their appearance, their wild behaviour, might have perhaps stirred the imagination and conjured up visions of the hordes of Attila the Hun, as effective in its way as the capture of military supplies and provisions. But after the defeat at Friedland and our retreat to the Niemen, when our own infantry, artillery and cavalry could barely contain the attacks of victorious Napoleonic forces approaching the frontiers of Russia that lay open and unprepared to repel an invasion, how could anyone hope for success by opposing fifteenth-century weapons to nineteenth-century cannonballs, shells, grapeshot and bullets – even if the warriors with their bows and arrows had presented themselves in unthinkable numbers!?

Be that as it may, French and Russians who came across these Bashkir horsemen were unanimous in greeting them with laughter . . . That evening stories circulated of adventures with Bashkirs during the course of the day. I myself was witness to one rather amusing episode. During a skirmish, we took prisoner a French lieutenant-colonel whose name I have now forgotten. To this officer's ill fortune, nature had bestowed on him a nose of extraordinary size, while the vicissitudes of war wished to have this nose shot through with an arrow which was embedded to half its length. We helped the lieutenant-colonel down from his horse and set him on the ground so that we could free him of this distressing adornment. A crowd of onlookers, including a few Bashkirs, gathered around the victim. Our physician grabbed a saw and prepared to cut the arrow in two so as to remove it painlessly from either side of the enormous bulge, when one of the Bashkirs recognised the arrow as one of his own and seized the physician by both hands.

'No,' said he, 'I would not let you cut my arrow. Do not offend me. Please do not. It is my arrow. I will take it out myself!'

'Are you raving?' We said to the Bashkir. 'How will you get it out?'

'Well, I will take one end and pull it out, and the arrow will stay in one piece.'

'And the nose?' we enquired.

'And the nose,' he answered, 'the devil take it!'

You can imagine the roar of laughter that greeted his words. Meanwhile, the French officer, not understanding a word of Russian, was trying to guess what was going on. He begged us to chase the Bashkir away, which we did. The affair was settled and in the end the French nose triumphed over the Bashkir arrow.

On 5 [17] June our situation did not improve. There was still no news about Lestocq and Ney; still the enemy advance guard's relentless pursuit; and still the selfless devotion of our troops to repel all enemy attacks! While discussing the outlook with one of my closest friends, Staff Captain Baron Diebitsch of the Life Guard Semeyonovskii Regiment, we happened to glance to our right and observed fifty or so Prussian hussars galloping in our direction. I set off briskly on my horse, Cossack-style, joined up with the Prussians and rode over with them to meet Bagration. They informed him that Lestocq had successfully got through the Gross Baumwald forest, that the French had fallen a good way behind him, and that they would be delayed even further on account of a narrow dyke that bisected the woods for more than two miles and which the Prussians had damaged and dug up in several places [to slow down the enemy].

We felt as if we had received a new lease of life! And fate had more to offer us. At that very moment, another dispatch arrived with no less happy news: our scouts sent towards Insterburg to keep an eye on Ney reported that he was no longer aiming for the road to Tilsit, but had changed direction instead towards Gumbinnen. So here, too, the skies were clearing. Matters were taking a new turn and our salvation was now assured.

Finally, towards the evening of the same day, our forces reached both Tilsit and the Niemen . . . Our army was deployed in battle order near the Dranghof church to safeguard the crossing of our heavy equipment. These events, so important to us, untied Bagration's hands and released him of the obligation to hold back Napoleon's forces, ten times superior in numbers to his own. Ney and Murat no longer menaced his rear and he could confine his efforts to fending off routine attacks against his front line originating from Wehlau.

This was the state of affairs when I was sent to see Bennigsen on the morning of the 6th [18 June] to inform him that our rearguard was no longer threatened, that our troops were safeguarded and in good spirits, that Murat had joined up with the main body of the French army, and that Ney's corps had turned towards Gumbinnen. When I arrived at the Dranghof church, I was unable to catch up with our troops. Having sent its heavy equipment across the Niemen, the army had also crossed, and the main headquarters was now located in Tilsit. Beyond the church, I ran into Major Ernest Schepping, one of the wittiest of my friends and companions.

'What's new, Schepping?' I enquired.

'What's new is that I am carrying a letter from Bennigsen to Bagration. He instructs him to use me to contact the French and offer them an armistice, until we enter into peace negotiations. There's the news for you, lad. Goodbye!'

I cannot express how this news affected me! It was not that the notion of armistice and peace were repugnant to me. On the contrary, the endless retreats, even when we were successful, the constant occupation of positions considered impregnable and their subsequent abandonment at the first appearance of the enemy, and the absence of offensive action – all this drove me to despair. I was genuinely tired, even sick, of such a war. Besides, I perceived the circumstances as they were, free of any deceptions and flattering. I was well aware of the glaring inequality of talent between Bennigsen and Napoleon, the disparity in numbers between our army and the enemy forces, the conviction among the larger part of our army that Napoleon was invincible, the material chaos that plagued us after the defeat at Friedland, the lack of supplies and the reserves, the enormous distance between ourselves and the militias that were still in the formative stage, and a host of other equally important circumstances. I recognised all this, but the casual words uttered by Schepping immediately erased all of these thoughts. I felt nothing except the shame of entering peace talks without avenging Friedland, and was quite beside myself with indignation, as if the duty of answering to our country for the grave wrongs to its glory and honour had fallen upon me alone.

In my madness, I rushed off to see Bennigsen to assure him of the excellent state of our rearguard and the possibility of our still continuing to fight bravely for as long as he found it necessary. As if everything depended on the rearguard alone! As if a handful of troops would be enough to engage a commander against whom an entire army was deemed insufficient! But such is youth!

I galloped to the headquarters, where I found crowds of people: Englishmen, Swedes, Prussians, French Royalists, Russian military and civil servants who knew nothing of either military or civil service, men of intrigue and without employment. It resembled a market-place for political and military speculators who had already failed in their previous hopes, plans and actions. Entering the house occupied by Bennigsen, I learned that he was still resting, but was expected to make an appearance shortly. Having nothing better to do, I went back into the street to watch the troops moving towards the crossing and preparing to burn the bridge. At that moment, as luck would have it, I ran into an acquaintance, whose sad aspect and bearing alone contradicted the measures that were running through my head. This pale and trembling apparition, learning of my intentions, believed that Bennigsen would listen to me, a twenty-year-old mad-cap, and agree to all of my suggestions. He was terrified. He began to lecture me about how reprehensible it was for a man of my rank (staff rotmistr of the Life Guard Hussar Regiment), so young and so inexperienced, to proffer advice to a high personage such as the commander-in-chief. Besides, everything had already been settled anyway and I would simply become the butt of jokes and ridicule and accomplish nothing. His remarks were absolutely justified and shook me to the core. They gave me serious food for thought. I looked around at the fashionable crowd that had gathered, reflecting that these were the very same people who were recently so confident that Napoleon could be easily defeated. It was enough to ensure that my lips would remain sealed. With hangers-on such as these, how could we even think of continuing our struggle with the enemy? Only then did I realise what sort of company I had found myself in and perceived how much these people who live under a real roof and rarely find themselves on the battlefield differ from those men who live under open skies and whom I had left two hours previously facing bullets and cannonball, and ready for never-ending struggle.

At the main headquarters everything was in a state of alert, as if the world was a half-hour from Doomsday. Only Bennigsen seemed unchanged. He was clearly in pain, but he suffered in silence, a manly, Roman-style distress. He resembled [Publius Cornelius] Scipio after his defeat at the hands of Hannibal at Ticinus. As soon as he entered the hall, I went over to him and conveyed

Bagration's message, without mentioning a word of the stupid thoughts provoked by my meeting with Schepping. Indeed, I was already cured of it by the good sense of that frightened officer and the petrified atmosphere at the headquarters, which sooner or later was bound to filter down to the troops under their command. The news that I had brought concerning the safety of the rearguard appeared to be a welcome gift for Bennigsen, because his face suddenly cleared. After a few questions and answers, my audience was over and I returned to my station.

In the meantime, throughout the 6th and 7th [18–19 June], our army continued crossing to the right bank of the Niemen under the protection of the rearguard which, regardless of Bennigsen's offer to Napoleon, continued to fight as it was hard-pressed by the French advance guard. Finally, all the troops had crossed the Niemen with the exception of a few dozen Cossacks who kept exchanging fire with enemy skirmishers. Orders for them to hurry and join up with the rest of the troops had been dispatched. At that very moment, French chasseurs à cheval and dragoons burst into the town. The Cossacks galloped off, not noticing that the foremost pursuer, with sword drawn, was Murat himself. They got safely over to the right bank just as he reached the bridge, which immediately burst into flames under the very muzzle of his beautiful horse! The imprudent paladin reined in his steed and returned slowly to the town. The Niemen now separated the opposing sides. During the subsequent armistice, Murat bragged about his hot pursuit and assured his audience that he was all set to gallop over the bridge to the opposite bank. 'Too bad that didn't happen, Your Highness,' answered one of our officers. 'We would have had one more prisoner!'

[...]

This is how the campaign of 1806 and 1807 ended. What an astonishing turnaround in less than two years! In August of 1805, France, which neighboured other countries of comparable resources and power, had been content to remain within its borders behind the Rhine. By early June of 1807 there no longer existed a single independent state between France and Russia; all had bowed before one will, that of the conqueror who gazed ever more hungrily from the banks of the Niemen at the land of Russia, which appeared as a blue line on the horizon. [From the Russian text in Denis Davydov, *Voennye zapiski*]

Vasilii Grigoryev

Wounded at the beginning of the battle of Friedland, Grigoryev managed to get out of the burning town and travelled on a half-wagon ahead of the battered Russian army.

3 [15 June]. In the morning the remnants of our battered regiments arrived at [Allenburg] but so did the French around 2 o'clock in the afternoon. So as our troops were moving out, the French were marching into the town, while we, the wounded, were dispatched in supply half-wagons [polufiurka] on the road to Gumbinnen* where we arrived well after midnight.

4 [16 June]. Today my batman, showing his great diligence, was able to unearth a piece of black bread and three potatoes, for which he paid a silver ruble. I ravenously devoured the potatoes and my hunger made [the unappetising] bread taste delectable. I then sent my batman to the hewaldiger general† to procure a permit for my return to Russia; I soon received this document. Through this official I also rejoined Staff Captain Peter Ivanovich Borozdin of the Kexholmskii Regiment, who had fallen ill with fever after the battle of Heilsberg, and with Lieutenant Jacob Ivanovich Sablin of the Guard Field Artillery, so we travelled together in the half-wagons that resembled coffins as they had no openings. Travelling in these on poor roads turned out to be a torturous experience.

5 [17 June]. We arrived at Insterburg, which was choked up with artillery park and wagons, much of which are already unsuitable for use. With a great difficulty did our batmen find a little bit of bread and butter for us, but they had to pay handsomely for them.

6 [18 June]. We departed at 4 o'clock in the morning and travelled on the road to Jurburg, where we arrived at seven o'clock in the evening. We waited for more than an hour to cross the [Niemen] river and, losing our patience, decided to ford it, followed by our wretched wounded soldiers. We spent the night in the half-wagons on the bank of the Niemen.

7 [19 June]. Despite our repeated requests to Major-General Marklovskii, the commandant of Jurburg, we were unable to secure any lodgings and were, thus, forced to continue our nomadic life in the half-wagons. There are unbelievably high prices everywhere and a rye bread cost four silver kopecks per pound while wheat bread, made by loathsome Jewish hands and smaller than a Muscovite saika,‡ costs one silver ruble. I tried writing a letter to my family but the heavy rain interrupted me since the canvass covering my half wagon offered little protection from it.

8 [20 June]. At last, I was given lodgings today and even though it was in a filthy Jewish shack, I cannot do anything but to submit to circumstances. To mark this news, my batman fought somewhere a few handfuls of grits and a goose; after experiencing hunger [for so long], this seemed indescribably delicious to us. After lunch I walked through Jurburg and found the desperate Neterfeldt, who was in a wretched condition since his wounded leg was

---

* Today Gusev in the Kaliningrad region.
† Head of the military police.
‡ Saika, from Estonian saia, was a type of wheat bread.

inflamed [gangrene] and he could not find a physician to operate on it. Zenin is still alive and he has been moved further ahead, to a village.

9 [21 June]. Today I was visited by Stepan Leontievich Osipov and Major Joseph Stepanovich Mendoza de Botello of the 24th Jager Regiment. We shared a humble meal and walked along the Niemen in the evening. We learned from the passers-by that a peace will be soon concluded.

10 [22 June]. Around nine o'clock I was unexpectedly visited by Prince N. M. Golitsyn and I spent a very present time with him, lamenting our poor comrades who are seriously wounded and yet abandoned without care and help.

11 [23 June]. The rumours about the conclusion of peace have become universal and caused widespread joy, both among us as we would be able to return to our families, and among the wounded and captured because of the prospects it offered to each of them.

12 [24 June]. We received reliable news about the conclusion of the peace [armistice] at Tilsit, which was located not far from us. This news so thrilled Captain Luknitskii, who served in our battalion and disappeared during the battle of Heilsberg, that he unexpectedly reappeared from God knows where, with his head bandaged and riding a civilian horse, and proceeded, like a herald, to inform everyone about the conclusion of the peace with the French and the impending return of the troops to Russia.

13 [25 June]. My comrades and I are on the road again and stopped at the village of Pegany, not far from Ariogala. This village consists of no more than twenty small and rather destitute stacks, populated by the Polish zhmuts* who are tight grips of the filth and poverty.

[...]

22 [June; 4 July]. I travelled to the village of Raseiniai, which is slightly larger than Ariogala and is populated by Jews. Here I rejoined my battered battalion, where just slightly more than 200 men have survived. We spent nine days here waiting for our stragglers who kept arriving from various places ...
[From the Russian text in V. Grigoryev, Podennyj zhurnal ...]

Nikolay Levshin

After being wounded at Lomitten, Levshin was evacuated to Jurburg and on the way there learned about the disastrous battle at Friedland.

On the way to Jurburg, we encountered the Izyumskii Hussar Regiment, which was hastening, at the trot, to protect our supply trains and the town of Jurburg. Under our very eyes, this regiment searched for the ford across the Niemen River and their courageous commander, General Yurkovskii, was first to rush

---

* Žemaitė or Samogitians are a part of the Lithuanian ethnic group.

into the river. He was followed by the entire regiment, in pairs. The hussars crossed the river facing great dangers. The transports were moving across the river on plaatschuits [small boats] directly in front of the city and we could see clearly as some hussars fell off their horses while others fell together with their mounts into the rapids and drowned helplessly; their bodies were carried away by the river's rapid current.

When I arrived, the city was in a terrible commotion. The hussars were pushing transports onto the road to Riga while the wounded officers were instructed to secure passes to wherever they desired, from Major-General Marklovskii. I got passport No. 238 to the town of Orel. In the street I unexpectedly met my brother Nikolay Pavlovich Levshin, who was wounded by a bullet to the right knee at Friedland. He suffered terribly but refused to have his leg amputated. We travelled together to Riga.

The entire trip from Jurburg to Riga proved to be a dreadful experience as we had to hear the incessant moaning of the wounded and dying. My late brother kept crying day and night. Somehow we reached Riga, where we were given a comfortable room in the house of Baroness Grotgus and placed under the care of the best local physician, Somener. He helped me recover and two weeks later I could stand on my feet. Yet, he had condemned my brother Nikolay to death – my brother's leg had to be amputated above the knee but he kept refusing it and consequently suffered greatly for more than one and a half months before dying on 10 [22] July, the very day when the Life Guard Jager Regiment, on its way back to St. Petersburg, entered Riga. A squad from the company where Nikolay served, escorted the mournful procession to the cemetery and, with three volleys fired over the grave, it paid its respects to the man who had sacrificed his life for the Fatherland. Lieutenant-General Kologrivov, who commanded the Guard Corps, almost all officers of the two Life Guard Jager battalions and numerous officers from other Guards regiments attended the funeral.

My late brother Alexander★ was lightly wounded in the hand and was present with the regiment. After Nikolay's funeral, he spent another nine days in Riga before leaving to catch up with the regiment. He then secured a furlough and went to Moscow to deliver the sad news [to the family]. This grief almost claimed the life of my mother, who was inconsolable for several months and, in fits of exasperation, she spat at and threw down holy icons and suffered from a violent fever.

Thus, I was left alone in Riga, mourning the death of my brother with whom I had always been very close. My only occupation were books while, in the evenings, before sunset, I walked in gardens and occasionally in the streets. [From the Russian text in N. Levshin, 'Domashnii pamyatnik . . . ']

★ Alexander Levshin was killed at the battle of Borodino in 1812.

Konstantin Batyushkov

The famed Russian poet, translator and essayist, Batyushkov left a rich literary legacy which also includes his various recollections. One such memoir is devoted to his close friend Ivan Alexandrovich Petin (1788–1813) who tragically died at the age of twenty-six (already a colonel) at the battle of Leipzig. In January 1807, Batyushkov, just emerging as a literary figure in the Russian society, decided to enlist as a junior officer in the St. Petersburg Militia Battalion. During the campaign, he developed a close friendship with the young Ivan Petin, who was a recent graduate of the elite Page Corps and served as a lieutenant in the elite Life Guard Jager Regiment. They were both wounded during this campaign and were reunited only after the battle of Friedland, when they reached the town of Jurburg.

I will not go into details of describing my joy [upon seeing Petin]. Only those who have fought under the same banner, shoulder to shoulder and have experienced the fortunes of war would understand me. In a small shack on the bank of the Niemen, without any money, help or bread (and I am not exaggerating this), and in terrible agony, I was lying on straw and looking at Petin, who was getting his wound bandaged. All around our shack were wounded soldiers, returning from the wretched fields of Friedland, and numerous [French] prisoners accompanied them. In the evening, the door of our shack opened and in came several Frenchmen, with menacing moustaches, in bearskin caps and with the haughty look of the victor. Petin was away at that moment so we invited the wounded to share our lump of putrid bread and our few drops of vodka. One of my comrades even shared his money with them – he gave them one of just two gold coins, a veritable fortune considering our circumstances. As is customary, the French showered us with kindness and praise and so when Petin entered the room, our loquacious prisoners were already unrestrained in their eloquence. Imagine our astonishment when in response to their greetings, Petin, reclining on a crutch, pointed to the door and told our guests, 'Will you please get out of here. There is not enough room even for the Russians, as you can plainly see.' The Frenchmen left the room without uttering a word but my comrades and I reproached Petin for breaking the rules of hospitality.

'Hospitality!, hospitality!' he kept repeating, his face turning red out of vexation.

'And you've got quite a nerve to mock us,' I shouted, raising from my bed.

'I have the right to deride your reckless cruelty,' he replied.

'Cruelty? But were you not cruel just a moment ago?'

'Maybe. But first you must answer my questions! Have you seen the crossing over the Niemen?'

'No.'

'So you have not seen what is happening there, right?'

'No! But what can the Niemen have to do with your behaviour?'

'A great deal! The entire riverbank is covered with the wounded. Countless Russians are lying on the wet sand, exposed to rain and dying without any help because all the houses are crowded with them. So would not it be better to bring here those warriors who have been crippled alongside with us? Would not it be better to feed the Russian who is dying from starvation rather than entertain those accurst braggarts? So do tell me! Why are you silent!?' [From the Russian text in K. Batyshkov, 'Vospominaniya o Petine']

Yakov Otroshenko

After the disaster at Friedland, Otroshenko, who commanded a company in the 7th Jager Regiment, retreated with his men to Wehlau, where he arrived a day later and began crossing the Pregel River.

All the troops crossed over the Pregel while I, with three [jager] companies, was tasked with remaining in the town because there was still a considerable number of stragglers and the wounded remaining. I burned the bridge over the Alle and deployed my skirmishers in the houses. During the night, enemy cavalrymen approached the [burnt] bridge but my men shot at them and they fled, losing two men killed.

Meanwhile, pillaging broke out in the town during the night. Soldiers broke down doors into shops with supplies and grabbed bread and various provisions. In one of the shops there was a barrel of honey [in one part of the store] and a barrel of tar [degot'] in another corner. The news that honey had been discovered prompted everyone to rush there with whatever they had in hand, be it a flask or a piece of bread. Those, whom fate directed towards the barrel of honey, grabbed as much of it as they could and then jostled to get out, fighting through the crowd, holding their flask high in the air and spilling their sweet syrup on heads and uniforms. Meanwhile, those who stumbled upon the barrel with tar initially took it for honey and started filling their flasks and dipping their breads in it but after tasting it and realising their mistake, they were throwing and spilling tar amidst the crowd.

Elsewhere, soldiers captured a supply store with different coloured covers [chekhol] for cloth items. There was no less vigorous jostling here as the soldiers grabbed covers of the colours that they had liked, without opening them or checking their quality. They emptied their knapsacks and filled them with these covers. On such occasions – in darkness and with soldiers from various regiments all mixed together – it is dangerous for an officer unknown to them to assert his authority. The following morning, I received orders to leave the town and burn the bridge over the Pregel. Our troops withdrew for several verists and halted. Now it was possible to recognise soldiers who had been involved in night-time plundering because their uniforms bore clear evidence of stains from honey and tar. Furthermore, our bivouac soon turned colourful as soldiers took [stolen] cases from their knapsacks and, after seeing their quality, angrily discarded them and bemoaned the things they had thrown out during the night. Later on, soldiers made colourful trousers out of these cases. [From the Russian text in Y. Otroshenko, *Zapiski* . . .]

Eduard von Löwenstern

[On 25 June 1807] came the meeting of the two Emperors at the Niemen. I watched this entirely remarkable drama from the shore, but you could not see the faces of the prominent people clearly because of the width of the river. Soldiers crowded along both shores of the Memel to see their monarchs standing together. But how different their feelings must have been: those there as victors, those there as vanquished. We, pushed back to our borders, felt humiliated, deeply hurt. Especially the Prussians had every reason to be very downcast. Of that beautiful large Prussia, once so marvellous under its Frederick [the Great], there remained for the present king only a small strip of land and one single city as a refuge for his family.

After the peace was concluded, we took up cramped quarters near Tilsit. Here I received the depressing news that again nothing would come of my officer's rank. The Emperor, dissatisfied with the entire campaign and angry about Bennigsen, had not confirmed his order and I, poor devil, who was totally innocent of the defeat at Friedland had to suffer for it and became, what I had already been in the camp at Launau – a junker in Major Potapov's squadron. As a consolation, I was awarded the Cross of St. George for the battle of Eylau. For better or worse, I had to be satisfied with my fate. Potapov's hussars greeted me with mocking laughter. I had to put up with all kinds of little practical jokes and repress my inner anger. [From the German text in Eduard von Löwenstern, *Mit Graf Pahlens Reiterei gegen Napoleon* . . .]

Nadezhda Durova

Tilsit. Here we were reunited with our regiment. Everyone with strength enough to hold a weapon is in the ranks. They say that we are going to Russia from here. And so the campaign is at an end, and my hopes and dreams with it: instead of splendid feats, I committed scatterbrained pranks. Will I someday have a chance to make up for them? Napoleon's restless spirit and the uneasy crown on his head assure me of the possibility. Once again he will force Russia to take up its formidable arms, but will it be soon? And what will I be until then? Can I really remain a common recruit? Will they promote me to officer without proofs of my nobility? And how can I get them? My uncle has our charter if he would send it. But, no, he will never do so. On the contrary. Oh, God, God, why was my life spared?

I was so absorbed in these lamentable reflections that I failed to notice the captain galloping up to the spot where I stood. 'What is this, Durov?' he said, touching my shoulder lightly with his sabre. 'Is this any time to be hanging your head and looking pensive? Sit alert and look cheerful. The Emperor is coming!'

And with this he galloped off. Words of command rang out, regiments dressed ranks, trumpets sounded, and we dipped our lances to our adored Tsar as, accompanied by a large suite, he dashed up to us on a fine horse. Our emperor is a handsome man in the prime of life; meekness and charity are expressed in his large blue eyes, greatness of soul in his noble features, and an uncommon amiability on his rosy lips. Our young Tsar's kindly face depicts a sort of maidenly bashfulness along with his benevolent expression. The Emperor rode past our entire formation at a walk, looking at the soldiers compassionately and pensively. Oh, how his paternal heart must bleed at the memory of the last battle! Much of our army perished on the fields of Friedland! [From the Russian text in N. Durova, 'Kavalerist-devitsa']

Alexsey Yermolov

A meeting between the Tsar and Napoleon was arranged in the middle of the Niemen. The Prussian king was left on the riverbank! Several days later, the Tsar visited Tilsit, where, in the middle of the French army, his escort comprised one battalion of the Life Guard Preobrazhenskii Regiment and two squadrons of the Life Guard Hussar Regiment. Peace was soon concluded; Napoleon had all to gain by it, but he showed respect to the Tsar. He also agreed to meet the Prussian king. Napoleon paraded his troops and, at the French camp, the Tsar was met with respect and honour on a par with Napoleon himself. The Emperor's suite included all his marshals and numerous generals. Finally, the Prussian queen was invited to lunch. This beautiful woman, with eyes full of tears though trying to seem happy, appeared before the same conqueror against whom she had once incited her armies. Meanwhile, the armies began returning home and the day for departure was set. Napoleon's entire Guard was in new uniforms (thanks to Prussia) and in incredible order. With a battalion of the Preobrazhenskii Regiment at the head of the column, the Imperial Guard marched past both emperors, who said their goodbyes and left Tilsit.

The troops of the rearguard returned to those divisions from which they belonged; all of us, serving under Bagration, quit this beloved commander with an expression of devotion to him. Besides complete confidence in his abilities and experience, we felt the difference in his treatment of us as compared to that of other generals. There was no one better at ensuring that his subordinates knew who was in command. The soldiers simply adored him. Having said goodbye to my comrades, I travelled back to Russia.

Thus, I served throughout this war as an artillery commander in the vanguard. Due to my good fortune, I did not lose a single gun, whilst many others, facing less trying situations, lost many. Only one of my guns was abandoned – that in the Pskovskii Musketeer Regiment, but even then, an artillery officer could not have been reprimanded.*

I enjoyed the benevolence of Grand Duke Constantine Pavlovich, who often praised my service. I also enjoyed the confidence and friendship of Bagration. He often gave me orders that surpassed my rank and nominated me twice to the rank of major-general, making every effort on his part for me to receive it; however, he was unsuccessful because, at that moment, promotion was mostly done based on seniority, not merit. In the meantime, I earned the respect of my comrades and the confidence of my subordinates. In short, new prospects opened up to me and I hoped to have less trouble than before. During the campaign, I received the following awards: a golden sword inscribed 'For Courage' for Golymin, the Order of St. Vladimir (3rd class), the Order of St. George (3rd class) for Guttstadt and the Passarge and the diamond insignia of the Order of St. Anna (2nd class) for Heilsberg. [From the Russian text in A. Yermolov, *Zapiski* . . .]

Alexander Shishkov

Infamous for his Slavophile sentiments and aversion to foreign influences, Alexander Shishkov was one of the leading Russian ideologues of the Napoleonic Wars. After a long and distinguished career in the navy, Shishkov retired from active service with the rank of admiral in 1798. He continued to serve in the Ministry of the Navy. In 1805, he was appointed head of the Admiralty Department of the Ministry of the Navy but soon clashed with Minister of the Navy Admiral Pavel Chichagov and was forced to retire in 1807.

---

* Yermolov's note: During the battle of Heilsberg, the enemy captured many our guns because I ordered my officers if forced to abandon guns, to open fire at close range to avenge themselves. I explained to them that it would be less harmful to lose a gun rather than to remove them prematurely and expose our troops. Officers were told about incidents, which had taken place earlier in the rearguard, when the batteries remained in their positions at all costs and were not captured by the enemy despite their efforts. I explained that if any officer, concerned not to lose guns, left his position, then our troops would inevitably be destroyed. I issued certificates to my staff officers when they recaptured guns seized by the enemy and they later received the appropriate awards based on these documents. My superiors were informed about my instructions, which absolved the officers from any responsibility for the lost artillery pieces; the Tsar himself was told about it and later kindly asked me about them.

Soon after the Peace of Tilsit, many received St. George Crosses, even though hardly anything was known about their exploits that earned them these awards. With our troops defeated and the peace concluded on humiliating terms, the distribution of these crosses led to plenty of derision and mockery. Even the persons who had received these awards seemed to attach no importance to them. Thus, on one of the holidays, many of them accompanied the Emperor to the church and stood outside waiting. A retired naval brigadier Kozhukhov, who had arrived from the village, happened to pass by them. An old man with a balding head, he was dressed in a frayed white uniform, which used to be worn in the times of [Emperor] Paul, with the Order of St. George (3rd class). Upon seeing him, the new chevaliers focused their attention on him and, as if the cross [of St. George] that he was wearing was different from theirs, they kept telling each other, 'Look at that old man! He must have received that cross not without merit. This award makes him even more respectable and stirs one to want to kiss his balding head.' I personally overheard this conversation and thought to myself, 'So that is how much respect people show towards the awards given in the times of Catherine!' The following day I went to my department, where I discussed with Count [Xavier] de Maistre how critically people perceived these untimely-granted awards. De Maistre took out of his pocket a piece of paper with poems written in French that, without much bile but with plenty of wit and justice, condemned the distribution of these crosses. After reading them, I handed the paper back to him but de Maistre told me that I could keep it if I wanted it. So these poems stayed with me. That day I dined with [Senator Alexander] Sablikov and met a certain Rodion Koshelev. After dinner Koshelev mentioned these same rumours spreading through the city. I added that there were already poems and epigrams written about this and showed him the ones that [de Maistre] had given me. Koshelev asked my permission to copy them but I told him that he could have the paper itself.

Several days later, I was visited by a police officer who acted on behalf of General Sergey Vyazmitinov [the military governor of St. Petersburg], inquiring about those poems and where I had obtained them. Surprised by such a visit and unwilling to cause any unpleasantness for de Maistre, if he was indeed the author of these poems, I told the officer that I would personally visit Vyazmitinov. I immediately went to him and told him, 'You have sent [a police officer] to inquire about the poems. It is true that I had them but finding nothing worthwhile in them, I paid no attention to them and thus could not remember who gave them to me.' Vyazmitinov responded, 'I have orders to find the author of these poems. And since our investigation stops with your name, I will be compelled to inform His Imperial Majesty about this. Of course, His Majesty would not believe that you are the author of these poems but you might experience His displeasure at this.' I replied, 'Well, what can I do if I do not remember [who gave them to me]?' and, bowing, I bade farewell to him. Forthwith I met Count de Maistre at the department and told him about everything that had transpired. He thanked me for my gracious silence but also told me that he would not be afraid to reveal the name of the person who wrote these poems. 'If that is so,' I told him, 'You should go to Vyazmitinov and tell him that.' He indeed went to Vyazmitinov and did that. But I have never heard if the author of these poems had ever been discovered or not. [From the Russian text in A. Shishkov, *Zapiski* . . .]

Bibliography

Batyshkov, Konstantin, 'Vospominaniya o Petine'. in P. N. Batyushkov (ed.), *Sochineniya K.N. Batyshkova* (St. Petersburg, 1885), vol. 2 http://books.google. com/books?id=YWEEAAAAYAAJ.

Benckendorff, Alexander, 'Vospominaniya . . . ', *Imperator* 11 (2007), pp. 2–6.

Bennigsen, Levin, *Mémoires du Général Bennigsen.* ed. Jean Jules Cazalas (Paris, 1907–8). Russian edition: 'Zapiski grafa L.L. Bennigsen o voine s Napoleonom 1807 goda,' ed. P. Maikov, *Russkaya starina* 12 (1896), pp. 481–518; 1 (1897), pp. 81–110; 2 (1897), pp. 253–72; 4 (1897), pp. 73–102; 5 (1897), pp. 299–316; 7 (1899), pp. 205–24; 8 (1899), pp. 453–66; 9 (1899), pp. 675–93; 10 (1899), pp. 213–29; 12 (1899), pp. 697–712; 1 (1900), pp. 259–72; 2 (1900), pp. 501–16; 3 (1900), pp. 745–67.

Bode, Lev, 'Moim dorogim detyam', in G. Lyapischev (ed.), *Rosiiskie memuary epokhi Napoleonovskikh voin* (Moscow, 2013), pp. 9–64.

Bulgarin, Faddei, *Vospominaniya.* Moscow, 2001.

Davydov, Denis. *Voennye zapiski* (Moscow, 1982). English edition: *In the Service of the Tsar against Napoleon: The Memoirs of Denis Davidov, 1806-1814*, translated and edited by Gregory Troubetzkoy. London, 1999.

Durova, Nadezhda. 'Kavalerist-devitsa' (St. Petersburg, 1836) < http://dlib.rsl.ru/viewer/01003823011#?page=5>. English Edition: *The Cavalry Maiden: Journals of a Female Russian Officer in the Napoleonic Wars*, translated by Mary Fleming Zirin (London, 1988).

Engelhardt, Andrey, 'Zhurnal biograficheskoi moei zhizni', *Russkii arkhiv* 6 (1895), pp. 200–16.

Grigoryev, Vasilii, 'Podennyi zhurnal vo vremya pokhoda iz S. Peterburga za granitsu v Prusskie vladeniya 1807 goda fevralya s 23-go for 25 avgusta', in G. Lyapischev (ed.), *Rosiiskie memuary epokhi Napoleonovskikh voin* (Moscow, 2013), pp. 70–120.

Grabbe, Pavel, *Iz Pamiatnykh zapisok . . .* (Moscow, 1873).

Ker Porter, Robert, *Travelling Sketches in Russia and Sweden during the years 1805, 1806, 1807, 1808* (Philadelphia, 1809).

Jackson, George, *Diaries and Letters of Sir George Jackson, KCH*, edited by Lady Jackson (London, 1872) <http://books.google.com/books?id=nhVp1N91dpoC>

Levshin, Nikolai. 'Domashnii pamyatnik N.G. Levshina', *Russkaya starina* 5 (1876), pp. 59–72.

Löwenstern, Eduard von, *Mit Graf Pahlens Reiterei gegen Napoleon: Denkwürdigkeiten des russischen Generals Eduard von Löwenstern, 1790-1837* (Berlin, 1910). English edition: *With Count Pahlen's cavalry against Napoleon: memoirs of the Russian General Eduard von Löwenstern (1790-1837)*, translated by Victoria Joan Moessner with Stephen Summerfield (Huntingdon [UK], 2010).

Mikhailovskii-Danilevskii, Alexander, *Opisanie vtoroi voiny Imperatora Aleksandra s Napoleonom v 1806 i 1807 godakh* (St. Petersburg, 1846).

Obolenskii, A., 'Vosponinaniya Knyazya A.P. Obolenskago (1780-1812)' in *Khronika nedavnei stariny: iz arkhiva Knyazya Obolenskago-Neledinskago-Meletskago* (St. Petersburg, 1872).

Osten-Sacken, Fabian von der, 'Iz zapisok feldmarshala Sackena', *Russkii arkhiv* 38 (1900), pp. 169–74.

Otroshenko, Yakov, *Zapiski general Otroshenko, 1800-1830* (Moscow, 2006).

Petrov, Mikhail, 'Rasskazy sluzhivshego v 1-m egerskom polku polkovnika Mikhaila Petrova o voennoi sluzhbe i zhizni svoei i trekh rodnykh brat'ev ego, zachavsheisya s 1789 goda' in F. Petrov, A. Afanasyev, et al.(eds), *1812 god. Vospominaniya voinov russkoi armii* (Moscow, 1991), pp. 112–355.

Polnoe sobranie zakonov Rossiiskoi imperii s 1649 goda (St. Petersburg, 1830), vol. XXIX.

Pushkin, Alexander, *Dnevniki. Avtobiograficheskaya proza* (Moscow, 2008).

Sherbatov, Aleksey, *Zhurnal knyazya Sherbatova*, RGVIA, fond 846, opis 16, delo 3166. Printed edition: Sherbatov, Aleksey, *Moi vospominaniya*, ed. A. Shiryaeva (St. Petersburg, 2006).

Shishkov, Alexander, *Zapiski, mneniya i perepiska* ... (Berlin, 1870), vol. 1.

Timofeyev, Vasilii, 'Iz vospominanii generala ot ifanterii V.I, Timofeyeva o srazhenii 23 ianvarya 1807 goda pri Preussich Eylau', *Voennyi sbornik* 4 (1907), pp. 1–14.

Vigel, Phillip, *Zapiski* (Moscow, 1891).

Volkonskii, Sergei, *Zapiski Sergeya Grigorievicha Volkonskago (dekabrista)* (St. Petersburg, 1901).

Wilson, Robert, *Life of General Sir Robert Wilson, from autobiographical memoirs, journals, narratives, correspondence, etc.* edited by Rev. Herbert Randolph (London, 1862) < http://books.google.com/books?id=ZEI6AAAAcAAJ >

Yermolov, Aleksey. *Zapiski A.P. Yermolova, 1798-1826* (Moscow, 1991). English edition: *The Czar's General: The Memoirs of a Russian General of the Napoleonic Wars*, translated and edited by Alexander Mikaberidze (Welwyn Garden City [UK], 2005).

Zhurnal voennykh deistvii imperatorskoi Rossiiskoi armii s nachal do okonchaniya kampanii (St. Petersburg, 1807).

Index